To
MARSHA (CRAFT) Robb
OL' HIGH School BUD.

Rich W. Vol...

3/2/13

THE DIRTY THIRTY

Richard W. Hudson

Bloomington, IN   Milton Keynes, UK

AuthorHouse™
1663 Liberty Drive, Suite 200
Bloomington, IN 47403
www.authorhouse.com
Phone: 1-800-839-8640

First published by AuthorHouse 8/29/2007

ISBN: 978-1-4343-0617-3 (e)
ISBN: 978-1-4343-0619-7 (sc)
ISBN: 978-1-4343-0618-0 (hc)

Printed in the United States of America
Bloomington, Indiana

This book is printed on acid-free paper.

Coverphoto by Richard and Shirley Hudson

CONTENTS

FOREWORD

This book is based on my experiences as a soldier in Vietnam from June 1969 to August 1970. The events herein are from my personal recollection and may not be taken as pure historical facts as to dates, units involved, and locations. As a lower ranking enlisted man, I was not informed of the battle plan or objective. I seldom even knew our location. Luckily I wrote down all the names of the firebases, towns and villages I'd been to on my Boonie Cap. This faded relic was my starting point for my research to ascertain where I'd been for my fourteen-month tour.

Writing this story, I realized I either did not remember or maybe never knew the real names of all my fellow soldiers. Nicknames or last names were the norm. I have rearranged the character's names and backgrounds while trying to maintain their personalities and level of involvement.

For years I was encouraged to write about my experience by family and friends and especially my wife, Shirley, who helped make it all come together. I was also assisted by Mr. Scott Breckenridge, now deceased, who helped me by sharing his own experiences and reference materials providing many insights as to campaigns and battle records.

Some of the incidents I remember were funny, some were horrifying and still are to this day. Mainly this is an account of the every day happenings experienced by most of the G.I.s who ever served in Viet Nam.

Mostly, I wrote this book for my Mother to atone for all the lies I told her in my letters.

PART I
THE FIELD

PFC Richard W. Hudson

1

'GUN-BUNNY'
June 7, 1969

'Jeez, why can't those guys hold it down', I thought. We'd been flying for the best part of 24 hours now, and thanks to that 151-proof Maitai I'd had in Honolulu, I'd managed to pass out for the last how many hours? I cracked open an eye and saw activity down the aisle of the 727. The stewardesses (who, we had decided, had to have been ex-W.A.C. Drill Instructors), were stowing pillows, cases, clothing and other articles into the overhead bins, and all the guys were milling around looking out each others windows. I sat up and looked left at Piggy in the window seat.

"What's goin' on?" I asked, sleepily.

Piggy (AKA Stanley Meyers, late of a small town in Northern California) said, "We're coming into Tan Son Nhut."

"What the hell's a tonsenoot?" I asked.

He told me, "It's THE major airport in Vietnam."

Vietnam!!! We're here!

I'd met Stan at the transfer barracks at Fort Ord two days earlier, and we'd become friends mostly because we were both kinda misfits. Me, at 5'5" and 120 lbs., he at 5'6" and 195 lbs. With round wire-rim glasses, he reminded me of a character in Goldman's, "Lord of the Flies", hence the nickname 'Piggy'. He'd read the book and understood the character and had taken no offense, and proceeded to call me by my army nickname 'Mouse'.

We'd spent three days of intensive waiting at Ord together, talking about hometowns, girls, cars and what we might do in Vietnam. We'd eaten crummy meals in the mess hall together. The last night there

3

out of complete boredom, we went to the post theater for a screening of "Chitty-Chitty Bang-Bang" which we agreed was boring and stupid, followed by the second feature, John Wayne in "Green Berets", which we agreed scared the hell out of both of us.

"We'll be on the ground in ten minutes, Mouse" he said.

With a bad hangover and equally bad case of stomach butter-flies, I gathered my stuff and prepared to enter "The War".

Upon landing, looking over Piggy out the window, I saw huge concrete hanger-type buildings, small corrugated shacks with sand-bagged blast-walls built around them, and more military planes, heli-copters, jeeps, trucks and personnel than I'd ever seen.

"Wow", I said, "looks like a pretty good size air base."

He laughed and told me Tan-Son-Nhut Airport is the biggest in all South Vietnam and serves Saigon and all the large cities there. (Piggy had studied at the post library at Ft. Ord.)

We finally taxied up to a concrete-walled, open-front building with a corrugated tin roof that professed to be the terminal building. The stairs were rolled up to the front and rear entrances to the plane, and the hatches were opened.

"Officers and over E-6 are to exit front, all others exit rear." said a voice over the intercom. We all gathered our stuff and headed in the directions indicated.

My first comment as I came out the hatch was "Whew, what's that smell?" Somebody behind us laughed and told us "Gun smoke, die-sel fuel, and burning shit". We found out later that that's exactly what it was. Also, the heat! 8:30 A.M. and it's probably 90°- hits us like a huge hand and I immediately start sweating.

After de-planing and another roster check, we load into what looked like prison buses with wire mesh over the windows (to keep out Grenades, we're told), and are driven through a gate with an oriental-looking roof on it, down some dirt roads between chain link, concertina wire, and dirt berms.

Piggy and I both have orders for the 1st Cavalry Replacement Center in Bien-Hoa, which turns out to be another base ten or so miles from Saigon. We roll along a paved highway looking out on the dirtiest landscape I've ever seen, strewn with cans, bottles, debris, small settlements of tin and cardboard shacks and, occasionally, a brick or concrete building set back from the road.

187 CAV Location Center – Bien Hoa

Some of these buildings have walls and gates and appear to be very old. Some have damage that I assume is from bombs or bullets. Finally, we roll through a checkpoint M.P. gate into Bien-Hoa itself and stop at a group of gray wood barracks by a flagpole flying a yellow 1st Cavalry flag.

Piggy and I are the only two guys on the bus destined for the Cav, so we're told to report to the sergeant in the CP, a low wooden building with sandbags halfway up it's sides, screens above with rolled-up ponchos on them, and a sandbagged roof. The sergeant inside eyed us, checked our names off a list, and told us to wait in the jeep parked out front. We went to the jeep and found the metal so hot, we sat on our duffel bags to keep from burning our butts.

The sergeant came out five minutes later, climbed in, and told us to hold on. He started-up and drove us between two of the wooden buildings along a road past what looked like a mess hall, then between two earthen berms that were at least thirty feet tall. We could hear planes and helicopters on the other side of these walls revving their engines, but the view was completely blocked by the berms. We came around a left hand 90° turn in the walls and came to a row of four G-P type tents with their sides rolled up to allow air-flow under them. Inside and around these tents were 25-30 other replacements in various stages of dress and undress, milling about in groups or singles.

The Sergeant took us to the last of the tents in the row and told us to take our gear into this tent, find an empty bunk, and settle in for the time being; we would be sent on to our permanent assignments the next day.

Inside, the tent was dark and stifling with the mid-morning heat. At first everything was in silhouette against the open sides of the tent and it was hard to pick out details, but we found two bunks empty in the rows of upper and lower sets. We claimed them and put our duffel bags on the dirt floor next to them. In the next row of bunks was a group of soldiers playing cards on a lower bunk, so Piggy and I walked over and asked where the latrine was and introduced ourselves to several of them. Piggy took off for the john and I started talking to this blond, medium height PV2 named Clark. Turns out he's from Louisville, KY (I'm from Lexington) and he was friendly and told me we were just waiting here till they decided where we were to go in the morning. He pointed out the mess hall, visible in the distance, pointed to some small culvert type bunkers placed along the base of the huge berm to our right and said they were in case of rocket attacks. Clark had an artillery survey M.O.S., and I was a 13A10 artilleryman, so we had some things in common. We sat in the shade of the tent and talked until Piggy returned, then we started B.S.-ing and passing the time best we could. Finally, at about 1300 another sergeant E-5 came to tell us to go up to the mess for noon chow, so we all trailed up to the mess hall for our first combat zone meal of mystery meat burgers and french fried potatoes. After chow we were told to return to the tents, pass the time, and stay in that area only.

6

As the afternoon simmered on at about 100°, we sat around the tent and talked. Two other guys, a PFC and a corporal, were in-country re-ups and had already been here for a year each, so they were answering a bunch of questions from newbys about what it's like in a combat zone. They'd both had non-combat jobs in their first tours. One, (the PFC), had been a company clerk with an aviation company. The corporal, a black dude named Jones, had worked in supply here in Bien-Hoa for a unit that supplied the mobile home quarters for officers. He was full of stories about Donut Dollies (Red Cross girls) that supposedly were allowed to visit officers in their quarters, the air-conditioned BX at the airbase,' and the abundance of good dope available everywhere.

At the mention of marijuana, several of the guys wanted to know if it was possible to score some dope. Jones told us that usually all you had to do was find a permanent party below E-5 rank and ask.

I looked over at Piggy and Clark and said, "Have you guys ever smoked?"

Clark said he knew some dudes in Louisville that did but he never had. Piggy seemed aghast that anyone would try it in a place where you could get killed so easily if you didn't 'keep your wits'. I'd never smoked either, but I decided that if I might get killed anyway, hey, what the hell, I'd try it. So we all decided, if we could get some dope, we'd try it while we're still in a safe place like Bien-Hoa.

At 1500 hours, the same E-5 came and told us to report to the Orientation Pavilion behind the C-P at 1530 hours for a speech by Sgt. Andrews. We all put our shirts back on and trailed up the path along the berm wall, past the mess area, to the main company compound. We found the Orientation Pavilion, an open-sided, roofed structure with bleachers. We took seats and waited another 15 minutes until Sgt. Andrews (E-6) came out the back door of the C-P and took his place at a lectern facing the bleachers.

Sgt. Andrews, (a 'Lifer' as we came to know them), was in his late forties. He was obviously a career man, dressed in starched, tailored jungle fatigues. He proceeded to inform us about the many ways of dying in Vietnam, from actually being killed in combat, to VD, to drinking ground-up glass in beer or Pepsi bought in a restaurant or along a road. We were reprised in the use of condoms, clean socks, malaria pills, clean ammo, and water purification pills. After about 45 minutes of this, he informed us that chow was to be at 1700-1800 hrs., and a formation with gear was to be held in front of the CP at 1830 hrs. After a ten minute warning about drugs, we were dismissed.

We had time before chow to go back to the tents, and anyone who'd been there long enough to unpack could gather gear for the formation. Piggy and Clark and I hadn't had time to take anything out of our bags, so we sat on a bunk and talked about Sgt. Andrews and his speech on the evils of Vietnam.

On the way to the mess hall Piggy said, "Wherever they put me, I should be safe in a bunker". Piggy was a FDC (Fire Direction Control) guy and they spent their war below ground in bunkers operating computers to direct artillery fire.

"How about you, Clark? Where do you suppose they'll put you?", I asked.

"Don't know, but I imagine we'll find out tomorrow when we get sent out", he said.

" I know where I'll go; I'm a gun bunny and I'll end up on a fire base somewhere with gooks trying to shoot my ass!" I lamented.

"You don't have to be in the boonies to get your ass shot in this country. It's as likely to happen right now as anytime", Clark said as we entered the mess hall.

After a meal of franks and beans, instant mashed potatoes, and warm Koolaid, we were standing outside the mess hall when a guy named Franklin came over and asked if anyone was looking for some dope. Piggy, Clark and I looked at each other, and decision made, I nodded yes.

Franklin said he knew one of the cooks could get us something if we'd go out back of the mess hall and ask for Louis. We talked and decided Clark would go instead of all three of us. Piggy and I would keep watch. We stationed ourselves where we could watch for Lifers and Clark disappeared around back of the mess hall. He and returned five minutes later and informed us we had a matchbox full of grass for $5. We both said "WOW" and decided that after the evening formation, we'd go back to the tent and find a place to smoke it.

At 1830 hrs we were in formation in front of the CP with our AWOL and duffel bags beside us. We were roll-called again. We then packed up our gear and were marched to the supply building (one of the gray wooden buildings) where we were issued our new jungle boots, fatigues, a poncho and liner, an 'Alice' pack, socks, T-shirts, and 'Newby' caps, all in deep new O.D. green. These new uniforms would I.D. us as FNGs as well as wearing signs saying 'Fucking New Guys'.

We were told to extract all personal items from our stateside issue and turn in our duffels and AWOLS with all khakis and stateside fatigues at the supply desks for storage in a facility in Bien-Hoa.

Dressed thusly in our new FNG suits, we left the supply point about 2045 hrs. and headed back to the tent area.

Having arrived back 'home', we were told that the rest of the evening was ours, to spend it reading, writing letters, or whatever. The latrines were open all night for showers, but hot water was turned off at midnight. We were told not to leave the immediate area as guards were on duty and you might get shot as a gook, though we couldn't imagine a gook being stupid enough to be walking around a big base like Bien-Hoa, even at night.

At 2230 hrs we were sitting in the tent, bored, but too excited to read or sleep. (Our first night in a combat zone). Clark said quietly, "I've got this matchbox of grass, where can we go to try it out?"

"I've got my tobacco pipe," I offered, "let's go over by the berm wall on the other side of the bunkers. It should be pretty safe there."

As casually as we could, we ambled over toward the bunkers, keeping watch over our shoulders for Lifers or officers. None were in evidence as we slipped behind the last bunker in the last row and squatted down to try our first DOPE!

I filled the bowl of my Dr. Graybow pipe with the rich, green contents of the matchbox, and after another brief look around, lit the mixture and inhaled. Whhoofff! I lost it completely and choked and gagged with a red face and tearing eyes. Clark and Piggy took turns slapping my back. I said, "Jeez, that shit is so strong!?"

Clark, not to be outdone took the pipe and called me a pussy. "Let a man show you how."

He took a big toke and burst out in a spasm every bit as bad as mine had been.

Watching this, Piggy said "I don't know if I want to try this or not", but Clark and I were adamant that he was a pussy if he didn't. So Piggy took the bowl and my Zippo and after checking out the area again, took a huge hit off the pipe. At the same time, sirens burst out all over

9

the world, it seemed. Piggy burst out a cloud of smoke and, with eyes as big as saucers, choked on the smoke and turned beet-red in the face.

The sirens wailed and we peeped over the bunker roof, assuming the M.P.s were right there to bust us.

Instead, we saw the entire population of the tents running full-tilt straight at us across the open area. We looked at each other in confusion.

Suddenly a voice to our left yelled, "Hey, you FNGs, get in this bunker, now!" We saw a head poking out of the next bunker and an arm waving us over. We ran over and the guy in the bunker pulled us roughly inside and threw us on the floor.

"Stay down" he said.

He looked back out the open end of the bunker, his back to us. No one else had run that far back in the row of bunkers, so we were alone in this one. When he turned back to us, we were still wheezing from the dope, and he asked, "What were you guys doing back there?"

"Uh, we were just talking", I said lamely. Meanwhile Piggy and Clark were still coughing and gagging.

"You guys smoking something back there? You were, weren't you!"

I said defensively, "Well, what if we were…"

Suddenly we heard explosions coming from the other side of the berm we were next to. The guy hollered "Look-out!" and dove to the floor with us. Then two huge explosions lit the whole area, making the dark cave inside the bunker glow like daylight. We felt a strong concussion break over us as we lay there. I think I was as scared as I've ever been. A minute passed and the Bunker Dude crawled over and peeked out of the opening. There were no more explosions and some of the sirens were winding down. "Holy shit" he said as he looked out. We gathered our wits and crawled over beside him and looked out the opening with him. What we saw, in the sizzling light of the drifting flares, was a huge, smoking hole in the open area between the tents and us. Also, the end of the tent where we were supposed to be was hanging in shreds with little bits of burning canvas falling to the ground around it and inside it.

I yelled, "What the fuck was that?"

Piggy and Clark, like a duet in harmony, said "Shiiiit!"

The Bunker Dude said, "That's the gooks! They aim their rockets at the chopper pads on the other side of the hill, and sometimes we get what falls short."

"You mean, they hit our tent and weren't even aiming at it?", Piggy asked.

"Sure, they just walk 'em across the area hoping to hit the helicopters parked on both sides. Spread 'em about 20-30 yards apart and they're pretty sure to hit something worth-while!"

"Shiiiit!" we all said.

The Bunker Dude said, "We'll just lay low here for a while in case they decide to lob a few more 107s in." We sat up and leaned back on the walls. The Bunker Dude asked, "What the hell you guys smoking makes you choke like that?"

"We picked some up from a guy we know", Clark said.

Bunker Dude smiled, "Guy named Louis?"

"Uh, yeah," I said.

"Let me see", he insisted, holding out his hand.

Clark pulled out the matchbox and handed it over. The Bunker Dude opened it and pinched out a little and sniffed it.

"Sheweee! How much you pay for this?" he asked.

"Uh….$5", Clark says.

The Bunker Dude's eyes gleamed in the flickering light and he laughed.

"That damn cook, Louis, he's still fucking over the FNGs!!!!"

"What d'ya mean, it's not enough for $5 worth?" Piggy asked.

"Not just that," he stated, "It's not even dope!"

"What?" we all three chimed.

"Hell no," he guffawed, "that's oregano!"

Me and Piggy and Clark looked at each other, feeling like true FNGs.

The Bunker Dude clapped Piggy on the shoulder.

"Don't feel too bad," he said, "you ain't th' first."

We sighed.

I thought, 'I've sure got a lot to learn!'

"Listen," he said after a minute, "you FNGs really wanna smoke some dope?"

He paused and we nodded.

"Well, you're in luck. My name is Dennis Dexter, from Philadelphia, P.A., and I've got some of Vietnam's best right here!" He pulled a big bag about 3 inches in diameter from his leg pocket along with a well-worn looking bowl.

"This is more like $5 worth, dudes, but I'll turn you guys on for free, cause you've already been screwed once tonight."

So, as it turned out, we still managed an introduction to the magic weed that night. When we finally left the bunker thirty minutes later, we were all so stoned that when we went to check out the damage to the tent we were supposed to be sleeping in, we were scared shitless but we couldn't suppress bouts of giggling. Some of the other guys looked at us strangely, but we knew that for once smoking dope might have saved our lives!

Everyone was standing around with their eyes bugged, checking out the blown-up tent and the hole in the field. Some guys had found pieces of shrapnel from the rockets and showed them around.

Dexter was a Permanent Party at the 'Reloc-Center', as he called it, and had been there for three months. He gave us the low-down on some things that he thought we should know.

He mentioned the Artillery unit down the road from us, and, how sometimes they had a fire-mission during the night. He explained how to tell the difference between "In-coming" and "Out-going" fire.

"Out-going's just a big 'Bang' or a bunch'a 'Bangs'. Ya don't hafta worry 'bout Out-going."

We nodded, understanding. This was serious shit.

"In-coming's whatcha hafta worry 'bout", he continued,

"If you're listening close, you could hear the "Whoosh-pop-pop" of the rocket as it flies over, an' maybe see the flame from its tail, but that's doubtful, cause they're traveling a thousand miles an hour."

I, at least, was absorbing his every word.

"Th' dead give-away, an' I DO mean DEAD," he paused for effect, "is th' sound."

I found myself holding my breath. I exhaled slowly so no one would notice.

"In-coming sounds like a truck-load of rocks, dumped all at once, from a hundred feet up! Kind'a a 'KRUMP'ing sound."

He used his hands to emphasize the enormity of the sound.

12

He had described the sound the rocket made as it took-out our tent.

We talked for several hours, sitting on our bunks in the dark tent.

We'd recovered our stuff from the damaged tent and moved to the other one. The smell of cordite and burnt canvas followed us.

Dexter left at about 0100 hrs. Things had settled down and most guys were in their racks sleeping, trying to sleep, or pretending to sleep. No one stayed in the damaged tent. I squeaked into my sagging steel cot and tried not to imagine what might be in store for me tomorrow. I figured I'd find out soon enough.

2

THE 'FIELD'

Morning still came early in the Vietnam army, so by 0730 we were back in formation in front of the CP, roll-called, and handed orders to our further assignments. Sgt. Andrews told us to check with the company clerk for the travel arrangements and to be sure to report to our units by the appointed time on our orders.

Piggy, Clark and I got together with some of the others and compared orders. Piggy's orders said "Bravo Battery, 1/30 Arty., Tay Ninh City". Clarks' were for "HHB 1/30 Arty, Phouc Vinh", and mine said "Delta Battery 1/30 Arty, FSB Jamie".

We were to acquire transport by reporting to the CAV LAISON unit at the aviation unit down the road. A bunch of the guys were already boarding a bus to the main airfield to ship to other CAV infantry and maintenance units.

The five of us who had orders to artillery bases gathered our packs and headed down the road to E/82nd AV, (Aviation). After seeing Clark and another guy board a chopper for Phouc Vinh, and Piggy and the other guy hop on another for Tay Ninh City, I was finally directed to a my own ride, a Huey 'Slick' that was winding-up on the line. This was to be my first flight in a helicopter and I didn't know what to expect. My butterflies and I climbed into the empty chopper and sat in the canvas sling-seats.

I had no sooner gotten myself strapped in with my pack under my knees when the crew chief jumped into the side door and waved his hand above his head, signaling the pilots to see how much shit they could scare out of their single new-guy passenger.

14

After 10-15 seconds of the engines winding-up to full speed, the rear of the chopper jumps up and I'm looking down at the ground through the front windshield. The helicopter shuddered all over and the loud thop-thop-thop of the blades is all I can hear. I look sideways out the side door and realize we're also traveling forward and rising slowly so that the revetments and other aircraft are sliding past at what's becoming an alarming rate. Slowly the ship levels out and we gain altitude like an out of control elevator.

We reach about 500 feet of altitude and begin radical forward motion, sometimes banking right or left until the ground is outside one side door or the other. I had assumed the doors would be closed for flight, but nooooo! They wanted me to enjoy the view and the lovely breeze coming in the open sides. I felt my breakfast churning, threatening to re-visit me, and within minutes, my teeth were chattering from the cold air.

After about ten minutes in flight, my stomach settled enough for me to begin to enjoy my first airborne view of the country. Green, green, green as far as I could see, just jungle or forest, interspersed with rivers or small lakes. There were some open, flooded fields broken by low walls that criss-crossed them, then much more jungle. I noticed small, almost perfectly round lakes, with water that sparkled light blue, like the Mediterranean Sea. This puzzled me and I made a mental note to ask about them the first chance that I had.

I didn't have much chance for reflection, as minutes later we banked hard left and I spotted a clearing on a small rise about a mile in the distance.

The crew chief, who had made the flight standing in the opening to the cockpit, holding hand-holds on either side of the door, turned and gave me a thumbs down, which meant, I assumed, that we were descending.

We over-flew the LZ once, circled back, then came in on an open area off to one side of the firebase. We came in fast, but I had enough time to get a look at L. Z. JAMIE.

'What a mud hole!' I thought to myself.

And it was.

I saw a bunch of brownish green bunkers, six 155 mm Howitzers in round dirt pits, some smaller 105 mm guns on the other side, all surrounded by rows and rows of concertina wire out to the jungle that surrounded three sides of the area.

As we came in over the landing area the pilot flared the ship to a halt and settled down to earth with a small jolt. The crew chief waved with both arms that I was to exit left, and do it quickly. I undid the seat straps, grabbed my pack and jumped out onto the skid. Before I could step completely off the skid, the rotors revved back up, the chopper started to rise and I was propelled out into the mud between two pieces of PSP (Perforated Steel Plate).

My brand new jungle boots immediately sank in about two inches and the blast from the chopper tried to blow me over face first. Somehow, I remained mostly upright and took three or four steps to regain my balance and almost ran into a Spec 4 standing there with a clipboard in hand.

"Who are you?" he asked.

"Hudson, Richard", I said and handed him my orders.

He looked them over and checked something on his clipboard. "Follow me."

As we walked between two low dirt berms into the LZ I said, "Jeez, what was their hurry, they gotta date or something?"

The Spec 4 glanced back at me and muttered, "The pilots don't like to stay on the ground long enough for Charlie to line up mortars on 'em!"

"You get a lot of incoming mortars here?", I asked, as I stepped around a mud hole that, to me, looked like it could be a crater.

"No", he told me, "But it don't take many mortars to make it damned unpleasant."

"I guess not." I agreed.

By that time, we'd come up on a low, sandbagged bunker differentiated from the rest only by the several antennae sticking up from the timbered and sandbagged roof. We stepped down two wooden steps to a doorway positioned behind a built-out blast wall. There was a rubber poncho hung over the opening. We ducked under the poncho and entered the combination CP (Command Post) and FDC (Fire Direction Control).

The room was maybe 15' x 15' with a 7' ceiling composed of heavy timbers and PSP with no windows. Around all the walls were

16

shelves cantilevered into the sandbagged walls. These contained several radios, landlines, rows of books and papers and files. Across one end of the room was a large folding table, eight feet long, covered by maps and overlays, coffee cups, a butt can, and somebody's half-eaten C-Rat meal. The other end of the space was taken up by two folding desks, at one of which was seated a large blond Sgt. E-8. There were five other people in the room, all engrossed in their routine and paid us no attention.

The E-8 looked up from his desk and asked the SP4 if the weather had come on that chopper. He told him "No, Top, but we got a FNG in for #3."

The 1st Sergeant looked at me and told the SP4 to see that I got settled-in and turned back to his desk.

"C'mon" the SP4 said and as we passed the other desk, he laid his clipboard on its surface and ducked back out the door with me behind.

When we were back out in the sun, the heat hit me again and I asked the SP4, "Is it hot or is it just me?"

He turned and smiled and said, "It's just you, cause it ain't near hot yet today."

I shook my head and said, "I can't wait."

He said "My name's Salo, I'm battery clerk here and general do it all for Sgt. Ambrose. Hudson, that your name?"

"Yeah, but you can call me Rich or I guess, 'Mouse', that's my nickname from basic."

"Mouse, huh. Well that's pretty appropriate, you're not much bigger'n one of the 'Joes' we hump out here." I thought that was pretty easy for HIM to say, since he was over six feet tall, though skinny.

"Joes?" Another new term.

"Projectiles, ProJos, 'Joes', ya know?"

"Oh." I said, like 'Sure, I understand.'

"Yeah, a 155 round weighs 97 lbs. and you can't be much more'n that."

"Well, actually I'm 120." I said defensively.

"S'alright." He continued as we walked. "You'll probably do better anyway. This ain't no place for a big or fat man. You'll make a much smaller target and the heat won't get you so bad."

"Well, the heat's got me bad already." I said mopping my forehead with my hand.

"Just wait, this afternoon will probably be 105 in the shade and we don't get much wind up here till the rainy season. Then tonight it'll drop down to 75 or 80 degrees and you'll freeze your butt off."

We arrived at one of the guns that bordered on the perimeter of the LZ, surrounded by its own protective berm about 30' in diameter and 4-5' tall. Set into the wall facing the jungle was a small sandbag bunker with a piece of PSP overhead and a small sandbag blast wall, blocking it from behind. Through the opening I could see an M-60 machine gun on a bi-pod set up in the opening facing out. As I looked on around, I noticed another small sand bag bunker dug into the inner side of the wall that I assumed was for powder charges and rounds, and six 4' x 8' sand bagged culverts with poncho doors and porches. These culverts were our sleeping quarters or 'Hootches'. There were two men per culvert when the gun was fully manned but I found out that the gun crew had never had more than eight guys at one time, and usually averaged six. Commanding the entire center of the area was a 14,600 lb., 155-mm Howitzer with O.D. green paintwork and brushed stainless bearing-surface tube gleaming in the hot sun. The smell of gunpowder and oil was everywhere.

There didn't appear to be anyone around until I followed Salo over to the hootches. Finally, in the gloom inside the culverts I could barely see heads and shoulders.

"Hey, Scotty! I finally got somebody for your crew, FNG and all!", Salo called as we walked up.

The guy he called Scotty crawled out and stood up. About 6' tall and stocky with dark curly hair and bright blue eyes, he also had the deepest tan I'd ever seen. He eyed me up and down, noting, no doubt, my FNG suit.

"Man, you really are new. How long you been in-country... uh..."

"Mouse Hudson", Salo filled-in.

"Mouse? Ha! Just what we need, a mouse!" Scotty laughed. "Well, welcome to the 'Dirty Thirty' anyway, Mouse." He stuck out his hand and I shook it.

He thanked Salo and he left. Scotty said for me to follow him and we'd get me set up to live on a LZ. Thirty minutes later, we'd been to the supply bunker where I got a steel-pot, Flack jacket, web belt and canteen, gas mask, four O.D. towels, an M-16 rifle and a basic load of ammo in a box. Scotty helped me carry all this back and stow it in the #4 center hootch which he said was mine.

"You might as well cool it here until about 1800 hrs." he said, "That's when we all get out and start making ready for night."

He must have seen the questions in my eyes and continued, "Around here there's no Day-shift/Night-shift thing. We get fire missions sometimes during the day, but not all the time. We are up most of the night on either fire missions or firing H&Is (Harassment and Interdiction). Any time we're not firing we get to eat, sleep and do P.M. (Preventive Maintenance) on the guns and equipment."

"Speaking of eating," I asked, "where's the mess hall and what time are meals?"

He shook his head and said, "We don't have a mess hall yet, but we've got a store of C-Rats in the little bunker next to the powder-store. Help yourself and eat while you can, 'cause I have a feeling we'll be busy tonight. The 2nd of the 7th boys went out on S & D, (Search and Destroy), this morning, sweeping North around Dong Xuai, and I think they'll find something to shoot at. If they do, we'll be firing support missions all night."

Right then I heard yelled commands from the other side of the LZ and Scotty looked intently and said, "Good, they're firing out away from us. If they change azimuths and fire over us, use your earplugs, those little poppers have a 'crack' that will really make your ears ring." Just then one of the guns fired and the tube blew a big smoke ring into the air.

"Registration Round," Scotty said, then added, "to see how close on target they are."

"BANG" went the 105 again.

"Second Reg Round for fine tuning." Scotty explained.

Then all six guns fired almost in synch followed by each gun firing as fast as they could re-load. Finally all firing ceased after each gun had fired six rounds apiece.

Scotty turned and explained, "That was a contact fire mission, when the Grunts spot a target or get into some shit, they call back to the FDC with the map co-ordinates. Then the FDC calls out to the guns on Lima-Lime (landline) and gives us the quadrant, deflection, type of round, fuse setting and what powder charge. The Gunners set up one tube for registration, pop off a round, usually Willie Peter (white phosphorous) for visibility, then, if needed, another round to adjust. Then if the rounds land close enough to the target, the whole battery will fire for effect."

"How do we know how accurate we're being?" I asked.

"We don't," he said, "we just fire th' co-ordinates, but we hear about it quick if we don't come close to what they want to get hit. We hear REALLY quick if somebody screws up and fires a short round or something that lands too close to the 'friendlies'."

I was beginning to wonder if I would be able to absorb all this new way of life quickly enough to keep from getting killed, or, at the very least, looking like the world's biggest idiot.

Scotty gave me a reassuring pat on the back.

"Don't worry." He smiled, "It'll come to ya. Now, I've got some shit to take care of, so just get your stuff squared away and hang out here. I'll introduce you to the other guys later when we're all out and about." he said and turned away toward the C-P.

"Hey, Scotty" I said. He turned back to me. "I've trained on 105s in AIT at Fort Sill, but I've only fired a 155 once, and I don't know how much I remember about it."

He rolled his eyes and said, "That figures, but after tonight you'll have plenty of experience. Don't worry. It's my job to aim the gun and fire it. All you'll have to do is keep us supplied with powder and rounds. See ya in a while."

"Yeah, thanks, I'll see ya," I said, and ducked into the hootch to see how I could arrange my stuff to make myself comfortable.

Ha! Comfortable is not a word to describe anything about living in a culvert.

First, you either sit or lay down because, even as small as I am, the overhead is too low to even allow squatting inside. Second, water seepage keeps the floor just a little damp at all times, so you use your poncho as a ground cloth and sleep rolled up in your poncho liner.

Ah, the poncho liner. Undoubtedly the best piece of equipment issued in Vietnam! It's an ultra light, camouflage blanket that will keep you warm when it's cold, keep mosquitoes off your hide, and when you get sunburned (which everyone did regularly), its satiny texture would

20

soothe the pain. Every gun bunny on the LZ tried to have at least two ponchos and liners to alternate back and forth, so you cold have one clean to sleep in while the other is drying out. It didn't always work out that way, but you keep trying. Life on an LZ, I found out, is a very tentative thing.

Around 1830 hrs, I'm sitting on top of the hootch watching as people all around start moving with a purpose. The other guys in my crew came out of their hootches one at a time and came over to see who the 'Newby' was.

First, Ralph Bechtal, from Worchester, Mass, came and introduced himself. He was a 5'10", 170 lb. ex-hippie who'd been in-country '93 days and counting. His main claim to fame was having been at Woodstock and smoked dope with Richie Havens.

Next was T.C. Manus, from Baton Rouge, La. T.C. had, like me, dropped out of college and gotten drafted. His pride and joy seemed to be a 1965 GTO that he was "building" in his Dad's garage till the call came. He was 20 years old, 5" 9" or so and about medium build. He had a round face, wide mouth, blue eyes and combed his hair down over his forehead. T.C. had been in-country for 32 days.

Then Scotty brought a guy over and introduced him as Jim Harris from Torrance, CA. Jim was about 5'8" but couldn't have weighed 135 lbs. He exuded an energy that seemed to infect everyone around him. I found out later that before coming to the field he'd been a speed freak back in the service battery in Long Binh, got caught and sent to the LZ Jim had been in-country for 191 days.

The last guy on the crew was a big guy, 6'2", 220 lbs. His name was John Buckstone. The son of a farmer from Hannibal, Mo., John was the only R.A. (enlistee) in our crew. John was a really good guy but was so innocent and gullible, the other guys were always pulling jokes on him and John, once he figured it out, laughed with the rest of us at his own foibles. But, I was told on several occasions, 'Don't piss him off or he'll crush you like a bug."

John was 'Short'. Not in stature, but in days left in-country, with only 92 days left on his tour. Vietnam was the most exciting thing that had ever happened to John, and to our amazement, he talked of re-upping at the end of his tour. We all told him he was crazy to put himself through the stateside shit, but who knows, it may have been the best

21

thing he could do as a career because, like he said of himself, "I ain't no rocket scientist".

After we'd sat around about 30 minutes and swapped a bunch of stories, T.C. stood up and said "I'm gonna get some chow. It'll be dark by 2030 hrs, and we've got an H&I list to shoot tonight." He walked off to the other side of the gun pit and started rummaging in some boxes just inside the door of the little supply bunker. He pulled out some O.D. green cans and studied the labels on them, selected something that looked good to him and walked back over to his hootch.

The others grunted and stood in singles and pairs and wandered over to do the same. I followed and looked through the box and pulled out some Beanie-weenies, (also, called beans and bangers), a turkey loaf meal and canned chocolate cake with frosting. I took this selection back to my hootch, and, not knowing the procedure, watched around and saw the other guys setting-up some sort of little stoves made from other C-Rat cans with holes punched in the sides. I walked over Buckstone's hootch next to mine and asked if he'd show me how to prepare a C-Rat meal that seemed to be a part of basic training that I must have missed.

He said, "C-Rats can be done several ways and can be right (pronounced RAT) tasty. It is all how you cook 'em and season 'em. Let Uncle John show you how."

He rustled around in his stuff.

"All ya' need is some salt, pepper, catsup if ya' got it, chili pepper if ya' got it 'r anythin' else you can come up with to cover up the natural, uh, flavor (?) of C-Rats."

He then reached into his hootch and pulled out an oiled ball of paper wrapped around a gray putty-looking stuff, broke off a little piece and put it into his stove.

"C-4 plastic explosive." He explained, nonchalantly, "We get it out of Claymore mines."

"Explosive? Mines!!??" I said as I stepped back.

"Naw, don't worry. It won't explode, even if you hit it with a hammer." He laughed. "Takes another explosion to set it off, like with a blasting cap," he said, "but if you light it, it'll sure cook your food. But you gotta be fast. In about 15-20 seconds it'll burn a hole in your meal can."

He lit the small piece of C-4 and it glowed a dim blue flame, then gained in intensity till it was on orange glow around a blue center. He then put his opened chili con carne can on top of the stove/can and immediately started stirring with his mess spoon. He poured in some chili powder from a small bottle he had ready, then stirred some more. After very little time I could see the contents begin to bubble and he took the corner of his green towel he had, conveniently, draped around his neck, and lifted the can quickly off the stove. The whole process took less than ½ minute and he had steaming hot chili that even smelled kinda good.

He gave me a chunk of C-4, and loaned me his little bottle of catsup till I got my own supply. He said catsup in the 'beans and bangers' would give it body and add to the taste. Shortly, I found out, sure enough it did.

Back at my hootch I used a small dessert can and pounded it full of holes for a stove and cooked my meal and wolfed it down. I was hungrier than I'd thought. I followed with the chocolate cake, which was dry and crumbly but tasted pretty good to have been baked during WWII. I washed it down with sweet, C-Rat Kool-Aid, and lit up one of the unfiltered Pall Mall cigarettes in the little four-pack included in the box. I only got about four drags on the cig and it burned down enough to burn my fingers. Boy, talk about dry tobacco! I'm not joking about these things being packed during WWII. I actually found a slip of paper inside a C-RAT box that stated it had been packed in 1944.

At 2000 hrs Scotty, who was an E-5 and the chief gunner on our crew, called us all together and laid out a tentative plan for firing our 'Harassment and Interdiction' list, better known as H&Is. These were set co-ordinates of trail crossings, former enemy sightings, and probable or possible VC grouping areas. The idea was to fire, on no set schedule, on these areas, hoping to either luck out and kill some enemy or at least discourage movement through the region and deny the use of the trails to the VC.

Scotty told me I was to be the 'Powder Monkey', and to go ahead and set out a bunch of 'Joes' from the pallet racks by the powder bunker and to un-box some fuses that were on a shelf in the bunker. This meant I was to unpack the powder charges in the bunker and cut the charge bags to the proper amount according to what the gunner ordered. Then I'd run the charge out to the gun after the round has been rammed into the breech. I'd give the powder charge to the assistant gunner who'd put it into the breech behind the round.

He'd then raise both hands above his head and call "clear". At that time the gunner closes the breechblock and calls "closed." Then the assistant gunner cocks the firing hammer on the back of the breechblock and inserts the primer casing (a small bullet-like brass blasting cap), into the hole in the breechblock. He then calls "Ready".

Then, the Gunner gets on the landline to the FDC, repeats the coordinates from the H&I sheet and listens for the quadrant, deflection, etc. He and the A.G. then crank the tube up or down and traverse left or right according to instructions from the FDC. The gunner then loudly calls "Fire in the hole!" to warn every one to cover up and be aware. He holds the lanyard in his left hand and takes up the slack in it.

Everyone else by this time has moved from between the trails of the gun and taken places on either side, well out of recoil range. (The recoil on a 155 is just under four feet and can shatter bones if one is stupid enough to stand in the way.)

The gunner stands just outside the right carriage wheel, listens to the landline and, on command, yanks the lanyard, firing the Howitzer. The tube belches orange fire and a grayish-white smoke ring. The tube recoils, stops, and returns more slowly to its extended position by means of a huge recoil spring and hydraulic suppressor. I was amazed that from my position behind the gun I could actually follow the trajectory of the round for the first 3-4 seconds of its flight.

The concussion from the gun is tremendous, raising dust from the floor of the gun pit and making us wince if we weren't wearing ear-plugs or holding our hands over our ears. If you happen to be in front of the gun for some reason, the blast can knock your helmet off and make your eyes bulge. You find yourself constantly trying to pop your ears after every round.

After firing, the gunner throws open the breech block, the assistant gunner comes back between the trails, bends and peers into the breech to make sure it's clear of the round and powder charge. He reaches around the breechblock and pulls out the primer cartridge, then calls, "Breech clear."

By this time, the two guys carrying rounds have another round fused and on the loading tray, ready to ram. The assistant gunner steps left against the trail, making room for the loaders. Then we start again.

Gunner calls "Mission! Round HE, fuse time, the four-number fuse setting, charge 1-10, ready ram!" At that time another round is rammed into the breech, another powder charge is inserted. The breech block is closed and the AG calls "CLEAR!". The gun is cocked, the primer is inserted, and everyone moves back for the next firing. Range, deflection and quadrant, "Fire in the hole" and "Boom" on command.

Sometimes we were firing individually and other times in a group of three or more guns firing in unison. We'd fire about 10-12 rounds in 30 minutes, swab out the tube, re-dig-in the spades on the ends of the trails, stack up more rounds on the ready racks, un-box more fuses, smoke a cigarette, and rest a bit. Then we'd go back and fire another sequence.

The entire time, I'd been kept busy humping charges and time passed quickly until I realized it was 0100 hrs. The nighttime air, as promised, had cooled to about 75°, and when we stopped for any period of time, we would become chilled as the sweat dried on our bodies.

Finally Scotty announced the end of the H&Is until 0600, when we would shoot the rest of the page on a different azimuth. He looked over at me and told me to rack-out now, and I'd be woken up if we had a "contact mission" or 0530, whichever came first.

I walked over to the row of hootches and the other guys were either crawling in to sleep, or sitting outside under their poncho porch-roofs, smoking and talking. Too keyed-up to sleep, I walked over to the end hootch where Harris and T.C. were sitting, brewing up coffee in a canteen cup over a chunk of C-4.

"Coffee?" Harris asked.

"No, thanks, man," I said "I've never been able to drink it."

"Man, I couldn't live without it," T.C. said.

"You guys do this, like, every night?" I asked.

"Pretty much," Jim said, "But then, sometimes we don't fire one round all night."

"Makes for pretty spotty sleeping, doesn't it?" I yawned involuntarily.

"Well, yeah," said Manus. "We'll have maintenance and details in the morning, but we'll get some down time in the afternoon. Better to try to sleep through the heat of the day, then work nights when it's cooler."

Jim lit another cigarette and said, "Shit happens at night anyway. At dawn 'Charlie' turns back into 'farmer Ho' or 'farmer Quang' and grows rice for the V.C., sells dope or his female relatives to G.I.s on the roadside, and appears to be a peaceful dude who wouldn't think of raising arms against the government forces protecting his ass."

Manus laughed and looked meaningfully at me.

"If the Gooks can't kill you with bullets or bombs, they'll get you with some strange kind of V.D from the 'Boom-Boom' girls in the 'villes."

"Boom-Boom girls?" I asked.

"Whores, man," Jim said. "They're all over, in the 'villes and sometimes out along the road."

"Selly pussy, 5 bucks G.I.'", Manus chimed-in in a sing song voice. "My sister number one virgin, G.I., she fucky but no sucky, or she sucky but no fucky, G.I., five bucky, ha, ha, ha!"

I laughed too and said "No shit!"

Jim's eyes were glowing, either from the strong coffee or the dim light of the flashlight with a red lens hanging from the hootch entrance.

"Yeah, but you're better-off if you just leave them alone and get yer jollies some other way. They're all diseased, man, and if you get THAT shit, you can forget going home. There ain't no cure for some of the bugs those girls are passing out."

"Yeah, but they sure are sweet lookin' little thangs," T.C. said; "But Jim's right, better not dip-it or your wick could rot off."

Just then Scotty got back from the C-P and as he walked past said "First call 0530, dudes, get some sleep while you can."

I walked back to my hootch and crawled in. I wrapped up in my poncho-liner and knew I would not be able to sleep. I watched some stars drift past a split in the poncho fly and listened to the ambient sounds of a firebase at night in Vietnam.

3

THE LEARNING PROCESS

Suddenly I heard a voice, far off.

"Hudson! Hey Mouse."

I felt a hand on my shoulder shaking gently. My eyes cracked open and I realized I'd been sleeping. I looked out at a dark shape in the doorway of my hootch and finally recognized Buckstone, the Assistant Gunner, by his huge shape.

"Grab yer socks, man, it's O-dark-thirty and time to go to work."

I peeped at my luminous Timex and it was 0532.

"Oh, man," I muttered and crawled out to a pitch-black morning.

Guys were up and moving about in the darkness. I could hear small noises here and there. Then a darker shape was right beside me. It was Bechtal, or 'Hippie', as he was known. He took me by the arm and led me around the gun.

"Scotty said for me and you to get ready to man the firing jack, we've gotta shift this pig to a different azimuth."

I said, "Sure, but I don't know what to do, so you'll have to tell me."

"O.K., no sweat," he replied. "Just listen up to Scotty and me and you'll figure it out easy enough."

We went to the front of the gun and squatted beneath the tube. A few seconds later Scotty peeped around the blast shield and said, "You ready Hippie?"

We answered "affirm" and Hippie said, "I'm opening the cock lever and you'll put the jack handle into the socket on your side." I felt around and found a round 3" long tube about 1 ¼" in diameter on the lower side about 6" up from the jack base, and inserted the 3' long handle.

"Okay, the lever's over; start jacking." he said.

I put my weight on the handle and pushed it down, then let it come back up. As the lever came up the jack let the gun come down about ½". Several repeats later we had the carriage wheels on the ground. A 155mm Howitzer has to be jacked-up off its wheels when fired, or the recoil will blow out the tires; therefore, whenever we changed azimuths, the gun had to be jacked-down, turned physically on its wheels, jacked back up and re-dug-in at the trails. Then the gun sights have to be re-aligned with a new set of aiming stakes pre-set in the concertina wire outside the gun pit. All this took about 30 minutes and when we were through, the eastern sky had lightened to a dull gray and I began to pick out details in the LZ around me. Two of the other guns had also shifted like us, but the other three were on our original azimuth from the night before.

As soon as we got the gun ready, Scotty called "mission" and we set to getting rounds, fuses and powder ready. I was pretty dragged-out and groggy as I went back down the two steps into the powder store.

Bechtal and T.C. were stacking rounds, Harris was fusing them, and as I passed I asked, "When do we get to eat and, like, take a shit and stuff?"

Bechtal paused long enough to tell me, "We'll be through with this set of H&Is in about an hour; then we'll take a break for chow." He pointed at the powder bunker and said, "Sooner you get those charges un-canned, sooner we'll get this over with." I turned back into the bunker and started taking the powder bags out of the metal canisters.

At 0730 we had fired about 25 rounds and Scotty stepped back from the gun and announced, "Alright, that's it for now. Break for chow till 0830, then get on your details."

Everyone turned and headed for the hootches. I was still standing by the powder bunker door. Scotty saw me and said, "Mouse, I need you to clean out the canisters and fuse boxes in the powder store. Take 'em over to that ¾ ton truck by the C-P and haul 'em out to the chopper pad by 1030 when the re-supply chopper comes in. They'll be bringing in fresh rounds for the guns and taking out the empties. Get some chow and then get on it."

28

"Sure", I said, and went to the supply bunker, got a scrambled egg/sausage C-rat box and went to my hootch and cooked it up. It tasted like cardboard and powdered milk (warm), which wasn't real appetizing either, but it filled me up and I wasn't quite as groggy as before. I visited the latrine next, a row of toilet seats mounted on a box over a row of 55-gallon drums cut down to 1/3 height, filled with diesel fuel. These were located right at the concertina wire, out on the 'Greenline' (perimeter) as far away (and downwind) as possible. On the way back, I stopped at the water trailer next to another gun pit and filled my canteen, then went back to my hootch and brushed my teeth, splashed water on my face and smoked a cigarette for the first time that morning. 0915. Time to get to it if I want to be out on the chopper pad by 1030.

When I went to the powder bunker, T.C. was just getting there and said, "You go get the truck and I'll get the empty cans out of the bunker." When I backed the ¾ into the gun pit, he had a stack of metal cans in front of the bunker along with all the empty fuse boxes. All the leftover powder and cardboard sleeves and trash was heaped next to the opening in the berm. These were to be taken out to the dump and burned later. We loaded the truck and I drove us out through the rolled-back concertina wire to the chopper pad.

It was 1010 by then, so we smoked some cigarettes and T.C. told me about his time so far in V.N. He had come straight to "D" battery or "Delta" as he called it, from the relocation center, but at that time it was on another fire base called LZ IKE. He said Jamie was pretty secure, but IKE had been pretty flaky. He told me they had had two 'SAPPER' probes in the first week he was there and the Gooks popped mortars into the LZ

"I sure was glad t' get off 'IKE'." he said. "Place had bad kar-ma."

1035 and we heard choppers in the distance.

Soon the dust was being blown around in a maelstrom from two huge 'Chinook' twin rotor helicopters, easing onto the chopper pad to set down about 40 feet from us. They had sling loads under them that had to be released before the choppers could land. This was done by the 'Blackhats'. Guys in distinctive, black baseball caps who were in charge of helicopter traffic and loads on the pad. Finally both helicopters were down and the side doors were opened. The Blackhats waved us over and we set to unloading boxes and bags of cargo into a pile on the pad.

When we had the first chopper emptied, it wound its rotors back up and took off in a red, choking cloud. We then proceeded to do the same on the second chopper, and it took off also. This all took about 20 minutes. When the dust had settled, the Blackhats left for the LZ and T.C. and I backed the truck over and loaded all the stuff into the back. We drove in to the CP, dropped off the bags and boxes to SP4 SALO.

"Hey, Mouse," Salo said as I walked in, "I see you got through the first night; how is it so far?"

"Well, I've had more sleep and better food, but I guess it's o.k." I said.

That done, we drove to each of the guns and left off about 20 boxes of four fuses each to each gun crew. Then we went back to the chopper pad and faced the sling loads. One was entirely composed of 155 'Joes' on four pallets. There were 100 'Joes' per pallet equaling 400 rounds, each weighing 97 lbs. The other sling load was an equal amount of powder canisters. We made eight trips back and forth carrying all this into the LZ and distributing it all to the gun pits.

When we finished it was 1330 hrs. We parked the truck back by the CP and dragged our tired butts back to the #3 pit. Scotty met us and said, "Good job, guys, take a break and get some chow. Unless we have a fire mission, rest up and stay cool."

'Cool! Ha!' I thought, 'The temp must be about 100 now.'

While T.C. and I were doing the re-supply, everyone else had been busy cleaning and oiling the gun, doing the routine maintenance on it and generally squaring away the area. The powder and trash had been picked up by a crew from another gun, taken out, and burned. Most of the guys were already in their hootches, except Harris, who, it seemed, never slept. He was sitting on the berm smoking and looking out at the jungle.

The day wore on in the heat. I got something to eat, then sat out on top of my culvert/home and watched everything going on around me. When the sun got too hot, (didn't take long), I got down under my poncho porch in the shade and dug out my paper and envelopes and wrote a letter to Mom.

'Dear Mom, I'm here at a big base, can't tell you where. Not because of security or anything, just that I don't know exactly where I am. I'm somewhere in Vietnam. Don't worry, it seems pretty safe where I am. Love, your son, PV2 Hudson.'

I sealed the envelope, thinking, 'Hell, I don't know if I'm in a safe area or not. They could probably be right out there in the tree line watching us, waiting till we weren't looking, then blow our asses away with rockets or mortars or God knows what kinda weapons they got!'

I put Mom's address on the envelope, stood and walked over to the CP to post it for the next mail. As I ducked into the dark bunker, Salo was sitting at the first folding table/desk reading a book, feet on the desk.

"Hey, Salo, tell me what our return address is here for this letter?" I said. "And where can I get some stamps?"

"You don't need stamps. Free mail service for us brave men at arms."

"Wow", I exclaimed. "You could save a fortune in postage if you wrote a lot of letters."

Salo rolled his eyes. He moved some papers around on his desk, found a card and handed it to me.

"Your address." The card read HHB1F30, Bat D, APO 91020.

I put the return address on the envelope and handed it to him.

"Thanks, Salo." I paused, then asked, "Hey, Salo. Does much … uh, you know… shit happen around here? I mean like rockets and mortars and stuff?"

Salo looked over at the crackle of one of the radios on the shelf, then said, "We get some shit, like mortars mostly early in the morning, or around chow time in the evening. They wait till the times when a lot of people are out doing stuff. More targets, I guess."

"Anybody, like, hurt or killed?"

"Yeah, in fact, you're replacing a guy that got shrap in his back and butt from a mortar nine days ago." He shook his head, then continued, "He was sitting on the shitter after supper about dusk, didn't hear the 'pop' and a 'short round' landed in the wire behind him. Literally blew the crap out of him. He was okay, though," he grinned, " just has an extra asshole now!"

"Are there a lot of gooks around here?" I asked intently.

"Man, there are gooks all over this country and we don't even know about half of 'em. Of course, there's gooks out there. You can hear 'em sometimes, at night when it's quiet. Moving stuff around out in the jungle. Don't know what, but probably their little mortar tube they use for our wake-up call."

"How long you been over here?" I asked.

"121 days to DEROS, man. Seems like forever." He said wistfully, "Man, if you want to learn to keep breathing, talk to Scotty, your Gunner. He's been in-country longer than anybody. Two tours. He's been there and back, several times. Scotty could tell you stuff, curl what little hair you got!"

I thanked him again and walked out of there thinking, 'Gotta remember, use the shitter during the middle of the day!'

When I got back to #3, the rest of the guys were emerging from their hootches and we all set about getting ready for another night of firing. I made a mental note to keep an eye on Scotty and try to do what he does.

'Maybe I'll learn something,' I thought, 'Maybe, just maybe, I'll live through this.'

4

"CAN'T WE JUS' CALL MAYFLOWER?"

The next three weeks ground by with a mind-numbing sameness. The weather was clear skies, hot and humid. I'd peeled my first two sunburns down to brown skin.

One high spot was hot chow once a week sent in by chopper in insulated field cans and coolers. Mostly it was roast beef, gravy, instant mashed potatoes, green beans and usually some form of cake for dessert. Not fancy, but a vast improvement over our usual fare of C-Rats.

We also got beer and soda! A whole pallet load a week, equaling about three cans of each per man per day. We had no refrigerators on the LZ but we did have a large ice cooler in a lean-to, back of the CP All the beer and soda was put into it among chunks of 100 lb. ice blocks also brought in weekly by chopper. The ration was on the 'honor system' and we all abided by it, because, if someone came up short on his allotment at the end of the week, from someone hogging too many cans, we all knew it would be a bad scene. Cool drinks are very important to hot soldiers. The ice only lasted about two days in the Southeast Asian heat. So by Sunday, we were drinking warm beer. But at least it was wet and wasn't the metallic-tasting water from the water trailer, although warm Pepsi has to be the be-all, end-all of nasty.

I'd gotten to know, at least in passing, most of the other guys on the LZ. Most of them were pretty good guys, though of course there were a few that everybody tried to avoid because these guys were either crazy or downright dangerous, either from ineptitude or being carelessly brave (we called it 'gung-ho').

There was one guy from Georgia named Heffelfinger. He was a really nice guy, but he'd fallen over everything on the LZ at least once, and was always injured in some way, but never bad enough to be sent off the LZ. He screwed up every job he'd ever done, including rumor was, burning down a mess hall in Bien Hoa before he was fired as a cook. Here, he was in Commo, a seemingly safe job. But we found ourselves tripping over the miles of wire he'd strung out, all over the LZ, when he hooked up our 'Land-line' system. Rumor also was, due to Heff's over-zealous capabilities, someone had talked to Canada on a field phone! We were afraid some day he'd fall over something important and take out a couple of other guys in the explosion. Everybody liked him, but his ineptitude brought about the 'Flying Heffelfinger of Fate' award, given to anyone who screwed up in a major way.

Then there was Brother Gray. A black guy from Detroit, or "Deetroit" according to him. He was always doing something to show that he was the Baddest Dude on the LZ. He didn't walk. He strutted with one arm straight at his side, 'Power Fist' ready. A slight hitch in his stride, designed, I guess, to show that he had rhythm, and he was 'Cool', but to me and most other guys, he looked like he had jock-itch, hitching around like that.

And, to show what a 'Big, Brave Bruthuh' he was, he'd wear a sparkling white tee-shirt at night, defying the snipers and the First Sgt.'s orders of "OD dress at all times!" 'Top' kept getting on his case about it, but Brother Gray was unfazed and did pretty much what he wanted. Unfortunately, the 'Bro' was the Supply Specialist, in charge of ordering all our re-supplies, so if you got him pissed at you and you needed, say, new boots or something, well, Bro Gray didn't know if any could be had or not. You might walk around in a broke-down boot for weeks before a new one your size came in. Gray was not popular with anyone but the five other black EMs in the unit. They formed their own little club and hung together at all times around the CP and Supply Bunker, "Dappin' 'n Slappin' n' Rappin'" (Jive-talk and elaborate handshakes involving the whole body, at times.)

I'd picked up on a lot of little things that made it bearable on the LZ. I'd fallen into the little habits most of the guys had adopted to help ignore the pretty much miserable existence we led. We learned that the more you can tune-out in your head, the easier it was to do our muscle work on the gun while eating stuff packed in 1941. All on average 4-6 hours sleep in 24. At the same time, you tried to be alert to the war around you. To be careless was to be dead. We regularly heard, either officially or as scuttlebutt, news of other LZs being hit with rockets or mortars. Some had had sapper probes (little invisible gooks that sneak into your LZ and blow stuff up). One LZ even had an all-out ground attack, where the regular N.V.A. soldiers had, en-mass, leaped over the barbed wire strung in the "killing zone" around the firebase, and came in shooting and throwing grenades. This attack had been repulsed, but not before three G.I.s were killed and 7 wounded. The body count for the N.V.A. was supposedly nineteen, but we had always heard that the gooks carry off their dead and wounded, so we assumed the kill count was probably higher than that.

It had been quiet around LZ Jamie and we all considered ourselves lucky to be only bored.

Then, on a Tuesday in July, word came down from DIVARTY (Division Artillery) in Bien Hoa. "D" Battery was to be split. Three guns were staying on Jamie, and the other three were to be moved to "IKE."

We were all gathered around Scotty as he delivered this news. I looked over at T.C. and said, "Hey, Top Cat, isn't IKE the LZ you were on when you first came in-country? The one you said was so flaky?"

"Yeah," he replied, "and I sure don't like the idea of going back out there. This place is like an R & R center compared to IKE."

Scotty looked at me and said, "You're the only one hasn't been on a hot LZ, Mouse. We were all on IKE 'til right before you came in. But it's been, what, five, six weeks now since we've been out there, maybe the gooks have moved on by now."

"I sure hope so," two or three of us said in unison.

Scotty looked at his watch and said, "It's about 1530 now. Lets get some rest until about 1800 hrs, then get your chow and pack up your personal shit. There won't be any H&Is tonight so we can get ready for the move. We'll pack up all the extraneous gear tonight, and we'll be taking the gun down at 0600 hrs." Bechtal told us "All movable gear is to be on the chopper pad by 0830. Choppers will start arriving about 0900."

"Hey Chief," Harris asked Scotty, "Do we hafta dump the bags?" He was talking about the hundreds of sandbags that made up our hootches and bunkers.

"No, all structures are to remain and, from what I understand, the pits and bunkers are still intact on IKE, so that's something anyway."

"Yeah," Harris sighed, "We won't have to fill all them bags back up, at least."

"You guys have done this before" I said. "How the hell do you move all this stuff?"

"One piece at a time!" Scotty said seriously. "Don't worry, the U.S. Army can expedite anything, anywhere, all we gotta do is work our asses off to get the shit out to the pad and the Blackhats and choppers do the rest."

By 0630 next morning we'd jacked the gun down and folded the trails for portage. We capped the tube and put a dust cover on the receiver group. All the ammo and powder was palletized on the chopper pad and all the aiming stakes, gunsights, general supplies, and various indispensable junk was boxed in metal or wood boxes and stacked to be taken out to the pad. One man from each gun was detailed to the CP to help pack up the radios and files and desks and stuff. Harris took off for that and the rest of us sweated and humped until about 0825. We had all the equipment sitting in the morning sun on the pad. Our personal gear was in a heap beyond the berm.

"How do we get the gun out here?" I asked, eyeing the opening in the berm that was not, I didn't think, wide enough to get the gun through.

"We don't," Bechtal advised me, "They'll hook it right out of the pit, and drop it into the new pit at IKE."

"The gun's the easy part," Harris said over his shoulder, "Its all this other stuff that's the pain; just be glad we don't hafta take all the sandbags with us."

"I am." I agreed.

A team of Blackhats had come in on a chopper early that morning and were now spreading net cargo slings in various locations around the pad, and instructing the gun crews to stack certain things in each sling. We'd gotten one sling stacked to about 10' high x 10' x10' when

36

one Blackhat jumped up onto the stack. We handed him the corner straps for the sling and he used a very large "D" ring from his tool belt to fasten them together in the center. He then went to each corner of the stack and pulled the strap tight and arranged the slack on the top of the stack. Minutes later the first chopper, a big, twin–rotor Chinook came in from the east to hover over the stack. Following directions from the Blackhat Sgt.'s handheld radio, a strap attached to the sling hook on the underside of the chopper was lowered. The Sgt. hooked the "D" ring to the hook on the main strap, tested it by hanging on it, then jumped to the ground and signaled the pilot to take up slack. The chopper eased upward till the sling strap was taught. Then he increased the pitch on the rotor blades and applied more power until the sling lifted from the ground. He gained about ten more feet of altitude and tilted out and away from the LZ gaining more altitude as he went. We, of course, didn't get to see any of this due to the huge cloud of dust blown into our eyes by the down wash of the blades. We turned away and hunkered down and held onto our steel pots to keep them from blowing off. Bits and pieces of paper and ponchos and loose stuff blew back into the LZ and had to be retrieved.

Less than two minutes later another Chinook came in low out of the east to hover over the 'Joes' and powder slings. These loads were hooked up in series, one above the other, with the powder above and the rounds below. This process took less than four minutes and we had all backed away into the LZ and gotten to watch the Blackhats work. Man, they were really good at their jobs. They seemed to know just how much each helicopter could lift and positioned the slings so the chopper could smoothly take up the weight.

The powder and rounds were less than a ½ mile away when another Chinook came in over our gun pit and a Blackhat had already hooked the three point sling to the portage rings on the trails and tube. He stood on top of the receiver and the pilot brought the chopper down to within 3' of the Blackhat's head. We saw a large hook descend from a square hatch in the bottom of the aircraft. The Blackhat hand-tested the connection, then jumped down from the gun and signaled the pilot. The chopper took up slack and whirled away in a huge cloud of dust, the nearly eight ton Howitzer dangling like a toy on a string.

The chief Blackhat came over to us and raised his eyebrows.

"NUMBER THREE?" he asked Scotty, who nodded affirmation. He waved us out onto the pad as a Huey with door gunners came in and settled on the PSP. Its twenty-foot-long rotor blades cutting the air above our heads as we filed up to the door and climbed into the open middle bay.

First Sgt. Ambrose and our BC, Lt. Stark, had joined us and there were eight passengers. There were four seats across the back wall, and one jump seat on either side of the door to the cockpit. The Lt. and the 1st Sgt. took the jump seats and Scotty, T.C., Bechtal, and Buckstone took the other four seats. I looked around in confusion when the crew chief motioned Harris and me to the little alcoves behind each door gunner. The door gunners manned M-60 machine guns protruding out of each side door, and behind each was a small nook with a shelf/seat and some tie down straps. I fit pretty well in my little nook. Harris, on the other hand, had trouble getting his long frame into the position required to fasten the straps around his middle. All secured, the chopper leapt from the pad with a blast of dust and sound and we were airborne.

I had a bird's-eye view over the door gunners' shoulders and watched LZ Jamie withdraw into the distance. As we gained altitude the heat dropped off and suddenly I was shivering.

"I'm cold!" I yelled, "Wow, I'd forgotten what it's like!"

My words were swept away in the wind, so no one heard, not even the door gunner, a foot away, but I was thrilled.

We flew at probably 5000 feet and, again, I got an overview of a beautiful panorama of green trees and jungle, with small splotches of farmland here and there.

We flew approximately north by northwest for about 15 minutes or about twenty-five miles.

I could see the cloud of dust for the last five minutes of the flight.

LZ IKE.

As we went into a high circling holding pattern, we watched as the Chinook with the ammo landed the sling and took off to the west. Then the other big chopper dropped the Howitzer into the pit, one of six ringing a small flat space on a terrace above a small Viet village of about thirty thatched-roofed huts. The other side of the LZ was fronted by a ravine about 30 feet deep with a hill on the other side of the gully that was a little higher (30-40 feet higher) than the LZ.

This little hill would have given an enemy a vantagepoint over the firebase, except there was no cover. The entire hill, all the way around had been completely denuded of foliage, so that from the air it looked like a red mound growing out of the trees. Finally, we swooped in and flared to a hover in the center open space of the LZ (there was no formal chopper pad) and we all exited the craft in a military manor very quickly, that is.

The helicopter wound up and was gone and we stood around for 4-5 minutes waiting for the dust to settle enough to see our surroundings.

The sight was not inspiring.

'Jeez,' I thought to myself, 'Jamie was an R & R center compared to this.'

The LZ consisted of six gun pits surrounding a flat open space about 200 yards in diameter. In the open space were four larger (15' x 15') dug-out bunkers with sandbag/psp roofs and ten various sized surface buildings with tin roofs and sandbag half walls with screens above. There were also two towers, one facing the village, and the other opposite facing the little hill. The towers were built of 6" x 6" wood beams with cross bracing and were about 30' high. The room at the top was about 10' x 10' with sand bagged half walls and tin roofs.

We could see a couple of guys in both towers and another unit (of Grunts) was occupying two of the empty gun pits. There looked to be about 35 men and a group of six mortars. They had moved into the arty bunkers and looked like they'd been there awhile. Long enough to have done laundry at least, as evidenced by the sox and skivvies and fatigues hung out on a line between the two gun pits.

My first impression was red dust. It settled like thick, red dew on the buildings, bunkers, and on the other guys and on me. I had a taste of red dust in my mouth from the air. The heat at ground level was still blazing, and as we perspired, red dust stuck to our skin. It had a gritty, oily feeling.

After a week or so I'd find out that it abraded under your arms and in your crotch and caused small heat blisters that itched, badly. But if you scratched, the rash quickly infected and before long you'd have running sores. You could wash the dirt off, but within an hour it was right back. The red dust was so powder-fine that it was always floating in the air, even when the helicopters weren't landing in the middle of us, stirring it up in red clouds.

We drifted over to the pit where our gun had been placed and scoped it out. Pretty much the same arrangement as on Jamie, except the Greenline side of the pit faced down the hill toward the village, about 300 yards off.

"Hey Scotty," T.C. yelled, "I see the V.C. 'ville is still there!"

Scotty looked up from the box he had carried into the pit from the stack in the slings.

"Yeah, its still there." He smiled. "Ya know, ya better go on and get the M-60 set up. Ya never know when the Mama-sans an' Baby-sans an' Granddaddy-sans from that 'v ille might attack!"

I was standing right by Scotty. I had to ask, "Is that really a V.C. village?"

"No, it's called Dong Wa or Dong Woo or something like that. It was originally one of the Fortified Hamlets that were set up to eliminate the V.C. effectiveness in this area. The theory didn't work very well though, 'cause a lot of the villagers were V.C. and would spy on the Friendlies to the local V.C. cadre. But, so far as I know, this ville has never been a problem. Ike's been manned by U.S. or A.R.V.N. (Army, Republic of Vietnam) troops for about two years now. We used to get some mortars and snipers on the hill over there, but Agent Orange took care of all the cover, so anybody trying to do anything can be seen and blown away."

"Who's Agent Orange?" I, the FNG, asked, "Some kinda spy?"

Scotty shook his head and snorted a laugh.

"Not WHO. What." He paused. I nodded.

"It's some kinda goo the Air Force sprays on areas where they don't want stuff to grow. It kills trees, brush, grass. You name it, it kills it!"

"Probably kills GIs, too." I said, dubiously.

"Nah!" he said, lighting a cigarette, "They say it's safe. I've been sprayed a couple times, my first tour. I'm not dead yet."

I wasn't so sure.

"Killer Goo, huh?"

"Yeah."

I changed the subject.

"T.C. said something about sapper probes last time you were here?"

We'd moved over by the gun, and he slipped the dust bag off the gun-sight and started fiddling with it.

"Yeah, a couple of nights we had movement in the ravine over there."

He nodded toward the other side of the LZ,

"We popped a bunch'a flares an' sprayed the area down with M-16s, but we never found anything but some cut concertina wire. Looked like somebody made it about half way and gave up."

"Think we're pretty safe here?" I asked, hopefully.

"Hell, Mouse, nowhere's safe in this whole fuckin' country," he said, exasperated, "least of all here."

I felt like I was bugging him, but I wanted to learn this stuff, it could be important!

"Now cut the Twenty Questions." he said gently and gave me a look.

He glanced around at the other guys who'd come into the pit and were gawking around and raised his voice.

"Lets get our shit into the pit an' get this gun operational! The other two guns AND the F.D.C. will be here A.S.A.P.... We'll havta help set THEM up, too."

"Let's get to it," he shouted, " 'fore Top starts chewin' on us!"

We got to it and by 1330 we had the gun "laid" (sighted in on the aiming stakes).

All the ammo was stowed in the bunkers, and we had strung our poncho-porches on our hootches and stowed our personal stuff.

Home Sweet Home.

Meanwhile, the other two guns were slung-in to the other empty gun pits and the crews were busy setting up. The whole base was a bee-hive of activity. Huey Slicks brought in clouds of dust and the F.D.C. 'pukes' (as we called them) and their equipment.

We ate our chow and Scotty sent Harris and T.C. to the CP to help, then told the rest of us to clean weapons and scope out the A.O. (Area of Operations) so we'd be able to find our way around after dark.

I went to my hootch and cleaned my M-16 even though I'd yet to fire it during the six weeks I'd been in-country. When I ran the patches through the barrel, they came out, you guessed it, red with dust. I figured it was going to be impossible to keep anything clean on this LZ.

By 1600 hrs, we were a completely operational firebase and everyone settled down, gratefully, for a siesta.

I was dreaming about my girlfriend Judy. She had come to my house (back home), and she was knocking on my door. I was sleeping inside (in my dream) and woke up (in my dream), wondering why she was knocking so LOUD.

I woke for real and someone was yelling "IN-COMING!!" as a huge "KARRUMP" sound came from somewhere inside the LZ.

I grabbed my steel pot and struggled into my flack-jacket before I eased my head out the end of my culvert and looked around. Scotty and Bechtal were cranking the gun around with the tube on a low trajectory. I stood up and saw they were aiming at a spot a little to the left of the gook village. Scotty saw me and T.C., who'd just crawled out, and yelled at us to get rounds and powder ready

"We've got an azimuth on those mortars an' if we can pump out some quick rounds we might get 'em!"

I ran toward the ammo bunker, with T.C. close behind. As I passed the opening in the gunpit berm, I glanced out toward the middle of the LZ and saw a pall of smoke over by one of the surface buildings and some GIs running toward it. Suddenly a huge gout of red-orange flame shot upward just on the other side of the CP and I saw clumps of dirt and rock fly out in every direction, accompanied by a deafening "KARRRUMP!!!"

The concussion lifted the red dust off the ground and nearly lifted me off my feet. I hit the dirt and low-crawled the rest of the way to the powder bunker

With T.C. scrabbling behind, yelling "Go on, Mouse! Go on, Mouse!"

Harris was already there as we crawled over and he had several rounds on the ready rack.

Scotty yelled "Fuse; Impact. Charge; Two. Round; H.E.!"

T.C. and Harris took the first round to the gun in the ramming tray and I ducked into the low bunker and hastily cut a charge-two powder bag and rushed it to Bechtal.

The 'Joe' was already rammed and Hippie took the white powder bags and stuffed them into the breech, threw his hands up and yelled "CLEAR." Scotty slammed the breechblock shut with a muffled clang which, oddly enough, sounded like the driver's door on my V.W. back home.

As Bechtal cocked the firing hammer and inserted the primer cartridge, another incoming mortar sailed in and hit on the hillside right outside our pit, between the barbed wire barrier and us. Dirt flew back over the low wall and rained down on us at the gun.

Unfazed by the noise and debris, Scotty looked around and shouted "FIRE IN THE HOLE!!!"

After a couple of seconds he pulled the lanyard.

The 'Pig' (gun) lurched with the recoil and the BOOM was tremendous.

We looked out across our berm toward our target and within seconds saw a bunch of trees jump into the air, then crash back down about a half-mile out. Scotty cranked another couple degrees of deflection, and T.C. and Harris arrived with another round.

I ran to cut more powder.

BOOM...BOOM!! The other two guns fired out into the same area and I glimpsed more trees jumping and falling over as I darted back and forth from bunker to gun. Then the cloud of smoke that quickly blanketed the area where our rounds were landing blocked our view.

We quickly fired three more H.E.s, adjusting slightly between each one, to blanket as much area as possible. The other guns did the same. Then we ceased fire and listened. The incoming had apparently stopped when we began firing.

T.C. was stalking back and forth muttering "Man oh man! I knew this place had bad vibes! The Gooks are gonna start on us as soon as we get here!"

Scotty came around the gun trail and patted him on the back.

"T.C., don't you recognize the Welcome Wagon when you see it? They just wanna make us feel at home."

He and Bechtal laughed but T.C. just scowled and said " Shit, my home's thirteen thousand miles away an' no way do I feel welcome in this crappy country."

At 1900 hrs things had settled down and we all had some chow.

Scotty had us all together by the hootches and told us we didn't have an H&I list tonight, but we'd probably get some contact missions. The 2/7th grunts were on sweeps out to our west, and could possibly hit some shit anytime.

I settled on my porch and started a letter to Judy. T.C. and Harris went over to one of the other guns to visit some guys they knew and Scotty and Bechtal went to the CP to drink beer with the F.D.C 'Pukes'.

I was still wound up from the incoming and had a hard time concentrating on my writing. I finally got up and walked out to the berm where Buck was sitting, looking out over the village to the west.

The sun was low on the horizon and the countryside and the village looked so picturesque.

"Man, it's times like this that make it hard to imagine we're in a war zone." I said, "look at that ville', looks so peaceful an' quiet."

Buck continued looking at the deepening sunset, and for a minute I thought he hadn't heard me, but then in a low voice he said, "Yeah, it looks nice." He paused for a drag off his cigarette, then continued,

"But them Gooks down there?" He nodded toward the town, now in deepening shadows.

"They'd jus' as soon shoot you as look at you."

He turned to me, blew the smoke from his nose.

"Knew a guy in another battery, went into a ville' that was supposedly 'friendly'. Him an a couple other dudes, sitting at an outdoor café kind'a thing, you know? Like tables out on th' sidewalk? Anyway, they're sittin' an' sippin' here in th' middle of town, an' this dog walks around th' corner of a building an' comes over t' th' table, where these guys are, an' wags its tail, cute as hell, ya know?"

I nodded.

"Turns out th' dog had a grenade hooked on its collar an' a wire hooked to th' pin in th' grenade. Somebody right around that corner waited till th' dog was right next to th' table, an' this dude I knew was bendin' over to pet it, an' they pulled th' wire. Three seconds later, Poof! Three dead G.I.s, man. Killed th' damn dog, too!"

He shook his head, sadly.

"Gooks don't even care about animals Man!"

The big guy actually trembled with suppressed rage.

"If they don't got no respect for little innocent animals, ya know they don't give a shit 'bout people, either! I know it's jus' th' way they was brung up, but, Damn, it jus' gets me, is all."

After a minute I said, "Buck, you think you'll get through this and get back home? You know, go back and work a job, get married, have kids and all?"

He seemed surprised by the question.

"Hell yeah," he said in no uncertain terms.

"Seventy one days an' a wake-up an' they'll play hell tryin' ta' stop me. I'll still have fifteen months ta' do in th' states, but then I'll be a free mayun."

His Missouri drawl was strong.

"I thought you were gonna re-up?"

"Shit, th' shorter I get th' more I think I better jus' get th' hell outta this FUBAR army an' go back to th' farm."

"FUBAR?"

He chuckled. "Means 'Fucked up Beyond All Repair'."

"There it is." I agreed.

We sat quiet for a while, till the sun had set completely and the village had disappeared into the gray twilight.

"Think I'll go and try to finish that letter I started." I said and stood to leave.

Buck stood, also, and we walked around the gun to the hootches.

As we parted he said, "Mouse, I've been here a long time, an' you got a long way ta' go, but if ya' jus' take it as it comes, one day at a time, you'll do okay. Ya' jus' gotta remember 'It don't mean nuthin'."

"Whadda you mean?" I asked.

"To yer 'Friends an' Neighbors' back home, man. The ones that seelected yer' ass to come over here. They don' care if you get yer shit blown away, as long as it ain't their kid. Think 'bout that if ya' wanna live. It'll piss ya' off so bad you'll get through anything jus' so's you c'n go back home an' say 'Fuck you, Jack, I'm back!'"

I laughed and said, "I'll keep that in mind, but I've been pissed off since my first day in Basic. Man, if I get any more pissed I'd be dangerous."

"It's good to be dangerous over here, maybe it'll keep ya' breathin'." He said and turned to his culvert.

I went to my own and finished the letter.

Done, I lay my head on my ruck as a pillow and snapped off my red flashlight and drifted off. 'Been a long day,' I thought as sleep took over.

5

'SAPPERS'

"CONTACT MISSION!" The call woke me in pitch darkness. I raised my arm and checked my luminous watch.

'Man, 4:30 in the morning!' I thought and rolled over to find my boots, pot and flack jacket.

A minute later I rolled out and ran past the shadowy images of the rest of the crew to the powder store.

By the dim ('Damn, need new batteries again') red glow of my light, I cut out the first charge, a 'charge three', and ran it to the gun and handed it to the A.G.

"Hey, Hippie, any idea what's up?" I asked, as he 'cleared' and the breechblock slammed shut.

He cocked the hammer and inserted the primer cartridge and joined me outside the trails.

"A 2/7th L.P. (listening post) has movement on the road...."

BOOM! The gun fired.

"....on the road out the other side of the ville' about two clicks. They want some steel on it A.S.A.P." He ran back and cleared the breech for the next round.

We fired ten rounds, then stopped and swabbed the tube and policed the area. By that time the sky was gray in the east as we all sat on the gun trails and smoked our first cigs of the day.

"Wonder if we got any of 'em?" I mused.

"May never know," Harris said "the gooks haul off their dead, wounded, trash, everything. Just to keep us wondering and screw up our minds."

T.C. spoke up.

"Yeah, th' little fuckers can just up an' disappear like they weren't never there. Scares lotta guys. Makes 'em think they're some kinda spooks or somethin'. But I know they're jus' flesh 'n blood, like anybody, an' we kill a bunch of 'em on a regular basis. But they never run outta gooks. Got a inexhaustible supply of 'em up north in Hanoi."

"There it is." We all agreed.

Scotty stood and said, "Get some chow and stand down 'till re-supply comes in at 0830. Also, the 2/19th Arty is bringing in three of their 105s sometime today and I heard from Salo another company of Grunts is coming in, so it's gonna get crowded around here."

"We expecting some shit?" I asked.

"Salo said there's been a build-up of Victor Chuck and NVA activity in the area an the Grunts will be doing sweeps and Search and Destroy around here. We've been advised to keep perimeter guard around our berms at night and watch out for movement around the LZ. I'll set the guard roster later. Right now I'm gonna eat." He turned and walked away.

"Yeah, like we already get too much sleep." T.C. said, sarcastically.

We all laughed and got up to eat our breakfasts. After chow we attended our usual details and watched the activity around us.

As the day wore on our population swelled as the 105s were slung into the empty pits. Then later the new Grunts came in on Chinooks and settled all around our pits, looking, in all their fierceness, like a tribe of Gypsies with weapons.

Grunts always look rag-tag and scruffy, carrying their worldly possessions on their backs. They live a hard existence, and it shows. They'd be open for derision, in any other part of the Army, but the look in their eyes warns anyone to keep their opinions to themselves.

At 1800 hrs Scotty rounded us up and assigned the guard schedule. I drew 2:00 to 4:00 A.M. and was advised to get some rest and don't, under any circumstances nap-out on duty. He had come up with a Starlight Scope, (a night vision device that looks like a fat telescope), from somewhere and spent an hour showing us uninitiated how to use it. I racked out by 2130 hrs, but I was a little wired and didn't get to sleep until about 2330.

At a little before 2:00 A.M. I was shaken awake by Harris.

"Guard, Mouse. Wake up."

Groggy, I crawled out and went to the M-60 bunker that faced outward down the hill toward the ville. Harris told me to keep my eyes open and to make a 'Sit-Rep' (Situation Report) to the CP every half-hour on the field phone.

He left and I was alone, peering into the dark night. I picked up the Starlight Scope. It's a dark green tube about 4" in diameter and 18" long. It has an eyepiece on one end with a little cover-cap that hangs on a little chain when not snapped in place. The other, bigger end also has a cap on its own chain. On the side is a 2"x3"x2" metal box with a switch in the middle labeled 'ON-OFF-STANDBY.' I flipped the toggle to 'ON' and waited about ten seconds for the mechanism to warm up and the images to resolve on the little screen inside the eyepiece.

I was looking at a surreal landscape done in shades of green and black. The images weren't distinct but I could make out the shapes of the roofs in the ville' and the line where the open 'Kill Zone' met the tree line. I scoped my entire area and found nothing out of the ordinary.

When I took my eye from the scope, I experienced the 'BIG GREEN EYE'. The eye I had used felt twice as big as the other and the green glow was burned onto my retina, like the dots from flashbulbs but more so and all over. My 'good' eye couldn't compensate for the brightness I was seeing in the other eye, so essentially, I was blind as a bat for five or more minutes until the effect wore off. I made a mental note to not use the scope unless absolutely necessary, or else be blind for a while.

I ducked down behind the sandbags and quickly lit a cigarette. I sat up and smoked it cupped in my hand, (to supposedly avoid making a target for a Gook with a Starlight Scope). I sat, watched, listened and realized it was about as quiet as I'd ever heard it on a firebase. As the night dragged on I dutifully checked my A.O. regularly and reported my 'Sit-Rep negative' to the CP every half-hour, which was roger-ed each time by one of the F.D.C. guys on duty.

At 0335 I was thinking how good it was going to feel to go back and sack-out. Suddenly all hell broke loose on the other side of the LZ.

I started and knocked my steel pot on the low PSP roof of the bunker. I immediately looked out the opening facing the Green-line and saw nothing, so I crept along the blast wall and peeked around the end. I saw flashes and red tracers flying in all directions, and heard M–16s and M-79 grenade launchers (or 'Bloopers') working out by the gunpit directly opposite our position.

Scotty was suddenly beside me and said, "What's up, Mouse?"

I said I didn't know and he pushed past me into the bunker. He picked up the phone, cranked it and talked to the CP for a minute while I peered intently out the gun-port at the quivery light and drifting shadows thrown by the parachute flares that were now up all around the base.

Scotty hung up the phone and turned beside me and said, "Crew on #1 reported movement in the ravine."

The firing had subsided to just a few 'pops' now and then.

"They were doing a little 'Recon by Fire'."

"I haven't seen a thing out here, man." I said, trying to act not nervous.

We took turns looking through the 'scope at our section of the KZ, but after about fifteen minutes we still saw no evidence of activity.

I told Scotty I needed to go wake up Buck for the next guard shift. He said for me to go get him, but to come back and stay with him until I was told otherwise. Also, I was to tell the other guys what was happening and that they were to stay in their hootches unless a mission was called.

I ran across the gun-pit, lit by the swaying flares, and found everyone gathered on Bechtal's porch, talking excitedly and pointing across the LZ. I arrived and relayed Scotty's message and as Buck and I ran back to the M-60 bunker, the others went to their bunkers and crawled in.

We ducked into the small space as Scotty was hanging up the field phone. He told us to do a Sit-Rep every fifteen minutes until the CP gave the 'All Clear', and then left. Buck looked at me in the dim light and grinned.

"Man, scared th' sheeit outta me when them guys let loose alla sudden like that."

I laughed and told him how I'd bumped my head on the ceiling. He laughed at that, too, and our tension was broken.

We settled down and took turns watching the perimeter. By 0430 all the flares had sputtered out and all was quiet in the enfolding darkness. At 0500 Scotty came by and told us that the CP had given the

'All Clear' and that I should rack-out, but Buck should stay there until first light at 0630.

I didn't have to be told twice. I was soon by my hootch and before crawling in I glimpsed the other guys apparently sleeping peacefully. Inside, I lay down and tried to relax but it seemed sleep was out of the question. I tossed and turned and just couldn't get comfortable.

Finally, at 0700, I gave up the effort, got up and heated a scrambled egg/ sausage C-Rat. Ate that and washed it down with warm powdered milk. This did not help the nasty taste in my mouth, so I took my canteen cup and walked out of the pit to the water trailer and brushed my teeth.

I smacked my lips and thought, 'There are still a few little pleasures left.'

I still felt like warmed-over shit, but at least my breath was good. I was halfway back to the gun when I heard excited voices from over by the CP, so I walked over to see what was going on. It was Salo, talking to our crew and some other guys. I stood beside T.C. and nudged him.

"What's up?" I asked.

He turned and said, "They got some gooks this mornin'."

"Wow, Really?"

"Yeah, two of 'em, in th' wire on th' slope up to #1 gun! Salo said they'd cut some of th' wire an' had satchel-charges strapped on 'em."

I heard Salo tell us not to run over there and gawk, but if we wanted to see some dead gooks, go in an orderly manner, two at a time from each gun.

On the way back to our pit Scotty said, "I heard this morning, we got some gooks on that contact mission last night, too."

Everyone exclaimed and asked "How many?"

"'Bout four, but some of 'em were in kinda pieces, so, they couldn't tell for sure. Got some rockets and equipment, maps an' papers an' shit, too."

I grinned around at the others and said, "Good to know we're not just shooting all these rounds out to kill trees an' bushes."

Yeah, man, "Harris spoke up, suddenly serious, "but that also means we've got a serious infestation of gooks in this A.O. They're like cockroaches, man, if you see one there's a thousand ya' don't see".

Harris and I were the first to go over to see the bodies.

51

When we got there, a lot of other guys were standing around talking and looking at a section of the K.Z. where three men were standing, looking down at, I presumed, the bodies. They were approximately halfway down the slope from the berm wall where we stood, but we still couldn't see anything.

We followed the general drift of people to an opening in the concertina wire into the K.Z. itself. We followed two other guys down slope, winding around the rows of lethal wire, being careful to avoid the trip flares and Claymore mines.

As we neared the place where the three guys were standing, I first heard flies buzzing. Then I saw the source of the sound. On the ground, still hard to see, even in the broad morning sunlight, was the first body. The head pointed uphill, on his belly, his brown-red skin the same color as the ground. He lay with his arms stretched out in front of him. He was partway under a strand of wire and had been cutting another strand when he was hit the first time. I looked close enough to see four bullet penetrations, two in the head and two in the shoulder. The head shots had exited the back of the skull and had taken a large chunk with them, leaving a bloody mass down between his shoulder blades. This is what the flies were so excited about, Buzzing and settling in a swarm.

"Sheeit!" Harris whispered beside me, "It's just a kid!"

I looked again and, sure enough, he was probably only 4' 6-8" tall and skinny as a rail. But the four, black, 10"x10"x3", canvas Satchel charges strapped to him told me this was no kid. This was a soldier, intent on killing as many of our guys as he could before the inevitable happened. He had to have known he'd be killed, as he carried no other weapons. He was dressed only in a loincloth and rubber 'Ho Chi Minh racing slicks' (sandals cut from old tires).

"Man," I muttered, trying not to breathe the stench already rising in the heat, "He was just gonna crawl in, throw the satchel charges an' then what?"

I wondered what kind of dedication it took to sacrifice your life for, what? The chance to kill a few G.I.s?

"Musta been stoned-out on somethin' pretty heavy, or just plain crazy." Harris said, shaking his head.

"Yeah.... Stoned is right." I turned away, the smell getting to me.

Harris was close beside me. As we made our way toward the other site, I wondered if I'd have that kind of dedication, or 'Balls' or whatever if I was ordered into battle against insurmountable odds, knowing from the start I'd be killed or at least captured. I sincerely doubted it. My estimation of these little M.F.s took on a whole new light.

About ten yards on down the hill we found the second body; or pieces of it. Looked like an M-79 grenade had landed right next to his right side, separating his right arm from the body. It was ten feet away, hanging in another strand of wire. The entire side of him was raw hamburger and what was left of him was bloated and misshapen and a bluish color under the dark skin. This one was about the same size as the first, and equipped similarly.

He had obviously been several feet to his right when the round hit, and had been lifted and thrown left until he was draped, face-up, on the 'Tangle-Foot' wire, with his remaining arm hanging up over his head, with only his hand resting on the ground. His blood was black on the wire and the ground around him.

Here, too, the flies were having a feast.

"Man, I'm glad I ate already." I told Harris.

"Yeah, me too," he replied, then "C'mon, I think I've seen enough."

He turned and walked back up the hill, and I followed a few yards behind him.

When we were back inside and walking across the LZ I said, "Well, that's two we won't have to worry about tonight."

"An' all his buddies are still out there, and probably pissed." He paused, "They'll be back and try again. Bet on it."

#2 Gun Pit - LZ Jaimie

6

VIETNAM IN A BAG

But they didn't. Not until eight days later.

Then it was mortar attacks morning and evening for four days running. No one was killed during this time but shrapnel hit several guys when a mortar blew out a blast wall in the building they were in on the other side of the base.

The gooks (probably some V.C. from the village, we all thought) would fire in from about a quarter mile out beyond the 'ville. About the same area where we'd killed the other gooks on the road.

The Grunts were doing daily sweeps of the area but saw no movement or evidence of the enemy. Still, every morning between 6:00 and 8:00 and every evening between 5:00 and 7:00 we'd get two or three 81mm mortar rounds come in and blow holes in the ground or a bunker. So far, none had landed in a gun pit, but we figured it was just a matter of time before they mastered their aim and then we'd be the targets. We always returned fire with two or three rounds from our three guns, but as far as we knew, we never blew anything away but jungle.

"They must have a tunnel or system of 'Spider Holes' to duck into." Scotty conjectured, but the Grunts never found them. Finally after four days they stopped. We don't know why, but they seemed to just lose interest in us (much to our relief.)

Then the jungle and hills around us seemed devoid of any moving thing except the Grunts, out patrolling. Things were quiet until the end of July, when we got orders to move again.

"Where we goin' now?" T.C. asked Salo that evening. Scotty, Bechtal, T.C. and I had gone over to the CP to see what we could find out.

"New LZ called St. Barbara, north of here 'bout ten clicks. Supposedly where the gooks went when they left here."

"Why we gotta chase 'em, man?" Harris said, not joking, "Lets make 'em come an' get us for a change."

"You wish, man." Salo returned, "But, fact is, the choppers will be picking up loads at 0930. That's A.M., dudes, so ya' better get packin'."

"Do we dump our bags this time, Salo?" Scotty asked.

"No, leave the structures as- is, but St. Barbara is a new base so you'll have to fill your bags for bunkers and hootches. The Engineers have the berms up and the dugouts in but no roofs or walls."

He looked around at the group.

"The Grunts have been there for a night and a day, already, so they've got the perimeter wired and booby-trapped pretty well, but there will be extra wire and stuff if you want to, like, embellish on their job."

A groan rose up from the crowd and one guy said, "Man, we gotta move all this shit again, Then we get to dig up half of Vietnam an' put it inna bag?"

I said, "Ya mean we gotta fill all our own bags?"

"Hell no, man." A guy called 'Lizard' cracked "WE gotta fill all them FUCKIN' bags."

Our crew walked back to our area, ate chow and hashed out our plan for the move. Scotty assigned details and we set about breaking down all the non-essential equipment and making stacks of gear in the order it was to be carried out to the pad in the morning.

At 0-dark-30 we broke the gun down for portage, stacked the ammo on skids and towed it out to the pad with the LZ's only vehicle, a little 'Mule'.

The 'Mule' is like a four-wheel-drive golf cart, only a little bigger. It consists of a frame, wheels and engine, under a flat platform about 5' x 8', with a drivers seat, pedals and steering wheel all in a little basket attached to the front. I am always amazed at how much stuff you can pile-on or hook-to and drag with a 'Mule' without even slowing it down.

The choppers arrived on time and 'Hooked' us out and flew us to our destination, LZ Barbera.

Barbera turned out to be a mere clearing in the jungle with a lot less space, even, than we'd had on Ike.

There were only three gunpits and the Grunts had put their bunkers in between our pits to complete a ring about 300 ft. in diameter. In the center of this small space was the F.D.C. or the hole where the F.D.C. would be. We were dropped into the LZ and all our gear was slung-in by the pit. Finally the gun itself was brought in by a Chinook and set down inside our berm walls.

After we'd all had a look around, T.C. said, "Man, I don't like the looks of this place AT ALL!"

"Yeah," Harris said "looks like the gooks could take a couple of good leaps over that wire out there an' be on us before we could say 'shit.'"

Scotty, always the Chief, said, "All the more reason to start filling those sandbags." He indicated several pallets of brand-new bags sitting by the F.D.C. hole. He picked out T.C. and me and told us to start on the CP bunker. We, of course, groaned but we grabbed our shovels out of the pile of equipment and proceeded to, indeed, 'Dig up Vietnam and put it in a bag.'

We used the loose dirt from the dug-out first, which made for much easier digging than later when we had to scoop out our own hootches. These holes were dug just deep enough to provide dirt to fill enough bags for side and back walls and two layers of bags for our PSP roofs. T.C. and I dug and filled all day, taking turns at the shoveling while the other guys took care of setting up the gun and getting operational. When they had us ready for fire-missions, they pitched-in with the hootches and powder bunker.

During a mid-afternoon break I said, "Man, I thought humpin' rounds was tough work, but it's nothin' like humpin' dirt!"

"There it is." T.C. agreed, wearily. "But at least we're diggin' holes, an' a hole is a good thing to have in Nam. Especially, on this flaky LZ."

"You think we'll get some shit here, T.C.?"

"I'd bet on it." He answered in his southern drawl.

"Th' gooks won't be able to pass up a sweet li'l target like us. Hell, our asses are flappin' in th' wind out here. Only thing we got goin' for us is, we're still close enough to IKE that our other three guns can fire support for us."

"Or us for them." I reminded him.

Later that night my words rang prophetic when we got a fire-mission on coordinates around LZ Ike as they were hit by an organized force of N.V.A. supported by 107 and 122 rockets. News we got the next morning, after firing almost continuously from 0130 to0530, was, the gooks had breached the wire, again in the ravine under #1 gun-pit, and had over-run the crew briefly. ARA and Mini-guns dispersed the attackers from gun-ships out of Phouc Vinh. (A large base to the south.)

One GI was killed and two were wounded, all on #1 gun. In addition, three structures, including the FDC were damaged or destroyed.

"I guess they were just lulling us 'til the guard went down, then we split the battery an' made Ike more vulnerable." Scotty observed, during our morning chow.

"Yeah," Harris said, still chewing beanie-weenies, "makes me almost glad I'm here." He paused, "But not quite."

We all remained tense and irritable for the next two weeks, but nothing else of consequence happened. The Grunts reported seeing signs of activity on the trails and streams in the jungle around us, and, sometimes, our LPs would call-in 'movement' in their AOs, but as far as we knew, they never came anywhere near Barbera. We fired some contact missions for the Grunts, and H&Is all night, most nights. The rest of the time, we were just left alone.

We weren't complaining.

Sandbagging LZ Ike

7

GUN-BUNNY HOP

Pig 'n Me

The third of August found us packing our bags for the move to LZ Odessa. Odessa was a carbon copy of Barbera, just slightly bigger, and situated on a hill, (or 'rise', as T.C. called it, "This ain't no hill.") The 'Rise' gave us a view over the top of the surrounding scrub-jungle. We were on Odessa long enough to fill about 10,000 sandbags and fire 300 rounds, then we were off to LZ JUDY.

"What a lovely whirlwind tour we're getting." I commented. Maybe Judy would be a nice place, 'cause my girlfriend back home was named Judy. No, Nada, Nix, it was another dirt-hole, probably thirty clicks west of Odessa, in the 'Fishhook' area, from what we gleaned from

Salo. Of course, this information meant nothing to me. I was only sure I was in Vietnam, somewhere. Just about everywhere I'd been in the last two months and eight days had looked almost exactly the same.

At JUDY, we rejoined the rest of the Battery. It felt good to be 'whole' again. Strength in numbers, we hoped. We'd avoided any hostile action against us for over a month, and we felt we'd been leading a charmed life since leaving IKE.

This calm period ended on our third day of occupancy, when a sniper shot a guy named Sellers in the thigh. He was Med-evac'ed to 15th Med in Bien Hoa, and we never saw him again.

Two more days passed before the sniper tried again, this time, only wounding a sandbag by the CP door as 1st Sgt. Ambrose was entering there. Naturally, this caused 'TOP' to have a major case of the ass, and soon he had the 2/7 Grunts out patrolling, day and night, looking for "The li'l Bastard", but to no avail.

The 'Lil Bastard' disappeared and could not be found.

Six more days passed without incident.

We, as usual, fired contact missions and H&Is, and we settled into the firebase routine of details, firing, eating and sleeping as we could.

On August 17th we were ordered to move again. This announcement was met with the usual moans and groans from all present, but Salo, holding up both hands to quiet us, said, "WHOA dudes! You might like this one!"

"Why, we going to San Francisco?" a voice from the crowd called out.

"Well, not quite," he laughed, "but we ARE going to a stand-down area, southwest of here about sixty clicks. Tay Ninh City ain't half-bad. It's got restaurants an' bars, an' even a steam bath, I heard."

We all grinned around at each other and jived about getting laid, showers, getting the 'Clap', and doing anything but the usual crap.

Salo quieted us once again.

"We'll still be a firing Battery..." he had to hush our moaning again, "but I do believe some 'free' time can be arranged so you guys 'n gals can absorb some of the local, ...uh...'culture', so to speak."

The excitement among us could not be suppressed as we walked back to our respective areas to pack-up once more for the move.

8

THE LIFE

"Hey Mouse, how 'bout a steam 'n cream?" T.C. yelled, stepping through the hootch door, "Hot water an' hotter ladies!"

"Sure, man!" I said, looking up from trying to polish, mostly unsuccessfully, my 'suede-look' boots.

"Wait five."

It was our second day at Tay Ninh City, and we'd already found out we'd have some adjustments to make to survive in this jungle.

The rules were different on firebases than in rear areas.

For instance these boots.

In the field the rough leather was OK, if not 'cool'. But in the 'City', if you were to be seen in public (meaning by the 'Lifers'), "Yer boots WILL be at least black, if not polished. Yer hair WILL be cut to Regs., an' you Will shave ever blessed day you are here. Is that CLEAR?" to quote the 1st Sgt. the morning we arrived.

We'd lived a camp-out existence for so long we'd hardly noticed how bad we smelled. In fact, we were downright crusty, so truthfully, a little cleaning-up was a good idea. (And felt good, too!) After a morning formation (of all things) we had been sent in groups of four to the Gook Barbershop (in a semi-trailer on blocks next to the PX). We'd also been advised, no more cut off fatigues, shirts or pants.

"The BRASS don't wanna see any sloppy-ass soldiers." 'Top' harranged,

"So I want everybody, especially YEW Private Gray," pointing to our leading dress-code offender, "to get yerselves STRAIGHT and STRACK. Be on yer best behavior! I know it's been a while since any o' yew've been in a bar or restaurant. Or around th'...LADIES, so ta speak.

But I'm sure it'll come back ta yew. If yew screw up here, it's th' same as it wuz back home. Yew WILL be arrested an' locked up! I DON'T wanna havta come down an 'git any of yew assholes outta th' Brig. If I DO, yew WILL be on my SHIT-LIST forever, NOW IS THAT CLEAR?"

It was perfectly clear to me.

T.C., Harris, Buck and I had already visited the PX and the barbershop. The PX wasn't much, a low, metal-sided building not much bigger than a corner grocery store back home. What it lacked in size it made for in volume. It was stacked and packed full of amazing (at least to us) stuff.

"WOW, man!" T.C. exclaimed, looking all around, then he dashed over to a rack by the check-out counter, "Candy bars an' nuts an' stuff! An' look!" He pointed to another rack, "Cigarettes, cartons of 'em!"

We were all like kids in a candy store.

We 'shopped' for a half-hour, and came away with treasures that I had not figured on finding in Southeast Asia. I got two cartons of ciggs, (Marlboro, Kools, Salems, and Pall Mall were the only brands available), a big bag of M&M's, shoe polish (to appease the Brass), a warm six-pack of canned Pepsi, and, most amazing of all, a small portable radio/tape-player that would run off 'D' batteries.

Man, I hadn't heard music in over three months, except drifting out of someone elses hootch.

I also picked up five cassette tapes. 'Santana, Black Magic Woman', 'Iron Butterfly', 'James Gang, Rides Again', 'Beatles, Yellow Submarine', and best of all, 'Chicago, Silver Album'.

I figured I was set for about anything as long as I had my 'tunes'.

The other guys got cigarettes and candy, too, but for some reason T.C. could not resist a loud, silk Hawaiian shirt with bright red flowers and multiple bright shades of green foliage.

Harris, Buck and I laughed and looked at each other with amazement, but T.C. insisted.

"We can have a real 'Luau' some night an' we can invite some other guys over, an' I'll be dressed like th' King of Hawaii himself."

We cracked up.

"Yeah sure," Jim said, between guffaws, "we'll just shoot us a water buffalo, dig a pit an' roast him in the ground wrapped in banana leaves. Think we can get banana leaves around here?"

He elbowed me.

T.C. looked hurt.

"Aw, y'all are jus' jealous 'cause I got th' best lookin' shirt in Viet Nam." He paused as we laughed that much harder. "Anyway, it'll feel good to wear something besides Olive Drab for a change."

With this we had to agree.

In fact, I went back in and bought a yellow Ban-lon shirt.

Next stop was the barbershop next door. Inside the OD green trailer were four barber chairs and four Gook Barbers. They wore white coats, black pants and sandals.

Buck whispered "I think I've seen those guys before, but they were wearin' black 'Jammies', then. I ain't lettin' any of 'em near my neck with a razor."

We each took a chair and got thoroughly sheared without experiencing a single casualty.

From there, not knowing what else we were allowed to do, we went back to the Battery area, where I was struggling to put a shine on those boots.

"You mean we get ta go to the 'Ville?" I asked, scrubbing away.

"Yeah, Top said we could, 'slong as we're back by 1900, so, come own, it's almost 1430 now!"

He was practically dancing with anticipation.

I gave up on getting a real gloss on the boots (they would have to settle for just black), and put them on and laced them up. I grabbed my steel pot and flack jacket, then turned to get my rifle when T.C. put his hand on my chest and stopped me.

"Naw, man, ya don't need no combat shit, nor weapon."

I looked at him doubtfully, but put my gear back on my bunk.

"You sure, man? I don't feel 'right', ya know? I mean bein' in Gookville without a weapon."

T.C. grabbed my arm and nearly dragged me out the door.

"I think it makes th' 'Lifers' nervous, 'round here, ta have us 'Peons' runnin' around with loaded guns, man."

We emerged into the hot slanting afternoon sun and walked the quarter-mile to the MP checkpoint at the gate to the city. We were waved through a wide, oriental-looking wooden archway with 'TAY NINH CITY' painted in red on a pagoda-shaped board across the top.

Tay Ninh was not really a 'City', to my way of thinking, at all. Though it did have more concrete or brick buildings than any other villages I'd seen.

The overall effect was low and spread out.

The tallest structures in town were two-story and looking back toward the base all you saw were radio antennas and one, tall, A-frame wooden building with a yellow 1st Cav patch painted on it.

The gate led straight onto the 'Main Street' of town. It was paved (so to speak), with an oily, compacted surface, similar to asphalt, only gooier in the heat. On both sides the street was lined with bars, shops, restaurants and all manner of 'capitalist' ventures.

T.C. and I walked along ogling both the city and the girls, (of which there seemed to be many,) we pointed and commented (Wow, look at that!) like a couple of tourists (which is what we were, come to think of it.)

The traffic on this hot, late afternoon was still pretty heavy, with lots of bicycles, motor scooters, pedi-cabs, trucks and cars, all intermingled with military vehicles from Jeeps to 5-ton trucks. It was noisy but exciting.

We came to a sort of square. Just three benches around a flagpole bearing the South Vietnamese banner, yellow and green, waving in the slight breeze that blew hot from the west.

We sat on one of the benches and I lit a cig.

I was sweating from the walk, but also because it was my first time in a VN town without a weapon.

I was paranoid.

"Do all these gooks look like VC to you?" I whispered to my partner.

He just shook his head and told me to "Cool it, man." He didn't seem concerned.

He jumped up and dragged me on down the street and around a corner into a side alley, darkened by the shade of the buildings. It was cool and dark there, and I couldn't stop my imagination from picking out potential enemies in the shadows.

"Wish I had my rifle." I said. "I feel naked."

"Yeah, but I could get used to it." T.C. replied.

"There it is." I said, relaxing a bit.

"THERE IT IS!" He practically yelled, startling me.

"WHAT?!" I gulped, ready to dodge for cover.

"The steam baths, man. There it is!"

He pointed to a gray stucco building on our left, about fifty feet on down.

It had been an impressive structure at one time, but was now down at the heels. The stucco coating that covered the entry and second floor galleries was chipped off in places, leaving the arched, brick columns on the façade exposed. All the downstairs windows were covered in plywood. A once-impressive wrought-iron gate that sported intricate and beautiful filigree and swirls guarded the double entry doors, but had, in recent years, had a layer of rusted expanded-metal sheet, with a diamond pattern, welded over its exterior.

A sign above the second floor arches proclaimed, in English and Vietnamese, TAY NINH STEAM BATHS and MASSAGE, in gold letters trimmed in red.

T.C. was rubbing his hands together, grinning.

"Oh, man, I'm gonna get rubbed the right way, for a change!"

We walked up to the doors, one of which swung open at our approach, and was held for us by a small, grinning mama-san.

She smiled her Betel-nut stained smile and waved us into a dark, lobby/foyer/waiting room with an ornate, carved bench along one wall, facing an equally ornate counter, built into the other long wall. At the counter was a beautiful girl-san in a flowery Aou-Dai (Vietnamese traditional dress).

"Welcome, GI, may I he'p?"

Her smile was dazzling white.

I was behind T.C. as we approached.

"We want th' steam bath, massage an' th' works!" His voice boomed in the large, marble-lined room (reminded me of our bank, back home.)

"That 500 piasters, or five buck, MPC." (military pay scrip)

66

"Yes M'am," T.C. said, and we both fished in our pockets for our money.

She counted our money and pointed to a door at the end of the counter, to our left.

She had a lilting, singsong voice.

"Go there to undressing room and you be shown. All tipping allowed for girls, for sure!"

We went through the beaded curtain and entered another tiled room with three wooden benches down the middle of the area. Old, paint-chipped wall lockers lined the walls. Another girl (or woman, it's hard to tell) was standing in the doorway at the other end of the room and saw us enter.

She rushed over and handed us each two towels from a stack by the rear door.

"You take off clothes," she pointed, "put in lockahs."

She pointed to the rear door.

"Then come!"

We looked at each other, giggled.

"You betcha, baby!" T.C. leered.

She withdrew to the front entry, poked her head through the beaded curtain and said something in Vietnamese to the counter-girl. Then she turned back, saw us still standing there.

"Rikky Tik! Clothes off! Veddy busy, veddy hurry!"

She clapped her hands to emphasize this statement, and went to the rear exit and stood with her arms crossed, waiting.

"See many GI nekkid," she added, smiling. "no big deal!"

T.C. and I smiled at each other and proceeded to undress and stow our stuff. The lockers had no locks and I didn't want to leave my watch and wallet in there. I was just getting ready to mention this to T.C. when the girl-san picked up two small, green drawstring bags and brought them to us.

"You put vallables in here, carry." She explained.

We did and then we followed her swaying rear end through the curtain on the exit and into the main hallway, also tiled that led back through the building. There were doorways letting off left and right, all with beaded curtains covering them.

As we walked toward the other end I heard slapping sounds and moans coming from the side rooms. This struck us both funny and we started giggling again as we followed the pretty girl to the door at the end.

"You go!" she said, simply.

She pointed through the door, indicating we should go right.

We entered another shorter hall that ended at a heavy wooden door with a thick glass insert in it and a sign that said 'STEAM'. We went through this door and into a cloud. The tile halls had been cool but the temperature in here was at least 150° or more. We peered into the steamy gloom and detected other ghostly shapes occupying the three-tiered wood benches that disappeared into the mist. We walked down the row and ID'ed the specters as some other GIs, streaming sweat with their towels wrapped around their necks or draped over their heads.

T.C. and I found a place, sat down, looked at each other and tried to stifle our snickering somewhat successfully.

We cooked about fifteen minutes, until the sweat was really rolling off us. I felt like my pores were a quarter-inch wide. I wasn't sure how much longer I could stand it and was about to tell T.C. I was going to have to leave when two girls materialized out of the fog, took our hands and led us out through another door.

'Thank God!' I thought. I was starting to feel like a boiled lobster.

We entered into a huge room with a large swimming pool. A fountain bloomed in the middle of the expanse of clear, blue, water. It looked very inviting. The girls stopped by the edge and said, "You give towels, you swim."

T.C. blushed and I said, "Oh Wow."

We handed over our towels and, partly out of embarrassment jumped into the pool screaming as we hit the coldest water I'd felt in over three months. I swear I heard my pores slam shut! I surfaced, gasping, T.C. popped up ten feet away, blustering.

"OH MY GAWD!"

The two girls were watching us, giggling with their hands over their mouths.

"Brrrrrr! It's co-o-old, but, damn it feels go-o-ood!" I managed and gulped air and dove under toward T.C. I had almost reached him, thinking I'd maybe pull his feet out from under him and dunk him, when I realized 'He ain't got no shorts on'. Too late! YUK what a view! I back-pedaled and thought, 'Hell, I don't wanna play water-games with no naked man!' so I swam, still submerged, to the edge, where I could see the wavery images of the two girls, standing on the very rim of the pool. I got my feet under me and shot up next to them and grabbed their arms and pulled them, squealing, into the cold water.

Submerged again I saw them surface to gasp and, YES, one of their towels had come off and she was wearing only skimpy white panties, her small, but beautiful breasts bobbing in the water. Even from under the water I could hear the girls squeals. I surfaced, blowing a stream of water at the girl without a towel and grinned at her hoping she would not kill me. They both shouted angrily at us but, from the looks in their eyes, I could tell it was pretend.

Soon the other girl had lost her towel, also, and was busy rubbing T.C. the 'right way'.

My girl had her legs wrapped around my hips from behind and was pretending, (I hoped), to strangle me. It soon turned into a neck rub that turned into a shoulder rub that turned into everything-below-that rub. After about five minutes of playing, involving a lot of touching and rubbing, the other girl squealed.

"GI no s'pose get rub in pool! Make watta, what you say, Gummy?"

We all cracked up, even the girl who said it.

Getting her breath again she continued.

"For sure! No get rub in pool, get rub in room, only! Pool numbah ten!"

With that, she climbed the tile steps up out of the water, T.C. close behind her. She wrapped her sodden towel around her dripping body. When T.C. emerged it was obvious, in a big way, that he'd been deeply affected by the attentions of the girl-san. My girl squealed and pointed, and the other GIs (two of them with their own girls) and I, burst out laughing as Li (or Lee, T.C.'s girl's name) screamed and feigned a look of horror and tried to cover him up with a wholly inadequate towel. Finally, accompanied by hoots, she gave up and pointed to his waving member.

"You come in room, I show you how FIX that!"

She winked and was chased from the room by T.C., like he was doing bayonet practice.

I climbed from the pool, affected the same way, but I was more discrete and donned my own towel as Kim (my girls name, almost every girl I met was named 'Kim'), emerged wrapping her towel on as she came up the steps. She could not have looked more beautiful, with water streaming out of lustrous hair so black and shiny. Water and hair cascaded down her back to her pert little rump protruding from the split in the towel in back. I followed her rump through the door back out into the main hallway and through a beaded curtain into one of the massage rooms.

The room, a closet, really, was six by eight with a low ceiling that had two parallel brass rails suspended from it, over a chrome and black leather adjustable massage table. The table filled most of the room.

The only other furnishings were a small round table with a bowl and pitcher (like my Grandma had), on it, and a two step platform, I guessed, so the tiny girl could reach her subject on the table.

The only decorations in the room were two colorful posters taped to the otherwise bare concrete walls. The poster's words were in Vietnamese, but they depicted Asian-looking men and women in colonial or maybe ante-bellum dress. Kind of like a Vietnamese 'Gone With the Wind' or something.

I wasn't allowed much time for study, before I was practically thrown onto the table by the tiny but surprisingly strong girl. It was rather painful to lay on my 'bayonet', which was still sharp, but she reached under the table and pulled out a bottle of scented oil and proceeded to beat me into submission. She used her hands, elbows, forearms, shoulders, and soon her feet, by hanging onto the brass rails, attached to the ceiling.

Somehow she pulled each of my muscles, individually, from my body, twisted and kneaded them, before snapping them back and beating them into place with small, clasped hands that made a sound like a rifle shot at each impact. At times I wondered if this could be beneficial, (it hurt like hell), but then she'd rub the pain away with smooth, sweeping motions. At times I would nearly drop off to sleep, only to be whipped awake by the next attack.

She flipped me over like a pancake and worked down the front of me to my feet and back up to my mid-regions where she slowed to a stop.

All during this onslaught, she'd been murmuring "You like?" or "GI feel good?" or "Ooh, big muscle!" and so on. Now as she paused she asked, "GI want pussy?"

I must have gaped at the direct question, after all, she was a very beautiful young girl, somewhere between fifteen and twenty five, and hardly looked the type to ask "You want pussy?"

She laughed at my look.

"Han' job, two dollah. Sucky, fi' dollah, Fucky, Seben dollah. You want?"

Of course I said, "I want!"

And I did!

The details of my choice need not be discussed here, but needless to say, she suck….uh…succeeded in relieving my last tension and I soon emerged from the room with a smile on my dopey face and my loose muscles hanging from my body like an ill-fitting suit.

Kim stuck her head through the curtain as I stood in the hallway outside.

"You like?"

Of course all I could do was nod and grin like a fool.

"That all, you dress now!" She pointed me down the hall to the dressing room.

As I was donning my pants, I looked up as T.C. entered through the curtain, also looking groggy and beat-up, but Li must've taken the edge off his 'bayonet', too, 'cause his towel fit, now.

"Jeez, man I just got my pipes cleaned like never before!" He muttered through a wide smile.

I said I had, too and we stood there for a minute with shit eating grins, which we could not get rid of the whole time we were dressing.

From the coolness of the foyer we walked back out into the evening heat of the street. As we turned the corner onto the teeming main drag through town I commented.

"I don't think I've been this clean since I've been in country."

T.C. nodded.

"Me neither, man, it was getting' where I couldn't sleep with myself for th' smell. Hey, how 'bout a beer on th' way back? I saw some neat-lookin' bars on th' way down."

I agreed that would be a great way to round off this day and soon we were entering the 'Tay Son Bar and Rest.' It was a neon-lit hole-in-the-wall a couple blocks back toward the base.

The room was barely lit and we felt our way to two seats at the bar an ordered a couple Bah Me Bah's (Bier 33). Bah Me Bah was the Vietnamese beer of choice among GIs. The 33 must've meant percentage of alcohol, because after two each we both had a major 'Buzz' on.

Several bargirls approached us as we sat drinking and suggested 'Good Times'. T.C., randy sucker that he is, was all for it, but I had to remind him that our time was limited. (We only had a half-hour to get back to the compound.) We passed on the bargirls, finished our beers and reeled back through the MP gate at 1855 hours. We split up at the hootches and I went in, fell on my bunk and slept like the dead all night.

Life in Tay Ninh was a vast improvement over conditions on the LZs.

We slept in walk-in hootches built of wooden ammo crates filled with dirt and nailed together to form walls. These were topped with PSP roofs covered with plastic sheeting and two layers of sandbags.

Our bunks were also made of ammo box wood, four to a room and covered with 2" thick army mattresses which were pretty hard but felt like a feather bed compared to what we were used to.

We also had hot chow, served in a real mess hall, which we were allowed to use by the 2/19th Arty, a 105 unit next door.

Weapons were not carried unless on guard duty and we had to make sure to shave every day, keep our fatigues clean and, of course, polish our boots.

We fired very few contact missions and only fired H&Is two evenings the whole time we were there.

All in all, it was a pleasant break from the tension and hard work of the 'field'. The only aggression we experienced was from afar. Between five or ten 'clicks' north of us were two mountains jutting up from the otherwise flat terrain, both visible from Tay Ninh. One night I sat on top of our hootch with T.C., Harris, Bechtal and Salo, watching, through binoculars, a ground attack on the peak of the largest mountain, named, I think, Nui Ba Ra. The smaller peak was Nui Ba Dinh.

Through the lenses we could pick out both red and green tracers flying about and the distinctive red streaks of B-40 rockets. As we watched the action, Salo, always a source of information, explained.

"The Army has radio relay stations on both peaks, covering most of III corps. 'Charlie' really likes to try to disrupt our commo. They hit the radio bases up there every two or three weeks an' try to do as much damage as they can."

We watched the flashes of rounds fired by 2/19th, landing on the hillsides, as well as the flashes of VC mortars landing on the very top of the mountain.

"Wow, man, they must be gettin' their asses kicked up there!" T.C. said as he took his turn with the glasses.

"There are only about twenty or thirty guys on each relay, but they've got the high ground an' it's fairly easy to defend, plus they get Arty support from here and ARA from Cu Chi, down south, if they need it." Salo said, lighting a smoke.

As if to prove Salos' info correct, we gasped as rockets seemed to streak out of the sky on yellow-white trails, followed by continuous red, wavy streams of mini-gun fire that snaked down, touched the dark jungle surrounding the base, then ricocheted thousands of spent tracers into the air.

"That's the gun-ships from Tay Ninh, working-out, now." Bechtal explained.

"Wow, I'd sure hate to be a Gook in the middle of all that shit!" T.C. said in awe.

"No shit!" Salo continued, "Those mini-guns fire a rate of 6000 rounds a minute and can cover a space the size of a football field in one burst."

"Wow!" we said in unison.

The 'Dirty Thirty', (though somewhat cleaner, now), languished in this comparatively peaceful lull.

We caught up on letters home and received back-mail from friends and loved-ones.

We'd cleaned up and (reluctantly) appeared more Army-like, much to the relief of the BC and 1st Sgt. Ambrose, who kept an eye peeled for anyone not behaving in a 'military manner.'

Most of us got 'laid' in town.

Some got drunk in the bars.

I, personally, visited the steam baths at least once a week, enjoying the luxury of sweating out the red dirt of Viet Nam, as well as the 'other' pleasures offered.

Kim became my 'Girlfren' whenever I came in, and, though I knew it was a sham relationship, it felt good to have a 'steady' girl who seemed to care only for me and for my pleasures.

At the end of the first week there, someone discovered that the 101st Rangers had an EM club in their compound that served hamburgers and beer, and, on Saturday nights showed movies on an outdoor screen. Any E-4 and below was welcome.

That Saturday night, leaving only Salo on radio watch, everyone trooped over there and thoroughly enjoyed an old John Wayne flick about WWII where John leads the Marines to victory on, I think, Iwo Jima. We whooped and kidded around like kids at a drive-in. ("Except there ain't no girls ta pick up." T.C. lamented.) It was great, even though the sound track was out of synch most of the movie and the film broke regularly.

It was a restful three weeks, but, of course, good things end, especially in the Army.

The first week in September, at morning formation, after the news of Ho Chi Minh's death on Sept. 3rd, ("Does this mean th' war's over?"—"Naw, man, some other Gook Mutha' will jus' take over."), Salo announced our impending move to another LZ.

9

THE HUNDRED DOLLAR WOUND

LZ MIMI was an instant replay of LZ JUDY, complete with sniper. Almost every day of the three weeks we were there, our new sniper, named 'Luke th' Gook', would creep up to our tree line and pop off two or three SKS rounds at us. Luckily, Luke was a terrible shot and never hit anyone, but he succeeded in keeping us on edge the whole time.

From MIMI we moved to DON. (DON? I thought the LZs were named after the Generals' wives or girlfriends. Who the Hell's this DON?)

DON was a combination ARVN-US base. We were on one side and 'Marvin The ARVN' was on the other. We didn't like the idea of half our perimeter being guarded by the South Viets who, we all agreed, were the sorriest group of 'soldiers' ever allowed to wage war.

DON was also 'Flaky' with a capital 'F'. So Flaky, some of the choppers hooking in our equipment received ground fire. ARA was called in to suppress the sporadic AK-47 fire from the surrounding jungle

First night there we got eight rounds of incoming mortars, and we were up all night firing H&Is and contact missions. And anticipating a ground attack that, thankfully, never materialized.

Buckstone had DEROS'ed while we were at Tay Ninh and we had been one man short on our gun for three weeks. The morning of the second day on DON, a little 'LOACH' (Light Observation Helicopter) swooped onto our pad and deposited our newest FNG.

Bobby Andrews, instantly nicknamed Andy, late of Boston, MA. He was as wide as he was tall, all muscle and no fat. He was about 5'7" tall, and 200-210 lbs. He had bright blue eyes and stubbly blond hair on a head that was joined to his body without benefit of neck. Andy was, also, brand new in country. I was no longer the 'New Guy'.

Andy, for all his mass, was a really nice guy and fell into our group without a hitch. He and I became close friends from the first night he arrived. Due to a hootch shortage he shared mine. He took up a lot of room in the small culvert, but then, I don't take up as much as the other guys, so I guess it equaled out. Still, he was as polite and considerate as circumstances allowed. That first night he was full of questions about the gooks, how much action we'd seen, the 'Lifers', the Officers, ("You mean they don't make you polish your boots?"). Man, this guy was NEW!

But mostly, he was concerned about food. He was aghast when I told him about our C-Rat diet, ("Oh, man, I'm gonna starve ta' death here!"). Eating was one of his favorite things and he was always 'scarfing' on the other guys' goodie-boxes they got in the mail, though, to be fair, he always shared his mom's cookies or cake with us. However, they were mostly crumbs by the time they'd traveled 13000 miles. His mom was an excellent crumb baker, and he would shovel 'em in with a spoon. Us, too.

Late one night, he shared a whole cooked ham in a can with Harris and me. I provided some semi-stale Ritz crackers, Harris got us some cokes from the CP cooler and we 'partied' on the porch of my hootch.

On his second night with the 'Dirty Thirty', Andy found out all about what it's like on LZs. It literally rained rockets. 107s; about fifteen of 'em in groups of two and three, all over the LZ, but mostly on the ARVN side. This was around 2330 hrs (11:30) and as the rockets were exploding, the other side of the green-line, manned by trigger-happy ARVNs, opened up with every weapon they had. Red tracers were flying, M-79s were thumping, and M-60s were rattling like to melt their barrels.

I was in my hootch, and Andy had been outside somewhere. After the first five or so rounds hit, there was a small lull, and I peeped out and saw Andy crawling, on knees and elbows, past the door about four feet out, his head gouging out a groove in the dirt, his arms hooked across his helmet. I could hear him saying "Oh, shit! Oh, shit!" I reached out and grabbed his ankle and he jumped two feet off the ground, with a loud "OH SHIT!" He looked back with huge round eyes glowing in the flare-light.

I yelled, "Get in here, Dip-shit!"

He scrambled around and as the next salvo of rockets hit, close, he knocked me over at the door diving in.

"JEEZ, man, we're gonna get killed!" He wailed.

"Maybe." I said, picking myself up, "But if not, as soon as this lets up, we gotta man the gun for return fire."

"Bull Shit! I ain't going back out there 'til its time for me to go home!"

I looked at him

"You want 'em to come back tomorrow night and shoot more rockets at us?"

"Well...no, man." he replied.

"Well then, we gotta shoot some rounds back and hope we either get 'em or scare 'em off, or sure-as-shit they'll be back tomorrow!"

"Well....you put it that way...." he agreed.

Finally, after a longer lull in the incoming, but with the outgoing still blazing away, we all emerged and gathered between the trails. Bechtal pointed me toward the M-60 bunker and told Andy to cut charges. I crawled into the small space and started checking out the tree line in the last of the flare-light that the Grunts had fired.

In my excitement, it seemed every bush and tree was moving. They were all NVA soldiers, headed right at me. I forced myself to calm down, with much difficulty, and looked again. It was only trees and bushes. I rationalized that if the shit was really coming down, the Grunts, in their bunkers to our left and right, would have opened up by now.

Our first shot was a six-gun salvo, followed by six more rounds each, fired at will. I saw that the guns were on a high trajectory, meaning the rounds would be landing close by. Sure enough, I listened and, among the out going fusillade and the continuing 'battle' on the ARVN side, I could hear the 'CARRUMPP' of the big 155MM 'Joes' landing not more than a 'click' from our perimeter.

A thick haze of gun smoke drifted above the trees, like storm clouds, sometimes reflecting the flashes of our explosions on their bottoms.

Finally, the ARVNs must have run out of ammo. Their fire petered out and all was painfully silent. After a minute I risked a peek over the blast wall and spotted Bechtal by the right wheel of the gun.

"Think that's all?" I asked him.

He shrugged and put the landline to his ear and turned back to the gun. Just then a mortar landed about ten feet outside the rear of our pit. Dirt and pieces of shrapnel blew into the pit and zinged off the gun shields and thudded into the sandbags of the bunkers. I caught a glimpse of the guys diving in all directions before I ducked back down into the bunker, where I landed facedown and buried my head under my arms. Some dirt rained down on my legs, which were still sticking out from under the overhead cover of the bunker, but I was still behind the blast wall.

I lay there several seconds, and all was quiet again except for some guys yelling in the next gun-pit. I heard Bechtal asking if everyone was all right and started to rise when I felt someone slap me on the ankle. I raised up and turned, expecting to see Bechtal. But there was nobody there. I raised up more until I could see over the wall and there's Harris just coming over from the gun. He saw me.

"You OK, Mouse?"

I was about to say "Yeah", but suddenly my right ankle was, like, on fire. I screamed (like a girl, Harris told me later), jumped up and fell over the blast wall, my helmet flying and I dropped my rifle, which clattered on the ground in front of a startled Harris, who was shocked to a standstill. By now my ankle was screaming 'PAIN!' and so was I, so I jumped up and started hopping on my left leg and trying to rip my right boot off with both hands. I jumped into Harris, knocking him down, and we both lay there in a pile, him trying to get me off him and me still trying to rip my foot off.

He finally maneuvered around and got me in a scissors lock between his legs and was trying to hold me there as T.C. and Andy rushed over.

T.C. hollered "What th' fuck?"

They thought we were fighting.

Harris yelled "I don't know, man, he just went nuts an' jumped me!"

They tried to pin my arms but couldn't pry my hands off my boot.

"GET IT OFF...GET IT OFF! GET IT OFFFF!"

"What, man, get what off?" T.C. asked, puzzled.

"THE BOOT, THE BOOT, THE BOOOOOT!!!" I screamed with tears in my eyes. Now smoke was obvious coming from my right foot.

"Shit, hold still!" T.C. said, trying to get a hold on my thrashing leg. He finally pinned me, and using his old Commo knife, sawed through the laces and pulled the boot off with a jerk.

Almost immediately the pain was much less, and I quit struggling so much. "WHEW, man! That yer foot?" T.C. said, wrinkling his nose. A really bad smell hit us all and Andy, this time, said "What th' fuck?"

T.C. had raised my ankle and peeled away my, still smoking sock.

"Jeez, Mouse, ya got a burn or somethin' on yer leg. Look!"

Sure enough, there was a blackened, wrinkled-up, circular mark on the back of my ankle, about the size of a silver dollar.

"Where th' hell'd that come from?" I asked, confused.

Andy bent over, picked up my boot and turned it over.

"Well, I'll be damned!"

There, imbedded in the side of the nylon boot-upper was a quarter inch thick piece of still-damn-hot shrapnel, melting away at the material, smoking in the dim flare light.

My eyes bugged-out!

"How th' hell'd that hit me? I was on the ground behind th' wall there. No way it could'a got me."

"Well, it did." Andy said, picking at the hot metal with his knife. It finally burned the rest of the way through and fell into the boot. Andy dumped it out into his hand, but it was too hot to hold so he dropped it on the ground beside me and we all bent down and stared at it as if it would tell us its story.

Almost in unison we all muttered "Well, I'll be damned!"

It took a while but we finally decided the chunk must've gone straight up, Lord knows how far, and come straight back down and hit my boot and stuck to the melting nylon 'til I felt it, seconds later.

Thankfully the mortar hurt no one else, but Bechtal decided I had been 'Wounded' and took me to the CP to see 'Top'. He explained to the 1st Sgt. what had happened and suggested that I should get a Purple Heart.

Sgt. Ambrose just said, "Bull shit! You don't git no Purple Heart fer no itty-bitty burn on yer laig, boy! Hell, won't even make ya limp!"

I tried with: "Yeah, but Top, I got hit, in combat by a piece of shrapnel, an' I got a wound!" I pointed at my black spot.

"Don' mean nuthin'," he said with a grunt, "I cut myself shavin' worse'n that, now git outta my CP an' let me git back ta' impotent stuff! GIT NOW!"

Dismissed, we walked out and over to the gun pit, me with my one good boot on.

"I still think you oughta get a 'Heart' for that." Bechtal commiserated.

"Well, thanks anyway." I told him, "I guess all I'll get is a purple ankle, but Hell, I've got my 'medal' right here."

I held up the ragged-edged chunk of metal, all black and gooey-looking with melted nylon. I saved it the rest of my tour and it was the subject of many a late-night debate, not to mention Show-off sessions for the FNGs.

I had to wear the boot with the hole in it 'til a new pair could be sent from the rear. This actually worked out fine, since the hole was right where my wound was, so it didn't irritate the tender skin and the burn healed in about three weeks, about the same time it took to get my new boots.

10

"SAME-O SAME-O"

On the same Chopper as my boots were promotion orders. Mine included.

'Wow, I'm a PFC.', I thought, 'but nobody but 'Lifers' wears rank insignia. Hell, nobody wears a shirt! What difference does it make?'

Also on the same Chopper were our orders to move to LZ JER-RY. (Another 'guy' name; hmmm.)

'DON' was to be abandoned so we were told to dump our sandbags and take them with us to JERRY for construction of hootches and bunkers. Dumping sandbags is not much easier than filling them, but, eager to be off LZ DON, we went about this back-breaking task with, if not zeal, enthusiasm. In the last three weeks we had been subject to three mortar attacks and two more 'Panic Attacks' by the ARVNs, so we figured LZ JERRY had to be better than DON is, Right?

No, not really.

We were on the ground by 1350 hrs, two days later, with all our equipment and our gun. All that was missing was the LZ. 'LZ' JERRY was a large hole in the jungle, a quarter mile wide by a half-mile long. Roughly egg-shaped, surrounded by a meager four strands of 'Concertina' wire and one stretch of 'Tangle-foot'.

Some obvious Engineer-types were working on it as we came in. Parked at one end of the egg was a D-8 Bulldozer/Back-hoe combo, sitting in the middle of a half-finished gun pit. In the center of the widest part of the egg were five round sandbagged bunker/fighting positions with three-foot tall walls, open-roofed.

In three of the bunkers were 80mm mortar tubes and crews of four. In and around the others were the Grunts, our Protectors. Several of them were still filling bags for another bunker under construction, but most were standing, sitting or laying around, apparently not doing anything in particular.

Hooking into LZ Jerry

We had six 155 Howitzers and ammo, and one gun pit that wasn't finished. Plus, the guns had been brought in no particular order, so, when we got our firing positions, we'd have to hand-push the 14600 lb. 'Pigs' across rough ground and stumped-off trees to our pits. Wherever that might be.

'Top' and the BC (Battery Commander) came in on a LOACH, looked around and the 1st Sgt. started pitching a bitch.

"Ah cain't believe we don't have PITS!" He began, "Goddamn Engineers been here since 'fore dawn! WHERE- ARE- OUR- PITS an' OUR- BUNKERS!"

He marched over to the Engineers, who, up until this tirade had been driving stakes for more barbed wire. They watched his advance with trepidation in their eyes.

As well they should.

Ambrose was a real Bad-ass when riled, which was most of the time.

Hell, he was a Bad-ass when he felt good.

He was 6' 1" and a solid 200 pounds of pure 'Lifer'. When he was pissed off, he seemed to swell and become even larger. His shoulders would hunch and swallow what little neck he had, and his blond, brush-cut hair would actually bristle as the muscles of his face and scalp would contort as he ground his surprisingly small, white teeth.

He came up to the E-5 in charge of the 8th Eng. Detachment, thrust his face within 12" of the much smaller man's, and repeated his tirade, ending this time with "I'M TOO SHORT FER THIS SHIT!!!"

The E-5 backed off a couple feet, glancing around, I think, for a place to jump to if 'Top' got physical.

"Top," he squeaked, "I've only got seven men here to work. We was supposed ta have ten more guys an' another 'dozer, but somebody in Tay Ninh screwed up an' this is all we got!" He ended with a palms-up, 'What- am-I-gonna do?' gesture.

The 1st Sgt. stood there glaring for another full minute. You could almost see the heat rising off him. The little Sgt. continued in a stammer.

"I radioed Phouc Vinh an' they're trying to get us some more heavy equipment…. probably by 1500 hrs, they said. Problem is, we don't have enough operators ta run the machines."

'Top' stood there and quivered a few seconds, turned on his heel and marched back to the Captain, waiting by the idling helicopter.

We were all standing around waiting to be told what to do as the 1st Sgt. and the BC conversed with their heads together. Then they gestured and pointed to different spots around the LZ, and talked some more. The Captain leaned into the Chopper and came back out holding a radio microphone. He spoke rapidly and listened to one earphone of a headset. We couldn't hear the words, but from all indications he was giving somebody a reaming.

He talked animatedly for 3-4 minutes and signed off.

He conferred with 'Top' again, accompanied by more pointing and hand gestures. With a final nod, Capt. Nord jumped back into the passenger compartment and the little chopper wound up for take-off. Sgt. Ambrose ran to where most of us had drifted into a group, and waved all the others to gather round.

When we were all around him, he said, "Goddamn Engineers fucked-up again, as usual. I need volunteers. Any y'all got 'sperience on heavy 'quipment, fall-in over heah!"

He pointed a spot to his left. Eight guys, including T.C., lined up.

He said "Good!" and turned and faced the rest of us. "We're gonna build this heah LZ ayrselves, looks like. I need ever' man wants a safe hole ta crawl in tonight diggin' an' fillin'. Me an' th' gun-captains'll lay out th' pits an soon's th' machines git heah, y'all..." he pointed to the 'volunteers' "... Git on 'em an' do yo thang!"

We all nodded or said, "Yes 'Top'."

He looked at his watch.

"We got us six hours ta set these guns an' get 'em pertected."

He went on and assigned each group tasks, digging the FDC, filling bags, digging latrines.

"Man cain't work if he's gotta shit!"

He put some of us helping the Engineers with the wire in the KZ (Kill Zone). He even rounded up some of the Grunts who were not busy at something.

"We got shovels'll fit yer hands, too, now MOVE IT!"

Nobody had the balls to say no to that man.

In less than a half hour, every man on JERRY was working feverishly, sweating and straining in the afternoon heat. My group got the task of moving equipment to the pit sites. No easy job as some of the sites were all the way across the wide expanse of rough, plowed up dirt.

At 1445 the first of a series of 'Green Giant' helicopters with two D-8 'dozers hung underneath arrived and deposited its load in a whirlwind of dust that choked and gagged every- body on the LZ.

We'd be breathing dust for most of the afternoon.

Capt. Nord's threats must've shook somebody up 'cause soon chopper after chopper swooped in bringing more men and equipment, not the least of which was a ¾ ton truck, which we commandeered to tow the guns and haul ammo and equipment.

Our guys and some of the Engineers were on the back-hoes and 'dozers and made quick work of the FDC hole. The crew there started filling and stacking the sandbag walls.

Then they started on the pits themselves and by 1630 the berms were up on all six pits. The backhoe manned by T.C., (Mr. "I should'a been a Injineer!"), himself, was making the holes for the powder bunkers at each site.

By 1800 hrs we had a semblance of an LZ.

The FDC walls were up and some guys were putting the finishing touches on the roof of sandbags. The pits were up and the guns in place. The equipment was still in piles, but the bunkers were almost finished and the hootch culverts were in place, though they still needed sandbags.

By 1930 hrs all the guns were 'laid' and sighted on the aiming stakes positioned in the now much more substantial barbed wire barrier around the base. The ammo and most equipment were stowed, but our personal stuff was still in a pile by the hootches, which still did not have sandbags.

We were fully operational by 2000 hrs when the BC flew in again, looked around at what we'd done in a mere seven and a half-hours, nodded his head and walked around to each gun pit, passing out 'at-a-boys' to the crews.

Nord had another 'pow-wow' with 'Top' and flew out again.

At 2045, we were told to lay off and get some chow and some rest.

We didn't have to be told twice!

I felt like a little old man, aching in every bone and muscle, as I spread my ground cloth and poncho-liner in my culvert. I HAD to get something to eat. I hadn't had anything but water since before we left DON this morning, and it felt like my stomach was digesting itself, and it probably was.

I settled outside my culvert opening and started cooking up some beef stew LRRP rations I'd gotten from a Grunt on DON, in trade for some paperback books that I'd already read. As my water boiled, I watched as the other guys either dropped like dead men, or ate chow, like me, or just smoked and stared out at the trees at the edge of our world.

I tried not to think about all the stuff I had hauled, carried, lifted, shoved and pulled today or all the stuff tomorrow. I just numbed my mind, ate my stew without tasting it and crawled into the dark culvert and slept undisturbed through the night. If 'Charlie' was out there, he thankfully ignored us that night.

For the next two days we embellished on our work. Roofing the culverts, building more bunkers and firing H&Is and missions in between. Every once in a while we'd eat or sleep.

The third day, Andy and I drew 'Green-line' duty, setting trip flares and grenade booby-traps in the wire along our stretch of the perimeter. The barbed and razor wire itself had been beefed up all around the LZ by the engineers, so we wore gloves and an extra layer of fatigues for protection, but we still got cut up pretty badly. Little slashes and stabs that wouldn't want to heal in this climate. Plus, the extra clothing made the heat almost unbearable, and soon we were drenched and the salty sweat would run into the cuts and.....well needless to say we were not happy campers.

We had worked our way into the last inner strand by 2:00 P.M. and here we set the 'Claymore' mines (Command detonated anti-personnel mines). These were a 'Last Line of Defense' before the very inner wire barrier. We were to set eight Claymores and I remembered back to some training session at Fort Knox, where they explained the 'Proper Procedure For Setting and Arming The M- (whatever) Claymore Mine'.

Between Andy's and my recollection, we set the first four by building a little hillock, about a foot or less tall (short enough to not be too obvious). Then you lay on your belly behind this mound and carefully place the mine, facing outward, on the other side of the hillock. Then you had to force the two little stake-like legs that conveniently folded out from the body of the curved mine into the ground to secure it.

While I placed the mines, Andy buried two strands of commo wire from each site, back to the M-60 bunker at our pit. These were to be attached to 'clacker' type detonators, but first I had to wire the other ends to blasting caps that were then inserted into holes, made just for them, on either side of the top of each mine.

I had just set the fourth one, and, according to procedure, I was "Low-crawling backwards to a safe distance behind the mine before rising, in case of accidental discharge". I was about eight or so feet behind the mound, when I heard a helicopter coming in low. Big deal! Nothing unusual about that on the LZ.

Being on the ground, I still couldn't see it.

It swooped into the LZ directly over me, no more than 40' up.

My world was suddenly enveloped in a swirl of dust and sound, both blinding and deafening. I was physically lifted three feet off the ground, then slammed back hard. I was dimly aware of dirt cascading down on my back and bare head (my helmet was blown off and found twenty feet away). I could do nothing but lie there, face down.

I was partially conscious, but all sound was washed out by a tremendous ringing sound. My muscles and joints felt like I'd been stretched out in many directions and allowed to snap back violently.

The dust started to settle and I raised my head slightly and turned it sideways, mostly to see if I could. Through the clanging/ringing sound I heard little tiny mouse voices yelling something incoherent.

I strained to hear what was being said and it suddenly seemed very important that I hear because someone, I could not remember who, told me to always be aware of my surroundings and to listen-up. I was trying to raise up a little so I could hear better when I was grabbed by the arm and held to the ground. My vision was blurry and all I could see of my captor was a (or should I say two, I was seeing double at the time) dark silhouettes against the brassy brightness of the sky.

The little mouse-voices were going again. Several of them, but I still could not make out what was being said or what they seemed so excited about. I was distantly aware of activity around me and I was turned over face-up and hands were touching me.

I was as limp as a dishrag and couldn't willingly move any part of my body.

I was picked up and carried, joltingly, some distance, then everything was dark.

Many things seemed to revolve around in my brain and for some time, (about two hours, the 'Doc' said) I was semi-conscious, but incoherent. Then I must have passed out or gone to sleep because when I finally opened my eyes, all I could see was a bright red spot in a sea of darkness.

"You still in there, Mouse?" a disembodied voice said.

I didn't know.

"Don' know, where am I? It's dark."

"You're OK," the voice returned, "You're in the CP. You've been knocked out for about eight hours and it's night-time, that's why it's dark."

The red spot moved and that's when I realized it's a flashlight with a red lens above me. Doc Sammon's face appeared in the dim beam.

"Lie still, you've got a concussion, that's why things will seem a little ... uh... unreal, for a while. Does your head hurt?"

"Like hammers hitting iron. I can hear you, but not very well." I said, trying to 'pop' my ears to make the shrill ringing go away but it didn't work.

"Well, just stay still here till you feel better." He said, looking into my eyes, "I can give you some aspirin for the headache, but I can't give you anything else because of the concussion."

Concussion?

"How'd I get concussed, Doc?"

"The mine went off." He said, simply.

Mine?

"What mine, Doc?"

"You were working on the green-line, setting Claymores."

"Oh...... Yeah."

I sort of remembered something like that

"Am I ...wounded or anything?" I asked, suddenly afraid.

"No, just concussion from the blast." He said, to my relief. "You were low enough to the ground you weren't hit, but it rattled you pretty good."

"No shit!" I agreed' still trying to pop my ears.

"Just lay still, now, for a while and I'll......" That is when I must have passed-out again.

I was dreaming about Judy, my girl back home. She had sent me some pictures of herself, dressed in Bikini bathing suits and sheer 'nighties' in alluring poses (a GI's wish come true). In my dream, she was soattired and walking down a street in a Viet village. I somehow knew this was a VC village and all the guys along the street, leering at her were VC, and she was in danger! I was trying to go to her and give her my fatigue jacket to cover up with, but my feet were mired in dream mud and she was walking away from me, smiling, unaware of the threat.

A couple of guys in black pajamas with AK-47s slung over their shoulders came around a corner and headed right for her. I was getting agitated and scared for her, but I could only move in slow motion. One of the VC unslung his weapon and, to my horror, aimed it at Judy and.... BOOM, BOOM, BOOM!!!

Jolted awake, I was breathing fast and I sat up.

My surroundings were lost in a spin.

I immediately felt nausea well up, but fought it back and closed my eyes.

I sat there for a while, feeling the world spin, even with my eyes closed. After a few minutes I dared open them again and the room was still going round but slower, now, and it came to me.

'The CP, I'm in the CP. Why? Something .... A mine...wounded? No, I'm cussed, no con-cussed'

I still had a headache and the ringing in my ears but not nearly as bad as...'when? How long have I been here?'

BOOM, BOOM, BOOM!!!

'What's that?'

I looked around the room, slowly by necessity, I found out that even small movement of my head set off bouts of the nausea. I finally got around where I could see the FDC guys at work at their plotting table and Salo sitting at his folding desk across the room. He noticed me sitting up so he rose and came over.

"How ya' feel now, Bud?" he asked

"W-what was that?" I asked, confused.

It took him a second to figure out what I was asking.

"OH, Fire-missions. You mean all those last night didn't bother you 'til this one?"

"UH....No. How long've I been here?" I stammered, having difficulty, I noticed, getting words to form in my mouth.

"Since 'bout 2:30 yesterday afternoon, and it's," he looked at his watch, "...11:45 now."

I shook my head, incredulous. Big mistake!

The room spun again and the nausea rose up.

When it settled a minute later and I opened my eyes, Salo had a concerned look on his face; he was reaching as if to keep me from falling off the cot I was sitting on.

"I-I'm OK…..I think." I said weakly.

"Jeez, your eyes rolled back and I thought you were gonna fall over, man."

"My head feels shitty, an' I'm really dizzy, but I think it's not as bad as last night, or ….whenever."

I waved my hand, not wanting to think too heavy just yet.

Salo said, "Be back."

He turned and left the room. A few minutes later he returned with Doc Sammons, who knelt down in front of me and talked while looking into my eyes.

"How's it goin', dude, feel any better now?"

His hand felt first my forehead, then my neck.

"Uh… yeah, I think so." I said "Still dizzy as hell, though."

"That'll pass, but you'll have the headache and ear-ringing for a couple of days."

I'm hungry, I suddenly realized, and said so.

"That's a good sign."

He took my arm and helped me gently to my feet.

"C'mon, I'll help you out, if you think you can walk."

My knees wobbled and I swayed from the dizziness every time I moved my head a little too fast, but with his help I made it back to the gun pit without falling. T.C. was the first to spot us and he ran to help, the others close behind.

"Mouse, man, we thought you was….."

He paused and looked down

"Well…hell, we thought you was dead, or real fucked-up. But th' Doc, man, he tol' us you was gonna be OK. You OK, man?"

I managed a small nod and a smile at the look on his face that said he'd really been worried. The others murmured greetings and moved as if to help carry me.

Andy pushed them all aside and took my other arm and he and the Doc took me to my hootch.

"He's gotta lay down till the dizziness goes away but he'll live." The Doc announced to the, obviously relieved, group.

T.C. beamed.

"He can lay on 'is ass all week, if he gotta!"

At my culvert, I managed to crawl in under my own power and collapsed in a heap. I shifted around and got stretched out. All the guys were staring in the door like I was some specimen in a zoo.

"Thanks, guys, just let me lay here for a while." I said, gratefully.

They all left except Andy, who sat down by the door.

"Man, you scared th' shit outta me!" he blurted with wide eyes.

"You flew up an' dirt an' shit went all over! I thought I'd done something that made the Claymore blow, but, honest, man, I hadn't hooked 'em up yet."

"Well what th' hell happened?" I asked, "I'd already put th' caps in and was backin' away."

"It was the chopper, man." He said, simply.

"Chopper?"

"You don't remember? Th' chopper that flew in over us?"

I shook my head 'No', regretting it instantly, the bile rising into my throat.

"Well, it did! An' Top told us it was the static electricity from th' 'Bird' set off th' caps. Good thing you were back away or you'da been.....'" He didn't finish.

I thought about it a minute.

"Static electricity, huh?"

"Yeah." He shook his head.

"Jeez!" I laid my head down and tried not to barf.

Next day I was sufficiently recovered, except for a nagging headache, for 'light duty', which meant helping Salo in the CP, filing papers, stacking books and sweeping out the bunker, etc. I felt pretty good, but had to watch out for quick movements of my head or bending over. Either would bring on waves of nausea. By evening, this too had mostly passed.

We fired H&Is 'til 0100 hrs with a couple of 'Contact missions' thrown in. Afterwards, as I was getting ready to rack-out, Bechtal came over and handed me two letters.

"These came while you were knocked out the other day." He said and left.

I crawled into my hootch, turned on my red flashlight and looked at my mail. One letter was from Mom and Dad and the other from Judy. I 'flashed' on the crazy dream of the other night and glanced at the back 'wall' of the culvert where her pin-ups were hung on the sandbags. I sighed and opened the perfume-smelling one first. I read it with a sinking feeling in the pit of my stomach.

Judy wrote that she was 'Sorry' but she'd met 'Someone Else' named 'Steve' and they were 'In Love'. Period. End of letter. End of relationship.

"Shit!!"

I wadded up that letter and threw it into the back corner of the hootch.

Angry, I snapped off the light and plopped down on my stomach, (making myself nauseous in the process), and tried to cry, but couldn't. I was pissed for a good two hours, wallowing around in my bed (of self-pity), thinking nasty thoughts, each punctuated by me uttering "BITCH" aloud.

Somewhere around 4:30 or 5:00 in the morning, I finally resolved my 'Love Crisis'.

'SHE's th' one's missin' out.' I rationalized. 'SHE don't know what she's givin' up!' I decided. 'SHE could'a had ME! HUMPH!!' I mentally blustered.

Besides, I wouldn't have to feel guilty about the steam baths, now!

Still couldn't sleep, so I sat up, looked outside.

Still pretty dark.

Snapped on the light, (getting pretty dim, gotta get new batteries).

I picked up Mom and Dads letter, tore it open and read the Home news.

Mom had injured her back at work. She had been to the doctor, but still didn't know if it was serious. She was 'managing' but with much pain.

Dad had my little VW 'Bug' up on blocks in the back yard and sent a picture of it, covered with a tarp and a dusting of snow.

I leaned back against the wall and tried to imagine 'snow'. Tried to 'shiver', like I knew I would be if I were standing there looking at the little 'Bug', instead of sitting here looking at a picture.

Guess shivering's out since this is the coolest it gets here and it's probably 80°.

Mom finished up with the usual 'Love and Support' phrases and, 'Damn', my eyes teared up. I usually kind of 'skimmed' over these little kindnesses, but, I guess I was at a 'low ebb' of emotions, feeling stressed and put-upon. Right then I was so glad to have someone back home who cared; people who loved me, no matter what, even long-distance.

I realized that my parents, even in the midst of their own troubles, took the time and effort to send me cheery letters. They played down their own problems to help me get through MY bad times, not to mention the regular supply of 'Goodie Boxes'.

They were helping feed my spirit as well as my body, and, sitting there alone in the dark I was grateful. I guess 'Moms and Dads' all over the world had done the same things for their sons since time began, but I felt special, somehow. Truly Blessed.

I turned off the failing light and lay down, finally drifting off to sleep, only to be shouted awake an hour later for a fire mission. I crawled out grumpy, but resolved to put the Judy-business out of my mind. I had more important things to deal with than worrying over someone who obviously never cared that much to start with.

The 'More Important Stuff' turned out to be three-plus more weeks of the three 'B's.

Beefing, Boredom and Bullshit.

October is one of the hottest, driest times of year in SE Asia, with temperatures well into the hundreds and oppressive humidity. Everyone wilted in the waves of heat that radiated off the hard, cracked red dirt of the LZ. Surrounded as we were by an almost solid wall of fifty-foot trees, filled in below with undergrowth, very little breeze filtered in to cool the air.

At mid-day the only shade was man-made. We're talking no-sleeping, mosquito-biting, salt tablet-eating, sunburn-peeling, dangerous heat.

Fights and arguments broke out among the men and there was even a stabbing over a stolen pack of cigs. The stabbee and the stabber left on the same chopper, one to hospital, the latter to LBJ (Long Binh Jail).

Two good things happened during this period.

T.C.'s Mom sent a box of the best cookie crumbs we'd had to date and the supply helicopters brought in ice in 100 lb. blocks almost every day. This was stored in a big cooler in the CP and was rationed out by the 1st Sgt.

"Oh, God, a cold Pepsi on ice!"

Most of us hadn't had regular ice in two or more months. Just a cold drink helped soothe a lot of nerves and cooled many a temper.

11

"LET'S HIT THE HO CHI MINH TRAIL, BOYS!"

First week in November we were told to move to LZ Mary, about 50 clicks west of JERRY.

"AW, man, ya mean we just got through buildin' this place an' now we gotta leave an' do it again someplace else?" a voice implored from out of the crowd gathered in front of the CP.

"Looks like it," Salo said. "Choppers will pick up on #1 gun at 1030 hrs; now, SADDLE UP!!"

Next morning we bade JERRY goodbye. With some regret, actually.

Even though it had started out rocky, we had made it quite comfortable in the twenty-six days we had been there (except for the heat). And on JERRY we hadn't seen 'Charlie' or 'Luke' and other than the stabbing and my Claymore accident, we'd drawn no aggressive attacks.

"Maybe it's too hot for the Gooks, too."

Then we said 'Hello' to 'MARY'.

MARY was a mirror image of JERRY except, in this area were the rolling foothills of a small range of mountains that were visible in the distance. The LZ was situated on top of one of these hills.

It had a good, established KZ around it, already-built hootches and bunkers and best of all, a breeze! After being down in the jungle low lands, being on even this small rise gave us a 360-degree panoramic view around the LZ, and the fresh, though still hot, breeze lifted our spirits.

We set up the equipment and guns and that evening took turns sitting on the berms looking out over the jungle that spread out to the next ridge line, a mile or so away. On a clear day, after the morning mist burned off and before the mid-day heat waves came on, we found that with binoculars, we could see a small village, and a piece of a road to our south; and to the north, a radio or TV antenna mast from another LZ or a village.

We'd been set up at MARY for three days when things started happening around us. 2/7th Infantry 'Grunts', who were patrolling north and west of us, started reporting trails and 'roads', well traveled recently, within a 'click' of the LZ.

These 'High Speed Trails' were camouflaged from view from the air, but clear and open for NVA/VC traffic to and from Cambodia, about thirty miles to our north. The Grunts hadn't encountered any activity on the trails yet, but they did discover a supply 'cache' only 500 yds. outside our perimeter. Most of the matériel found at the bunker was destroyed on-site, but some got carried back to the LZ to be taken to DIVARTY, in Bien Hoa, for 'study and evaluation'.

Of course we knew the AK-47s and SKS rifles, and even a 51 cal. anti-aircraft gun, were destined to become 'War Souvenirs' for some of the Lifers in the rear.

But not all the good stuff got away.

Inevitably, some items were smuggled out and got distributed among us common dudes. For three packs of cigarettes, I got an NVA rucksack from a Grunt who had a case of them. I used it to pack my tape player and all my tapes and other personal stuff.

Other odd items found their way to us, including an NVA battle flag that Sgt. Ambrose confiscated and hung in the little room on the back of the CP that served as an NCO 'club'.

In the second week on MARY, The Grunt's LPs were reporting night-time movement on the trails, and sensors and indicators were picking up somewhat heavy traffic through our entire area of operations. We were posting guard on our perimeter each night but, still, there was no contact.

Then on the following Sunday, (I remember because the Chaplain had made his rounds for Non-Denominational services that morning), we got a series of mortar attacks. The first came at 1830 hrs and consisted of six rounds that impacted at various locations around the LZ. One of the locations was Gun #2, just 50 yds. from our pit. Two guys I

96

didn't know were killed and their gunner, a guy named 'Bear', whom I did know, slightly, was cut up by shrapnel.

'Bear' and the bodies were lifted out in a half-hour,

At 2000, six more rounds came in and hit mostly outside our pits in the KZ. This time we had a general idea where the first barrage had come from, so we fired out and hoped to catch them before they could break down and move. It was quiet for a while after that and we assumed we had either gotten them or at least scared them off.

WRONG! At 2330, as we were getting ready to fire our H&I list, six more mortars came in and blew away one of the Grunt fighting positions on the green-line.

Two Grunts badly wounded.

The other five rounds were at random around the LZ but no other casualties were reported.

We fired some retaliation rounds, of course not knowing the outcome, as usual. Then we fired our H&I list and in the lull afterwards, I was sitting on my hootch roof talking to Andy. He asked me what I thought was going on with all the activity in the area. One of our favorite pastimes was to conjecture about this subject, whether or not we actually knew any thing. Andy was the 'New Guy' and looked to us 'Hardened Veterans' for advice and counsel.

"I think we're gonna get some 'shit' soon." I said, wearing my 'Veteran' look.

"Ya think?" Wide eyes.

"Nah, I don't know," I answered, "But we got all th' bad signs. An' I've got a feeling. All this could be just more bullshit to keep us scared and cautious, or it could be a warning to keep out of 'Charlie's' woods. We ARE right smack-dab in his way, here."

"Whadd'ya do.... I mean.... To keep from getting ...scared?"

"I don't do anything. I'm scared all the time." I answered, honestly. "Hell, I'm even scared to take a shit in the daytime. I believe if yer not scared yer stupid. Stay away from guys that act like their not petrified when th' shit comes down, 'cause they're the ones'll get killed or get you killed." Sage advice from an 'Old Hand'.

We shot another page of H&Is at 0130 hrs and since there was no more incoming, we all 'racked-out' except T.C., who was the guard on the M-60 bunker.

It had been really hot that day and was still in the 85-90 degree range, so I slept out on top of my culvert, to catch some breeze. I was awakened by pop-flares and an M-60, chattering over by #6 gun.

I glanced at my watch as I rolled off and crawled into my hootch for my 'pot' and flack jacket. It was 0430, and except for the flares, it was still pitch dark.

While rummaging for my bandoleer of M-16 ammo, I heard someone outside yell "GAS....GAAASSS!!!"

I lit my flashlight and looked around some more for where I'd stashed my gas mask. I located it back under the gook pack with my tapes in it, and by the time I'd opened the carry-case and started slipping on the rubber mask, my eyes were stinging and starting to water.

'Oh, shit' I thought, 'This is it, we're gonna get hit!'

I'd just got my mask on and adjusted when I was hit from behind and knocked into the rear wall of the culvert. I scrambled onto my knees and turned to see what had hit me. It was Andy in the red glow of my light, eyes streaming and nose running, throwing my poncho liner and stuff around, muttering "Where is it? Where th' Hell is it?"

"Andy! Yer in th' wrong hootch, man!" I yelled, "Your hootch is over there!"

I pointed out and left.

"Mouse! Man, that you? You seen my gas mask? I can't see shit!"

I said, "Wait one." And climbed over him (no easy task in that small space), and got out and dived for his doorway and found his mask by his bedroll and carried it back and put it in his hands. He'd been rubbing his eyes, which were now swollen and even redder in the light of my red lamp.

"Don't rub 'em, man, it just makes it worse. Here, put on yer mask an' it'll get better."

I helped him get it adjusted and quickly he was still coughing, but breathing easier.

"My eyes, man, they're burning terrible." He managed after a few minutes.

"You got a good dose, but it'll ease off after a while." I tried to soothe him.

I turned and crawled out again to find Bechtal and Harris already on the gun, looking like bugs in their masks. They were cranking quads and deflection.

It looked to me like we were going to fire straight up into the air. This told me we were trying to get our rounds close in to our position.

The Howitzer will not fire downhill from level ground. It only has a 5 degree deflection below 0 degrees or level, so in order to get rounds close-in, you fire on a high trajectory, with a small charge, and lob them in on target, like mortars do.

Bechtal finished his settings and turned to me. His voice was muffled through his face gear.

"Where's Andy?"

I pointed to my hootch.

"In there, he got a good dose of gas, but he's got his mask on, now, so he'll be OK"

"Well, get him out and over to the powder store, he can cut #1 charges with his eyes closed. Then get yer ass to th' M-60 bunker an' keep yer eyes peeled. Th' Grunts are reporting movement all around the perimeter an' #6 has already had a probe into their wire below them."

I turned to go and he grabbed my arm.

"If you spot any movement out there, use the land-line an' report it to the CP, an', listen-up now, don't fire the M-60 unless you absolutely have to. The gooks always target automatic weapons first. Use yer M-16 on semi, or, better still, th' M-79. Got that?"

I nodded affirmatively.

"Send T.C. back here, I'm gonna need some strong arms ta' ram rounds into this vertical tube." He motioned to the gun with his head. "Keep a sharp look-out, now, an' if you see anything, an' I mean ANYTHING, move out there, tell me first then th 'CP, OK?"

I nodded and took off.

I double-timed to the berm where I found T.C., looking like a big, dirty, alien in his mask. He was gazing intently out toward the trees at the edge of his visibility.

He turned as I entered.

"Wow, man, I jus' talked to Salo on th' phone an' th' Grunts're reportin' movement all 'round us an' #6 already has dead gooks in th' wire!"

"Yeah, I heard!" I said, out of breath, "Bechtal said for me to relieve you so you can help with th' gun. You seen anything goin' on out there, yet?"

"Hell, with th' flares swingin' around, it looks like everthangs movin' out there, but I ain't seen nothin' ya' could shoot at."

We both peered out the small window into the darkness.

"Well, ya better get on back an' help on th' gun, I'll keep watch here."

He gathered his stuff and left.

Alone again, in the dark.

'Shit, we're gonna get hit!'

The words kept running through my mind, but I was strangely calm.

I set my rifle and my taped-together magazines on the sandbags to my left, then checked the M-60 and found it locked and loaded, safety 'on'. I ran my hands down the ammo feed-belt, feeling for kinks or twisted rounds where they unfolded from the metal box. Last, I opened the wooden ammo crate where the grenades and flares were stored.

Also stored there was an M-79 'Blooper' (grenade launcher), and several bandoleers of the oversize bullets for it. Using my red light, I arranged the rounds in groups on the sandbags around me, for instant access.

I turned off my light and waited a few seconds for my vision to adjust, then peered out at the ghostly landscape, lit by a few pop-flares still drifting down. Everything looked the same as before.

Thanks to our small breeze on the hilltop, the gas had pretty much dissipated and drifted away across the LZ, so I lifted my mask and tested the air. It smelled strangely metallic but it didn't burn my eyes or nose Slowly I removed my mask, greatly relieved to breathe air only tinged with diesel fuel and shit and gun smoke, and laid it close-by.

The Howitzers were banging away behind me, but my attention was on the tree line on the other side of the KZ, about a hundred yards out.

Our rounds were landing some hundred yards further out, blowing big holes in the forest, and I could see debris flying in the flashes of the explosions.

100

As T.C. had said, the trees seemed to be moving and swaying, due to the drifting light of the flares. I strained my eyes to try to pick out anything that might move out of sync with the trees.

I could hear the Grunts in their fighting positions to my right and left, moving around and talking softly, and I felt somewhat reassured, knowing I wasn't really alone.

'Hell, we got probably 300 armed men on this LZ.' I thought.

But then I figured, 'But there could be thousands of Gooks out there! An' we won't be able to see 'em 'cause they're th' same color as th' damned dirt!'

I strained my eyes even harder.

After about ten minutes, the outgoing had about petered out and the last flare had sputtered out and it was real dark again.

Off to my right, at the limit of my vision, I saw the distinctive red streak of a B-40 rocket, emanate from the trees and extend across the wire in a continuous hissing line and disappear from my field of sight. Followed by a bright yellow flash as it found its target, and a 'Ke- blam!' detonation.

I couldn't see, but I figured it must've hit between our pit and the next one, in the Grunt areas.

Instantly, M-16 fire went out on full auto, as the infantry 'hosed-down' the area of trees where the rocket had come from. Red tracers pinged and flew in all directions, and flares went up again all round.

As this was going on, mortars began falling inside the LZ, impacting with their usual 'KARRRUUMP, KARRUUUMP, KARRU-UMP!!!!' Sounding, to me, more like loads of gravel being dumped than explosions.

During this fusillade, I heard several more 'KE-BLAMs' of B-40s, but I couldn't see where all this was happening, so I watched my sector intently.

Pretty soon, I felt a tightening in my gut as I thought I saw a shape, moving just inside the trees. I closed my eyes and opened them again and looked. Now there were four shapes in the trees and they were moving right to left opposite the flare-light drift. I reached and grabbed the phone and rang the crank for the CP, never taking my eyes off the now distinct shapes. Someone picked up on the other end.

"CP."

I think my voice was shaky.

"CP, this is Pit #3, ...uh... I've got definite movement in the tree line at my 1:00 position, moving right/left. Four, no, ...Five individuals, copy?" Another one had appeared as I spoke.

Then a voice I recognized as Salo's.

"Roger that, #3. Hold your fire till the Grunts open up. Copy?"

I acknowledged and hung-up.

As I watched, the shapes turned into men carrying rifles, wearing green uniforms almost, but not quite the same shade as the surroundings. I saw at least twenty men materialize and advance on our outer strand of wire.

I quickly popped my head around the back blast-wall and waved, frantically, to Bechtal, by the gun. He saw me, shrugged and raised his hands, palms out, with a questioning look.

"Gooks, man!" I whispered as loud as I could to be heard, "We got Gooks in th' wire!" I pointed outward, "Heads up, man!"

I ducked back in and looked out to see that the NVA soldiers had now fanned out and were working at the outer strand of wire. There was a bright flash and a 'THUD', as one of them set off one of our grenade traps. The flash illuminated two of them flying backwards, into the relative darkness of the jungle.

At almost the same time, another soldier set off a trip-flare that illuminated the whole group.

The Grunts, left and right, opened up with M-16s on semi-auto, three and four round bursts, picking targets The Gooks started to scatter and I grabbed the M-79 and chambered a HE round. I'd only fired a 'Blooper' once, in training, but at this range, it's almost like firing a BIG shotgun.

My first round went high and exploded in the trees. My second hit right behind two NVA who had turned and were running back for the shelter of the jungle. In the flash I saw them both knocked down.

'Shit, I hit 'em!' I thought.

One lay still, but the other was crawling off as the Grunts centered their fire and stitched rounds across both soldiers and then they were both still.

By the time I'd reloaded, the Gooks still alive had vanished back into the gloom, so I picked up the binoculars and spotted five bodies, still in the open space, not moving.

Behind me, the Howitzers started up again and this time the rounds were landing, seconds later, only 50-75 feet out in the trees. A lot of trees fell or were blasted up in a maelstrom of debris, including brush, limbs and tons of unidentifiable stuff.

The flashes, even viewed through the trees, were blinding, if you were stupid enough to be watching it happen. Most GIs, myself included, had our heads buried behind something solid.

I felt the earth rumble, as if a couple of freight trains were passing at great speed, right outside my bunker.

After six rounds, spread across their sectors, the guns, one at a time, fell silent.

I ventured a look at the trees as the dust settled, and, through the thick drifting smoke, from what I could see, the jungle looked like it had been hit by a…what? Hurricane? Tornado? Herd of wild, crazy bulldozers? Hell, all three and more!

Meanwhile, more shit was coming down over by #6. I could hear their M-60 Rattling away, and a lot of M-16 fire. Gook mortars were still coming in, but not with any regularity, and they all seemed to be centered on the opposite side of the LZ from us. The Grunt mortars were popping and they seemed to have the enemy tubes on the run. They were only stopping to fire off a round every once in a while.

I heard another 'KeBLAM' over there and their machine-gun suddenly went quiet.

'Don't use th' M-60 'less you have to.' I thought of what Bechtal told me. 'They target automatic weapons first.'

The Howitzers fired up again, this time concentrating on the other side of the perimeter, for another devastating barrage of light, sound, and ground shaking.

The night was lit brightly by 155mm 'Lume' rounds, floating high and turning the night into a silvery day.

My AO was clear, as far as I could discern, so I crawled out and carefully stood up behind the blast wall and looked around. The LZ was blanketed with a heavy, greasy, cloud of smoke, through which visibility was limited to flashes of light from explosions.

I could barely discern red and green tracers flying around somewhere around #6's area.

I saw Bechtal waving for everybody's attention.

"Listen up people! We're gonna get ARA and Gun-ships on-station in 'bout two minutes! Keep your heads down! They WILL be firing in th' tree line! REPEAT, ARA an' gun-ships on th' tree line in TWO MINUTES! Get your heads down!!!"

I ducked back inside, glad at that moment to be in the small enclosed bunker. I still got down as low as I could, lying on my belly with my head up just high enough to see between two sandbags. Soon, over the almost continuous din of small arms fire, I heard the familiar 'Thwopping' sound of helicopters. I ducked down even further, peeking through a crack between two bags.

I could see upward through the gun port opening, but all I could see in the sky was a solid cloud of smoke.

Suddenly, like lightning from the clouds, bright yellow streaks of fire.

Three! No, four, five, six!

The 40mm rockets came crashing into the jungle with a drawn-out hissing and rumbling that shook the ground under me.

The steaks were accompanied by red 'snakes' of mini-gun fire in continuous streams, that hit in the trees and ricocheted like welder's sparks in all directions.

In a brief clear spot I caught a glimpse of a flying shark with a big red grinning mouth with rows of white teeth, spitting fire at the jungle.

Hell, it even scared me!

I ducked my head really down this time and listened as the 'COBRA' gun-ships laid waste to everything in their paths.

I had no idea how many of them were up there, but they seemed to be working all around the LZ at once. The 5.56 mm mini-gun bullets were flying in all directions, including into the LZ, thudding into the sandbags and sometimes clanging off a piece of equipment.

The outgoing fire from the LZ had stopped completely, but the noise level hadn't abated at all. If anything, it was louder. I couldn't believe the sheer volume of rocket, mini-gun, and Auto-blooper (M-79) fire could come from those choppers.

'Heads down, my ass!' I thought, 'I'm diggin' a hole!'

After about four or five minutes the noise suddenly stopped, as if on a given command, (which it probably was) and the sudden silence made my ears pop. It was like the whole world held its breath for thirty seconds or so.

I could hear the crackling of fires out in the jungle.

Then I heard somebody, probably the 1st Sgt., Yelling "ALL CLEAR! ALL CLEAR! MAN YER GUNS! ALLL CLEAARR!!"

I raised up, slowly, and looked out at the perimeter, still bright in the flares.

I couldn't imagine anything could still be alive out there.

The trees, even at a distance, looked shredded. Limbs, leaves and pieces of debris were still falling or drifting down into the smoky dust left by the explosions.

I believe I felt …humble… I guess, and damn glad the gooks don't have helicopters! I heard a Grunt outside, with obvious awe in his voice, say, "MAN, I gotta get me one o' those!!"

His companions laughed and so did I. My tension was broken.

I suddenly realized I was soaked in sweat and mosquitoes had been feasting on my bare arms and chest. I hadn't even noticed till now.

I kept my eyes on the green-line as I reached up and got my plastic bottle of 'Bug-juice' from the elastic band on my helmet and rubbed my arms, chest and neck down with the oily fluid. It's really nasty stuff but it keeps the bugs off. As I was doing this I heard Bechtal yelling.

"Hey, Mouse! You all right in there?"

His head appeared around the blast wall and I waved him in.

"Yeah, man, I'm OK. Didja see th' show?"

"Hell, no, man! I was busy rubbing my face in the dirt between th' trails."

He settled next to me and peered out through the gun-port.

"Were there really Gooks out there?"

"Hell Yeah! " I said, "I got a couple with th' M-79 while th' Grunts were firin' 'em up!"

"No Shit?"

He looked at me and I pointed out to where the two were laying, now partially concealed by fallen scrub trees.

"Hell, Mouse killed a couple o' Gooks, man!" He said as he looked out with the binocs. "Shit, guess they'll think twice before the try US on, again!"

"Those two won't even think once, any more." I said.

He looked me in the eye and said, "There it IS! Man!"

Less than an hour later, the sky lightened in the east as the dawn came on.

We'd all stayed in our positions, ready to fight, but the NVA must have reconsidered and fallen back. All was quiet except for low talk from the Grunt fighting positions and the clanking and whirring sounds as Harris, Bechtal and T.C. cranked the gun down for a swabbing and Andy threw out the empty powder cans.

I knew my eyes were red and they felt like they had gravel and sand in them.

Finally, the light improved enough to pick out details and I checked the KZ one more time. The dead NVA soldiers were still there and the Grunts were emerging from their hidey-holes to point and discuss the action with others that gathered to see.

Harris poked his head around the blast wall and told me to stand-down.

I crawled out and, at first, I had a hard time walking after being cramped up in there for almost three hours. I stretched loose and took a look around.

The morning mist was heavy and still mixed with the smoke from all the 'fireworks'. It made my remaining 'bug-juice' feel even greasier on my skin and the smell of Cordite hung in the air. (Or it was up my nose, because that's all I could smell the rest of the day.)

The first thing I noticed was the large hole in the side of #2 pit, allowing full view of their gun, which was off its jack and pushed to the rear of the pit. I knew a few of those mortars last night had sounded mighty close, but MAN.

I saw Harris standing, leaning against the wheel of our gun, so I walked over.

"Is everybody OK?"

He nodded.

"How 'bout damage?"

I was noticing some large chipped and dinged spots on our gun's paint-work.

He nodded toward #2.

"Two guys killed. Mortars." he said, simply.

He nodded again, this time toward the rear of the pit, where two shapes were stretched out, covered with ponchos.

He didn't say anything else, so I walked past him and went slowly out of the pit. I stopped, took my helmet off (man, those things make yer neck tired) and lit a cig. I heard Andy call.

"Hey, Mouse."

He walked up and stood next to me.

We stood there, smoking, not talking, for a while.

Everybody was doing just as we were.

Guys walking by with cigarettes dangling, far-off looks in their eyes.

In the somber gray light, most everyone looked like Zombies.

Some people were moving pretty fast, putting out some fires around the LZ or running who knows where.

Almost every face I saw had that same, dazed look, like those dead guys in that movie, 'Night of the Living Dead'.

Suddenly, I don't know why, a thought flashed through my mind.

A scene from another movie where that black guy 'Rochester', you know, he was Jack Benny's butler? Anyway, he'd been captured by a voodoo cult in some jungle, somewhere, and turned into a Zombie. In the scene he was walking around, kinda stiff-legged, with his arms out front, like he's sleepwalking, moaning, "I am a Zawmbie, I am a Zawmbie."

I started chuckling and turned to Andy, who looked at me like I was nuts.

I told him about the 'Rochester' thing and nodded around at the 'Zawmbies' around us and he started chuckling, too. Bechtal walked up just then and looked at us both strangely, so I told him and Andy did the 'Zawmbie' walk and he smiled, condescendingly.

"Funny-boys. You guys are nuts!"

I had to agree.

"C'mon, you guys," Bechtal said, "let's see what's happenin."

We walked along behind #2, avoiding the bodies, and inspected their gun. Their Gunner, guy named Smitty, was there and filled us in on details. Both the guns tires were shredded and there was blood smeared down the left trail. According to Smitty, the round had landed right in front of the gun and the blast had toppled it off its jack. Shrapnel had scarred and dented the blast shields and come in under the gun to get the asst. gunner and the loader.

The hole in the berm was from the original B-40 that I'd seen.

Bechtal 'dapped' Smitty.

We walked out through the hole and came to the Grunt fighting positions between #2 and our gun. The Infantry guys were busily pulling up sandbags and looking under them like they'd lost something.

"What's happenin'?" Bechtal asked one of the soldiers.

The Grunt, the ever-present cigarette dangling from his mouth, looked up.

"We're lookin' fer Jacobs' toes, man. He thinks they can sew 'em back on, but I don't know."

His eyes were like holes burned into a wooden face.

"Toes?" Andy had to ask.

"Yeah, he weren't all in th' hole when that mortar," he motioned toward a large hole in the wire, "went off over there. Took th' end o' his foot off, clean, boot an' all, an' if we can find 'is toes, they'll go out wit' 'im on th' chopper. Maybe they CAN sew 'em back on." He shrugged.

I looked around my feet to make sure I wasn't standing on 'Jacobs' Toes'.

Andy and Bechtal did, too.

From there we went out into the middle areas of the LZ.

Everywhere there were signs of destruction.

Mortar craters, like twenty-twenty five feet apart. One had missed the back wall of the FDC by three feet and had shredded the wall but hadn't penetrated the two-sandbag thick construction. Smoke still lay thick on the ground and drifted up from the CP wall as well as two other Infantry bunkers nearby. One of these had taken a round right on its roof, but, again, the blast failed to penetrate to the inside. The occupants, the Grunt LT and a Sgt., were plenty shook up and temporarily deaf, but otherwise OK.

Before we even got to #6's pit, I could tell things had been much worse over here. The gun was still in place but their berm had been blown down across a twelve foot span where their M-60 bunker had been. We learned, from one of the three 'Bunnies' that had survived the night, that three consecutive B-40s had killed the M-60 gunner in his bunker and wounded another guy on the berm.

Then a mortar had hit directly on the roofs of the culvert hootches and killed their Gunner and cut up the other two guys on the gun. He was the only one left not wounded or dead on # 6, he told us, because he'd been in the powder bunker, cutting charges, when the "Shit came down."

We heard the sound of choppers approaching and watched as two Med-Evac 'Slicks' swooped-in and flared to a landing in the center of the open space. About fifteen guys piled out and gathered into a knot to one side as the Medics and others rushed to load the wounded into the first chopper and the dead into the other. In a cloud of dust, the helicopters jumped away and were gone.

"You're gonna need some help getting your crew set up," Bechtal said to the new #6 Gun-chief. He motioned for Andy and me to go on.

"Yeah, I guess so." The Spec-4 said, "I'd really appreciate some help, thanks."

He smiled and they walked over toward the knot of new guys to pick out some replacements.

Bechtal looked back over his shoulder at us.

"If you need me, yell, OK?"

We nodded affirmative.

Andy and I circled #6 pit to the green-line side and looked out over the, now mangled, barbed and razor wire barrier.

There were, I counted, seven NVA bodies in the tangled strands. Some weren't complete bodies. I swear, part of one was hanging in the crotch of a scrub tree at the edge of the KZ. All I could see was a leg, with no boot on it, attached to part of a torso, lodged about twelve feet up. How it got there, and where the rest of him went, I could only guess.

Seeing this made me queasy.

"God, I may never eat again." I mumbled.

Andy had already turned away, but I could see in his expression, that he felt the same way. I followed him around past #1 and #2 pits, back to ours.

Outside our pit, the Grunts had worked their way out to the dead enemy soldiers in our wire, and were standing around out there, smoking and joking. I asked Andy if he wanted to go with me to look at them, but he refused, saying he'd "Had enough of that shit." I went to the open access gate and wound my way through the maze of rows of concertina, and came up on the Grunts, who were talking among themselves or looking at the bodies.

Three of the gooks were draped in various positions across the coils of wire, while the two that I'd got with the M-79 were about twenty feet beyond at the edge of the tree line, partially concealed by debris. I wove on out to the edge, bent over and pulled away a mangled bush covering the first ones' body from the waist up.

He was face up on the ground with his left arm in a very unnatural position under him. His eyes and mouth were open and the flies were already buzzing and lighting on his face. I gulped involuntarily, and looked over at the other one, about ten feet away. He was face down and spread-eagled, pointed out from me toward the jungle.

His entire back was a mass of blood and tissue. I didn't bother to examine him any closer. My stomach was weak enough.

It dawned on me that these men, (though they looked like boys in play uniforms), were soldiers, like me, doing what they were told to do. This time they'd paid the price, while I was able to stand here and look down at what was left. Another time, it could just as well go the other way around. I wanted to feel superior, the victor, heroic or something. No go.

I did my job! It was kill-or-be killed, after all. But all I could feel was a hollow, sick, guilt, like I'd done something wrong. I wasn't a very religious person, never had been, but I believed in God, and I'd broken the first commandment. The one, I was always told, was the most important one. My upbringing and beliefs affected me more than I thought they would.

No one else was near, so I bowed my head and said a small prayer for these soldiers and all soldiers, who'd died at the hands of other soldiers. And also for the men (myself included), who lived through the fighting, knowing that they had lived at the expense of another's life.

12

THANKSGIVING

The Grunts had started 'Sweeps' at first light and had come up with twenty-nine more bodies from the jungle surrounding LZ MARY. There were supposedly blood trails, many of them, headed north towards the Cambodian border, but no contact was made. The enemy had evaporated like water.

They brought the bodies into a clearing, just outside the perimeter, straight out from #1 gun pit. Counting the eleven from the barbed wire, there were forty NVA bodies lined up in the sun by 1000 hrs, when the first chopper-full of officers came in to view them. The corpses had swollen and turned an ashy-blue color and flies were getting thick.

By 11:30, when the second load of Officers and photographers left, the smell was getting unbearable, and a special detail of iron-willed/stomached men moved the bodies aside and a large pit was dug with the little Bob-Cat 'dozer that had been brought by chopper to mend our berms. The bodies were then pushed, very unceremoniously, into the hole, limed down by the 'Graves- Registration' detail, and covered over and packed down by the 'dozer.

All this, of course, was within plain sight of anyone who cared to watch, and, of course, we all did. I'll tell you, it gave me a very strange feeling, seeing such an ignominious end to our brave 'Combat Action'. The other guys, also, were somber and serious and went about their business with brief glances at the red patch of raw earth in the little clearing. What had been a major turning point in a lot of men's lives, mine included, had been tamped down with the red dirt, in such a business-like way by the Army's 'Green-Machine'. I felt the whole thing; the attack, the dead men, the officers and photog's, the burial, all the cowardice

111

and bravery of the last eight hours, was obliterated, cancelled, and made unreal. I wasn't alone in this. I saw it in the faces of all the guys I talked with that day.

By evening, most of the repairs had been done to the berms and perimeter wire. #2 gun was declared too damaged and was hooked-out by Chinook at 1700 hrs., along with its crew. The Grunts immediately took over their pit for their little three-tube mortar battery.

After evening chow, at dusk, we were all sitting around in front of our hootches, and small talk turned to the battle last night and conjecture as to what we might expect tonight.

"Salo told me they think we did a lot of damage to the Gooks last night." Bechtal said between sips of coffee. "They think they di-di mau'ed (retreated) back up to Cambodia."

"Man, I hope so!" Andy said earnestly, "I nearly 'freaked' last night when they hit us with th' gas! Shit..... I was....."

He paused as Harris and Bechtal burst out giggling.

"WHAT?" he looked at them, confused. They only laughed harder.

Finally Harris got himself under control.

"That wasn't enemy gas, man, that was jus' some 'Dufus' over by #6, got 'is gas grenades and 'is flares mixed up an' gassed himself an' most of the LZ, too!"

By that time we were all hooting and Andy got defensive.

"Well, hell, it still burned like hell, Gook gas or not!"

Harris, still chuckling, rose and said "I'm gonna sack out, didn't get much sleep las' night an' I'm bushed." He turned toward his end culvert.

"Good Idea." Bechtal said, rising, also. "We all better get some rest, th' S-2 could be all-wet 'bout th' Gooks not coming back tonight. One way or another, we're firing H&Is from midnight to 1:00 A.M.," groans from the group, "So get yer winks while ya can, ladies."

Andy mumbled as he crawled into his culvert.

"Man, ya don't get much rest around here!"

He collapsed in a heap inside, with his feet still sticking out the door. As T.C. walked past on his way to his hootch, he kicked Andy's booted foot.

"Better tuck them thangs in, I don't wanna be lookin' 'round fer YER toes, man."

The feet disappeared quickly, and T.C. and I laughed.

"An' keep yer gas-mask handy, too!"

More giggling.

I crawled in and considered writing a letter, but I couldn't decide how I'd describe my experiences of the last twenty-four hours, without scaring the crap outta my Mom. Or, really, whether I wanted to. Some things are better left unsaid, for all concerned. I opted for sleep and found no problem passing out like a drunk on New Years.

The following several days were uneventful.

We followed our usual routines and cleaned up from the attack. A new #2 gun was brought in with a new crew, and after the Grunts were evicted, (with much grousing on their part), it was set up in the original pit, (with holes now repaired).

November 28th came and it was Thanksgiving. It was a very strange concept in Viet Nam. Word came from Salo that we were to receive a real 'Turkey Dinner W/ Fixins', so almost everyone, (except Andy of course), skipped our C- Rat lunch to leave room for the Real Thing.

At 1500 that afternoon, a Chinook from HQ Battery in Phouc Vinh, brought in a portable banquet and a contingent of cooks, who proceeded to set up a serving line in a GP-Medium tent with the sides rolled up. We all stood around and watched in anticipation as the food was prepared for serving. Most guys already had their mess kits in hand and were jockeying for position near where the line would obviously form at the door. Good-hearted banter flew in volleys throughout the crowd of hungry GIs.

The Battery Commander, Capt. Nord and his aide, met with the Battalion Commander, Col. Johns, who flew in from Long Binh for the festivities. They shook hands on the chopper pad and joined the other officers and high NCOs in a separate tent where their food was served by none other but the Mess Sgt. Himself, who was then asked to join their group to eat. All of this was duly recorded on film by a cameraman from Stars and Stripes.

At last they were seated and eating and this was the signal for the Enlisted Ranks to do their thing. We queued up and our food was dished into metal mess trays with US ARMY silverware. It was hot and steaming.

"Man, smell that smell!" Smiling Andy said, poking me in the ribs with an elbow.

"That's some real, like, stateside food, man! Like Mama used ta make!" he smacked his lips.

I couldn't help myself.

"Man, I didn't know your Mom was a Army cook, but now I think about it, it figures. Is she a Mess Sgt. With th' Rangers, 'r what?"

T.C. chimed in from behind.

"Naw, man! She's in th' Navy, ain't she? Ya know she all'ays DID like th' sailors. HAW, HAW!!"

We all laughed and Andy play-acted hurt.

"You guys shouldn't make fun of a guys mother, man." He stuck his chest out.

"My mom's the BEST, man, I'm sure she's servin' up th' turkey right now to my whole family. Everybody comes ta our house for T-Day an' we all eat 'til we explode! Then we lay around th' living room an' watch football on th' Tee-Vee, an' th' kids an' women play games 'r something. You know, like Monopoly 'r Parcheesi 'r some such shit."

A wistful look had come over his face as he said this, and the look spread to the other faces around him. We were all mentally picturing our own families at home, trying to enjoy the Holidays without us. How worried they must be for our safety. For most of us, it was the first major holiday away from home.

"Man, I really miss that." Bechtal said, looking at his shoes.

They didn't want us clustered up eating at tables, so we took our food with us back to the pit and the Chaplain came by and said grace for us and we dug in.

"One Thanksgiving without Uncle Ralph an' Aunt Gloria is almost worth it to me," Harris said with his mouth full, "even if I gotta be in this shit-hole. Every year, soon's they show up they start a fight an' pretty soon everybody's mad at everybody. Arguin' an Yatta-ta-yatta-ta. Goes on th' rest'a th' day. Takes all year for all of 'em to forget what they was fightin' about. Then it starts again every Thanksgivin'. MAN, every blamed year!"

We all laughed at his version of 'Thankfulness.'

Andy nodded.

"I got some cousins like that, always stirring up some shit. It really pisses my Mom off. She keeps threatening to not invite 'em, but every year she gives in 'cause they're Uncle Jack's kids, an' Uncle Jack was the Family War Hero from Korea, an' she shows respect for him by puttin' up with his rotten kids. THAT'S th' kinda Mom she is, ya know?"

Andy looked around and we all nodded agreement.

"At my house," I began, getting kind of wistful myself, "it's usually just my Mom an' Dad, an' my sister an' her husband, if they can make it in from Arkansas, an' me. We usually play some kinda board game all afternoon, too, after stuffin' ourselves. It's usually Monopoly. I used to think it was boring, but, man, I'd give anything to be puttin' houses an' hotels on good ol' Board Walk, right now."

"Still sounds boring to me." Harris laughed.

We all laughed as the end of the chow line wove past us.

"I'm for seconds, anybody else?" Andy said, picking up his tray.

"Yeah, me too, wait up!" Bechtal said rising.

I turned to T.C.

"Any dessert? Did anybody see any dessert in there?"

T.C. shook his head 'No', sadly.

"'Jeez, I'd love a piece of pumpkin pie, right now, with whipped cream on top. Or pecan pie, hot with butter pecan ice cream meltin' on it."

My mouth watered.

T.C. rolled his eyes.

"Man, you just made me hungry all over again! HEY GUYS, wait fer me!"

He jumped up and followed the others to the line for seconds.

I leaned back against the sandbags, and my thoughts were back in Lexington, Ky. I could picture my family, enjoying the meal, praying for me, I'm sure, laughing and talking, and the whole time, there's my chair, empty.

'Man, that's really depressing!' I thought.

115

13

"SGT. WILSON, I FEEL SICK."

Not much actual 'News' of the world filtered down to us on the LZs and firebases. Other than some weeks-old Stars and Stripes Army newspapers, which were generally slanted toward in-country events, our only access to world news was magazines or hometown papers sent by somebody's parents or whoever, in a 'Goody-box'. We also got hearsay from the new-guys in town, the FNGs, who'd just come from the States.

One such 'Green-Weenie' was Zeke 'the Beak' Warner, of NYC, a new Commo guy. He had a Time magazine with stories and pictures of the 'Peace' marches in Washington. Other cities, too. The article said 400,000 people had marched to the Capitol steps, protesting the war and demanding the withdrawal of the troops in Viet Nam.

At first we all thought, 'Right on, man, end this muthah an' we'll all go home!' Then we read about the demonstrators waving NVA flags and signs saying that WE were the 'Oppressors'. That WE were committing atrocities on the 'Innocent Villagers' (Hell, WE didn't even KNOW any innocent villagers!) We couldn't understand! The protestors seemed to be showing support for the VC and the NVA!

"HEY!" Andy yelped, and grabbed the well-worn magazine.

"We're only over here to protect THEIR right to protest, an' THEY'RE rootin' for th' Gooks?"

He looked closely at the article in the book and shook his head.

"Man, those long-hair 'mothers' got it ALL wrong! They oughta' bring all those Hawks an' Doves over here an' let 'em get a load of what we're goin' through. How we gotta live. Man, they don't give a SHIT 'bout th' war, 'cept some of them or their kids might get drafted, too, an have to come over here an' get killed by th' same precious Gooks they're tryin' to protect! MAN, what a SHITTY war!"

He threw down the magazine and stalked off.

"Right-on." T.C. said and looked at me.

"There it is." I agreed.

December arrived and it was as hot and humid as any August back home.

We'd been on LZ MARY for a full four weeks; very unusual, for us 'Nomad Artillery'. We'd gotten ourselves settled in and complacent. There had been no enemy action in our area in over two weeks.

Sgt. Ambrose was 'short' and was shuffled back to the rear for his last two weeks before rotation. His replacement, 1st Sgt. Wilson, an E-8, was a huge, bald, very black man, whom, we all assumed, had been a basic training drill sergeant, because his attitude toward E-4 and below personnel was strictly Lord/peon. He the Lord, we the peons. On his first day in battery he reamed out almost everyone he came across. We had a bad feeling about Sgt. Wilson.

Our Battery Commander, Capt. Nord, rotated two days later, to be replaced by a ROTC Captain, fresh from the States, named Capt. White.

Capt. White made Sgt. Wilson look like a liberal. He immediately passed down orders that all military dress codes be strictly enforced. "All men WILL shave daily. Haircuts WILL be regulation."

Needless to say, these edicts raised the ire of a lot of us 'peons', and we bitched, for all the good it did. Pretty soon, there were a bunch of ex-SP4s and ex-PFCs, busted a rank for insubordination consisting of wearing flip-flops during the day or not blousing ones boots, or even not wearing a fatigue jacket on a 100° day. The 'Wilson and White Show' was obviously determined to clean up the 'Dirty Thirty' even if it cost the morale of the whole Battery.

And it did.

It was about this time that I started to feel sick. Stomach cramps, diarrhea, and a general low-grade malaise that the medic claimed was either " Bad water, C-rats, mosquitoes, heat, or all the above. I got some antacid pills and advice to eat more salt tablets and to take my 'Pink Pill' (Anti-malarial), every day.

My illness proved to be the cause of my first run-in with the new 'Top'.

After three days of feeling bad, I went to the CP and asked Salo if I could go to the rear for a medical checkup. He had to get permission from Sgt. Wilson, who came at me like a storm.

"There's nuthin' wrong witchu, soldiah. Yer jus' lookin' fer some soft time in the rear wit' th' ladies. You look healthy enough t' me an' we cain't spare none o' y'all goldbricks 'cause we ain't gittin' no mo' replacements. Request denied!"

I said, "But...Top..."

"Git yer sorry ass outa my CP an' git back t' yer work, TROOP!" He glared.

With a shrug at Salo, I left without another word.

It seemed from then on, every time the Sgt. saw me he had to remark about my 'laziness' or call me a 'Goldbrick' (His favorite name for most of us). He would go out of his way to irritate me, criticizing my work or calling me a "Sawed-off runt". He'd obviously taken a severe dislike to me, and, truthfully, I felt pretty much the same for him.

Second week in December we moved back to FSB JAMIE.

The difference between a 'Fire Support Base' and a LZ, is a FSB is an even bigger dust/ mud hole. JAMIE had expanded somewhat, but the base was still pretty much the same as it was six months (a lifetime) ago when I first saw it.

We set up in our old pits and us 'Old Timers' amazed the FNGs with stories of ground attacks and mortar/rocket attacks during our last visit here. (Mostly untrue, of course.) The best improvement to the base was a mess hall, with hot food. Not wonderful food, but a vast improvement over C-rats.

The first week on JAMIE was routine except for the 'TIME' and 'LOOK' magazine reporters and cameramen who arrived one morning and stayed 'til the next day. They took pictures and interviewed some of the guys. I didn't get an interview, but the 'TIME' guy had us on #3 gun to pose, (sort of), during a fire mission. I think my back was turned when he snapped it, though.

The second week at Jamie was highlighted by an alert around 2:00 A.M. one night. It was called in by T.C. who was on berm-guard. He'd heard rattling noises out at the dumpsite about 50-60 yeards out

118

from our position just beyond the tree line. The rattling went on for about ½ hour and was heard by Bechtal, Harris and myself.

Permisssion was given for recon-by-fire and T.C. opened up with the M-60 for about 200 rounds, spraying the entir area with tracer. No more rattling was heard that night.

The next morning, at first light, T.C. and I went out to the dump to check for dead V.C. or whatever.

'Whatever' was a 300 lb. Bengal tiger lying on his side on the heap of junk and trash.

He'd been scavaging for food, obviously. He was no looker before, being slat sided and kind of moth-eaten. The sixty or so holes from the M-60 rounds had not improved his appearance, but to us he was a real big-game bag.

Wildly excited, we ran back and borrowed a mule and fecthed a rope and Harris to help. We went back out and towed the big dead animal into the LZ and stopped by the CP.

A crowd gathered to view the remains. Many "ooh's" and "aah's" were heard as the tiger was examined by the curious onlookers.

Our cook, a Sgt. Lester Skanks had experimented with taxidermy in civilian life and volunteered to skin the beast.

"We'll save the hide and hang it on the CP wall." Captain White said.

"Maybe we can change our name to 'Tiger Killers'!" Someone offered. Another in the back muttered, "Tell the 1st Sgt. there'll be a black hide hangin' up next to it if he don't ease up!"

Before they butchered him up, I scrounged up a pair of pliers, and after much work, I pried out one of his big fangs to keep as a souvenir. It was nearly 3" long with the root. The exposed part was an ivory color and the root a bright white. Later a Viet carver in Phouc Vinh made the root into a Bhudda image for me and drilled it so it could be worn as a necklace.

I wore it for a while, but quit when it stabbed me in the chest when I rolled over on it in my sleep one night.

The skinning job looked like it had been done by wild animals, but we hung the remains on the CP wall and it was only recognizable as a tiger skin because of the color and stripes.

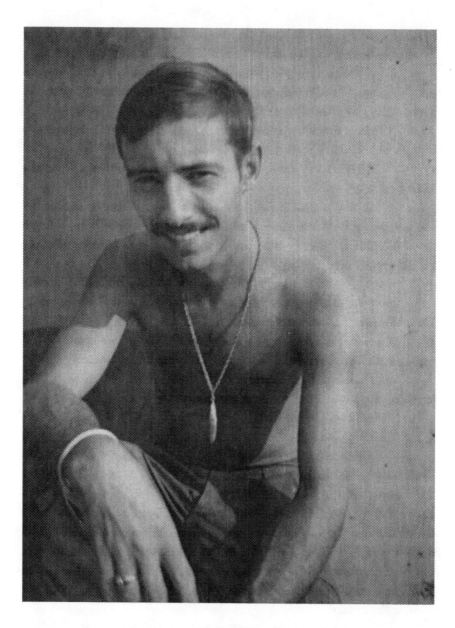

Tiger Tooth Necklace

My 'Goldbrick' illness had not improved, even with the better chow. In fact, I'd begun to throw-up my meals on occasion and my weight had dropped from 125 to 115 pounds. I got up my nerve and went to Sgt.

Wilson again and told him I thought I really should get checked-out by a doctor, but he blew up at me again and nearly threw me out of the CP physically, calling me names the whole way. I decided, then, that it was going to be useless to try again until I could show someone else, preferably an officer, how sick I was.

Days and weeks went by and I got to where I could predict when I was going to lose my breakfast, lunch or dinner. I was still eating my meals, but I couldn't hold it down for more than two or three hours, sometimes less if I was straining or working hard. After three weeks of this I was down to 110 pounds.

But it was 'Christmas'!!

There was a general cease-fire declared for the holiday and a Chaplain and a group of 'Doughnut Dollies' (Red Cross girls) arrived with a Christmas tree, and a little show consisting of songs and dances by the girls and a Christmas sermon by the Chaplain to hopefully enlighten us sinners and set us on the right track. But mostly, we just lusted over the girls, ugly as they were. We got a big meal, (replay of the Thanksgiving one), that was pleasant, but it only served to make me miss home even more.

After the meal, Capt. White actually got some of the Lt.'s together, not wholly voluntarily, I gathered, to sing Christmas carols, off key, in front of the gathering, and encouraged everyone to join in. Most of the men sang along, but I heard Sgt. Wilson, in the back, talking to a E-7 from the Grunts, "Shit, no officer ought'a be up makin' a fool o' hisself, front'a these here Enlisted Pukes."

Andy heard him, too, and elbowed me.

"Some people just don't have no fuckin' reverence for Christian holidays."

He winked and I smiled.

New Years, 1970, came and went, the high point being the 'Mad Minute' on the green-line at midnight Dec. 31st. Word went out and everyone brought their weapon(s) to the perimeter and on the stroke of midnight, we all fired as many tracers as we could round up, creating our own fireworks show. It was magnificent. We could even see tracers from two more bases within five miles of us. We were facing some major weapon cleaning, but it sure made us feel better. We let off as much steam as smoke.

121

By the second week in January, my illness was acute. I was down to 105 pounds, and even Doc Sammons agreed there was something besides the usual shit wrong with me. Doc petitioned for me to Sgt. Wilson, but, again, I was refused in no uncertain terms.

"Nobody leaves this LZ 'less he's dead!" Quote, unquote.

Then, one hot, hot morning, as me and 'Duck' Wisner were loading 'joes' into the truck on the chopper pad. Fate gave me the chance I'd been waiting for.

By 1030 hours that morning, the temperature was already hovering in the 100-degree range. I was up in the bed of our five-ton truck, stacking the re-supply rounds as 'Duck' handed them up. We were sweating profusely.

A 'LOH' (loach) helicopter swooped in and landed on our pad, carrying, none other, but our Battalion Commander, whose name I wasn't aware of, but I could see the silver eagles on his shirt collars, even at a distance. As the Colonel emerged and stood on the PSP, the First Sgt. ran out to greet him, (Capt. White being somewhere else, I presumed).

Wilson and the Colonel, due to the intense heat radiating up off the steel plates of the pad, walked over and were taking advantage of the only shade available.

Right beside my truck.

As I'm working, I can hear them talking, but I can't see them for the wooden stake-rails on the sides of the truck bed. I stacked another 97 pound projectile and I felt my stomach roll over, and I realized it's time for my morning chow to depart. I started to the OTHER side of the truck to heave, but then an inspiration hit me.

'Maybe I can make a point of this!'

I figured if I puked where an officer, like the Colonel there, sees me, the 1st Sgt. will have to admit I'm sick.

'Right?' Seemed so at the time.

I lurched to their side, clutching my belly and dumped the entire contents over the rail. I, honestly, did not realize how close to the side of the truck they were standing, or the Sgt.'s exact location.

If I'd aimed I couldn't have made a more direct hit on Wilson's head.

It was truly horrifying to me, to the Colonel, and mostly to the Sgt., down whose face, neck, and torso my greenish glop was streaming.

Blustering, the big Sgt. reached up and grabbed me by my shirtfront. He pulled me easily over the bed rails and stood, still unable to speak coherently, shaking my limp, soon-to-be-dead body in mid-air.

The Colonel, who had stepped back a couple of feet to avoid the splatter, stepped closer and looked at me, and the dripping NCO.

"What's wrong with that man, Sgt. Wilson?" He asked, incredulity in his voice.

Wilson, not holding his rage in very well, spluttered.

"There's nothin' wrong with 'im, sir, 'es just a Goldbrick allus claimin' t' be sick!"

He shakes me 'til my teeth rattle.

Then the magic words I'd longed to hear:

"A man does not puke on his First Sgt. unless there is something seriously wrong with that man!"

The huge man stopped shaking me and drilled me with his eyes.

"There's nothin' wrong wit' 'im YET, But there WILL be."

He threw me to the ground where I lay, dejected, seeing my life flash before my eyes. He took out a green hanky and started trying to wipe the mess off his face, but the cloth was totally inadequate for the task, so he just smeared it around.

The Colonel looked first at me, then at Wilson, drilling us with iron-gray eyes.

"I want this man off this LZ and checked-out by a doctor in the rear."

Wilson sputtered again.

"But.... But, Sir....."

"AND," the Colonel continued "I want a written report from YOU, Sgt., within one week, as to what's wrong with him. IS THAT CLEAR?"

The officer was scowling, now.

As bad as I was feeling, I was smiling inside at this turn of events.

"YESSIR!" the Sgt. could only answer.

"He'll go out on th' re-supply chopper tomorrow mornin', SIR!"

'Uh-oh,' I thought, 'I won't live 'til tomorrow, if the Top gets me alone.'

"Not soon enough!" the Colonel said.

(Oh thank you, thank you, sir!)

He looked at me as I picked myself up from the dust, trying to look soldierly and pitiful at the same time.

"Son, get your gear. I'm going straight to Bien Hoa from here, I'll drop you off."

I couldn't believe my luck.

He turned back to Sgt. Wilson, who was still mopping his bald head with the handkerchief.

"He'll ride to Bien Hoa with me and report to 15th Med. Make the arrangements, Sgt., and remember that report. Now, get moving, both of you! I don't have all day."

"YESSIR!" we both replied.

Sgt. Wilson gave me a withering look, but walked past me into the LZ, his shoulders hunched, still wiping his head.

I looked at the Colonel.

"Sir, I really didn't mean for that to happen.... It just suddenly...."

"If I hadn't been here," he looked at my name tag, "Hudson, you still would have ended up at 15th Med. The First Sgt. would have mutilated you for that, and I wouldn't have blamed him."

I think he smiled a little at that. I didn't tell him that if he hadn't been here in the first place, none of this would have happened.

"I'll just get my stuff, sir."

"You do that, Hudson, and be quick, I'm lifting off in..." he consulted his watch, "ten minutes."

I nodded and ran to the truck bed, grabbed my rifle and steel pot off the bench, gave a surreptitious wink to Wisner, who'd been keeping a low profile, listening to this exchange with unbelieving ears. He grinned and peace-signed me and gave me a thumbs-up.

I wasted no time getting my stuff. I literally threw it all into my duffel, told Bechtal and Andy the situation and to ask Wisner for the details, and left on the run. I hoped I wouldn't run into Wilson on the way. I was back at the 'Bird' in seven minutes flat.

The Colonel was already strapped into the co-pilots seat and the pilot thumbed me into the back passenger compartment, where I strapped myself into the canvas sling seat and we were off in a cloud of, hopefully, the last LZ dust I'd ever see.

We verticulated to 50 feet, then tilted forward and swooped in a circle over the FSB, allowing me a last look at my buddies on #3, all waving and shouting unheard good-byes. I also got a final look at 'Top'. He was just emerging from the CP. The last thing I saw on FSB JAMIE was the 'Don't let me ever see you again' look, plain in Wilson's eyes, even at that distance.

I hoped I'd make his wish come true.

END OF PART ONE.

PART II
THE REAR, SORTA...

14

FROM A ROCK TO A HARD PLACE

The flight to Bien Hoa was exhilarating.

I was flying high in more ways than one.

After we'd cleared the tree line, we continued to climb as we buzzed in a bee-line across ten miles of jungle in less than nine minutes. Soon we were at 10,000 feet over flat farmland dotted with paddies and dikes.

Up here the air was crisp and cold and I shivered with more than anticipation. My teeth chattered within minutes as the sweat dried on my soggy fatigues and body. My mind was racing with excitement. Finally, I was out of the 'field' and on my way back toward 'Civilization'. (At least relative to what I'd been used to). My last seven months had been spent on one firebase or another, and, face it, one hole in the jungle looks pretty much like any other. Except for one night in Bien Hoa, and two weeks in Tay Ninh City, my sight seeing had been limited to looking out the doors of helicopters in-between LZs.

I was just thinking, 'Hmmm…. 15th MED,….sounds like some kinda hospital. Wonder if I'll do some hospital-time?'

Then, the same thought occurred to me that would have occurred to any twenty-one year old male….

'NURSES! Man, hospitals have NURSES!'

I spent the next little while dreaming of being attended to by lovely young women in white uniforms with halos shimmering around their heads. I wasn't sure what was wrong with me, but, believe me, at that time I was hoping it was serious enough to require some extended hospital-time.

My reverie was interrupted when the bottom fell out of our flight and we descended into an immense, sprawling, military base. We literally fell onto, not the airport, as I'd expected, but a small chopper pad in the middle of a group of low buildings and tents. The PSP pad had a large Red Cross painted in its center.

'Guess I'm here.' I thought.

When we bumped down, the Colonel swung around in his seat and motioned for me to come forward. When I was close he yelled over the engine noise.

"Son, this is the MED-EVAC pad for 15th MED."

He pointed to a GP tent along one side.

"Report to the tent over there and they should know what to do with you."

I said "Yessir!"

I turned to get my stuff, but he reached out and held my arm lightly.

"Son, I don't advise puking on any more NCOs."

I paused, gave him a weak smile and nodded.

"No sir."

"I doubt it would have the same….effect….it had this time." He continued.

"Uh…no sir…I doubt it, too, sir."

I stammered, not sure if I was in trouble or not. I think I saw a small gleam of humor in his eyes.

"Hell of a way to get off an LZ, though, private, now get off my 'bird' and report to the duty-person."

I didn't see his name tag or hear his name spoken, but I really liked that guy. He seemed like a really straight dude…. for an officer.

I "Yessired" him again and jumped out onto the PSP and the little 'bird' jumped off before I took two steps, dusting and stinging me with tiny bits of sand in its downwash of wind.

I ran to the tent and peered into the gloom inside the door. I could pick out some furniture in the dark interior; a desk, a chair, a gray bank of filing cabinets, a dark shape behind the desk.

I "Ahem'ed" and the shape looked up and now it's a dark shape with round glowing eyes. Then I realized it's the light from the doorway reflecting off his glasses.

"Uh...hello.... I'm supposed to check-in here, I think... for some tests or something."

I stepped through the door, letting my eyes adjust to the darkness.

"Name?"

"Uh... Hudson, R, PFC, 'D' Battery, 1/30th Arty."

The shape looked up at me again, flashing his round glasses and a row of white teeth.

"Hudson?" He burst, "Is that really you?"

He came around the desk and grabbed my arm, looked closely.

"Well, I'll be damned, it IS you, Mouse!"

I looked behind those round reflectors of his.

"PIGGY!"

He shook my arm and I grabbed his shoulder and shook him.

"Well, how the hell....?"

He released me and shook his head.

"I only lasted two weeks in the field and had a heat stroke. Pretty bad. Almost died. They brought me here an' I've been here ever since."

"Wow, man, that's really tough." I said, sarcastically, looking around the small, but nice, tent.

"Yeah, really tough." He laughed. "C'mon, I'll take you over to the ADMIN building and get you processed-in and find you a place to bunk."

He took my arm again and led me through the other door out into what was, I swear to God, a movie set for M*A*S*H, complete with the flagpole with the PA speakers announcing the evenings movie. John Wayne, of course, in 'They Were Expendable', of all things.

"Jeez, it's good to see you, Mouse." He said as we walked, "You been in the field all this time? What, six months?"

"Closer to seven, man, yeah, whole time." I shook my head, sadly.

"Well, you're looking.....well.....Shitty, really." He suddenly stopped and looked me up and down.

"You're not wounded or something, are you?"

"Well, thanks, you're lookin' wonderful yourself," (and he was!) "No, I'm not wounded, just sick. Lost a lotta weight."

"Wow, no shit! You must be, what, 110 pounds, now?"

"105, man. Can't eat, or when I do, I can't hold it down. But my main problem was pukin' on a First Sgt."

"YOU WHAT?" He was incredulous.

"Long story, I'll tell you later."

I laughed at the look on his face.

"Can't wait to hear this."

We continued on to a tin and screen building with 'ADMIN' over the door. He led the way inside and got some forms from a clerk-typist for me to fill out. Which I did while he talked to another clerk or somebody in the next room then he came back and we handed-in my papers. I was assigned a bunk in a tent two buildings over, away from the chopper pad. Piggy walked me over there, and along the way filled me in on my prospective roommate.

"Grunt, named Williams. Black guy. Nice dude, but don't play cards with him for money."

"What's he in for?" I asked.

"Wounded both legs, but not too bad. He's ambulatory, but slow."

"Don't play cards with him, huh?" I asked.

"Never, unless you don't like your money."

We entered the little six-man tent, but nobody was there.

Williams was obviously the sole occupant, judging from the lack of gear on any of the bunks except one, which was strewn with Supremes tapes and general stuff. Williams was out somewhere, I supposed.

I picked a bunk against the other screened wall and stowed my stuff while Piggy quizzed me on my in-country adventures. Of course he wanted to hear about the first Sgt. Thing.

"Wow, man, I'm hungry. I'll tell you over chow, OK?"

We walked over to the mess hall and I had a plate of roast beef and gravy on toast. As crummy as I felt it tasted pretty good. I knew I'd lose it later but it was worth it. We talked as we ate and I told Piggy the 'Puke Story'. He nearly fell off the wooden bench laughing.

"What balls!" he kept repeating between guffaws. He struggled for breath. "You're lucky you're not in LBJ (Long Binh Jail).... or dead!"

He told me he'd gone from the replacement center, not to an air conditioned TOC on a large base, as he'd expected, but to an FDC bunker on LZ ANN, south of CU CHI. He said he'd always had trouble with hot weather, and the stuffy bunker had been too much for him and he'd had the heat stroke. He came to at 15th Med as a patient. After his recuperation, it turned out they needed a clerk and Piggy'd talked his way into a transfer. He'd been here ever since.

"It's not the Howard Johnson, but this place sure beats the LZs."

My mouth was full so I nodded affirmative.

"We got hot showers, hot food, Army food, but hot. An' we can go into Long Binh or Bien Hoa City to the bars or the 'Steam 'n Cream.'"

"Sounds great, man, so you'll be here for th' duration?" I asked.

"Guess so. What d'ya think they'll do with you?"

"Depends what's wrong with me, I guess. I hope I don't hav'ta go back out to the firebases though. It's a shitty life out there. Day-in day-out sweatin', livin' like animals in the dirt. An' you get shot at, too. Just to keep it interesting."

He wanted to know about the 'getting shot-at' part, so I told him about the ground-attacks and the guys that were killed and about my shrapnel, (I promised to show it to him later).

We sat and talked until the Mess Sgt. Ran us out at 1330 hrs.

Piggy had to report back to work, so I was left to my own devices for the afternoon. I stopped by the CP and inquired about the location of a PX so I could pick up some stuff. Then I headed off to explore a little.

I walked slowly in the intense, wavering heat, down the dusty peneprimed roads, past acre after acre of unit compounds, heli-pads and storage lots. I saw the usual jumble of military-type buildings interspersed with French-Vietnamese stuccoed structures. These were set back behind crumbling brick walls that had massive iron filigreed gates, and signs in English and Vietnamese over the entrances. Everything was so....neat, if not particularly clean. So different from the firebases I'd seen where everything was piled in a heap and definitely not clean. I also had to remember to salute officers, something we never did in the 'Field'.

At the PX, I picked up some candy and some paperbacks, and two 'Genuine Vietnamese oil paintings', depicting Sam Pan-type boats and a rice paddy scene. They were really beautiful in their bamboo frames and I mailed them home to my Mom as a belated Christmas present. She got them in May.

I felt conspicuous in my sun-bleached fatigues and 'suede-look' boots that hadn't seen polish since Tay Ninh. I figured I'd better clean up my act before some 'lifer' jumped me.

Back at the tent, I stowed my stuff and again inquired at the CP about some new fatigues and boots and a barbershop. I set off for the 'tonsorial parlor' first, which was another semi-trailer with gook barbers, just a couple of blocks from the Med compound.

After being coifed and shaved, I hit the unit supply room at 15th MED and, miraculously, obtained two sets of 'Extra Small- Short' fatigues and a new pair of boots.

I had a shower, (Ahhh…hot water), and soon changed into my new uniform, (Retaining my well-worn ball-cap so-as not to look like a FNG), then wandered over to Pigmy's little tent by the chopper pad to visit.

When I arrived, two MED-EVAC birds had just deposited a group of wounded Grunts and all the medical personnel were rushing about tagging and inspecting and stretchering-out the most serious cases. Piggy waved as he wound his way between the knots of people, checking names and noting them on a clipboard. I stood back and watched until everyone had been accounted-for and dispersed.

Piggy came out of his office and looked me up and down and whistled at my new attire.

"My, my, my, aren't WE strack, tonight!" he laughed.

"Bet you say that to ALL th' boys."

He said his duty-day ended at 1700, in about an hour, and told me about a small gook tailor shop close-by where I could get name tags and rank insignia sewed on.

"The Brass is pretty lenient on Grunts and Field-guys in dirty fatigues and boots and no rank tabs, but if you're gonna be here any length of time, you'd better have a day-uniform to stay out of trouble."

"Yeah, that's what I figured." I said, "The less I'm noticed, the better."

"It's too late to go over there tonight, but try to go first thing tomorrow, 'cause, no shit, if they notice you and get pissed, they'll have you burning shit or painting something, sick or not."

I told him thanks and that I'd wait in my hootch 'til he got off and maybe we could find something to get into tonight. He said "Sure" and went toward the Admin. building.

Back at the tent I finally met Chris Williams, my elusive hootch-mate. He was a light-skinned black guy from Detroit. He had a smooth, handsome face with odd, up-slanted green eyes that made him look like he was always pulling some kind of joke on you, or something. He smiled as we 'Dapped', (Soul brother hand shake), and he had the whitest teeth I'd ever seen, adding to the 'Cheshire cat' kind of look about him. He told me later that his dad was a dentist back in the world and if he let anything happen to his teeth, his dad would "Have his ass." We hadn't talked for five minutes before he asked me if I wanted to play some cards.

Remembering Piggy's warning, I replied, "Uh.....no thanks, uh...maybe later." I sat on my bunk and opened my new book from the PX, a John D. McDonald mystery called 'The Quick Red Fox'. I read until 1730 when Piggy showed up.

We decided to go on over to the mess hall and 'have it over with.' I couldn't believe they were so disdainful of the mess hall food. To me, unused as I was to real, cooked food, it was delicious. My appetite seemed to be returning, and so far I'd managed to keep my lunch down, I realized.

After a meal of sliced beef, (Mystery Meat), with gravy, (Brown Shit), and peas and instant potatoes, (Green Marbles in Pus), with a glass of warmish powdered milk, (Dry Moo-juice), we walked out into the still-hot early evening air and smoked cigarettes on the bench out front of the mess.

Williams limped badly and walked with the help of a cane. He told us about the mortar round that took-out the two guys in front of him and left shrapnel in his leg, in an ambush on a jungle trail.

We swapped 'Back-home' stories and 'War Shit' for about an hour, 'til it was almost dark. Piggy told us about this unit out by the perimeter road that had a regular EM club with a bar and a pool table and they were showing a movie tonight. Only thing was, it was about a quarter-mile away. Too far for Williams to walk.

"We could probably 'hitch' a ride out on the road, if your game, Chris." He offered.

Chris agreed, so we decided that that was the plan and went to our hootches to get our stuff. I grabbed my steel pot and flack vest and was reaching for my rifle when Williams looked up and saw me.

"We ain't goin' to war, man, we're goin' to see a movie. Put that shit back an' put on a ball cap. You'll get arrested carryin' heat in Long Binh."

"Even at night?" I asked, incredulous.

"Shit, anytime, man. The Lifers 'round here can't fuck with us proper if we're carryin' weapons. Only time you'll carry 'round here is on guard duty, if you're here long 'nuff to get on th' roster."

"Makes me nervous to not have my weapon, man. Just in case, ya' know?" I mumbled as I put my stuff back in the wall locker and donned a cloth cap.

"Yeah, me too, man. Ya' get used to it though. I still get paranoid sometimes, too, but it's too true, I'd prob'ly get pissed and shoot some o' these lifers if I had a gun, so it's for th' best, man. Don't need no more trouble than we already got." He said philosophically.

"There it is, man." I agreed.

We hitched on a ¾ ton that took us to within a block of our destination. We walked the distance along a razor-wire barrier around a group of cinder block buildings with tin roofs. Some of the buildings had window air conditioners poking out and this made me think about how cool it was in the old 'Kentucky Theater', on Main street back in Lexington.

I wondered if I'd ever be that cool again.

We came to an entry gate that was completely blocked by a huge PFC wearing a helmet liner and a .45 Colt on his hip.

"Hey, Stan," he said, obviously recognizing Piggy, "Come ta' get whipped at pool again?"

"Hey, Johnson. No, we just wanted to check out your movie and sip a beer or two. Is Lulu in there?"

"Yeah, him'n ever'body else, 'cept me. I got th' duty tonight. These guys witch'ya?" He motioned to Chris and me.

"Yeah. This is 'Mouse' and Chris, they're patients at th' MED."

We nodded our introduction.

134

"Well, G'wan on in. You know where it is. I git off at ten, mebby I'll see y'all later." He smiled and stood aside for us to enter.

I'd been looking around as they talked and I'd noticed something funny. There was a distinct lack of the usual military signs that adorn all unit compounds. There wasn't even a sign over the gate announcing what unit this was.

'Hmmm…very unusual.' I thought.

Almost all units have their slogans and designations posted, like the 'FIGHTING TOMCATS' or the 'FLYING BULLSHITTERS' or something. Even the 15th MED had 'SOLDIERS OF MERCY' on its sign, but this isolated, guarded compound had no such announcement. There weren't even signs on the buildings to tell which was which. Very curious.

"Hey, Piggy, what kinda place is this, man." I asked, noticing that all the guys I'd seen here weren't wearing a unit patch or rank tabs on their uniforms.

"This is a CID unit." He replied, "Kind of like th' MPs but more undercover and… spooky…. Ya know?"

"CID?" Williams burst, "Why'nt you tell me we was goin' to some 'SPOOK' unit, man, I got a pocket fulla WEED, man. If we'd got searched at th' gate 'r somethin' I'd be watchin' th' movie at LBJ, man, Jeez!" He looked around nervously.

Piggy reassured him.

"Won't be a problem, as long as you're with me, but you shouldn't be carryin' that shit around with you, man, ya never know what's gonna happen."

"Hell, I was hopin' ta turn you uptight white dudes on later, man." Chris explained.

"Well, that's cool, man," Piggy agreed and I nodded, "but keep it hid an' try not to look suspicious."

"Hell, I'll just act like I'm shittin' my pants, 'cause I WILL be." Chris moaned.

We all laughed as we came up to a door of a building that looked just like all the others except this one had 'INNA GADDA DA VIDA' blaring from behind it. Piggy pulled it open and a cloud of cigarette smoke puffed out at us and we were nearly knocked down by the 'Iron Butterfly' on the stereo.

The building housed two rooms, maybe 15'x 20' each. The first room had a long bar along the far wall, a row of booths lining the other. The center space was filled in with tables and chairs, almost completely occupied by GIs in all forms of dress from fatigues to Hawaiian shirts and shorts with flip-flops.

All the furniture, the bar and even the walls were made of ammo crate wood, burned with a blow-torch to accent the grain of the wood, then heavily varnished.

At one table, a lively card game was in progress with six players, all wise-cracking or studying cards held close to their chests. A large pile of MPC notes was on the table.

Chris elbowed me and said, "There's my action." He walked over and watched as the hand played-out.

Piggy and I went to the bar and he held up two fingers to the bartender for beers. I told him I'd better stick with coke or something, since I'd probably have to go in for blood tests tomorrow, and I didn't want a blood-alcohol level to pop up and mess things up. We gave the other beer to Chris and I ordered a coke.

The back-bar was made up of plywood shelves, arranged around a 4'x 6' mirror. The shelves were loaded with odd looking beer cans, war souvenirs like NVA helmets, 20mm cannon shells, a mortar round of undetermined size, and even a plastic hula-girl. On a long shelf over the mirror was, believe it or not, a German 30 cal. Maxim machine gun, complete with bi-pod and ammo feed belt.

It made for a real homey atmosphere.

At the end of the bar in the corner, protruding from the wall, was a huge old Sears Cold Spot air conditioner, struggling to keep up with the heat from the packed-in bodies, not to mention the cloud of cigarette smoke. There were at least 30-35 guys in that room alone. From my van-tagepoint, looking through the wide doorway to the other room, I could see the pool table and just as many men jammed in there, too.

"Popular place, huh?" I ventured to Piggy.

"Yeah, it's like this almost every night."

He sipped at his beer.

"I don't come over here very often, but their company clerk is a good friend of mine, even if he does beat me at pool every time I play him."

He pointed to a man shooting pool in the next room,

"That's Lulu at the table, now."

"Lulu?" I giggled, "Doesn't he get a hard time with a name like that?"

Just then the guy straightened up from his shot and I could see that he was at least 6'8" tall and weighed probably 260 pounds.

"Oh! No, I guess not!" I ended.

Piggy chuckled.

"His name is Louis and he's from Louisville, Ky., hence, Lulu".

We both laughed and sipped our drinks.

The pool game ended and he spotted us by the bar and came in and slapped Piggy on the back, almost knocking him down. Piggy introduced us and I told him I was from Lexington, so we spent a half-hour talking about back home and stuff. Then he took us into the poolroom and found us a place at some tables in there, and introduced us around to some other guys, some of which Piggy already knew.

The bullshit was flying fast and thick and I was actually having fun.

First time in forever, it seemed.

I watched the pool games going on and decided this was no place for amateurs. $50 and $100 bets were going down and some of the shots were incredible. Williams found us after a while and leaned against the wall by our table.

"Did ya get to play?" I asked him.

"Play?" He laughed, "I don't 'play' when it comes to cards."

He whipped out a roll of MPC bills and wafted them in front of me.

"With me it's serious business."

"I guess so!" I said and whistled.

"Did you win all that in just..." I looked at my watch, "...just 45 minutes?"

"No." he smirked his Cheshire cat's smile.

"I lost the first five hands, just to soften them suckers up. I won this in the last two hands. For intelligence guys, they sure ain't very intelligent."

He ran his thumb over the edges of the bills, riffling them,

"Two hunnert forty-six bucks."

I whistled, appreciatively.

At 9:00, Piggy asked Lulu what the movie was tonight.

"Charlton Heston in 'Sparticus'. Some kinda gladiator flick 'r somethin'".

I said I'd seen that back in 'The World' and it was boring.

Piggy had seen it, too, and Chris didn't like "Cut-'em-up" movies, so we finished our drinks, bade farewell to the 'Spooks' and left to go back to the MED.

Outside, the darkness had cooled the air to a tolerable 80° or so. We walked slowly, due to Chris's gimp, along the perimeter road and when we were well away from everything, Chris whipped out a cig and lit it.

Except it wasn't a cig, it was a joint, done up in a cigarette tube, complete with filter.

He took a big toke and held it out to me. I went to wave it away but he insisted.

"I risked my ass to bring this with me tonight, just to turn you dudes on, least you can do is smoke it with me."

I protested that I had blood tests tomorrow and....

He thrust the joint at me.

"Shit, don' mean nuthin', man."

'What th' hell,' I thought, 'what'll they do, send me to Vietnam?'

I took it and we walked as we smoked. We each got three hits off the joint before the filter started burning. I was floating and Piggy started giggling at nothing. Then we were all three giggling and everything suddenly seemed funny.

We stopped about halfway back so Chris could rest his leg. We plopped down on a partially collapsed bunker wall and Chris told us this story about when he was in a car wreck back in 'The World'.

He was driving his daddy's car and this old lady had plowed into him from behind, tearing off a bumper and a taillight. He had to go home and tell his dad and ol' dad had exploded and grounded him for a week, even though it wasn't his fault.

Piggy and I laughed all the way through, especially the part where he'd told his dad the little old lady was a "blind ol' bitch!".

"Hey! It ain't funny, man!" He kept repeating, but that just made us laugh that much harder.

"I wuz in real trouble, man, it really wasn't funny at all!"

We couldn't help it, we were ripped and couldn't stop laughing. Pretty soon he was laughing, too. Laughing at us for laughing at him. We cracked-up 'til our sides ached and our mouth muscles were tired from grinning.

By the time we got back to the tent, Chris was limping pretty badly and he collapsed on his cot with a whoosh of breath. Piggy and I sat up and BS'ed a while 'til I suddenly realized I was ravenously hungry.

I dug into my ruck in the wall locker and brought out the candy bars I'd gotten at the PX today.

Piggy's bloodshot eyes lit up.

"WOW, man, you ARE gonna share those, aren't you?" eyeing my bag of M&M's.

"Sure, dude, here."

I took a big handful and handed the bag over.

Piggy ate a bunch and handed the bag to Williams, who 'snarfed' the remainder of the little bright-colored treats.

That done, we proceeded to eat two Hershey bars, an entire can of salted peanuts and some stale saltines that Chris had in his locker. By 2330 hrs we were stuffed and laying back telling bullshit funny stories. I showed them my chunk of shrapnel.

"Man, I haven't enjoyed an evening like this in a long time." I said to the ceiling as I lay on my back on my bunk.

Piggy said something in response, but I didn't hear him. I was asleep.

15

JAN 25,1970

6:30 A.M. Reveille recorded on scratchy tape and blasted over the twin loudspeakers mounted on the flagpole in the center of the compound. I got up bleary and stiff. I hadn't slept that hard in months.

I still had on my fatigues from the night before and they were pretty rumpled from being slept-in. It was too much trouble to change, so I grabbed my shaving kit and towel and drug my butt through an early morning fog, both literally and figuratively, to the shower shack.

All four shower stalls were in use, creating a fog indoors, too. I wiped a clear spot on the mirror over one of the two sinks and looked at myself, sticking my tongue out.

'BLEAH!'

I looked like I felt.

I stripped to my T-shirt and pants and ran tepid water in the bowl and splashed my face several times to wake up enough to shave and brush my teeth. During this process it occurred to me that I hadn't thrown-up a meal since yesterday morning, even with all that junk I consumed last night. Out on the LZ I would have lost it sometime during the night, or definitely first thing this morning. So far, I'd had no indication of the rolling, sick feeling that I'd tried, mostly unsuccessfully, to get used to these last several months.

'Oh great!' I thought, 'I've been sick for months, an' finally get off the LZ for tests, an' suddenly I'm not sick anymore? Shit, I bet they run every test known to mankind an' don't find a thing wrong and send me right back out to th' 'Boonies'.

I had been worried that I was really sick or something, but, now, I was worried that I might NOT be sick enough to stay in the rear,

140

where, I had to admit, life was a lot more...pleasant. Still crude, but...pleasant.

Hell, I'd even stay sick just to be able to shave and shower, not to mention all the other perks available.

I looked once more at my not-fatally-ill looking face, shook my head and grabbed my stuff and left.

At 0700 there was a formation in the open yard in front of the CP, where details and orders were handed out to the able-bodied patients. A guy in front drew 'Shit Burning' detail, three others got mess hall clean up, and another guy was told to report to the 1st Sgt. for "Paint-work" of some kind.

I lucked out and didn't draw any work, but my name was called and I was told to report immediately after chow to the 'Lab' in building #6. Several other guys got similar instructions and we were dismissed.

I spotted Piggy entering his tent/office. I yelled and he waved me over.

"I talked to the company clerk about what they're going to do with you." He began.

"Yeah? What did you find out?" I asked, eagerly.

"They're gonna run tests all day today, and you'll ship back to your unit tomorrow or the next day."

Any hope I had was gone.

"Crap, I knew it was too good to be true," I shook my head, "I could have gotten used to the kind of life around here."

"Yeah, it's too bad, Mouse." He commiserated. "Well, I've got some stuff I gotta do, so I'll see you later or this evening, OK?"

I ate a bowl of Frosted Flakes in the mess hall then went looking for Building #6.

It was directly behind the CP, a low, cream-colored wooden building with the usual tin roof. I entered into an anteroom with a bench along one wall and a long counter mounted in a pass-through in the other wall. The clerk behind the desk took my name and waved me to the bench where I languished for a half-hour. My butt was just getting really numb from the hard, wooden seat, when I was summoned through a connecting door, along a hallway and into an examining room, where I waited another half-hour. Not knowing what to do, I sat on the paper covered table complete with stirrups, (Bet they don't use those much!), twiddled my thumbs and read the labels on the boxes and bottles on a shelf and in a stainless steel cabinet against the wall.

Finally, a SP/4 came in and after entering my name, rank and serial number on a form, wrote down all my symptoms and recorded my height and weight and took my blood pressure with one of those squeeze-bulb things. He laid out some syringes and containers on a tray, thanked me, and left.

Another half-hour went by.

Eventually, the door opened and a major doctor came in. I don't mean a Great Doctor, I mean a doctor who was a Major. I jumped up to attention but he off-handedly waved me back down as he studied my form on his clipboard.

He questioned me on the length and severity of my illness and I told him about the 'green shits' and throwing up and my weight-loss. He 'Un-huh'ed' me and 'Mm-Humm'ed' several times, then proceeded to suck most of the blood from my body with the various needles on the tray. He handed me a small plastic cup for a urine sample and a little cardboard cup for a stool specimen and told me to go to the latrine and obtain them. I was to give them to the clerk at the front desk as I left.

I wanted to ask him if he had some idea what my problem was, but he turned and left before I could.

At the latrine I learned I still had the runs, (maybe there's still hope), and my pee had a very strong odor. Of course that could also be attributable to the goings-on last night.

After filling my containers and dropping them off with the clerk, I was told to report to the CP for details.

At the CP I was told to stand down 'til further notice, so I asked the clerk about going to the tailor shop to get my insignia sewn-on. He said that would be fine and dismissed me.

I went back to my tent, put on my old fatigues, folded the new sets, tucked them under my arm and headed out toward the PX. I found the tailor shop tucked in beside a warehouse on the same street as the PX.

Two old Vietnamese women ran the shop, one of which I tried to explain what I needed in 'pidgin-English'. She had me write my name out on a scrap of paper.

"Return fifteen hunnert hour. Pick up. Fi' dollah."

I wandered the base for about three hours and saw many wondrous sights. I watched C-130 cargo planes taking off and landing at the airstrip and discovered the Air Force BX (the equivalent of our PX). It was a sort of air conditioned super department store with a built-in café that sold hamburgers, fries and soft drinks and even milk shakes!

Man! Sick or not I had to have a burger and a chocolate shake.

The cold drink made my teeth ache and my sinuses hurt, but it was delicious.

I saluted a General as he passed in his jeep.

I saw real American, or at least Caucasian, women in civilian dresses, skirts swaying with their walk. I tried not to stare a hole in them, or mentally picture them naked, but I wasn't really successful.

At 1400 hours I went back to 15th MED and checked with the CP to see if I had any more tests or duties. The clerk told me "No" but to make sure to be at the evening formation at 1700 hours.

I stopped by and said hello to Piggy, then went back to my tent for some cigs.

Williams, who'd been up and gone that morning, was lying on his bunk, reading. I elaborated about the BX and he agreed it was a great place, but warned me not to wear 'field fatigues' over there or sometimes the 'Air Farce' lifers, as he called them, would give me some shit. I thanked him for the advice and told him I was just going over to pick up my new uniforms at the tailor shop.

I picked up my clothes at 1500 hours and, while there, bought some new PFC collar tabs from a display case filled with rank insignia from PVT E-2 through Major, unit crests, CIBs, Airborne wings and all manner of military accoutrements. All these could be had in either bright brass or cammo black. I chose black, since I assumed I'd be back in the field tomorrow.

Later, back at the tent, I changed into my new uniform. I lined up for formation at 1700, but again, no orders or details were given to me. I went to the mess hall and ate an ARM, (Army Regulation Meal), for supper, as opposed to a LEG, (Lousy Eggs and Grits), for breakfast.

Piggy found me in the tent an hour later. I'd been writing a letter home, but put it aside when he entered and asked if I wanted to go into 'Town' with a bunch of other guys.

"Sure!" I answered excitedly, "You mean, like really into 'Town'?"

"Yeah," he smiled, "Th' bus will pick us up at 1830, drop us off in town and pick us back up at 2030 and bring us back."

"That's not much time." I said, putting away my writing stuff.

"Well, there's a 9:00 curfew on enlisted personnel, but two hours is plenty enough time to get laid and have a beer and look around a little."

"I guess I'm up for that!"

I grabbed my cap and we met the bus on the road in front of the PX.

And what a bus! It was ancient. Probably a French make, with evil slanted eyes painted over the headlights, lips and teeth on the bumper and wings down the sides.

It clattered to a stop, smoking a blue cloud and we boarded for the trip out the main gates of LONG BINH BASE.

We passed through the shantytown of tin shacks, made mostly of castoffs from the Army and Air Bases, that comprised the bulk of LONG BINH CITY. We crossed an open flat area about a quarter mile wide and came into the larger, more modern city of BIEN HOA. There were shanties here, also, but they were interspersed with larger, more conventional houses and buildings obviously dating to the French Occupation. After a half-mile or so, the buildings got bigger and taller and we were soon in the downtown of a city that, at first look, could have been any small city in the US, but only at first glance.

All the signs were in Vietnamese with English, and even some French, translations. The larger buildings had six or seven stories of offices or apartments above street-level shops of every description, from fish markets to antique stores. The shop windows were loaded with all manner of merchandise, ranging from chickens and piglets to ancient, valuable, Vietnamese artifacts. There was a mixture of Eastern and Western clothing stores. There were restaurants, Bars, food markets, and many shops that I had no idea what they sold.

The streets were thronged with vehicles of every description. Bicycles, scooters, trucks, jeeps, limousines, and even a few carts drawn by water buffalo.

The most prevalent transportation was the Lambretta three-wheel motor-cart. There seemed to be an endless variety of home-conversions of this vehicle to suit the individuals needs. Some, of course, were made into cabs that seated up to eight people. There were box-type and flatbed trucks hauling huge loads of goods; tiny busses, painted like their larger counterparts, in garish Dragon-designs and colors. Little garbage trucks hauling away the ever present refuse of a large city.

All this traffic was weaving, intricately, around thousands of pedestrians, many of which were carrying their own loads of who-knows-what on their backs.

We came to a roundabout with a fountain in the middle, faced all round by stately three and four storied buildings of French design surrounded by brick or stucco walls. Soldiers guarded their ornate iron gates.

Our bus wheezed around the circle and turned onto another of the four wide boulevards that intersected here.

We drove another four blocks and the bus stopped in traffic and honked its horn, which bleated like a wounded water buffalo.

I looked out the window to see what was going on. An ARVN MP ran from a building on our right just ahead and started routing the pedicabs and handcarts that were set up along the curb.

When the area was clear, the driver pulled the bus into the space in front of a two- story gray stucco building with a sign on the front in Vietnamese. I asked Piggy what place this was and he answered simply, "Bus Stop." The bus doors opened and the GIs poured out onto the wide sidewalk, all talking excitedly. Piggy and I were among the last to exit and had to hurry to follow the group of other GIs who were walking purposefully toward the next corner.

Dusk was imminent as we turned right into an even busier street lined with bars and restaurants, most sprouting florescent or neon signs that hung out over the sidewalk,

Advertising such exotic names as 'The Texas Bar', 'The American Restaurant and Bar', 'BIEN HOA Lounge', and some just said 'BAR'.

There was even a 'Pussy Cat Lounge'.

"Welcome to Downtown Gookville!"

Piggy smiled as I gaped at all the color and activity.

Floating on the evening breeze was a cacophony of music, screams, laughter and singing. There were Vietnamese 'Hawkers' outside most of the bars inducing the passers-by to try the pleasures offered in their places. Most of these guys looked to be no older than twelve or thirteen but I saw one physically drag a 200-pound soldier through the door of a bar. Obviously if they could not talk you into entering, they weren't above forcing you inside.

The street was crowded with bicycles, pedestrians, (mostly GIs), and pedicabs, but there were a huge number of teenage or younger 'Boy-Sans' on Honda motor bikes, all wearing some kind of bush-hat or cowboy hat. They would zoom dangerously through traffic and screech to a stop to talk to a group of soldiers here or there. Their conversations were very animated and involved a lot of arm-waving and loud singsong 'Pidgin English'.

Piggy explained that these were the 'Saigon Cowboys'.

These pint-size entrepreneurs were the main outlet for the huge 'Black Market' operations of the larger cities and could sell you anything from drugs to guns to their 'sisters', who, of course, were touted as a "Numbah-one Virgin!"

"Believe me," Piggy explained, "there aren't many virgins left around here. Best bet is to tell 'em to fuck-off or you'll get 'screwed', alright, but you won't get kissed."

"No shit?" I asked, innocently.

"No Shit!" He continued, "The 'Cowboys' are the most devious crooks in the country. Most of their 'Sisters' are either diseased or downright ugly. An' if they can't talk you out of your money, they'll pick your pocket or lure you off to some alley where a gang of them will suddenly appear and beat the crap out of you and take everything you own."

"No shit?"

"No Shit! Listen, I know a couple of pretty nice bars and a good 'Mama-san' who runs a clean 'House', so c'mon, lets get th' show on th' road."

He walked on and I followed.

We had to fight off several 'Cowboys' along the way, and mini-skirted girls offered "Good times" from doorways or windows. Hawkers grabbed your arm and tried to drag you into their establishments. You'd have to pry their hands off and tell them to "Fuck off", then endure the curses and taunts from these slick little hustlers. The closest I'd seen to this was Bourbon Street, in New Orleans. But even that wild town paled in comparison to this crazy place.

Finally we stopped in front of the 'Imperial Bar'. Eight-foot tall dragons rose up on either side of the door.

"This is a good place," Piggy declared, "let's go in."

We were met inside the door by a tiny 'Mama-san' of indeterminate age.

"Ahh, Corporal Meyers, so good see you!" she smiled a Beetle-nut greeting.

"Good evening, Mrs. Lei, This is my friend, 'Mouse'. Is there a table available?"

The lady tittered at my introduction, putting one hand to her mouth, and said, "Oooh, yes, of course, there always table for you and friend, Corporal.....", she tittered again

"...Moose... This way, prease."

I glared at Piggy. He grinned back.

Mrs. Lei, (pronounced 'Lee'), was dressed in a shimmering green Ao Dai, a traditional Vietnamese outfit consisting of a well-fitting long dress with long slits up the sides, over contrasting white trousers made of silk, with gold slippers on her feet. I noticed the materials color changed to blue highlights where it curved over her still shapely body as she led us through an inner beaded curtain into a spacious dining area with a tall ceiling. Dangling fans slowly stirred the air from above. A long carved bar filled the far wall and tables filled the open space remaining.

There was a table available. In fact, all the tables were open. Other than two 'Papa-sans' sitting at the bar and a younger version of Mrs. Lei behind the bar, we were the only American customers. Actually, we were the only customers, I figured out as one Papa-san got up and went through a curtain into, I presumed, the kitchen, and the other came over to take our orders.

Mrs. Lei hovered.

"What you like, Corporal Meyer an' Corporal...tee-hee... Moose?"

We ordered 'Bah Me Bahs'. Piggy asked for some peanuts. Mrs. Lei translated for our waiter and he nodded his head and wrote on his pad as he left for the kitchen.

A few minutes later he returned with two sweating bottles of beer and a wicker basket, lined with waxed paper, full of shelled peanuts. I took a long swig of my brew and, though bitter and rather strong, it was cold and surprisingly good. I took a handful of nuts from the basket and popped them in my mouth and attempted to chew them. They had the consistency of rubber pellets and were salty as hell. I chewed for a while and the look on my face must have clued Piggy. He laughed.

"They're steamed," he explained, munching a mouthful himself, "very salty, very nourishing."

"And very long-lasting." I added, after washing the lump down with beer.

"Put them in your mouth and drink your beer through them." He told me, "The salt makes the beer foam and you burp a lot. Burping is very polite in Vietnam. It means you're enjoying the food."

I tried it and it worked quite well. I almost immediately emitted a loud, involuntary belch. I tried to stifle it with my hand but the bargirl must have heard it, she smiled when I looked her way.

Mrs. Lei emerged from the back room and came to our table, smiling.

"You enjoy?" she asked with a small bow.

We both answered "Yes, mam." And I was tempted to burp again, but held off.

She turned to me and asked if I was new to Vietnam.

"I'm new to Bien Hoa, but I've been in-country for seven months," I answered, "in the field."

She nodded as she spoke.

"Ahhh, veddy bad! Many bad thing happen in feed. My family, in Plei Ku, in north. All time VC come, take all food."

She gestured with her hands as if pulling something.

"Take son, too! Off to north. Not see him t'ree year now. VC veddy bad. Veddy numbah ten!"

We nodded in sympathy and agreed.

"VC veddy bad!"

She talked to us for a while and told me about the various "Sight-sees" in the city and also in Saigon, should I happen to visit there.

We finished our beer and stood and bade Mrs. Lei goodbye. She escorted us back through the curtain to the door.

"Veddy nice meet you corporal....tee-hee-hee....Moose."

She patted me on the shoulder.

"Y'all come back now, heah?" She said as we stepped out onto the sidewalk.

I did a double take.

She sounded like an impression of Granny Clampet on the 'Beverly Hillbillies.'

'Wonder where she learned THAT?' I mused

In the half-hour we'd been inside, dark had fallen and the traffic had dropped off to mostly civilian pedestrians and bicycles. I saw an MP jeep a block up the street, but there were no other motorized vehicles in sight. Also, most of the neon and lit signs on the street were dark, and the main source of light was from the shop and bar windows or an occasional dim streetlight.

I elbowed Piggy.

"Man, it's kinda ...spooky...out here after dark."

He smiled in the dim light.

"Yeah, they turn off the signs an' stuff after dark so they don't draw rockets."

"Wow, you even get rockets here in town?" I asked.

"One or two a month, usually."

We passed a crowded restaurant packed with ARVNs and civilians, the smell of Nouc Mam sauce drifted out the door and over us, causing us to walk a little faster to get out of the stench.

"Right before Christmas," Piggy continued, "we were getting about fifteen a week, just to shake us up. But they're aimed, mostly, at the Air Base or the chopper pads way off over there."

He pointed to the west.

"If any hit the city it's usually a 'short round', though they do sometimes."

"What's to keep the VC from just walking in here during the daytime and hangin' around to blow stuff up at night?" I asked.

"Nothing." He answered, seriously, "In fact, a lot of these people around us are probably VC."

"No shit?" I looked around at the shadowy shapes that were passing us.

"Is it... you know.... Safe to be out here... I mean ... unarmed in th' city?"

"Yeah, I think so, at least for a few more days... 'til Tet."

I looked at him quizzically.

"What's Tet? I've heard guys talk about it and wasn't that when th' gooks really tore th' place up last year?"

"Tet is like the Vietnamese New Year, sort-of, and yes, last year th' VC an' NVA launched an all-out offensive on all the major cities and bases in the south, including here. I've heard the stories. How they blew up a bunch'a stuff on the airbase, took over a radio station in town. Then they occupied a whole section of town and had to be blasted out house-by-house for a couple days. A lot of US guys were killed, an' even more VC. It was supposedly a huge victory for the Americans, but I'm not sure. Seems like the morale has been at an all-time low ever since."

"Wonder if they'll try again this year?"

"Maybe or not. Who knows. The gooks are known for doing the exact opposite of what we think they're gonna do. Anyway, we'll know on January thirtieth, that's when Tet begins."

"I'll be back in the 'field' by then, I guess. Wish I could stay here, though, this has been like a vacation."

We stopped in front of a darkened building, set back from the street behind a stucco wall with an iron gate that was open into a court-yard.

"Well if you've enjoyed yourself so far, you're gonna love this!"

He gestured with his thumb toward the gate.

"Welcome to 'Mama Hos' Ho-house."

He bowed at the waist and waved me through the portal.

I won't elaborate on what went on in Mama Hos' fine establish-ment, except to say it was the finest use to which I'd ever applied ten dollars.

At 2100 hours, we were back at the bus stop and, judging from the grins on the other soldier's faces, and their boisterous attitudes, we'd all had a pretty good time in town.

Except, of course, for the one guy who, drunkenly, kept explain-ing to anyone who'd listen, "Fuckin' li'l gooks! Ripped me off, man. Reached right in my pocket an' ripped me off. Whole month's pay, man. Goddamn l'il shits." And so on.

Back on the base, Piggy came on back to the tent with me. We met Chris at the door, just leaving for a shower.

"Got orders on yer bunk, Mouse,"

He gestured with his head toward my bed,

"Looks like yer 'Air Mobile' again, man."

He shook his head and left.

"Aw shit!" I moaned "Here I go again, back to th' field."

I tore open the envelope with reluctant fingers and read the contents out-loud.

"PFC Hudson, report by 25 Jan '70, 1600 hrs.,…blah, blah… Phouc Vinh SVN, HHB 1/30 ARTY…. Temporary unassigned duty… blah, blah…indiv sec own trans.?"

Piggy translated, "Headquarters Battery 1/30. Individual secure own transport. You'll have to report there by 1600 hrs."

"I don't know where Fuck Vinh is, man. How'm I supposed to find this place when I don't know where I am now?" I said angrily, my former good spirits shattered.

Piggy commiserated.

"No sweat, man."

He put his hand on my shoulder,

"You can catch a ride on one of our MEDEVAC birds tomorrow, I'm sure. They fly all over that area and can take you right into Phouc Vinh. It's only about eighty clicks northwest of here. Check with me in th' morning and I'll arrange your flight and see you off, OK?"

I slapped his shoulder.

"I really appreciate it, man, Jeez, a Headquarters Battery. Wonder what that's like? Know anything about Phouc Vinh?"

"Not much, 'cept it must be a good sized base, cause it has its own mobile surgery unit and a big air field there. Also… uh,"

He stammered.

"What?" I said, worried.

"Well… it gets rocketed a lot, I heard. In fact, they call it 'Rocket Alley'."

"Oh great! Instead of getting' shot, I can get blown-up!"

"Hell, you can get blown-up here, man!"

He punched my arm.

"Don't mean nothin' here nor there."

"Well, there it is, I guess."

16

JAN 26, 1970

After 6:30 reveille, the Three S's (shit, shower, shave), and a bowl of cereal in the mess hall, I stood in formation and received my orders confirming my reassignment to HQ in Phouc Vinh. Also, included in the envelope was a medical report stating that I was being reassigned due to "Extreme allergic reaction to Cordite."

'Cordite?' I thought, 'Isn't that an ingredient in gunpowder?'

I went to see Piggy.

He read through the report and translated some of the medical terms, which boiled down to:

"Hell, you're allergic to gunsmoke, man."

"Gunsmoke?"

"Yep!" he grinned.

"No place worse than an artillery firebase to be allergic to gunsmoke,"

I grinned, also.

"Is there?"

"Nope."

"Well, I guess that shoots my 'Gun Bunny' career, huh?"

"Sure does."

He slapped my back and we both laughed.

"I got you a flight. I talked to the guy in Flight Ops and there's a regular 'Personnel Transfer' bird at 0930, going straight to Phouc Vinh. Sorry I couldn't get a later one, so's you'd be able to hang around a little longer, but that's the only one there is 'til tomorrow. We can try one of the other AV companies down th' road, if you wanna..." he offered.

152

"No thanks, man, guess I'll go on an' get on with it. At least I'm not going back to the LZ. A headquarters battery's bound to be an improvement. At least I hope so."

"Well, I've got shit to do, so, it's been good, ya know?"

He stuck out his hand and dapped me.

"Yeah, real good, man," I agreed, "Thanks for the tour, if you ever get up to ol' Fuck Vinh, I'll return the favor."

We laughed and said final good-bye's, and after packing my duffel and dapping Chris at the tent and wishing each other luck, I walked to the chopper pad and waited out the time on a bench in the shade of a building, reading my MacDonald novel.

At 0945, a helicopter started up in its revetment by the pad. A crew chief was standing out in front of the nose apparently looking around for someone. I ran over with my gear and asked if this was the flight to Phouc Vinh.

He nodded.

"You Clark?"

"No, I'm Hudson. I was told I could hitch a ride with you to Phouc Vinh, That alright?"

"Oh, sure, that's fine, but you seen anybody else waitin' around? We're supposed to take another guy on transfer to the med unit up there."

I was about to answer no, when a captain came running full-tilt around the corner of a building. He saw us and started yelling.

"Wait! Wait! I'm late! I know I'm late!"

The Crew Chief looked sidelong at me and yelled back.

"C'Mon Doc, we've been waitin' over fifteen minutes for you!"

"Oh God, you've waited that long for me?"

He skidded to a halt in front of us.

"Thank God you waited," he gasped breathlessly, "I've got to be in Phouc Vinh by 11:00 or the party will be over."

'Party?' I wondered.

The Warrant Officer hustled us into the passenger compartment of the Huey with the big red crosses painted on the doors. We quickly settled ourselves into the sling seats on the firewall and strapped in. The pilot revved the engine and we rose from the enclosure, tilted forward and quickly gained forward and vertical movement. I saw that the Captain was having a struggle with his duffel bag that yawed and thumped him in the wind coming in the open doors. I tapped him on the shoulder and using hand-signals and yelling showed him how to tuck his gear beneath his knees.

He stowed his stuff, and when we reached altitude and the engine noise abated somewhat, he thanked me and told me it was his first helicopter ride.

'No shit' I thought.

"It's kinda weird at first, but you'll get used to it!" I yelled

His name was Dr. Clark and we, (mostly he), talked, (yelled), the whole flight. I found out that the 'Party' was a going-away for the doctor he was replacing. The shindig was starting at 10:00 and he hoped to be there to say goodbye to his friend. I told him about my new allergy and that I'd been reassigned because of my illness.

"Don't worry, it may just be a temporary reaction. They sometimes are." He replied, helpfully.

"I sure hope not, sir, I'd kinda like to stay at HQ than go back out in the field."

"Can't blame you for that." He smiled.

After about a half-hour of flying, we circled-in above a fairly large village with mostly grass or tin roofed houses. They were laid out on a regular street-grid with square blocks. There were even some divided streets with median strips down the middle, though, even from the air I could tell they were obviously growing wild from lack of maintenance. There was a large white cathedral with manicured lawns, and a sprinkling of red tile roofs on larger houses near the central market street that ran through town straight up to the gates of the Army and Air Force Base. I could see it took up four times the space of the village. At this time of the morning the town's streets were thronged with people and vehicles, all intent upon their own purposes, rushing in all directions.

The Base was no exception. As we swooped over the rows of everything from tent-cities to wooden slat, sandbag and tin huts and hootches, to well-built concrete buildings, the streets were alive with movement. There was a C-130 cargo plane just coming in on the long PSP runway at the airstrip, and a smaller 'Caribou', taxiing for take-off. I caught sight of a good-sized PX alongside a chain-linked-in compound of mobile homes, obviously ranking officers quarters, judging by the air conditioners hanging from their windows.

I was just getting a good feeling about Phouc Vinh. It looked like it might be a busy but peaceful place. Then, out the other side of the chopper I spotted an artillery unit set-up in the usual style with berms and bunkers, though from this distance, I couldn't tell what kind of guns they were.

Phouc Vinh Arial View

'Uh-oh.' I thought.

I secretly hoped those guns had nothing to do with my new unit.

Farther off to the left, I saw a group of tracked vehicles with huge, long barrels.

'Oh shit!' I thought, '175s and 8" howitzers. More smoke!'

My 'good feeling' was fast evaporating in the hot breeze coming in the door as we set down on a chopper pad next to a ram-shackle wooden building that had obviously had not seen paint in years, if ever. A sign, hung on the porch roof, proclaimed 'Phouc Vinh Airport'. A Jeep and driver were waiting in the shade next to the building.

The Captain and I jumped off the chopper and hurried out from under the whirling blades. The Jeeps driver ran over to us and saluted.

"Captain Clark?" he yelled over the wind and noise of the winding-back-up helicopter.

The captain nodded.

"I'm yer driver, sir!" He grabbed the duffel bag right off Clarks shoulder, ran to the vehicle and tossed it in the back.

As the chopper took off behind us, the captain asked me where I was going and did I need a ride.

No jeep was there for me.

"If it's not too much trouble, sir."

He asked the driver if he knew where HHB 1/30 was.

"On th' way, sir."

We both hopped in, him in front, me in back with the bags, and took a wild ride between heli-pads and runways, on the bumpiest roads I think I'd ever traveled. I had to hold on with white knuckles to keep from being thrown out, and not just on the turns, which were made, I swear, on two wheels. The guy seemed to be drawn to every pothole and bump, and was not inclined to slow down for any reason. The poor jeep crashed and jarred like it would fall to pieces any minute and I held on for dear life.

After a mile, which thankfully only took about forty five seconds, I was deposited, shaken but not stirred, on the dirt road outside red painted gate posts emblazoned with our red and gold 'Flying-Horse' unit crest, and the words HHB 1/30 ARTY painted in yellow. I thanked the captain and saluted and they drove off in a cloud of dust, the jeep clanging and banging into the distance.

I stood there a minute, looking around at my new surroundings.

The 175s and 8"ers were directly across the road in an open field, and the ARTY unit I'd seen from the air, a 105 unit, I saw now, was right next-door.

"Figures!" I mumbled to myself.

I turned a complete circle 'til I was facing the compound again. The yellow painted iron-pipe gate was standing open, (inviting the unwary), so I picked up my bag and walked between the posts and down dusty road into the unit itself.

Unit Crest - Striving

Inside the gate, on the left and right were wooden buildings with tin roofs and sandbags halfway up the walls, the upper half of which were made up of wood slats slanted downward to repel rain and sun, while allowing air to pass through to cool the interior. I doubted that it worked very well in this heat. It was already 90° and not a hint of a breeze. The smell was the same as any other Army base I'd been on. Diesel fuel and burning shit, but the compound seemed clean and well laid-out.

To my relief, I didn't see a single Howitzer in evidence.

As I passed the first row of buildings a smaller road took off to the right and curved left out of sight beyond two low ammo box structures with sandbag roofs. Each building had a sign over the door. The first was marked 'FDC/TOC' and the other was the 'S-2'.

On my left, just off the main road, was a smaller wood shack with its own sign that said 'S-5'. Farther down was another set of wood-slat buildings, the CP on the left, mess hall on the right. The CP was what I was looking for so I walked on down and entered through a wooden screen door that creaked on its hinges.

Inside it was dark and comparatively cool, it took a moment for my eyes to adjust. A clerk was rummaging through a lower drawer of one of three big gray filing cabinets, but straightened up when he heard the screen door bang shut behind me.

"Help you?" The Spec-4 asked, arching his eyebrows of his rather handsome, dark, vaguely oriental face, broken by a white-white smile.

His nametag read 'Tabaranza'.

"Hudson, PFC, reporting from 'Delta' battery."

I handed over my orders. He pulled them out of the envelope and read them, looking puzzled as he finished.

"What are we supposed to do with you?"

"I'm not sure, myself." I answered, "I was told to report here for 'Temporary Unassigned Duty'," I quoted the orders.

"I'd better get the captain," he said, "see what he says."

He told me to wait and went to a solid wooden door in the back and knocked. I heard "Come!" from behind it and he entered and closed the door behind him. A minute later he came out and pointed with his thumb toward the other room.

"Captain Johnson will see you now."

I thanked him and went in.

I removed my steel pot, came to attention, and saluted.

"PFC Hudson, reporting as ordered, sir."

He "At eased" me and waved me to a metal folding chair by his desk. As he perused my orders, I perused him. He sat ramrod straight behind his regulation wooden desk, a tall man of average build, with thinning hair and wire rim glasses that gave him a professorial look.

'Dennis th' Menaces' dad!' I thought.

"Hudson," he said after a couple of minutes, "it appears we're stuck with you."

"Uh... yessir." I said lamely.

"Have you had any other training besides your primary MOS?"

"No sir. Just artillery, sir, I've been in the field since I arrived."

"And allergic to gunsmoke?" he raised his eyebrows.

"Guess so, sir, I've been pretty sick." I shrugged.

"Are you sick, now?"

"No sir, not since I left the LZ."

"Hmmm..." he went back and read my medical report again.

"Well, that's good I guess. Tell me, what did you do in civilian life, what was your occupation?"

"Well, sir, I was a professional musician and worked for a four-color lithography company as a 'Set-up' man, a kind of a printer, sir."

"Hmmm...." He said and rocked back in his chair, scratching his chin.

After a moment he looked at me.

"I'm sure you know we don't need musicians."

I nodded.

"But," he continued, "you say you did printing?"

I nodded again.

"Like on signs, and things?"

"Yes sir, well... no sir... I mean, not really signs and stuff, but we did do like banners, and I did some artwork for the set-ups and some of the camerawork, too."

He rubbed his chin some more, thinking.

"Well...that's not really very helpful, but, I'm sure, First Sgt. Anderson will find something for you to do, you'll report to him in the morning in his office here at the CP. Any questions?"

159

"No sir...I mean, yessir. Who do I see about quarters?"

"Specialist Tabaranza can take care of those details."

He nodded toward the outer office.

"Oh, and welcome to Headquarters Battery, Hudson."

He smiled and dismissed me with a wave of his hand.

I thanked him and saluted and went back out into the outer office where Tabaranza was now busy thumbing through an army manual. He looked up with a questioning look and I shrugged. I told him that he was supposed to get me billeted, and that I was to report to the 1st Sgt. in the morning.

"OK, Hudson," he stood up and took his cap off the top of one of the file cabinets, "come on then, we'll find a place for you to sleep and I'll show you around."

He held the screen door for me, so I picked up my bag and rifle and followed him out into the noonday sun.

We walked across the road and around the left side of the mess hall as he recited the hours for chow and informed me that Sgt. Carbone, 'The Master of the Mess', didn't allow any between-meal snacks. I nodded at this and told him I was just happy to have meals that weren't out of cans.

He asked if I'd been out in the field and I told him, briefly, where I'd been for the last seven months. He told me he'd been at HQ his whole tour and he was "Getting Short", with eighty days and a wake-up.

Beyond the mess was an open space, mostly devoid of vegetation except for tufts of sickly looking grass-like plants that sprouted here and there about waist high. Standing in this open space that sloped slightly down toward the rear of the compound, I could see that the main road curved past the EM latrine, which was positioned right on the rear perimeter fence. Then it went through a wire gate into what must be a motor pool, judging from the variety of trucks, jeeps and vehicles, parked in rows in a big fenced-in lot next door. Not to mention the big green Quonset-style motor pool tent that stood just inside the gate.

Another small dirt road took off to the right from the main one outside the motor pool gate and was the continuation of the road I'd seen as I came in the front gate. Between this road and the motor pool fence were two ammo-box buildings with sandbagged roofs, each with six doors on either side. Each set of two doors had a single ammo box blast wall that protected both doors. These would be the Enlisted barracks. They, like all the other buildings, were painted a medium gray

This side of the road was a tin shower shack with a water tank on stilts in back of it, and, up a ways, parallel to the mess hall, there was a long sandbag and slat building with a sandbagged roof, that I figured must be the NCO hootch.

But what really drew my attention was what was behind the EM latrines, outside the fence. A road, a bunker, some rows of barbed wire stretched through a partially cleared field. Then trees and bamboo clumps.

"Damn, we're right on the greenline!" I grumped.

"That's Bunker #42..."

Tabaranza pointed to the structure directly across the road from the middle of the compound.

"That's Tower November...."

He indicated a stilted, thirty five-foot tower adjacent the rear of the 105 battery next door. Then he pointed to another bunker on past the tower about a hundred feet.

"And that's Bunker #43. We pull guard duty on those three every three days, in rotation with the 2/19th."

He pointed again.

"That's the 'Popper' unit next door."

There was another bunker and a tower visible past #43 on the curving perimeter road to the left. To the right of #42, the perimeter road jogged outward and disappeared around a stand of rubber trees, while an interior road continued on straight behind our motor pool and on past some helicopter pads visible beyond, putting #42 on a 'corner', so to speak.

We walked on past the shower shack and across the road to the end door of the first gray hootch building.

"There's an empty bunk in here you can take, but two of the night shift FDC guys are sleeping right now, so be quiet and try not to wake them, OK?"

I nodded and said, "Sure."

He turned, waved and said, "See ya." And walked back toward the CP.

Bunker #42 (Bravo 4-2)

I unslung my duffel and ducked under a heavy wool army blanket that was hung over the door, into the darkened bunkroom. The space was about 8' by 12' and in the gloom I could pick out two sets of two-tiered bunks, one on either side, separated by a bank of four metal wall lockers along the far wall. Along the wall adjacent the door was a chair and a plywood writing desk nailed to the wall under an ammo box cubbyhole cabinet. Two footlockers were along the wall to the left.

I stowed my bag in a corner and put my rifle in the wooden rack on the wall to the left of the door. I stripped off my fatigue jacket and tossed it on the inner upper bunk, both lowers being obviously occupied, judging from the light snoring sounds emanating from there.

Rummaging through my gear, I pulled out my poncho liner and my book. I tossed them up, also, and climbed the end railings into the small space, (less than three feet below the ceiling), and using my jacket as a pillow, I settled back, figuring to read until lunchtime. There was a 12" gap, covered by screen, between the tops of the outer walls and the roof eaves, to allow light and air to enter. I started to read the adventures of Travis McGee, but soon, I must have fallen asleep in the relative cool of the darkened room.

I must have really passed-out, and I didn't wake up until the other guys were up and making noises in their lockers. I raised up and peered at my Timex, a gift from my Dad when I left the US.

'Wow, it's 5:30 already,' I thought, 'I slept through lunch!'

The other two guys, one short and stocky, the other extremely tall and skinny, were engrossed in their stuff and, I guessed, hadn't noticed me yet. I swung my legs over the edge of the bunk.

"Hi, guys, I'm Rich Hudson." And smiled.

They both looked up from what they were doing. The shorter one spoke first.

"Wondered if you were gonna sleep on through th' night. My name's Don Bowers an' this skinny dude's Gaylord Fukijima, or 'Fuk' for short," (Pronounced 'fook'), "though there's nothing short about him."

I jumped down from my perch and shook hands with both men.

"You both work in the FDC?"

Fuk spoke up.

"Yeah, night shift, 10 to 6 A.M., so we work all night an' sleep all day, what d'you do?"

"I'm not sure." I answered, "I just came in from D battery. I've been in th' field for seven months, but I got sick and they sent me here."

"Well, Hudson," Bowers said, "if you're hungry, we're headed for th' mess hall for breakfast, or supper to you, you're welcome to join us."

I grabbed my hat and jacket and we trooped over to the chow hall and, since it was rather late, the line was down and we got our food almost immediately. We sat at one of the tables with a slick, checkered oilcloth covering, and ate and talked about our experiences so far in VN.

Bowers was from a small town in Indiana named Princeton, and Fukijima was Hawaiian, which explained his dark skin, oriental features and name. Fuk also had a huge, white smile, which made me like him immediately, without knowing why. Bowers was friendly, but kind of stuffy and reserved and I felt like he'd be hard to get to know. They'd both been at HQ their whole time in-country, Bowers for eleven months and Fuk

163

for four. They finished their chow and took off to 'Take care of business' and left me alone to tour the battery complex after chow.

I exited through the back door of the mess into the open area outside, lit a cig and stood looking around. The sun was low in the sky behind the big green motor pool tent and the air took on a mauve tint as the light was filtered through the rubber trees beyond the road. I felt 'The Call', so I ambled down to the latrine and found the 'piss tube', a kind of outdoor urinal made from a metal powder canister imbedded, end up, in the ground and 2/3rds filled with gravel. Thus relieved, I walked down to the motor pool and looked around, but nobody was about, so I turned around and headed back up the main road toward the CP

Where the road started to curve back up toward the front gate, there was another small dirt track and a thick stand of bamboo and brush to the right blocking the view of the green-line. I turned onto the little road, intending to see where it went. After I'd walked twenty feet, I noticed a path that led into the brush and decided to see where that went instead.

The narrow footpath wound back and forth and the thick, more than head-high, weeds made it almost night-dark inside the copse. I inhaled the thick, pungent smell of jungle as I walked warily along. I secretly wished I had my rifle with me, and subconsciously began looking for booby traps. I was really getting a little spooked in there, despite knowing I was on a huge base, surrounded by armed men. Inside there though, with all views blocked by dense vegetation, I could have been on any jungle track in the heart of the 'Boonies'.

After about thirty five or forty feet, the path suddenly ended at a four-foot high crumbling sandbag wall. I cautiously peeked over the wall and realized that it was a very old bunker, completely surrounded by scrub bamboo and brush. It was round and about eight feet in diameter with no roof. Inside, the bare, hard-packed dirt floor was raised to within two feet of the top of the wall, allowing anyone inside to see over the top of the vegetation, but still allowing him room to duck for cover behind the low wall. The bunker itself was completely hidden by the bushes.

I climbed over the wall and was somewhat relieved to see Bunker #42 off to the right and Tower November to the left, with a swath of brush twenty feet wide, a barbed wire fence, and the perimeter road between them and me. I realized that this little bunker was completely invisible from all vantage points, except maybe the top of the guard tower, but it was probably eighty or ninety feet away, and in the failing light, I doubted even they could tell if anyone was here.

I moved to the front wall and sat with my feet hanging over the outer edge and sighed. The sun was down on the horizon behind the trees across the road, but shafts of light were playing through the branches and glinting off metal roofs, barely seen in the undergrowth below. The metal roof of the tower was also glowing red from the final rays of this day, but all below that was in deep twilight. The bugs were starting to buzz around, but they didn't interrupt my reverie.

I was suddenly aware that I was completely alone! That is a rarity in the army, especially in Vietnam. I had always appreciated the solitary moment, the quiet times alone in the woods or late at night back home. I tried to pretend I was there, now, on a rocky-top in Red River Gorge, or atop Natural Bridge, near Slade, Ky, watching this spectacular sunset, as I had many times before in my short life.

The sky above me had turned to a clear, purple-blue, and the rays of the dying sun flew up only to be absorbed by the heavy darkness of impending night. I lit a cig and just actually enjoyed the solitude, but, oh, how I longed to be home.

I faintly heard voices from the tower and the nearest bunker. Guards prepping for their night shift. I also heard the sound of an engine, faint but growing stronger by the minute, coughing and chugging from off beyond the trees where the sun had now almost completely set. Soon I saw the source of the sound, as a pair of headlights appeared, going east, but not on the perimeter road, as I'd expected, but outside the KZ, on a road that wasn't visible from where I sat. The four-foot tall elephant grass that grew outside our barbed wire barrier hid it. I was surprised to see in the remaining light, that it was one of those brightly painted Vietnamese busses sputtering along at about fifteen MPH, its yellow paint and evil looking eyes glowing through the twilight.

"Bus is late tonight." A soft voice said from behind me.

Startled, I jumped and swung around to see a figure materialize from the bamboo on the path I'd used. Medium height and build with a buzz cut and a heavy black beard shadow that I knew no razor could ever make disappear. He stopped as he reached the bunker wall and peered at me from the gloom.

"Oh, sorry, man, I thought you were Weitzel." He said as he climbed into the bunker.

"Uh… am I not supposed to be out here, or something?" I asked, not knowing.

"No, man, s'alright. This place don't belong to no one, so anybody can come out here, I guess. Me an' Jon-Jon come out most nights, an some other guys, too."

"Yeah," I nodded, "nice place to get away."

I sort of resented the intrusion, but, hey, it's not my bunker.

"My name's Leonard, Terry Leonard, who you be?"

"New-guy in battery. Just came in from the field today. Name's Hudson, but everybody call's me Mouse."

He smiled at that and stuck out his hand, which I dapped.

"Well Hey, Mouse. You get high, man?"

"You mean like, smokin', man?", trying to act innocent, not knowing anything about this guy. He wore cut-off fatigue pants and an army-green athletic T-shirt and no rank pins, just a metal peace symbol around his neck.

"Yeah, smokin', man, ya smoke…. Like dope?" he said, eyeing my PFC tabs, and, I guess, feeling safe enough to ask outright.

"Well… not on a regular basis, but…. Yeah, I have, sure."

I tried to make it sound as if I had vast experience.

"Great!"

He whipped out a rather large bag and a bowl.

"Let's get high. We won't wait for Jon-Jon. He's late, won't wait!"

He started packing the bowl with the pungent smelling weed.

"I heard that!" another voice came from down the path, "Late, won't wait, my ass!"

Another figure appeared at the wall.

"Don't be startin' no bowl wit'out yer main man, man!"

He saw me. His bright blue eyes, visible even in the near dark, narrowed.

"Hey, man, I'm Jon-Jon Weitzel, hoodefuckeryu?"

By then it was full dark, but I had no trouble picking out the man behind the voice. Dressed in a clean, white athletic shirt, with skin almost as white as the shirt and a silvery-blond pompadour hairstyle, John Weitzel glowed like a specter in the night.

He looked at me, his invisible eyebrows raised.

"Did I hear you say 'Mouse'?" He looked at my new fatigues, "You a FNG, 'r somethin'? You ain't much bigger'n a mouse." His fatigue pants were a soft green, not quite white, but definitely not O.D.

"No, man," Leonard interjected before I could speak, "He's in from th' field, he's cool."

"You a NARC?"

Weitzel leaned in close and watched for my response.

"A what?" I said, taken aback.

Leonard waved his hand in dismissal.

"Naw, man, he ain't no NARC. He's been in th' boonies, so he's cool."

I didn't exactly see the logic in Terry's defense of me.

"Uh... yeah, man, I'm just a gun bunny. I'm not a ... NARC 'r anything else. What's a NARC, anyway?"

Jon-Jon looked at me even closer.

"CID, Cop, Gendarme, you know, Fuzz, man."

He was one of the most intense people I'd ever met.

Just then Terry lit the bowl and passed it to me. As I took a hit from it, Weitzel, seemed to relax a little, so I passed it to him, smiling and holding the smoke deep.

"Well... at least ya ain't no bogart." He acquiesced.

After the bowl had gone around several more times, and I was getting a real buzz, Terry nudged me.

"What're you doin' back here at HQ, Mouse, did'ja have'ta kiss some lifers ass 'r somethin' ta get sent ta th' rear?"

I didn't know whether to take offense, or laugh, so, being as stoned as I was, I laughed.

"No, I got real sick an lost a lot of weight. Oh, an' I puked on th' 1st Sgt."

They both did double takes on each other and busted out laughing.

"You did...WHAT? On a First Sgt.?" they said simultaneously.

So I told them the 'Puke Story' and afterward, I guess I was a member of the 'Club'. Weitzel slapped my back.

"That took real 'Balls', man!" Then he looked thoughtful.

"That's one thing I ain't tried yet," he scratched his chin, "but it's worth some thought."

I looked questioningly at Terry and he explained.

"Jon-Jon's tryin' for a 612 discharge, man. Tryin' ta convince th' Army he's too crazy ta be a soldier."

"But..." I shook my head, "you have to be crazy to be here in th' first place!"

"That's what I tol' 'im,"

Terry shrugged.

"That he's here BECAUSE he's crazy, but he don't listen. He's always doin' goofy stuff around th' lifers, tryin' ta get kicked out o' th' Army, but I don' think it's gonna work"

"Sure it's workin', man, them lifers think I'm so weird they avoid me like th' plague." Weitzel bragged.

(I found out that Jon-Jon did a lot of bragging.)

In my stoned condition, all this made some kind of sense, and we all cackled and joked around for awhile, 'til I got the 'munchies' and told them I was heading back to my hootch. I told them where my quarters was and they told me they were in the next ammo-crate building down toward the motor pool, and for me to stop and visit the next day. We all 'dapped' and I slowly found my way through the, now pitch black path in the bamboo.

I ambled back to the hootch by the light of a sliver of moon, rising in the east. I was thinking as I walked, about the weird people I'd met so far in the Army. And that Terry and, certainly Jon-Jon, were certainly among the weirdest.

I liked them, all right, but, man...!

Leonard was undoubtedly the most unmilitary looking dude I'd run across, with his love beads and peace symbols. He was from Terra Haute, Indiana, of all places. He was one of the few RAs, (voluntary enlistee), I'd ever run across, and, unlike Jon-Jon, Terry was perfectly content to serve out his tour so he could save enough money to buy a new Chevy Camero when he got back stateside. He claimed he could have any chick he wanted in a car like that. (Though looking at him, I had my doubts). Terry had seven months remaining in his tour, and a year to do in the states.

Jon-Jon was not just unmilitary, he was downright radical. He was from South Chicago, with a thick, Big-City accent, and even though he wasn't into the love-bead thing, just his bearing and definitely his dress was arrogant and certain to piss-off a bunch of lifers, not to mention officers. I wondered how he got away with it.

I found out later, it was due to sheer nerve. Jon-Jon had lots and lots of nerve, and a pure hatred of the Army and its systems. Even though he'd only been in-country for a month, he'd already convinced most of the NCOs that he was insane, probably even dangerous. So, according to Terry, They all pretty much left him alone, assigning him details that took him out of the compound just to keep him out of sight, so they wouldn't have to deal with him.

Weitzel was not in the least concerned with how a 612 discharge would look on his record.

"Everybody back in th' city KNOWS I'm crazy, won't be a deal, ya know?"

17

JAN 27, 1970

Back in the dark, empty hootch, (Fuk and Bowers were on duty), I rustled around for my duffel and found my flashlight, which I always keep right on top. I flashed it around and took my first good look at the room. The first thing I noticed was, right over the little writing desk, there was a small, metal shaded lamp attached to the wall.

'Wow!' I thought, 'Electricity!'

I snapped on the lamp, turned off the flashlight, and felt very sophisticated. There was another light fixture hanging from the ceiling in the center of the room, just a bare bulb, operated by a pull chain, but the desk light was all that was needed and gave the room a cozy feel.

The little desk, illuminated by the lamp, had a thick piece of glass cut to fit the top as a writing surface over the rough plywood plank. Under the glass was a group of photographs. A pretty blond girl, early twenties, holding a laughing baby. They were smiling and waving at the camera. Same girl, younger, with Bowers beside her, both dressed up for a party or a dance, his arm around her. A group family photo, ten older folks with the blond and Bowers, in his uniform, all mugging for the shot.

Along the other edge were pictures of the Fukijima family in Hawaii. Mom, I assumed, was the short, fat one, smiling that wide, white smile, and Dad was the tall, strong looking guy with his arm around a uniformed Fuk. They were standing on a beach with the ocean as a background. A couple of others showed Fuk in the baggiest, floweriest swim trunks I'd ever seen. His legs looked like long pipe cleaners and he was holding up a surfboard that was three feet taller than he was.

Fuk

In every shot, though, he was with a different beautiful girl. And I DO mean beautiful. One of my socks covers more area than all the bikinis in those pictures.

"Wow! Ol' Fuk does alright!" I mumbled as I moved around, checking out the rest of the room.

Rifle rack, with only mine there now, by the door. Four bunks, four gray metal wall lockers, four footlockers, and a woven grass rug that covered the cement floor between the beds. Pretty Spartan, but, hell, it seemed like a luxury suite to me.

There were no other decorations around the room, except on the wall beside Fuk's lower bunk on the right. There must have been thirty photos of MORE beautiful girls, all hanging on Fuk like he was the king of Hawaii, or something. There was more flesh than sand showing in those beach shots!

'Man, what's he GOT?' I thought.

Lying in the corner of Fuk's bunk was a guitar.

'Hey, maybe he'll teach me some songs.' I thought as I stripped to my skivvies and made ready for bed.

I'd always wanted to play guitar, and I did know some chords from playing around with my dads old Silvertone back home, but having been a trumpet player in bands hadn't left me a lot of time to pursue other instruments.

I snapped off the lamp and using my flash, I climbed into the upper bunk over Bowers', spread my poncho liner and flopped down with a sigh. I looked at my watch and it was already past midnight. My first day in the rear had been pretty good. As I drifted off, I wondered what would be in store for me tomorrow.

About 0400, I was aware of my hootch-mates coming in and making noises, preparing for bed, but I must have drifted off again, because when I opened my eyes, light was reflecting off the ceiling above me. Brighter light than it should be.

I checked my watch and it was 7:45. Oh, Man. I'd slept through reveille and probably the morning formation, too! Crap!

I swung down from the bunk, being careful not to waken the sleepers, threw on my fatigues from the night before, checked my beard stubble in the little mirror outside the door, (Pretty thick, but it'll have to do!), and headed at a dead run for the CP.

I arrived at 0800, just as Tabaranza was entering the front door.

"I think I slept through reveille and formation!" I said, out of breath.

Tabaranza smiled.

"We don't do formation or reveille, here. Not since last month, when some ballsy gooks sneaked into the trees outside the wire and fired a couple of mortar rounds in as we were all lined up out here. Put the fear into the NCOs."

"Wow," I said wide eyed, "Anyone hurt?"

"No. Lucky they were bad shots. Blew away some dirt on the road outside the mess hall and knocked down the blast wall outside the Briefing Room, but that's all. No more reveille or formations since. The CQ's supposed to wake everyone, now, but I guess you got skipped, being new and sleeping in the 'night-duty' hootch. It's OK, though, you're just in time to see the First Sergeant."

He waved me in, walked to an open door on the back wall and leaned in.

"PFC Hudson to see you, Top."

I nodded my thanks as I passed him and entered the office where the Sgt. was seated behind his desk.

I could only see him from the waist up, but Sgt. Anderson was an imposing figure. He was looking down at some papers, and the first thing I noticed was his perfectly round little, pink bald spot, surrounded by thick bristly black hair. When he looked up at me, his head was also perfectly round with little pink ears jutting out to either side. His face was smooth, almost devoid of planes, except for a small, out-thrust chin at the bottom. His features, small black eyes and narrow thin line of a mouth, were pinched-up around a reddish, bulbous nose. He had no neck. Massive shoulders started right below his ears and transitioned into enormous arms covered in thick black hair. His fatigue jacket was tight across his chest and the rolled-up sleeves were tight enough around his arms to pinch-in the skin.

I stood at attention.

"PFC Hudson, reporting, Top."

He looked a hole in me for a good thirty seconds, then lowered his head again and waved his hand slightly, which I assumed was an 'At Ease', so I stood, waiting, but didn't relax much.

Ruffling through the sheaf of paper in front of him, he mumbled.

"Don' have enough shit comin' down 'round heah!"

His accent was southern, broad. Georgia, maybe? He looked back up, his beady eyes burning holes in my fatigues.

"Now what'm I s'posed t' do wit' a sick Gun-bunny?"

He shook his head (as much as is possible with no neck), and I shrugged.

"Don't know, Top."

"You ain't even a very biggun, either, are yew."

It was a statement, not a question, so I didn't answer.

He consulted his papers.

"Well, accordin' t' this re-port, ya ain't caused no real trouble…
'cept for th' …inceedent concernin' First Sgt. Wilson."

(My reputation had obviously preceded me.)

"We won't have no repeat o' that heah, WILL WE BOY?"

I snapped-to and almost yelled.

"NO, TOP!"

"Good." He said simply and waved another 'at ease'.

I 'at eased' again, but not very much.

He stood up, walked to a basket on top of one of the four file
cabinets along the wall to my left, and reached up for a sheaf of paper
that was sticking out. I said 'reached up' because he was only 5' 6" tall.
Only an inch or so taller than me!

'And he was making fun of MY height?' I thought.

It looked like there had been an accident at the 'People Factory'
when he'd been built, and he'd somehow ended up with the wrong legs,
(not to mention, no neck). From his shoulders to his toes he was absolutely triangular.

He looked hard at me as he turned and came back to his seat, to
see if I was checking out his height. I kept my face impassive.

"OK, Hudson, what c'n yew do 'sides shoot a Howitzer an' belly-
ache?"

"Well, Top…I was a …uh…trumpet player in bands. I was a
professional musician."

He waved his hand as if to dismiss that thought.

"Ain't no bands 'round heah, 'cept in Saigon, and if'n I cain't go
t' Saigon, YEW sure ain't gonna, neither. What else?"

"I…uh…worked in a print shop as a press operator, an' I did
some art work." I said, trying to be helpful.

"That ain't no he'p, neither."

He picked up a Styrofoam coffee cup and spit tobacco juice into
it.

"Can yew drive a jeep?"

His beady eyes looked hopeful.

"Well, sure, Top, I'm a good driver."

"Good," he seemed happy, "Re-port t' Lt. Cravens in th' S-2.
They need a driver an' yew c'n he'p th' Ell Tee with whatever th' hell it is
that he does. Tell 'im I sent ya. GOT THAT?"

I snapped-to again.

"Yes, Top!"

"Good, now beat-it!"

I did.

I remembered the S-2 sign on the side of the TOC building from the day before, so I walked on up the road and entered under a rubber poncho door curtain into a two-room office, lit by overhead shaded bulbs. There was a counter that wrapped around the two outer walls, covered with books, folders and stacks of papers. Two Spec. 5s were seated in green folding chairs at the counter, sorting papers. A PRC-25 radio was set up and hissing next to the door into the other room where I could see a 'Butter-bar' Lt. seated at a desk in the glow of a gooseneck desk lamp. No one seemed to have noticed my entrance.

"I'm supposed to report to Lt. Cravens?" I said to anyone who'd listen.

The guy seated by the radio looked up and casually waved toward the other room.

"In there."

I entered and waited in the light from the single overhead bulb until he looked up. "Yes?".

At attention, I saluted.

"PFC Hudson, reporting as driver for the LT sir."

"I don't have a driver." He said, looking confused.

"No, sir, I AM your driver. Th' first Sgt. sent me."

The guy looked even more confused for a moment, then as it sunk-in, he smiled and said, more to himself than to me,

"Well, it's about time!"

I thought he meant I was late reporting.

"I'm sorry, sir, I didn't hear reveille an' nobody woke me up an' I...."

"No, no,...uh...Hudson, is it?" he interrupted and I nodded.

"They've been promising me a driver for weeks, now, and I guess they've finally seen fit to provide one."

He was smiling, now.

"That's great, private, where's your jeep, I need to go to DIVAR-TY."

"Uhh... I don't have a jeep, sir. I'm, I guess, supposed to drive YOUR jeep."

He looked frustrated for a moment, then angry.

"We don't have a jeep, private." He said softly.

"Well, you have a driver, anyway, sir." I said helpfully.

"Yes, I have a driver, thank you, private."

He scratched his chin and thought for several minutes, then took his hat from the out-box on his desk and stood.

"Come with me, Hudson."

He strode from the office out onto the road with me trailing behind. He led me back down to the CP and I assumed he was taking me back to Sgt. Anderson, but, no, we went on past and around to the motor pool. We walked into the service tent where three guys were working on a 'Deuce and a half', (2 ½ ton truck).

An E-5 in greasy coveralls was standing on the driver's side front fender and yelled "TEN HUT!" The other two men, inside the cramped engine compartment tried in vain to straighten up to attention. One, a tall skinny dude, clanged his head on the underside of the hood.

The LT said "At ease, Sgt. Holly, can I have a word with you?"

The other two men went back to their chore and Sgt. Holly, the E-5, jumped down.

"What c'n I do for you, sir?"

"Sgt., is that jeep still out back, and if so, could we take a look at it?"

Holly grinned.

"Sure, LT, its back next to my trailer, behind those oil drums. Go on out and look all you want."

We walked out the far end of the big round tent and around the corner to a miniature junkyard. Piles of rusty vehicle parts, partially dismantled jeeps and trucks, and an old, used-to-be truck-mounted mobile command center, sitting on blocks next to a stack of 55 gallon oil drums. This was Motor Sgt. Holly's quarters, his 'trailer'. Past the drums, the LT pointed.

"Well, this is it."

"IT" was a jeep, M151A1 Ford, or at least part of one. It wasn't quite as bad as the other two I'd seen coming in, but most of its major components seemed to be there, (that is if you didn't consider wheels a 'major component').

"Uhh…what is it, sir?"

He grinned this Catbird grin.

"Your Mission!"

"Mission, sir?"

"Do you know anything about mechanics? Working on cars, Hudson?"

I nodded, looking at the wreck dubiously.

"Well…yes, sir…uh…some."

Actually, my dad was an automobile mechanic back home, and I'd spent hours in the driveway helping him do stuff to our cars, and I'd done most of the engine work on my little VW. But this? This would be like making a jeep from the ground-up.

"Do you think you could make something like this run?"

"I really don't know, sir, but…"

I glanced around the yard and muttered, "It looks like most of the missing parts could be gotten off the other wrecks, and what we can't find, we could requisition from supply."

This brought a short laugh from the Lt.

"Fat chance, Hudson. That's why most of these vehicles are here. Lack of parts and lack of interest. Don't expect much help from supply, but Sgt. Holly will be more than happy to help you any way he can, I'm sure."

"Well," I said, "if he'll let me use his tools, and help me with th' heavy stuff, sure, sir, I'll give it a shot."

He slapped me on the back.

"Good, Hudson! Your mission, then, is to restore this vehicle to running condition, if possible. If anyone tries to divert you from your mission or impede you in any way, you are to tell him to see me. Is that understood?"

I nodded.

He smiled.

"After all, a driver can't drive without a vehicle, now can he?"

"No, sir, I guess he can't!" I smiled back.

"Good!"

He turned back toward the motor tent and I followed.

"Get the motor pool men to get this junk out of the way so you can get started on MY jeep, Hudson!"

"Yes, sir!" I said and split off from him to get some help.

Sgt. Holly said that as soon as they finished their job on the big truck, they'd come and move the barrels. To kill time, I wandered around the mechanics bays, trying to figure what tools I'd need, and their location. After that, I walked back out and took a close look at my 'Mission'.

'Man, what've I gotten myself into?' I thought, looking at the hulk dubiously.

The body was pretty much intact except for: wheels and tires, brakes, gas tank, seats, drivers side windshield glass, top, hood, most of the engine except the head, and manifolds. The radiator was there but no hoses or fan. It did, amazingly have a starter and generator still attached, though whether they worked or not, I didn't know.

Thankfully, the transmission was still there, the gearshift sticking up through the floor with no knob. And then there would be the small details like mirrors, gas can, side curtains and a hundred other things that make a jeep a jeep. It was pretty stripped.

"Hell, it's REALLY stripped!" I mumbled, thinking, maybe I'd bitten off more than I could chew, this time. Then I thought, 'Well it's still better than being a gun-bunny.'

I rolled up my sleeves and started perusing the piles of debris for possible salvageable parts. I'd found some possible good stuff and had just loaded it into the small rear area of the jeep, when Holly and his two helpers showed up on a forklift and they started moving the oil drums out of the way.

While Jim and Ralph, the two 'motor-monkeys', were loading the barrels, Holly and I looked at the other salvage vehicles. He was really helpful and pointed out a bunch of stuff I would be able to use.

"The LT's been trying to get somebody to fix this junker for a long time, now."

"How come you guys," I indicated his helpers, "don't do it. I mean you're the motor Sgt. an' all."

He pulled two rusty seat frames out from under an old Chrysler ¾ ton.

"We stay too busy doing maintenance and repair on vehicles that are 'Farmed-in' from other batteries and even other units. Like we just had a track-mount APC that came in from 11th AC, up th' road. Needed a top-end rebuild on one o' those big Cadillac engines they got. That took a week, by itself. No way we could get even near this jeep in th' next month."

We dumped all the stuff we'd found into the jeep. By that time, the path was clear of drums. Jim swung the forklift around and picked up the jeep, side-on, on the big steel tines, and carried it to the tent and put it on wooden beams that were already set up just inside the open end of the hangar-like building. It looked even more pitiful, standing alone than it had in the junkyard.

Holly told me to help myself to the tools, but laid down some basic rules. Any tool used gets put back where it was found, in as clean or cleaner condition. Parts in the yard were fair game but the stuff in the little wood storage shed out back behind his 'trailer' was his domain. I could use some of it, but only with his permission. I told him I had no problem with that and he wished me luck and went back to bossing Jim and Ralph around at the other end of the tent.

I picked out a selection of tools, thinking 'So now I'm a mechanic, I guess.'

One really bent-up wreck had three good wheels, so I took the rolling jack out and soon had them stacked next to my 'mission'. I found an only slightly bent hood slid up under a burned-up ¾ at the very back of the yard and spotted another half-broken-out windshield in the bed of a 'Deuce.' I carried these back and made a pile next to the jeep and stood there pondering until my stomach reminded me I hadn't had any breakfast. My jacket was hanging on one of the grease rack timbers, and I reached in and took my watch out of the pocket. I'd been so engrossed in my parts hunt that it was already 1:45 and with a groan, I realized I'd missed lunch, too. I wasn't used to a set schedule for meals.

Jim was walking by just then so I asked him if chow was over.

"Yeah, man, ol' Carbone, cuts it off at 1300 sharp." He informed me.

"Well, shit!" I groaned, "I guess I'll have to wait 'til 5:00 to get somethin' to eat."

"No sweat, man. I was just goin' to my hootch for a bite, myself. C'mon," he motioned, "I got plenty."

We walked out through the gate and to the first EM barracks. His room was the first door on this end, facing the 'pool'. He entered and came back out with an aluminum pan, a C-4 stove and several packages of something I'd never seen. They looked like brown vacuum-packed plastic bags.

"Chili con carne, roast beef an' spuds 'r spaghetti?" he asked.

I asked him what those bags were and he explained they were 'LRRP' rations. (He pronounced it 'LURP'.)

I still looked questioningly, so he said, "Long Range Recon Patrol', man, freeze-dried. Just add boilin' water an' voila, eats!" he smiled and I did too and told him to make mine spaghetti, "With meat sauce?"

He said "Sure!", and proceeded to fire up his stove and put on a pan of water to boil. The expert way he did this made me think he'd probably spent some time in the field, so I asked him how long he'd been in-country.

"'Bout four months, man, how 'bout you?"

"Seven months an' counting," I replied as he handed me a packet labeled 'Spag. W/ meat, Tom. Sce. And printed instructions on cooking.

"I've been on the LZs the whole time, 'til I got sick."

"You don't look sick,"

He removed the now-boiling pan, tore open his packet, and poured in a little steaming water and stirred with a spoon.

"'Cept yer a li'l skinny."

Immediately the aroma of roast beef wafted by and my stomach growled. He handed me the pan and told me to do the same. I did and a few minutes later I had a bag of delicious-smelling spaghetti, to which I added a dollop of ketchup from Jim's 'pantry' for 'body'. As our food cooled a little we mixed up some warm cherry Kool-Aid for drinks, and I told him about my allergy and how sick I'd gotten to lose twenty five pounds over two months.

"Bummer, man," he commiserated. "th' LZs I was on were enough to make anybody sick."

"You were a gun-bunny, too?" I asked.

"Naw, man, I was a mechanic at Cu Chi for a couple months, then I moved with th' maint unit to a RVN base at Dong Xuai. I was standin' next to a SP (self-propelled) fuel cell when a welder fired his torch to braze a seam. There must'a been some gas fumes still in there, cause that sucker split wide open and blew me 'bout twenty-five feet an' busted my right eardrum. Th' welder went straight up 'bout th' same distance and had burns on most of his body. Bad news, man!"

By this time I was digging in to the spaghetti and with my mouth full replied, "MMMmmFFfth!", meaning, 'Yeah, real bad'.

"Anyway, I transferred in here 'bout a month ago." He continued, "Not a bad gig if ya keep low, know what I mean?"

Still chewing the delicious food, I nodded and swallowed.

"Man, either I'm real hungry or this stuff is really good." I smiled.

"Th' LURPS got th' best rations in th' whole damn army."

He nodded, as he took a big bite of his still steaming roast beef, chewed and wolfed it down.

"I got two cases of 'em on a trade for two good three-quarter tires. I got ten flavors! Besides these I got beanie-weenies, chicken ala king, uh... chicken 'n noodles, an' some others I ain't tried yet. Sure is good, ain't it?"

"Hell yeah! Got flavor an' everything!" I said between bites.

We ate for a while with only a few "MMM"s and groans between us, then washed it all down with the Kool-Aid. Finished, I pulled out my cigs and offered him one.

"Holy shit! You got Larks!" He said with a double take.

"Yeah. My mom sends 'em to me, a carton a month in my 'care-packages'."

We lit-up and he inhaled the smoke and savored it before blowing it out his nose.

"Man, sure beats those dried out PX Winstons! I used to smoke these in high school. Don't think I've had one since."

He took another long drag.

"They still taste like cherry blend pipe tobacco."

We smoked and talked for a while and I found out his last name was Lynch, he was from Torrence, Ca., had been working in a filling station 'til he was drafted, had a girlfriend named 'Willow', of all things, and was into stealing.

It was my turn for the double take.

"Just from th' army, though, man." he said.

"What d'ya steal from th' army?" I wanted to know.

"Well, hell, anything you need." He said seriously.

"You don't mess with another GI's shit, you know, personal stuff, but, say you need a ….wheel for that junk jeep of yours? You could, like, requisition one from Central Supply, An' you MIGHT get one in six months, or maybe never."

I knew how long it takes to get a pair of boots.

"Well," he continued, "Every jeep in th' US Army is s'posed to have an extra wheel hangin' on th' back, AND a spare gas can, AND they're s'posed to be locked down an' th' driver's s'posed to have th' key."

I was absorbing all this.

"Well, the driver loses th' keys an' cuts th' locks off thinkin' he can get another lock from supply, SO, since supply ain't got no locks, most o' th' jeeps spare wheels and gas cans ain't locked."

'Made sense.' I nodded, he continued.

"If somethin's not LOCKED in th' army, hell, they EXPECT for it to get stolen. They know what a bunch of degenerates us soldiers are, SO, somewhere in th' system there's a replacement part for anything that is stolen."

I shook my head, laughing.

"Then th' dumb ass driver, th' one who cut th' lock off in th' first place, ALLOWING th' tire to get stolen, has a choice of 'A'; ordering one from supply an' waitin' six months, OR, 'B'; steal one off th' NEXT jeep that's got a dumb ass driver."

I'm cracking up, can't believe this guy.

"Then that dumb ass steals th' NEXT dummy's an' so on 'til th' last one comes around and steals YOUR'S!"

Now we're both laughing hard.

"Then the cycle's complete," I added, "So, in essence, there's RE-ALLY only one dumb ass driver in th' army who's COMPLETELY without a wheel, so, let HIM order one from supply!"

"I like th' way you think… and your cigarettes."

He smiled and dapped me.

Thus fortified with LURPS, we went back to the motor pool and I jumped into my project with both feet. Jim helped me off-and-on. By 5:30 I had brakes, thanks to Sgt. Holly's storage room, and three wheels mounted. I got greasy and it felt pretty good, especially knowing that the shower was waiting for me afterward.

18

TET

The next couple of days passed in a routine. I was still in the night-duty hootch, so each morning the CQ would quietly shake me awake, I'd dress, do my S's, have breakfast, (I found my appetite had returned), then report to the S-2 and the LT.

Every morning I'd go to the Survey shack and borrow the S-5 jeep, drive the LT to Division Artillery, (DIVARTY), drop him off, then drive to the Meteorology Station at the air strip where I'd pick up the weather reports and forecasts. Then I'd go back to DIVARTY, pick up the LT and we'd go back to HQ. After that, if nothing else came up, and nothing HAD so far, I'd go straight to the 'pool' and get greasy.

Jim and Ralph turned out to be good Buds. They helped me on some of the finer points on the engine. Like how to bash dents out of a valve cover with a ball-peen hammer. And, after much scrounging in our yard and a quick trip to the big DX yard by the POL fuel point, late the second afternoon, we had the engine running. Not purring or anything, but it started!

Lynch found me an Army Manual, (there's one for everything), on the M151A1 ¼ ton Utility Vehicle, (Jeep), and after deciphering the Militarese nomenclature, I found it very helpful as it described, in minute detail, every procedure for the repair and maintenance of that vehicle.

Next morning, as I was fine-tuning the carb and timing, Lynch showed up with TWO practically new wheels and tires, and a spare gas can! He didn't even have to steal them, as they were on a blown-out jeep that had just been pulled into the DX yard that morning, while he was there looking for some other stuff for Sgt. Holly. He said he was lucky to get the parts because "There were guys all over that wreck like vultures, man." He proudly presented them to me along with two shiny new brass locks and grinned.

I mounted-up my fourth wheel and the spare and the gas can, (all properly locked, thank yew). I spent the rest of the day hammering-out the hood, bolting the, so far bare steel seat frames to the floor, and struggling with the rubber bead around the glass in the windshield frames. By 6:30 that evening, I had, except for a lack of a muffler, headlights, and a million other small items, a passable, road-worthy jeep. Ralph, Jim and I took it on its virgin cruise all the way around the perimeter road that evening, to the POL where I filled it with gas, like a proud teenager with his first car. Jim had brought along a joint and we smoked it as we drove around the south side of the base where the road was somewhat isolated by the airstrip and the chopper pads.

"Man," I exclaimed as we rounded the curving road to face the deepening sunset, "I feel like I'm back home, cruising around town, 'cept I know there aren't any girls to pick up."

Jim laughed, "You got THAT right." He passed the joint to Ralph, who was rattling around in the back.

"You wouldn't get any girls, anyway, in a sorry-ass jeep like this," Ralph said, holding the smoke. He blew out a cloud and continued, "Man, at home I got a '64 GTO, 389 with three 'Deuces', scoop on th' hood, four-on-th'-floor, fifth in th' dash an' a whore-in-th'-door. Th' girls jus' CREAM for that car, man. I've always got a babe with me, even as ugly as I am."

"You got THAT right, too!" Jim joked.

We got to talking about girls and I told them about my "Dear John" letter.

"Real bummer, man." Jim nodded sympathetically, "But there it is, man. If you ain't there to pay attention to 'em, women'll dump your ass in a heartbeat."

Ralph and I agreed, nodding sagely.

"You oughta find you a cute li'l Baby-san over here, marry her and take her home an' train her to be th', like, perfect wifey-poo." Ralph suggested.

"No way, man," I said laughing, "She'd probably turn out to be VC an' blow my ass away, along with th' whole neighborhood."

"Yeah," Jim chimed-in, "an' you'd havta learn to eat hamburgers with Nouc Mam sauce, too, man."

We were Hoo-Hooing as we drove back into the motor pool as the sun was going down and the twilight was getting all purpley, as it did every evening, lately.

We parted at the pool gate and Jim hesitated long enough to tell me to be at the tent at noon, the next day, as he was driving a Deuce to Bien Hoa to pick up some parts at the Service Battery, There.

"If yer LT an' Sgt., Holly say it's OK, you can be my assistant driver, an' I know about a Gook upholstery shop outside Ben Cat that'll cover those ol' rusty seats for you for 1200 piasters (about ten dollars) each. It's practically on th' way, cool?"

"Cool!" I said.

The second evening there, I had spent alone in my hootch, as Fuk and Bowers worked all night. I wrote letters home and informed everyone of my new assignment, that I was in a considerably safer place, now, and for them not to worry.

The third evening, I joined Jim and Ralph on the roof of their hootch. It was a very fine place for watching all the goings-on for a quarter mile around us from the tree line of the jungle out beyond the Dong Xuai road to the north, nearly to the end of the runway at the airfield, to our east. North were the chopper pads of the E/82nd AVN GRP (according to their sign), and south was the 2/19th Arty., the 105 unit next door, and beyond that the 11th Armored Cav. Beyond that were more chopper pads. We had an almost clear view of the curved half-mile long section of the Green-line road that passed the back of our compound. We watched the traffic of the guard details changing over at all of the six bunkers and five towers that we could see spread along the wide, mostly cleared perimeter. We watched as C-130s took off and landed at the airstrip. We couldn't help but notice them, since their landing glide path came right over our heads just before they touched-down on the wavering PSP runway. The roar overhead was quite tremendous, and we felt a momentary blast of heat from their engines as they reversed and applied the airbrakes just before landing.

Did I mention that Phouc Vinh was not a quiet place? Between the 105s next door and the 175s and 8"ers across the road we averaged at least six or seven fire-missions a day. When they were firing east or west or south, away from us it wasn't too bad, but when they changed their azimuths to north, and fired across us, man, especially the eight-inchers, they raised the dust in the streets and shook mirrors off the wall and books off shelves. Their 200-lb rounds creating a vacuum felt even at ground level, as they soared, roared overhead. It seemed I spent a lot of time popping my ears, though I'd been doing THAT since I'd been in country, anyway. It didn't really bother me, used as I was to the din of a firebase, but the other guys kept bringing my attention to it by complaining of the noise.

This is not to mention the helicopters continually buzzing and whopping about everywhere. There was, it seemed, a huge volume of traffic in and out of Phouc Vinh at all hours. It was somewhat quieter at night, but not much.

Anyway, we're sitting in home-made ammo box chairs on the roof, watching all this go on and eating Jim's LURPs, (I had chicken and noodles, which was as tasty or better than the spag w/ mt sce had been.) It was now full dark and I was enjoying the pin prick lights of the planes mingling with the stars and smoking an after dinner cig. Jim and Ralph were sipping cold cokes from their, (honest to God), refrigerator in their hootch. They were discussing, animatedly, the American involvement in the war or some such shit. It was about 2200 hours and I was just considering getting up and hitting the sack.

Out the corner of my eye I saw a bright flash in the distance, over by the airfield. I was just opening my mouth to yell 'Incoming', when we all heard the old familiar "KARRUMMP" of explosions. Out of sheer habit, I 'hit the dirt'. Then I realized I'm on a roof. By the time I got to the ladder on the end of the barracks, Ralph was halfway to the ground and Jim was starting down the ladder. While I waited my turn, I looked back toward the airstrip and saw three more blasts, each one a little closer to us than the last.

"I think they're walking 'em down th' airstrip!" I said over my shoulder as I started down to the ground.

"Which means that any 'short-rounds' will land around here!" Jim said

He pointed toward the culvert bunkers by the motor pool gate.

"Get yer War-shit an' c'mon down here, we'll be waiting."

I looked toward the green-line and in that instant I saw flashes and then the trails of at least four more rockets as they lifted up from the jungle and headed in.

"Shit, I saw 'em pop-off, man!" I grabbed Jim's arm, hard.

"What?" he said and looked where I was staring, but of course it was too late, the rockets were landing now and they were even closer than before, from their sound.

"I saw 'em pop-off," I repeated, "They're coming from out there," I pointed to the exact spot where I'd seen the launches, "'bout a click straight out from Tower November, in that real thick bunch of trees out past the road."

Jim told Ralph to go on to the bunkers and grabbed my arm and pulled me up the road yelling "C'mon, Mouse, we gotta tell the S-5 where th' gooks are so they can direct th' 105s in on 'em. C'MON, HURRY!"

We ran up the road and as we rounded the corner of the NCO hootch, we saw the S-5 jeep careening out the front gate on two wheels, on their way to view the first impact holes to determine what azimuth the rockets came in on.

"Shit, they're gone a'ready!" Jim said and stopped. "We needed to tell th' Survey guys where th' rockets came from so they c'n tell the Arty where to shoot!"

I thought about this for a second, then said, "Why don't we tell 'em ourselves?"

"Hell yeah!" He grabbed my arm again and drug me to the TOC and through the door where Bowers and Fuk were sitting, talking quietly on two separate radios. The Lt. in charge got up and asked what we wanted.

I explained and, on a big map showing a detailed grid section of the Phouc Vinh area, I pointed out the spot where I'd observed the incoming fire. The officer thanked us, wrote down the co-ordinates on a slip of paper, and handed it to Fuk who grinned at me while Bowers gave me a thumbs-up. They got on the radios and started relaying the position to whoever, and, feeling like we'd really done something, we went back out into the street, where the sirens were now howling and 'lume rounds were up all the way around the perimeter. And where the rockets were still falling, the last two falling across the road just beyond the 175 unit lit up the area and Jim and I dodged back down the road to join Ralph and probably some other guys in the relative safety of the bunkers. As we passed my hootch, I told Jim to go on and I'd be right there after I got my 'War Shit', and I ducked into my room and grabbed my pot and flack-jacket and my rifle and bandolier, AND my gas mask. (Ya never know!)

Seconds later I emerged from my door and had run maybe fifteen feet when I heard, "SwoooOOOSH...KARRUM_BLAM!!!" and the world lit up seemingly just on the other side of the NCO hootch from me. "OH SHIT!" I must have yelled as I skidded face first to the ground, and my stomach was pummeled by the concussion. Dirt and debris rained down on me for a few seconds, then I was back on my feet running full tilt down the road. Fear put wings on my feet and as I passed the gap between the NCO hootches and the shower shack, I glanced left between them and saw the rear quarter of the mess hall in flames. 'WHOA!' I thought and somehow managed to run even faster.

I entered the bunker like a runner sliding into home plate. Jim, Ralph, Sgt. Holly and four more guys I didn't know were there. I heard the 105s finally let loose with their first salvo of six guns, all, I hoped, aimed directly at those little gooks out there that were causing all this shit. I heard a very satisfying series of explosions outside the wire, and hoped to hell they'd killed every single one of them.

"Jesus, man, did you see what got hit?" Jim asked as I leaned up against the curved wall, breathing heavily.

I told them, between gasps, about the mess hall.

"Shit! There goes chow!" somebody said in the dark.

"How bad, Hudson?" Holly asked.

"Well, it's on fire." I replied.

Holly thought for a minute, then said, "Lynch, you Hudson and Ralph get out th' portable pump. Th' one that's under th' tarp under th' workbench in th' service tent. And get all the rolled hose, intake and outlet, we've got. Get it ready to load into whatever vehicle I can get to first and I'll be there in a minute. Got that?"

We all nodded and Jim asked, "What're we gonna do, Sarge?"

"We're gonna fight that fire, if we don't want to starve." Holly answered with a grin.

189

Between the three of us we had the pump and hoses out by the time Holly backed in driving my old jeep that had been parked next to his 'trailer'. We threw the equipment into the back and piled in wherever we could and the Sgt. spun the tires in the gravel as we went 'Hell Bent For Leather' to the now really flaming mess hall.

It wasn't just the mess, now, but also the wash house out back of there. The heat was intense as we pulled up within thirty feet of the inferno, approximately halfway between the wash house and the shower shack. Holly yelled for Ralph and me to roll out the intake hose and attach it to the water tanks on the back of the showers. Then attach the other end to the big pipe on the pump, with the wrench that was in the tool pouch on the side of the unit. I laid out the hose, shinned up the metal tower, (about 15'), and clamped the quick connecting fitting to the dump valve on the tank, which was holding about a thousand gallons of water. Ralph had the other end secured by this time, and Jim had the high-pressure outlet hose attached and Holly was manning the nozzle, I could see in the flickering light of the blaze.

"Hot damn, I always wanted to be a fireman!" I yelled, as I cranked-on the valve and I heard the water slooshing through the hose.

Ralph pulled the rope and started the pump and Holly lurched with the sudden pressure, but got it under control. He started systematically hosing the back of the main building, as the wash house was almost a total loss by now. Only the back room of the mess hall, where Carbone's office and the storage room was located, was fully engaged.

Less than five minutes of hosing, with the help of a couple of the cooks with extinguishers, and the flames were subsiding. Then they were out except for smoldering embers among the wreckage. The wash-house was burned-out now, too, but only because there was nothing left to burn. Acrid smoke blanketed the area stinging our eyes and making us cough.

I heard someone quip that it smelled "better'n some of Carbone's cookin'."

Somebody else hollered, "WHOOPS, burned th' beans again Carbone?"

A little 'Fireman Humor', I guess, but it was lost on the big hairy Mess Sgt. He was walking around yelling at everybody, pissed-off as hell.

At Holly's signal, I shut down the pump and in the ensuing quiet, my first thought was; 'Any more in-coming?' I listened for a full minute and there didn't seem to be any more explosions, either near or far.

Carbone finally quit fussing and came over to our little fire brigade and yelled, "Y'all done done it, boahs! Put it raght out! Thank yew, thank yew, boahs!"

He pumped Holly's hand like a pump handle and slapped us all on the back

"Y'all c'mone in heah an' see if I got 'ny coffee 'r somethin t' give yew fine boahs fer yer valiant efferts!"

He took Holly's shoulder and guided him, with the three of us behind, through the busted screen door on the side of the building. Inside, it was dark, smoky and smelly. The electricity was off and in the light of our torches, from the serving line back was a sooty, wet mess. (Well, it IS a 'mess' hall, I heard someone else say.)

Carbone launched into another tirade about "Them Yankee Gooks." meaning the North Vietnamese, I supposed. He alternated between ranting and praising us for five minutes or more, until Holly got us out of there to secure the equipment.

We rounded up our stuff, took it back to the pool, and stowed it. By that time it was 12:30 A.M. and I excused myself and went immediately to the shower to take advantage of what little water was left to clean the smoke smell off me. The CQ came around and told me, just as I was getting ready for bed, there was a red alert on 'til further notice, but exhausted as I was, I ignored it and went ahead and racked-out. About 2:30, I was awakened by a fifteen minute burst of small-arms fire from the RVN side of the base. They had 'lume rounds up and it sounded like WW2 over there, but it petered out in a bit and I went back to sleep 'til 0700 when the CQ woke me as usual.

I reported to S-2, as usual, and, through eavesdropping on the radio traffic and tidbits of info gleaned from the S-2 guys, I learned that our base wasn't the only one hit last night.

Bien Hoa and surrounds, including Long Binh, had been subjected to a three hour long rocket and mortar barrage that caused considerable damage. A whole section of the city had been taken over by the VC and as of 9:30 A.M., they were still being routed out by house to house fighting.

Saigon hadn't gotten off unscathed, either. They'd had a number of rockets impact around the Air base and sapper units had caused some damage in several areas, but the, so far, sketchy reports didn't specify to what extent what was damaged.

RVN units on the southern perimeter of Phouc Vinh reported sappers in their wire at 0230 hrs., but no bodies had been found yet, so it was assumed, at least by me, that 'Marvin the ARVN' was just nervous and popping-off at shadows.

Thus passed the 'TET Offensive of 1970'.

We'd gotten off light, I was told, compared to the '68 and '69 TETs, when all the major bases were attacked and many soldiers, from both sides, had been killed.

On the drive to DIVARTY with the Lt. that morning, I was able to view some of the local damage from last night's attack.

Two helicopters were still smoldering in their revetments on a chopper pad we passed. Several storage warehouses on the Air base were sending huge, black clouds into the sky. An 8th Engineer unit was crawling all over the airstrip, patching holes in the PSP runway. Back at our unit, Sgt. Carbone was bossing the clean up on our mess hall, and had served a rudimentary breakfast even this morning. I'd had Frosted Flakes and powdered milk, myself. The smoke smell was still almost overpowering.

Lt. Cravens was chatty that morning and had told me of the situation in Bien Hoa, which reminded me of my proposed trip with Lynch today. I asked him if it would be all right for me to go, and, after a little thought, he said it would be OK, as all the roads between here and there were swept every morning, and surely, by noon it should be safe.

He was really pleased that I'd gotten the jeep running. (We were riding in it for the first time). I mentioned that the main reason I wanted to go with Lynch was so I could get the seats for the jeep upholstered. We were sitting on rubber ponchos folded over and tied onto the steel springs with string, which was far from comfortable.

He beamed.

"Well, by all means you may go, Hudson, and be sure not to get black or dark brown covers. Third degree burns can be gotten from dark seats left in the sun, so make them tan or lighter."

We returned to HQ at about 10:30, so I collected my combat gear at the hootch and piddled with the jeep in the motor pool until 12:30, when Lynch drove in a Deuce and hollered, "Let's go, Mouse!"

I grabbed my gear and climbed into the cab of the huge truck. I'd barely got sat down when Jim popped the clutch and we roared out of the pool. Hanging on in the swaying cab, I said, "Hey, Jim, is this trip a good idea, man, what with all th' shit happenin' in Bien Hoa, an' all?"

"Good idea or not, those parts have to be picked up today, or th' Sarge is gonna pitch a bitch." He yelled over the engines roar, "It takes two hours to drive down, figure two hours there, including our side trip to the seat shop, an' two more hours back. So we'll hav'ta haul ass if we wanna be back here by dark. I DO wanna be back here by dark, how 'bout you?"

"By all means, driver, haul thy ass!" I replied.

19

ON THE ROAD

We barreled out of Phouc Vinh onto Highway Thirteen.

Jim's singing was loud but off key about a foot.

"Sounds like a country song, don't it?"

He was in a high ol' mood as he shifted through the gears and brought us up to speed, (about forty-five MPH), on the fairly smooth, but narrow road.

We'd passed through the gate and out of Phouc Vinh and into the countryside. The view on this stretch consisted of a 200' plain of sawgrass about four feet tall on either side of the road, then trees. Tall trees, 60 to 100' tall. I could see that there didn't seem to be any undergrowth beneath them and they were growing in even rows, and evenly spaced apart. This seemed odd so I commented on it.

"Rubber trees, man." Jim said, reaching out and raising his side of the flip-up windshield, letting the wind blow full on him on this hot day.

I said "Yeah?" as I did the same. 'Man, that feels good' I thought, 'Smells better, too.' The air out here was considerably fresher, without the diesel/shit tinge of the bases.

"Yeah, this was part of th' Michelin Plantation when th' Frenchies were here."

"Michelin, like in tires?" I asked, studying the trees closer. They had a whitish, smooth bark, and what foliage they had, smallish yellow-green leaves, was all on the top third of the tree, leaving the straight trunks, maybe two feet in diameter, bare for fifty feet or more.

"Sure, yeah, tires an' stuff." he nodded.

"I've got a set of Michelins on my VW back home." I said.

"They might've come from one of those trees over there."

"Wow! That's weird, man." I said kind of in awe.

There wasn't much traffic on the road, just some Lambrettas loaded with goods headed for Phouc Vinh. Shortly we came upon a broke-down gook bus, painted bright yellow with red, green and blue decorations. It was sitting half off the road with its hood up and surrounded by Mama-sans, Baby-sans, pigs and chickens. The passengers, I presumed. The driver tried to wave us down but Jim only shook his head and peace-signed him and drove around him speeding up again. The drivers curses, (or I took them to be curses, in Vietnamese I couldn't tell but the tone was right), faded off behind.

"Couldn't we have stopped to help him?" I asked.

"Man, I don't stop for nothin' out on th' road, 'cept maybe Boom-Boom Girls. Th' Dinks get you to stop an' you're a sittin' duck for whatever kinda ambush they wanna pull, from a command-detonated bomb to a cute li'l girl with a nice grenade for the GIs. Don't even slow down if you don't know th' situation. A moving target is much harder to hit." He advised.

Seemed like a pretty cynical outlook, to me, but I deferred to his road-savvy, he seemed perfectly comfortable driving around in a possibly hostile environment, and what he said made sense. I certainly didn't want to get killed for helping-out a stranded motorist.

Ten miles farther down the highway I first saw a sign on the right that said 'Phouc Hoa', then the village itself. We went straight through at a slower pace due to the chickens and baby-sans in the road. It was mostly tin or wood huts with grass thatch roofs. Nothing distinctive, just an average gook ville.

We're past the village now and the trees and brush have closed up right on the shoulder of the road to the point of brushing my rear-view mirror. It's cooler and dark in here and a little spooky since this is my first actual jaunt out among the populace, but Jim is still singing, in the key of M, 'Little Old Lady from Pasadena'. Jan and Dean or the Beach Boys, I think. He seems perfectly comfortable, and the breeze coming in through the windshield is wonderful, smelling like a musty forest, so I relax and enjoy the ride.

A quarter mile on we round a tight, right curve and the road widens out approaching a steel suspension bridge over a wide river. To the right of the bridge is a strip of open space alongside the road, like a parking area under the trees. Parked there are two APCs with several GIs walking around and a group of Vietnamese girls in Ao Dai's, their motor scooters parked in a row behind the APCs. They 're talking animatedly to the soldiers who are smiling and aping around as soldiers do around girls the world over.

"Pepsi-Girls an' Boom-Boom Girls." Jim commented.

"Pretty Girls!" I rubber necked them as we passed. Then I turned back to Jim and said, "You mean you can get laid, right out here along th' road?"

"Well, back in th' bushes, anyway, but, sure! I'd stop if we had more time."

"Damn!" I said in awe and took a final, longing look in the mirror as they passed out of sight behind some trees.

'What a wonderful country!' I thought.

"I've been down here before," Jim said, "an, th', girls are usually pretty clean. You c'n get screwed, buy dope, Pepsi, an' lord knows what-all from those pretty li'l girls. And, you c'n swim in th' river, if you don't mind th' leeches."

He chuckled, as I looked over and shivered.

The bridge had a steel grating roadbed that sang under our tires and a sign on an overhead girder that said 'SONG BE'. The span had once been painted blue but was peeling heavily with wide rusty streaks and patches. The yellow-green color and the fishy smell of the river reminded me of the Kentucky River, where we used to fish and swim when I was a kid. The bridge even kind of looked like the one on old US 68 that crossed the Ky. just below Harrodsburg. Of course, here, instead of soaring limestone palisades on the banks, like back-home, we had scrub jungle that hung thickly out over the river, creating deep shadows in the eddies of the murky water.

We rumbled through another quarter-mile 'tunnel' of thick jungle and suddenly emerged onto a broad plain of rice paddies and fields of grass. The paddies were dry now, but their mud dikes still delineated the boundaries of each area that was flooded during the rice-growing season, I supposed, if there was such a thing. The paddies seemed to stretch for miles in every direction, and the land was so flat you could SEE for miles in every direction. The day was bright, sunny with little puffy clouds and I was enjoying 'sight-seeing' for the first time in RVN. But of course, every silver lining has a cloud in it.

The next town on our little map that was clipped to the dash was PHU GAIO, but before we got there we passed a large cemetery on the right. It was surrounded by a low stone wall that was crumbling in places, and had many aboveground crypts, made of stone or cement, that looked very old. Some were pagoda-like structures while others looked similar to our own mausoleum-type tombs and all were grown-up in ivy or creepers that draped like shrouds around the pointy terraced roofs and hung down over doors. I was surprised to see a few Christian crosses and some Catholic shrines among the statuary, but they were obviously much newer than their Buddhist neighbors and were not as overtaken by foliage. I thought this pretty neat so I snapped a few pictures with my Ansco camera, which I had remembered to bring at the last moment.

I saw the ornate, stone entry gate coming up and was all set to take another snapshot, when I noticed a group of tough-looking RVN soldiers, dressed in their tailored 'Tiger-stripe' fatigues and full battle gear. They were standing next to a pile of, maybe six or seven, bodies of, I presumed, VC from their black pajamas and the stack of AK-47 rifles that lay beside them. I was shocked for a minute and forgot to take my picture until we were on past. The RVNs were taking turns posing for their own cameras, and as we rumbled by, one was holding one of the dead guys by the hair, raising his face so it was visible in the shot, and mugging a big smile.

"Wow, what a great memento to show th' grand-kids when he's older." I commented.

"Yeah," Jim sneered, "Th' RVN Marine Rangers are some really tough dudes, or THEY think so, anyway."

Now I felt strange sightseeing in a country where people, from both sides, died every day along the very road we were travelling. It sort of took the gleam off the day for me and we rode quietly for the next couple miles, 'til we went through PHU GAIO and turned left onto a hard-packed, but unpaved road.

We had to reduce speed, as the road was not as smooth as the highway had been and we jounced along at thirty-five to forty MPH. Jim reached out and pulled the throttle setting knob on the dash and said,

"Hey, Mouse, slide over here and take th' wheel for a minute."

Hesitantly, I eased over and grasped the wheel, which was jerking with the bumps in the non-pavement, in my left hand. Worried, I said, "Man, I don't think I can hold it very long!"

"Jus' long enough for me to step out an' take a leak. Hold 'er steady now!" he grinned.

I grabbed the wheel with both hands from the middle of the wide bench seat and held on as he opened the driver's door and stepped out onto the running board and pissed a stream into the wind blowing past us.

I managed to hold a straight course for the thirty or so seconds it took for him to climb back in and take over for me.

"AHHH!" he sighed as he settled back into the drivers seat, "First wet pavement they've had 'long here for a while."

"Did'ja ever think 'bout stoppin' and findin' a bush?" I asked as I slid back to my place on the passenger side.

"All th' bushes along here got gooks in 'em," he replied, "so I jus' piss on 'em as we go by."

I shrugged and went back to watching the countryside go by. There wasn't much to watch along here, though. Flat grassland stretched to the horizon with only occasional trees or clumps of bamboo to break the monotony.

We roared past CHA BUNG, TAN PHU and several side roads before we came to a triple fork in the road. At the fork we took the middle road, crossed another river on a concrete bridge, (the Song Dong Nai), and entered a forest of huge trees. The road actually wound between the trees, with very little undergrowth beneath the dark canopy of green that spread above. The air was refreshingly cool on my face.

On my side, I saw a huge, old Vietnamese truck parked way back among the trunks, partially loaded with giant sawed logs. Next to the truck appeared to be a camp-site and not far away was a group of men, (Lumber-gooks, Jim called 'em), working with a big ol' hand saw with handles at both ends, pushing and pulling it back and forth. The saw was about a quarter of the way through the five-foot diameter tree that they were cutting.

"Takes 'em about a week to saw through and fell a tree," Jim explained, "then another week to dress it an' load it. All for about 200-300 dollars that gets split however-many ways. They'll sell it to an exporter in

Saigon, an' he'll sell it to a company in th' US or Europe and by the time it reaches th' retailers, that log's worth probably ten thousand dollars."

"Hell of a mark-up!" I said.

"That's Asian Teak, one of the most valuable woods in th' world."

Another two miles along we turned again, right, on an even smaller dirt track that wound through sparse scrub jungle. We eventually ended up at a small village named TAN PHU. It was located on the picturesque Song Dong Nai River. Not really THE river, it was a tributary, small and muddy with a rickety wooden bridge spanning the stream. It really wasn't very picturesque, either, at one close look. The open trench sewer ran down both sides of the road within ten feet of the front doors of the huts, and as far as I could tell, ran straight into the sluggish waters of the river. Women were washing clothes, beating them on the rocks along the far bank, in the water of that river, but I WILL say, they at least had the good sense to do it upstream of the trenches, even if only by twenty feet or so. YUK!

Jim guided the truck through the 'down-town' section and turned right on a road that paralleled the waterfront, such as it was. A few spindly wharves with three sampan boats tied to them, and metal shacks with Vietnamese signs, probably proclaiming the equivalent of 'Joes Fish Market'. We pulled up in front of a faded pink stucco building with double garage doors that faced the river across the street. The prevalent smell in the whole area was the sewers, and the constant buzzing of flies was the loudest sound, almost drowning out the lap-lap of the river.

Jim jumped down from the driver's side, and I crawled over the rail into the bed from my side and handed down the two steel jeep seats we'd loaded in Phouc Vinh. I burned my hands on the hot, freshly painted, metal. I jumped down and we carried the seats into the shady garage bays where a Papa-san named 'Loy' or 'Loi' greeted us with nods of his head.

He said, "He'p?"

I explained what I wanted and he showed me a bundle of rather dirty material samples, from which I picked a tan Naugahyde and a brown piping that I thought, and Jim agreed, looked rather snazzy. Loy or Loi grinned widely, constantly ducking his head until Jim and I were doing it, too.

"Ten dollah down, you come back fi' day, ten dollah you pick up seats, yes?"

I agreed, slipped him his 'ten dollah' in piasters, (gooks weren't allowed MPC except for work on the bases), and we left on the road we came in on. We turned right again on the main road, and within eight miles we were entering the west side of Bien Hoa City. We ran alongside the Song Dong Nai River for about three miles, into the 'City' itself.

Shacks on stilts, wharves, some warehouses, old and rusty, sampan flotillas and a few large boats covered almost every square foot of water and bank area along that whole stretch. Traffic was bumper to bumper with jeeps, trucks, Lambrettas, motor bikes, bicycles and pedestrians, with the occasional water buffalo-drawn cart to make sure we didn't go too fast, so I took some pictures of the 'Local Color', of which there was much.

We bypassed the main part of the city by taking HWY. 51, a real four-lane concrete road, to the south to the turn-off for Long Binh. We entered the huge base through the south gate and drove across the, typical-looking military mega-base, to the 1/30th Service Battery, located almost on the northeast edge. Luckily, Jim knew the way, 'cause I couldn't have found it with a map and a psychic.

We arrived at 3:00, and while the service battery guys were getting our requisition together and loaded on the truck, Jim and I walked to a nearby PX and got some snacks, cokes, cigs, and stuff. On the way back stopped at an ice-cream stand, (CAN YOU BELIEVE IT?), and got those little cups of vanilla with the cardboard tops like we used to get in elementary school, complete with the little wooden spoons. I sucked my spoon and I don't remember that plain ice cream tasting that good, ever! It was so cold it made my sinuses hurt.

By the time we got back, the truck was loaded and ready to go, so, Jim signed the REQ- orders and we headed out, back to ol' PV. We left out the north gate this time and soon were jouncing along the road past the Tan Phu turn-off and at 4:30, we crossed the Song Dong Nai Bridge, headed north through the waving grasslands, where I learned to piss off MY running board.

Jim, a real talker, and I, (no slouch either), shot-th'-shit the whole way, aided somewhat, by a big joint that he'd brought along. After that, we snarfed a bunch of those snacks we'd bought at the PX. Anyway, the time passed quickly.

Lynch was the type of guy who gets to know a lot of stuff, by knowing the right people to ask the right questions of, at the right time. He told me, the next time we come south to Bien Hoa, he'd heard of a USO club in a place called 'Zee ON', or 'Zion' or something like that, that served steaks and French fries. He didn't know exactly where it was, but it was supposed to be somewhere close to the road to Bien Hoa.

He also told me the best places to get laid in Phouc Vinh Ville, where to buy opium in Dong Xuai Ville, about the Boom-Boom girls at the Song Be bridge, and all about his 'Ultimate Plan' to steal an entire motor pool tool-set, and ship it home, piece by piece, so he could open a custom car shop when he got back to the world. He already had a complete set of sockets and a ratchet handle at home, (according to his brother's last letter), that he had mailed in three packages, marked 'Souvenir goods. He'd wrapped the stuff in aluminum foil to disguise their shapes, and had marked them 'Shrapnel' on the forms.

The sun was red on the horizon when we crossed the Song Be bridge. The girls were not there this time. I guessed they were home changing into their black pajamas, for their night jobs as VC-ettes.

At 6:30 we pulled in through the gates of Phouc Vinh. We drove straight to the motor pool in our unit compound and parked the truck next to the tent for unloading in the morning. Jim signed-off on the 'Trip-Tic' and turned it in to Sgt. Holly, who was really pleased to have the truck-load of parts, not to mention the 'Rum-Soaked Crooks' cigars Jim had got him from the 'Big PX'.

"Points, man," Jim commented as we walked out the gate, "they never hurt, an' ol' Holly's a good guy, for a lifer wanna-be." He chuckled.

We caught the tail end of chow, (cold beef stew), at the partially repaired mess hall. Afterward, as the twilight settled into deep purple, we decided to go to the old bunker and check-out who was doing what.

Terry L. Weitzel and some guy named Randy were there smoking when we arrived. The bowl came around to us a couple of times before Ralph showed up with Fukijima in tow.

"I didn't know you smoked, man," I said to Fuk, "Does Bowers smoke, too?"

201

"Oh no, man." He flashed me his glow-in-the-dark smile, "Bowers is one straight dude, man. He doesn't smoke, drink, screw-around or up. Lifers love him, but he's cool, he don't ask an' I don't tell."

The bowl passed us again and he turned to me and asked, "Where you from, Mouse?"

"Kentucky, man."

"Wow, you guy's grow horses on farms an' shit?"

I laughed, "Yeah, sorta."

"You a jockey or something?"

He looked down from his 6'2" at my 5'5".

"Naw, man, I can't stand horses, but I worked on horse farms in my early teens. Good pay, but those thoroughbreds are some mean horses. They'd as soon step on you or bite you as look at you and you don't dare mistreat one. They cost more'n you'll make in a lifetime."

"Yeah, I imagine! I'm from Hawaii, small village, and suburb of Honolulu. I worked in a swim-suit shop on th' beach an' played in a band."

"Yeah, I saw your pictures on the wall in th' hootch. MAN, some good lookin' chicks!"

He nodded, smiling, "Man, they're everywhere, an' all lookin' for real Hawaiian dude to make love to on th' beach at sunset. It's great, man."

"You play that guitar?" I asked Fuk, but Jim spoke up from his place on Fuk's left.

"He sure does! He knows Peter, Paul an' Mary songs an' a buncha Simon an' Garfunkle stuff. Him'n Terry, here, get together sometimes an' jam. Terry plays th' Harmonica. He's good, too!"

"Hey, Fuk," Terry interjected, "I got a new harp from home th' other day. Why don't you come down later an' we'll play some tunes, man."

"Yeah, sure, cool, man." Fuk replied, "I got th' evening off 'cause Bowers's breakin' in a new guy to replace him next month, so I'll come for a while."

"Ok if I come, too?" I asked, "I was a trumpet player in bands back home, an' I can play guitar a little, but I'd really like to learn, like, some more songs an' stuff."

"Ha! Sure, man," Terry boomed, seemingly unconcerned that we're smokin' dope here. Fuk shushed him and he continued in a whisper, 'C'mon down with Fuk, man, we c'n re-lax on th' couch an' pick 'n grin."

"You got a couch?" I asked, incredulously.

The 'couch' turned out to be a warped 4' x 8' piece of 3/4 plywood, curved its entire length nearly ninety degrees. The 'back' was nailed to the hootch wall outside their room, and the 'legs' were concrete blocks under the 'seat'. It was surprisingly comfortable for four or five guy's to lounge back into the curve, but lack of padding was a concern for my skinny butt.

Fuk brought his 'ax', as he called it, and Terry brought out his harp and they played mostly blues, but some folk songs, for an hour or so. Jim and I brought some of the snacks we'd bought at the PX today, and those disappeared quickly among six guys.

Fuk let me play his guitar and I blasted out with my version of 'Summertime... an' th' livin' is easy.', my best tune. Terry played a good solo and I sang one verse and Fuk sang the other. We harmonized on the 'hush pretty baby, do-o-o-n't you ca-ry...' part.

We laughed as the other guy's applauded, and I handed the 'ax' back to Fuk.

He clapped me on the shoulder and said, "Hey, wow, man! You're pretty good." He thought a second then said, "Listen, I'm going on R&R in a week, to Japan to see my Honorable relatives. I could, maybe, pick you up a guitar an' bring it back, an we could play all th' time, OK?"

"Wow, sure, man," I said, somewhat overwhelmed, "I mean, if it's not too much trouble. An' if you c'n find one that's pretty good and not too ... you know... expensive."

And so it was, two weeks later Fuk returned from R&R, much partied-out and broke, but with a nice looking, and sounding, Japanese guitar for the equivalent of twenty six American bucks. It had a label inside, written in Japanese that he translated for me that said 'YAMAHA', Made in Tokyo.

"Don't they make, like, motorcycles?" I asked.

"Yeah, but guitars, too." He said, "I'll meet you at Jim's hootch after chow an' we'll jam some before I have to go to work. OK?"

"Sure, OK!"

New Guitar Man

In the past two weeks, since it looked like I'd be here for a while, after all, I'd bought a Sony reel to reel tape player/recorder, along with several pre-recorded tapes and some blank ones, at the Phouc Vinh PX.

I brought it down to Jim's to record our jam session, but every time we'd get something good going with the tape running, the 105s would open up next door with a fire-mission, and blow the recording. We had fun, though, and I learned a lot from just watching his fingers as they literally flew up and down the fretboard.

Weitzel and Ralph showed up late and we sat around talking after Fuk went off to work.

"I'm th' craziest dude in this whole unit!" Weitzel crowed, "I'm gonna make these lifers think I'm so crazy, they gonna let me out o' this green Mutha' on a 612 discharge. 'Un-fucking- acceptability to military life', an', man, do I find military life un- acceptable."

"I think that's 'Un-adaptability', Jon-Jon." I added.

"Whatever," he waved me off, "I'm gonna burn shit an' volunteer for all th' really shit details. I'll bad-mouth any lifer that gets in my face. When I get through, they'll think I'm so nuts, I'm dangerous, an' they'll let me out."

Terry and me looked at each other and grinned.

"But… you'll still be doin' all th' shit-work, man." Ralph said, thoughtfully, "Why'nt ya jus' pick a fight with a NCO 'r somethin'. 'R jus' shoot yerself in th' foot, 'r puke on th' first Sgt.," he giggled, "like Mouse, here, did!" Maybe Ralph wasn't as dim as we'd suspected.

"Oh, no, man, I'm not givin' 'em a excuse to lock me up or ship me out! An' I SURE ain't gonna damage MY precious skin t' satisfy them fuckin' lifers. Hell no! I'm gonna do what they tell me t' do, but in a way that'll blow their lifer minds!"

The BS was still flying when I left at midnight. I carried my guitar and tape machine back to my hootch and conked out shortly after.

The next couple days were spent mostly on the jeep, after my morning duties with the LT, and the little vehicle was starting to look military, with its new (to me) top, bumpers, and many more parts that I'd managed to scrounge from several different sources. I'd even tried my hand at stealing, and found I had a penchant for it. I snagged a passenger side rear-view mirror off a Colonels jeep that was parked next to me at DIVARTY, one morning, with the driver snoozing inside at the wheel. Two little screws quietly removed with my Phillips-head screwdriver, while I was still seated in my vehicle, and, "You snooze, you lose, buddy."

To dress the jeep up a little and to cover up some rust spots on the windshield frame, I painted a small Cav patch on the left side of the flat panel under the glass, a 'Striving to the Highest' unit crest on the right, and the name 'HEY JUDE' in the middle. The name was in honor of my Ex-girlfriend, Judy. She was an EX, but she was the only girl in my life, and besides, I still had all her scantily clad pictures, which I still enjoyed.

My Jeep

One afternoon, the LT needed to go to the Service Battery in Long Binh, so we left at 12:30 and drove the same route Jim and I had followed. We also sidetracked at Tan Phu and picked up the newly up-holstered seats from 'Mr. He'p' for the balance of 120 piasters. He did a great job on them with the light tan vinyl and dark brown piping and, most of all, the new padding! The Lt. and I immediately stripped off the tied-on ponchos and gave the old rusty seat frames to Mr. Loy-Loi, and we smiled and sighed as we sat on them for the first time.

"Oh, my," he grinned, "that beats the hell out of having a spring up my ass!"

As we turned back onto the main road to Bien Hoa, I brought up the subject of the USO club at some town named Zee On, or something, and how nobody seemed able to find it.

"We passed the turn-off a ways back, before we turned off to Tan-Phu, Hudson."

I asked him to point it out to me on the way back, and he did. It was marked with a sign that said 'Di An', with an arrow pointing down a road to the left.

He saw my perplexed look, and explained to me that in Vietnamese, 'D' is pronounced 'Z', as in 'Diem', and 'A' is 'AHH'.

"In fact, Hudson, since it's," he looked at his watch, "5:30, and near supper time, let's go and check out this USO club."

"Sure, sir!" I answered readily, and turned onto the little road. In less than a quarter mile we crossed a railroad track, (the first of those I'd seen in country), and entered a large hamlet of probably 2-3000 people. Right at the edge of town sat a (swear to God) brick, Greek Revival building with four tall, Corinthian columns across the wide front porch and a big sign over the side-lighted door that read 'DI AN USO'.

The Lt. said, "This must be the place." as I swung the jeep into an empty parking place alongside several other jeeps in the shade next to the porch.

Even before we got out of the vehicle, we heard strains of music, obviously live, coming from the tall open windows of the club, and the aroma of BBQ and grilling steak assailed our noses.

"This is SURE th' right place, sir!" I said, my mouth already watering like one of Pavlov's dogs.

As we walked up to the front door, I held back a minute and the LT looked back and said, "Is something wrong, Hudson?"

"Well...sir... I've never... uhh... dined, you know, with an officer, or anything, I mean... is it OK, an' all?"

"In a USO club, we're all like civilians, sort of," he explained, "Unless you're too good to eat with me."

"Oh, no, sir" I blurted, "For a steak, I'd eat with ANYBODY!"

"Say what?" He laughed.

"Oh hell, sir, you know what I mean, don't you?" I stammered, embarrassed.

"Yeah, come on Hudson, let's get us some of that food, and listen to some dinner music while we eat!" He led the way.

Inside it was cool and rather dark. We were in a large entry hall with a curving staircase to the upper regions of the former plantation house on the right, and a wide doorway on the left leading into a large ballroom filled with small tables for four on a highly polished linoleum floor. In the large room it was much lighter, due, in part, to the sun streaming in through the 12' tall open windows at either end in combination with the 20' tall ceiling with the improbable florescent lights hanging down. The far wall was mostly taken up by a stage, raised about three feet above the floor, and a small hardwood dance floor off to the right side. Some twelve or thirteen soldiers, and some Americans in civilian clothes, were seated at the tables in groups of two or three, all either eating or drinking and all watching a Sgt. E-5 dance with a very ugly, but smiling USO girl.

They were twirling merrily to a rendition of Nancy Sinatra's 'These Boots Are Made For Walkin', sung squeakily, by a tiny Thai girl with a heavy accent. She was dressed in the tightest, shortest, red leather or vinyl mini-dress I'd ever seen. Almost all the soldiers at the stage front tables were mesmerized trying to see the remaining two inches up her skirt as she gyrated above them. I can tell you, she wasn't hired for her singing voice.

The band providing the surprisingly good music behind her, a seven piece group comprised of drums, lead and bass guitars, an electronic keyboard of some kind, and a trumpet, sax and trombone, was all little Thai guys. They had slick, longish black hair, all sported tiny pencil thin mustaches, (except li'l Nancy), and were dressed in silk balloon- sleeved shirts in riotous psychedelic colors, and red vinyl pants that were as tight or tighter than li'l Nancy's skirt. They were really rockin' through a sax solo while Nancy gyrated on stage ala Tina Turner, affording all the soldiers wide open shots at what she was wearing or not wearing under her skirt.

The LT and I walked along the inner wall to a pass-through window, set into the wall about halfway the length of the room, where a sign said 'Order Food Here'. Alongside the window was a painted menu board offering hamburgers, hot dogs, steak, three kinds of potato chips, French fries, soft drinks and beer. We both ordered the steak and fries and walked to a table at the edge of the dance floor and sat down with sweaty cold cans of Bud, to await our food.

The band wrapped up 'Boots' with a flourish and Nancy was bowing low repeatedly, during the drawn-out last chord, allowing looks DOWN her low cut dress and eliciting a pretty rousing applause from the audience.

208

We clapped, too, and sipped our cold brews, and the band switched to 'Blood, Sweat and Tears', 'God Bless The Child', sung by a little oriental David Clayton Thomas, in a tie-dyed T-shirt and tight, ragged bell bottom jeans. He was really good, even with his accent, and the horn section had it down. I was surprised and pleased. I had not expected ANYTHING like this, and expressed it to the LT. As we watched the USO girl select another reluctant partner from the crowd to dance, practically dragging him out to the middle of the floor and prancing around him, forcing him to move, if only in circles.

"This is quite nice, Hudson." The LT said, grinning at the antics of the hapless victim on the dance floor.

"Better'n some of th' places I used to play in th' States." I commented.

"Oh?" he asked, "You're a musician?"

"Yes, sir, a trumpet player. I played in big bands and rock bands back home in Kentucky."

"I thought Kentucky was known for 'Bluegrass' music, Hudson, not Basie and Ellington."

"Not all of it, sir. Around Lexington and Louisville th' big thing, now, is R&B. You know, Otis Redding, Wilson Pickett, James Brown. In fact," I sipped my beer, "my last band was set up exactly like this one."

I nodded at the Thai band.

"Three piece brass, guitars and organ. We played at clubs all around and fraternity parties. We were better'n these guys."

I indicated the 'Nancyettes'. He laughed.

"You didn't have their accents to overcome."

"No, sir, but I've heard worse singers with lousier pronunciation than his."

David Clayton-san was just finishing up 'Gah Bress da Chile...' so we both hooted and clapped and the soldier on the dance floor dipped, and almost dropped, the USO girl. She, in the spirit of a real trooper, regained her balance, laughed, and shook his hand.

Our food came then, steaming hot on a real porcelain plate, with real silverware, (stainless, really). The aroma was almost overpowering. Steak, (cut unknown but who cared), smothered in onions, and another whole plate of fries heaped between us. We grinned at each other and dug-in as the band struck up a rather strange version of 'On Top of Old Smokey'.

"Quite a repertoire, too." I mused, around a mouthful.

We gobbled like a couple of field hands, not talking or even looking around for ten minutes. My concentration was completely taken by the total enjoyment of the slightly under-cooked meat and wonderfully greasy potato chunks, washed down with cold beer. AHHH, HEAVEN!

When finally there was nothing but some fat trimmings and a couple stray onion strings left on my plate, I looked up and realized the LT was already done and leaning back in his chair, watching the girl drag out another soldier to dance to Elvis', 'Are You Roansome Tonigh'. The music was good and the floorshow was better as the soldier stepped all over the girls white tennies with his muddy jungle boots. He had really gotten into his first female contact in probably months, and wanted to hold her close, but he kept trodding on her until she was holding him away stiff-armed and limping. The soldier kept apologizing, the whole crowd was laughing, and someone, one of his friends, I hope, yelled over the bedlam, "Don't kill 'er, Tommy, she ain't no VC!"

The song finally ended and with a final apology, he led her back to a chair and even offered to rub her feet for her, much to everyone's amusement, but she just smiled, refused, and fell back to rest a moment.

"That's probably harder work than we give her credit for." I mused.

"And more dangerous!" The LT added, still laughing.

The band shut down for a break and the LT stood up and asked,

"Another beer before we go Hudson?"

I had a buzz from the first one, so I told him, since I'm driving I'd better just have a coke.

He came back a couple minutes later with two beers.

"But, sir, I'm drivin..." I protested, as he set the sweaty can on the table in front of me.

"No you're not, Hudson, I've decided I'm going to drive us back to Phouc Vinh, so enjoy your beer."

"But, sir, you're th' officer, an' I'm s'posed to be your driver..." I began.

"I waited a long time for that jeep, and I don't see any reason I can't drive it!"

The Lt. obviously had a buzz, too. He seemed pretty happy.

I protested some more about how we could, Hell, I could, get in trouble....

"If anyone says anything, you have my permission to tell them I ordered you to let me drive and I'll take full responsibility, OK Hudson?"

"Well... OK, LT." I surrendered and drank my beer. If he wants to drive that bad, who am I to argue with an officer.

We literally swilled our beers and walked out to the parking area a few minutes later. The sun was almost down, but the air was still hot and muggy. The LT stood admiring the new seats, speaking more to himself than to me.

"Excellent! Excellent!"

He ran his hand over the smooth new vinyl and slid behind the wheel as I got in on the other side.

'Oh, man, th' Looie's got a buzz-on, too.' I thought to myself as he started up and backed carefully out of the space, smiling the whole while.

'Maybe he's not too bad...' my thought started.

He spun the tires in the gravel lot and took off like a bat out of hell, leapt the RR tracks, and flew down the road, winding up through the gears 'til we were going fifty MPH. (I wished I hadn't taken that forty-five MPH governor off the carburetor!)

We slid to a dusty halt at the highway and he looked over.

"Really runs well, Hudson, you've done a superb job on this!"

"Thanks, sir, but..."

I was thrown back in my seat as he swung left onto the pavement, accelerated through the gears, and soon had the jeep screaming along at sixty MPH on the straights and making some turns, I swear, on two wheels.

"GOING A LITTLE FAST, AREN'T YOU SIR?"

I yelled over the whining four cylinder.

"WE'VE GOT TO MAKE UP SOME TIME, HANSEN, IF WE"RE TO GET BACK TO PHOUC VINH BY DARK!" he screamed back, "BESIDES, THIS IS FUN, ISN"T IT?"

I wasn't sure how much fun it would be to run into a tree or flip over at fifty to sixty MPH, but he seemed to be handling it expertly, so I just shut-up and held on.

We'd just passed the sign for Phouc Hoa and rounded a curve when we both saw an obstruction in the road ahead and I yelled.

"ROAD BLOCK, SIR!"

I was glad the jeep had brand-new brakes as the LT stomped them and brought us to a sliding sideways halt within feet of the two MP jeeps that were nose to nose across the road. We showered dirt on two burly MPs that were standing, arms crossed by the vehicles.

"OH, Oh!" I said.

"OH, Oh!" the LT said almost simultaneously.

The MP, a SSG in a white helmet and arm band, walked slowly over to the drivers side and checked us out, noticing, I'm sure, our re-spective ranks.

"Sir," he began, "I just got a radio call from a MP post down at Phu Gaio. They said a jeep went by there so fast, they didn't even have time to get on the road before it was gone. That wouldn't, by chance, have been you, would it?" His sarcasm was thick.

"Uh, yes, sergeant, probably was. But we're late getting back to Phouc Vinh and I was trying to make-up time." the LT explained, rather lamely.

"Is there an emergency, sir?" the Sgt. wanted to know.

"Well...no, Sgt. We were, I mean I was in a hurry."

"Is this vehicle signed-out to you, sir?" he asked.

I spoke up, "I'm the assigned driver for th' LT, sergeant, but I was... I mean we were....." he didn't let me finish, which is good because I had no idea what I was going to say.

"Then why is the Lieutenant driving, and driving badly, I might add?"

"Well...I..."

Lt. Cravens cut me off.

"Sergeant, I ordered Hudson to let me drive to make better time going back to base. If there's a problem, I'll take full responsibility."

"You certainly will, sir," the MP stated, pulling a pad out of his pocket, "You'll get th' ticket."

He filled out the form and had the LT sign it and admonished us to "Slow down" and "Let your driver drive you, sir, it's th' ARMY way."

The LT nodded and we switched seats before I drove off at a sedate thirty-five MPH all the way back to Phouc Vinh.

Along the way I commented, "Who'd of thought you'd get a speeding ticket in Vietnam?"

The LT shook his head and said, "Who'd of thought, indeed."

20

BACK TO THE FIELD

The last week of February, 1970, started off strangely anyway. It rained. Hard. Also, the daily temperature was lower, too, only 90-95° during the day, instead of 100-105°; a real 'cool' snap. But of course, every silver lining has a cloud in it.

On Wednesday of that week, I was in the motor pool, as usual, fiddling with the jeep. Sgt. Jackson, the E-6 from Survey, appeared in the service tent and announced that Ralph, Jim and I had 'volunteered' for a 'sandbag detail' out on a LZ the next day and we were to report to the CP at 0630 sharp.

"But Sarge…" we protested.

He held up both hands for silence.

"It's only for th' day, ya lazy asses." (His favorite term for enlisted men.)

"You'll fill them bags for th' gun crews, an' leave them time t' do other shit. Then YOU pukes'll come back t' your cozy hootches, an them 'Bunnies' gotta stay out there. Least ya c'n do is help 'em build some bunkers t' get in out th' rain, now that th' season's comin' on!"

"Well, I've been there, an' I would've appreciated some help, too, so you can count me in." I said after a moments thought.

Jim and Ralph grumbled, but said they'd be there, too. Later, we found out that Terry Leonard, Weitzel and Jack Pagans, a guy from Survey, were going out, too.

"Gonna be a real party, with Terry an' Jon-Jon along." Ralph giggled.

Next morning a 0715, we were on a helicopter headed out to LZ Remagen IV, a new firebase near the 'Fishhook' area, west of An Loc.

We each carried our 'Basic Combat Load' of rifle, 500 rounds of ammo, canteen, poncho and liner, towel, mess kit and two C-rat meals. We each had a small rucksack for personal items, too. I had a couple pairs of dry socks wrapped in a plastic bag in my ruck, knowing what wet muddy feet feel like. I also had a couple of PX nutty-bars for energy.

Ralph and Jim had socks, an extra towel, and a couple extra Lurp packets.

Pagans was a new guy, never in the field before, and he'd brought some comic books and candy bars and was embarrassed when Terry made fun.

"We surer-n-shit ain't gonna have no time t' READ, dummy, an' them candy bars'll be puddles o' shit in plastic when th' heat hits 'em out here. HAW! What a ditz!"

What Terry said was true, but I felt bad for Pagans, as he just didn't know any better.

"Leave him alone, Terry, he'll learn this shit on his own, just like we did. An' whatta YOU got in your pack that'll save our asses in a fire-fight, huh?"

I couldn't help trying to irritate Terry, cause he irritated so easily.

"Man," he got all haughty, "I got th' most important piece o' equipment a soldier needs. I got my tape player an' my Jimi Hendrix tapes!"

"Oh, yeah!" Jim retorted, "Th' gooks are scared t' death of Jimi!"

"Wouldn't be a war without ol' Jimi!" Ralph joined in.

Turned out Jon-Jon had a clean, white T-shirt and a bag of dope in his ruck.

'Real useful shit, too.' I thought.

I warned him not to "smoke that shit in th' field, 'cause most guy's don't want some stoned-out dude who'll fuck-up if th' shit comes down."

Jon-Jon, his usual smart-ass self, called me a "tight-ass" but shut up when Jim and Ralph both agreed with me. And Ralph, an accomplished 'Doper', himself, said he'd kick Jon-Jon's ass if he caught him ripped.

Also on board the chopper were two pallets of empty sandbags and lots of shovels.

Oh, man!

Remagen IV was just a roundish clearing cut out of the jungle, and looked like many other crude LZs I'd seen. The Chinook set down in the middle of the clearing and we got off and muscled the pallets out the tail hatch onto the muddy, red ground, into which our boots sank two inches as soon as we stepped out. At least there was no dust in the monsoon season.

Being the 'Ranking' PFC of the group, I went off and found the 'CP' hole, for that's all it was so far, and was directed to an E-6 Engineer named Kelly who told us what we were to do. We were broken up into pairs and sent to different locations to fill bags for separate projects. Jim and I got the FDC bunker, and by 10:30, we'd filled enough to stack a four-foot tall wall around the hole. The 'Fill-pile' that came out of the hole was a mass of mud from the rains yesterday, and it was more like pouring it into the bags, than shoveling. We were soon covered head to toe with red slime that soon dried in the sun and became stiff, crumbling off our sweaty bodies and making our boots and fatigue pants weigh a ton.

Sgt. Kelly came by and watched us for a while and told us that 24 hours ago, this had been a solid jungle. His Engineer unit had worked all night clearing the LZ and now the six guns of 'B' battery were set up in the pits and firing missions as the berms and bunkers were constructed around them.

As we finished the FDC walls, Kelly came back and, with his back-hoe operator, began putting the roof beams in place to support the overhead, and sent us to the #1 pit to fill MORE bags to cover the hootch culverts. On the way we spotted Terry and Jon-Jon, covered, like we were in red mud, working on the #3 powder-store. Terry's tape player blasting 'All Along The Watchtower on the berm nearby. Pagans and Ralph were over by #6 doing the same thing.

216

Sandbag Detail

By 1600 that afternoon, we'd used up all the bags on the pallets and built two bunkers, Thirty-six culverts, and six powder stores. A hell of a day's work and we were all exhausted. The gun crews were appreciative, and slapped our backs before we flew out at 1630, back to Phouc Vinh.

I didn't envy those guys back there. Tonight, when the rains quit, about midnight, and every drip falling from a jungle leaf sounds like a whole bunch of other things, crawling around out in the bushes, they're going to be out there to hear it all. And they'll be as scared as I was, every night, for almost seven months. And they'll endure it, most of 'em, 'cause almost always, it's just a drip in the jungle. Almost always.

We landed in a rainstorm at Phouc Vinh, and our 3/4 ton truck that was at the pad waiting to take us back to the unit, didn't have a canvas over the back. By the time we rode the ¼ mile to the compound, we were drenched, and teeth-chattering cold, but at least most of the mud sluiced off us. The rain felt kind of good, even though the huge drops stung when they hit, and you had to look downward to keep from drowning.

We were dropped off at the CP and we all crawled off to our hootches. The mess hall had saved some chow for us, but Jim and I were the only ones to take advantage of it. Everyone else just stayed in their hootches. No party at the ol' bunker tonight. It was all I could do to just brush my teeth and crawl into the rack by 8:00. I slept like the dead.

Next morning, I reported to S-2, drove the LT around and when we returned, Rojeski, the S-2 specialist, told me I had to report to the First Sgt. for a 'Special Detail'.

Walking down, I wondered, 'Special Detail? Oh, man, what now?'

Of course I expected the worst, but actually, Top wanted to tell me that the Battery Commander had admired my artwork on the jeep windshield, the Cav patch and Unit crest, and wanted to know if I'd paint some on his. I told him "Sure!" if I could get some more paint and maybe a better brush or two. Top wrote a note and told me to give it to the Sgt. in supply "an' jis tell 'im what yew wont. We gonna keep th' Cap'n happy, boah." Miracle of miracles, I actually got something I wanted from the supply room.

I spent the rest of the day masking and painting on the BC's jeep and when I finished up at 1430, and Capt. Johnson admired it with a smile, he gave me the rest of the day off.

Not wanting to hang around HQ and maybe get sucked into another detail, I went out on the main road and thumbed a ride on a Deuce to the PX. While there I ran into Tabaranza, the BC's driver. He was driving the Captains jeep with my artwork on it. He praised my talent, too, and asked me if I wanted to go into Phouc Vinh village with him, to pick up some stuff at MACV headquarters. I said "Sure!"

Out the north gate was the sleepy village of Phouc Vinh. There was a District School in session with little uniformed kids playing in a fenced yard in the shade of a huge tree, the school mistresses in sparkling white Ao Dai's directing them. A little farther, past some thatch roofed stucco houses, was a small business district with shops, bars and restaurants. Some street vendors, plying their wares in the dusty road, under bamboo umbrellas or galvanized tin shanty roofs attached to the side of their carts, held up by bamboo poles. There were gaudy tropical flowers growing in some of the door yards and among the stalks of bamboo that seemed to separate most of the houses. The perfumey smell of the flowers did little to mask the other aromas wafting from the houses and the shops. Nouc Mam sauce was prevalent, but also frying chicken or pork, the musty animal smell of some water buffalo in an empty yard just off the main road. There was an underlying smell of sewage, probably due to the sanitation facilities that were mostly comprised of out-houses, and in some cases, slit trenches out back of the houses.

Somewhere, there must have been an electric generating plant, because most of the businesses had lights and some had electric signs. Some had running water, too, piped from the central well that was used by the populace, who carried their water home in big round jugs on either end of a stick balanced across their shoulders.

The road through the business area ended abruptly at a cross street that went east and west. Across the road was the main market house, obviously, as evidenced by the number of trucks parked at a long dock unloading goods. We sat at the 'T' for a couple minutes while two trucks maneuvered around a cart pulled by a water buffalo. Looking east I saw a long straight road lined with huts and houses. Looking west, the same except for the tall white spire of the Catholic cathedral I remembered seeing from the air as I flew in. The trucks finally managed to honk their way around the cart and we turned left, and eventually passed the huge church, which was surrounded by a low stone wall with well-kept grounds. There was a group of mama-sans raking the sandy paths among the plantings.

Past the church were more houses, of a poorer order, with pigs, chickens and baby-sans playing in the road. Then after a short section of scrub jungle we turned right into an arched stone gate guarded by an armed ARVN soldier, and pulled up in front of a stucco French plantation house with wide porches around the three sides of it I could see. Closed wooden louvered shutters covered all the floor to ceiling windows off the porch and a yellow MACV flag hung from a standard attached to one of the porch posts.

Henry jumped out and went inside and I waited in the jeep and smoked a cig. About ten minutes later, he emerged carrying a cardboard box that clinked, I noticed, as he set it in the back.

"Cognac." he answered my raised eyebrows.

"No shit?"

"Yeah," he climbed back in and started the jeep, "The NCOs really like that stuff. They're having a big party tonight and the first Sgt. has this friend at MACV, Sgt. Towers. He supplies the booze."

"Wow, privilege of rank, I guess."

"Yes, he and his 'Haole' friends have a big party once a month."

"Haole?" I queried.

"Hawaiian word." He answered, "Means 'white'." He laughed.

I laughed, too. "So you're Hawaiian?"

"Yes, sure. From Maui. My daddy was Portuguese, my mamma Hawaiian."

Henry was a very Strack dude. Spit-shined boots, tailored creased fatigues, black hair always combed neatly straight back. He had black piercing eyes that looked at you out of a smooth shaven, burnt-sienna face with vaguely oriental features. He was a Spec.-5 with ten months in country.

"I'm getting way short." He explained, "Two months, I'll be back on th' beach at home, checking out 'wahini's', you guys'll still be here, marking time."

Some of the guys called Henry a 'Suck-Up', 'cause he was favorite of the lifers, drove the Captains new jeep and had his own hootch next to the BC's quarters. But most people liked Henry 'cause he was so good natured and easy-going. If anybody I ever met in Vietnam had his shit together, it was Henry.

On the way back to the base, we talked about our respective homes and families. He told me that there were no mosquitoes in Hawaii and that they "Chew on us Hawaiians like candy."

I told him they chew on us Kentuckians pretty good, too.

He dropped me, at my request, back at the PX and I hoofed the quarter mile over to the airstrip and sat on the bench of the 'Terminal Building'. I watched the C-130s and Caribous take-off and land, and pretended I was waiting for one to take me home. There was a lot of action on the flight line. Choppers coming and going, people in uniforms coming and going, tow vehicles buzzing about. I saw a white civilian-looking plane come in and land right at sunset. Its only markings were a red PA & E on the tail. It taxied directly to a hangar at the far end of the flight line and was towed in without anyone disembarking. The hangar doors were shut after the plane was inside. 'Hmmm, curious'. These planes were reputed to be CIA operated and, according to rumor, carried guns, drugs, and any other illegal thing you could imagine.

As I was just thinking about getting up and heading back, a 'Charlie-Alpha', (Combat Assault), group of six Huey gun ships, flared-in on the line and deposited eighteen of the grungiest-looking Grunts I'd ever seen. Bowed under the weight of their 'Alice' packs and weapons, mud-lines up to their chests, the expressions on their faces told a story that gave me the shivers. They all grouped up around the door of the last ship in line and helped unload two body bags, obviously occupied. With two guys on either side gripping the rubber, they carried them off around the corner of a building, their shuffling steps raising little puffs of dust on the PSP.

I walked back to the unit along the dusty roads between the chopper pads, in the deepening dusk. My thoughts were on those Grunt's faces. As bad as it had been on the LZs, what I'd seen and done was like nothing compared to what those guys had been through. Should I feel guilty because I'm in a better situation? No, of course not. But I do.

21

CHANGE OF STATUS

The Army has more ups and downs than most elevators. Sometimes when you're feeling really low, something happens that makes you think things might be OK after all. Then, inevitably, you get shot down again to an all-new low.

The next morning, I reported to the S-2 and Rojeski, the Sp.-4 in charge, told me to report ASAP to the CP. I walked down the road thinking, 'What now?' The First Sgt. waved me into his office as soon as I walked in the screen door.

"Hudson..." he began.

'Oh, shit!' I thought.

"Lt. Cravens says you been doin' a pretty fair, (pronounced pert' far), job as 'is driver."

"Yeah, Top?"

"An' th' BC's real pleased wit' th' stuff you painted on 'is jeep, an' all."

"Really?" I stammered, "Uh... I mean thanks, Top."

"Don't thank me, son. They both recommended I put you in fer Specialist four, (Spatialist), an' I did, an' you are." He actually smiled.

"I'm ...what?" I said, confused.

"A damn Spec-four, Boah!" The smile was over quickly, "Git yer insignia changed ASAP, heah?"

"Uh...Thanks, Top." I murmured, as the news sunk in.

"An' yew got a new job, ta' go with it." He continued.

"New job?"

"Sgt. Carbone needs somebody t' drive rations fer th' mess, so one o' th' other Spec.-4s is gonna drive th' LT, an', startin' day after to-morry, yer drivin' fer th' mess hall."

"Why day after tomorrow, Top?"

He smiled again, "'Cause yer off duty tomorry, 'cause yer on guard-duty tonight. Re-port t' th' CP at 1930, wit' yer basic load."

My head was spinning as I hoofed back up to the S-2.

'Shit, Guard-duty? Hauling rations? Somebody else driving my jeep? Spec.-4?'

I think what bothered me most was somebody else driving MY jeep that I'd practically built by hand. I felt like a jilted lover.

I drove Lt. Cravens to DIVARTY for the last time, and on the way, I thanked him for the recommendation for promotion, and told him I was sorry to not be his driver anymore.

"Well…" He admitted, "That's mostly MY fault."

"What d'ya mean, sir?"

"Captain Johnson got in rather a …snit, about that…speeding ticket incident. He's limiting my trips to within the base and Phouc Vinh village. No more road trips, so I won't need a full time driver. I'm sorry, Hudson. It's no reflection on you. I hope they haven't put you on some crappy duty because of MY mistake."

"Oh, no, sir." I said quickly, "Driving rations for th' mess can't be THAT bad, sir."

"Oh? No… I suppose not." He agreed.

On the way back to the unit, he let me stop by the PX to pick up my new rank insignia and I spent my lunch hour ripping off the PFC stripes and fastening my Spec.-4 tabs to my collars.

At the motor pool that afternoon, Jim and Ralph were working under, (or over), a Deuce-and-a-half. Jim crawled out just as I walked in and he looked at me and at my collars.

"Hey Ralph, c'mere an' look at our new Specialist we got here."

They both congratulated me and I told them about my new job driving rations.

"Wow, man. That's a pretty easy gig!" Jim said.

"Yeah," Ralph added, "That doofus, Thomas? He's been doin' it for a couple months, an' Carbone tol' me he could screw-up a wet dream."

"Yeah, Mouse." Jim said, "You won't have no problem. All you gotta do is pick up th' supplies for th' mess hall at th' Ration Point down behind th' PX every morning, an' deliver it back here, an' pick up th' ice for th' coolers, an' such. No sweat, man. Ol' Carbone's a pretty good ol' dude, for a New York wop, an' if you get on his good side, he'll treat ya right!"

"Yeah, Mouse, Carbone's OK." Ralph added.

"AND…" Jim continued, "when you get to know th' guys down at th' Ration Point, You'll be in line for some MAJOR tradin' an' 'wheeler-dealer-in'" A gleam came into his eye. "Too bad 'bout your jeep, man, but that ¾ over there," he pointed out a pickup truck with a canvas cover over the rear bed, "is th' mess hall vehicle, so I guess you'll still have a ride."

I fiddled around in the motor pool the rest of the day, had supper at 6:00, then reported to the CP at 7:30 dressed in my soldier-suit, ready for guard detail. Henry Tabaranza was the CQ and the other two guys on my bunker, (#43) were Jack Pagans and 'Nick' Nickerson, both survey guy's from S-5. Six other guy's were there to man Tower November and Bunker #42, among them I saw Rojeski from S-2 and Clark, (whom I'd come in-country with at Bien Hoa), but the rest I'd seen around the Battery, but didn't know personally.

Now, I'd walked a guard-post in Basic at Ft. Knox. It was a sort of formal affair, where you wore a special uniform called OG's. They were 100% wool and guaranteed to itch enough to keep you awake all night. There were special procedures for saluting with your rifle and calling out, "HALT, who goes there?" There was a lot of standing at attention and answering questions about the chain of command and the Code of Conduct.

Well, scrub all that in Vietnam.

We were picked up at the front gate by the Sgt. of the Guard, tonight a Corporal Stevens, in a ¾ ton truck, and dropped off at the posts. The detail coming off duty taking our places in the truck. Our only instructions were, "Stay awake and NO BULLSHITTING ON THE RADIO!" It was completely dark as we mounted the bunker, and we used our red lensed flashlights to see as Jack and Nick, who'd both been on guard-duty before, showed me the procedures for hooking up the detonators for the Claymores, (twelve in-all), and how to operate the radio. We hauled up three boxes of M-60 ammo to the upper level, which was a sandbag walled box, six feet square, on top of the bunker, roofed with corrugated tin. I loaded the machine gun while Nick and Pagans brought up the M-79, with its bandolier of oversized bullets, a box of pop-flares and the Starlight-scope. Pagans came up last carrying a PRC-25 radio, that fit into a niche in the wall with its eight foot antenna extending out past the edge of the roof.

Jack put on the headphones, flipped some switches, dialed some dials, and keyed the microphone.

"Tango November, Tango November, This is 4-3, Over."

I couldn't hear the return transmission, but he must have been acknowledged, because he continued,

"November, 4-3, Commo-Check, over."

Then shortly,

"November, that's a rog', I have you 5-by-5, too, thank-ya-much, out. 4-2, 4-2, 4-3, Commo-check, over."

He listened a minute.

"Copy, 4-2, I got you Lima-Chuck, how me?" a pause, "Rog', 4-3 out."

I'd never had much chance to use a radio on the LZs, just field phones where you talked like you were using a regular phone. All this 'Phonetic' code-talk sort of mystified me and I said so.

Nick and Jack spent about ten minutes explaining 'Radio Protocol' to me. I'd learned the 'Phonetic Alphabet' from Alpha to Zulu, in basic training, like all soldiers do, but had no reason to use it much. It all seemed so... complicated, but they told me that the SOG would come down on me if I didn't talk right on the net. So I spent a considerable part of the night, listening to the transmissions over the radio and mentally translating the code until, scarily, it began to make some sense to me.

"It's not all Army bullshit, though." Nick told me.

"Hell, no," Pagans added, "it's about our only form of entertainment, out here in th' dark."

"What d'ya mean?" I asked.

"It all starts out pretty much strictly by- th'-book, for th' first watch or so..." Jack started.

"Yeah, then, when it's late and everybody's getting bored," Nick said.

"An' th' SOG isn't likely to be monitoring th' net," Pagans interrupted.

"Then things start to get … interesting." Nick finished.

"Interesting how?" I inquired, getting a crick from looking back and forth, trying to soak this info up.

"Sooner or later," Jack.

"Probably later," Nick

"Yeah, some guy somewhere'll start BS-ing." Jack.

"Funny call-signs, goofy names," Nick

"Or just some weird shit. Anyway, it chain-reacts and pretty soon th' BS is flying around," Jack

"An' it'll drive th' SOG nuts, an' he'll start yellin' over th' net an' shit," Nick.

"An' th' great thing IS, he can't tell where th' traffic is comin' from," Jack.

"Or who's doin' it." Nick

"It'll quiet back down for a while," Jack.

"Then start up again on some other weird ass thing, later." Nick

"It's kinda our way of making sure th' SOG don't get any more sleep than WE do." Jack finished.

Jack and Nick were from the same hometown. Milwaukee, Wis. They'd been best friends since grade school, graduated High school together and enlisted together right after, so they'd been together for most of their lives. They were always finishing each other's sentences like both their brains were required to get one complete thought. Listening to them was like watching a tennis match.

We decided on shifts, and since I was the 'new guy', (though I had more time in country than them), I drew the middle shift, midnight to four, considered the 'bad' shift because your sleep is interrupted in the middle. I sat up talking with them until 10:00, then went down the ladder to the cots in the lower room and sacked-out. I slept heavily 'til 12:00, then I was shaken awake by a yawning Pagan. Nickerson was snoring in the other bunk. Jack took my warm spot, told me to make a 'Sit-Rep' to the tower every half-hour and conked. I climbed up to the upper floor and groggily tried to look out.

Have I mentioned how dark it gets in Vietnam?

Man, it was black up there. I groped around a little and located the radio, the M-60 and stuff. I carefully lit a cig down below the wall, and even the glow from my lighter was enough to ruin my night-vision for several minutes. I sat and smoked, cupping the butt to hide the glow from the tip, and eventually I was able to distinguish the ground from the sky. I could barely make-out the tower to my left and if I looked back toward the base, I could see the outline of the roofs of the buildings. Everything else was black.

I groped around some more and came up with the Starlight Scope. I propped it on the wall and flipped it on. Looking through it was like looking at a scene in murky water, lit by a florescent green sun. I carefully picked out all the landmarks I'd observed earlier, marking out my AO. After a while I could ID details like clumps of bushes, trees and the stakes holding the barbed wire. The scope worked pretty well, once you got used to the green glow, except when you pulled away and tried to see normally, the 'Green Eye' caused almost total night blindness for about five minutes. I decided not to use the scope any more than necessary, and to try to depend on my night vision only.

At 12:30, I called in a 'Negative Sit-rep', meaning 'Nothing is happening'.

At 1:00 the overcast skies opened up and a torrential downpour soaked the area, including me even though the tin roof marginally protected me.

At 2:00 the rain had stopped, and mist or fog was rising from the roads and bushes, lending an eerie, drifting, look to everything.

At 3:00, the clouds had parted, revealing a multitude of stars and a quarter moon. Nothing had happened except the Sgt. of the Guard had blasted by in his jeep every hour or so, and I'd smoked a half pack of cigs.

Early on, I'd unplugged the headset from the radio and switched to the little audible speaker on low volume. The 'phones' made my ears sweat.

A crackling transmission squawked from the speaker.

"Chicken Man to Earth… Chicken Man to Earth…over."

I jerked my head around to listen, then, shortly, a reply.

"Chicken Man, this IS the Earth…over."

"Earth…Chicken Man, what is your status…over."

"Chicken Man...Earth, we are currently Sierra Bravo, that is, Straight and Bored, do you copy?"

"I got a big 'Rog' on your Sierra Bravo, Earth, we are 'Same-o Same-o, though maybe not ENTIRELY Sierra."

I heard giggling in the background before he unkeyed his mike.

"Chicken, this is Earth, Be Advised, the Sierra Oscar Golf passed this location zero-five mikes ago, headed west, I repeat....west. Do you copy?"

This, I was sure, was meant as a warning to be on the lookout for the Sgt. of the Guard, who was patrolling the perimeter.

"Earth, Chicken, I have solid copy on that location Chicken Man fears NOT the lowly Sierra Oscar Golf, as I soar high above the.... mundanities....is that a word?...."

More laughter in the background.

"...of the powers of REMF!"

'Man, this guy's a really good bullshitter,' I thought, waiting for the next transmission, 'And really stoned, too!'

Another voice popped in with more laughter in the background.

"I got a Roger on that 'Soaring', Chicken Man, How high ARE you guys...over?"

"This is The Chicken Man, we are as high as a chicken can fly, and..."

I heard coughing behind him.

"....YES, we are gaining altitude steadily!"

More hooty guffaws before he clicked off.

A southern 'Corn-pone' voice came next.

"Whur I come f'um, chickens don' fly, jes' why IS that, Chicken Man?"

Chicken Mans voice came back, imitating the hick.

"If'n y'all'd feed yer chickens on hemp seed, yore chickens c'd fly, too!"

Big burst of giggles behind that one.

A new voice came on, much louder than the others.

"Perimeter net, this is the Sierra Oscar Golf. DO NOT, I repeat, DO NOT BS ON THIS NET. If I find out who you are, there WILL be trouble in River City, that starts with K and ends with P an' that stands for 'PURE HELL' DO I MAKE MYSELF CLEAR? Over."

One of the original voices, "Chicken, this is Earth, receiving some sorta static on this end, how you...over?"

"Roger on that static, Earth. Must be the Rings of Saturn I just passed. I'll call back when we've rounded Uranus...over."

"Hey Chicken Man," came still another voice, "MY anus is AL-READY round!"

I laughed out loud!

The SOG busted in again promising recriminations if caught BS-ing on the net or smoking dope on duty. (Like it's OK to smoke dope OFF duty!) Anyway, all was quiet again 'til I woke Nickerson at 4:00 A.M. and rolled into his warm spot on the cot and promptly zonked-out.

At 8:00 A.M., Nick woke me and Pagans and we wearily un-hooked the 'Clackers' on the Claymores, packed up our stuff and loaded onto the truck that brought the 'Day Guard' out. We rode back to the CP where we were dismissed for the day and soon I was in my own bunk, snoozing away. For once, all three bunks were occupied in the night-duty hootch.

I slept 'til noon and woke to the roar of another downpour of rain. The smell of ozone, for once, overpowering the usual Army-base smells. It was coming down in buckets, so I didn't bother with a shower. I got one anyway, sloshing over to the mess hall for SOS, (Shit On a Shingle), and warmish Kool-Aid. I was at a table with Pagans, (Nick was still sacked-out), telling him about the Chicken Man jokes last night, when Sgt. Carbone, (My new boss), came over.

"Unnerstan' yer t' be mah new drivah, Hudson!" he bawled in his usual twang.

"Yeah, Sarge. I'm supposed to start tomorrow." I said.

He went on to inform me, in no uncertain terms, that I was to re-port to the mess at 0630, at which time he'd hand me a requisition sheet to take to the ration point, and outlined my duties as "His" driver, which included hauling "His" ass around when he needed to go. I told him I understood and he left with a final "DOAN BE LATE, BOAH!"

Still raining as I walked out, so I dodged to the eaves of the NCO hootch, followed that relatively dry path to the end, and ran across to my hootch. Bowers and Fuk were still sleeping, so as quietly as possible, I stripped to skivvies and climbed into my bunk. I plugged in the head-phones to my tape player, listened to 'Blood, Sweat and Tears', and wrote a letter to my Mom and Dad, complaining of the weather, army life in general, and asking them to send 'More Goodies!' Then I read my book until I must have dozed off, 'cause when I awoke again, my hootch-mates were up and doing stuff.

Fuk saw me stir.

"Wow, man, don't see much of you this time o' day. Th' Duty keep you up all night?"

"Pretty much, but it wasn't too bad." I said, swinging my legs over the side of the bunk, reaching for a cigarette.

"After chow, you wanna play some tunes, man?" he asked.

"Yeah, sure, man." I said, sliding down from my perch, "I'm gonna take a shower first, then eat, so…" I looked at my watch, "'bout 6:30 OK?"

He said that'd be fine and left.

Bowers was sitting at the little desk writing a letter. He looked up and said,

"You and Gaylord are playing music?"

I nodded.

"I heard you guys are pretty good."

"Fuk is," I answered, "I'm just learning, but he's teaching me all kinds of stuff."

I stripped off my skivvies, donned my towel and flip-flops, and grabbed my shower kit out of the wall locker.

"You guys can play here tonight, if you want to." He said, "Rojes-ki's coming over and we're playing chess, but you won't bother us, and I'd like to hear some live music tonight. OK?"

Bowers was a really quiet guy, and this was the first whole, long sentence he'd said to me.

I said "Sure, man." and smiled.

Everybody said he was a real square, but he'd always been OK, as far as I'd seen, and I figured there's a place in the wide world for the 'Squares', too.

I went off to the shower shack. It had stopped raining, at least temporarily, but the mud in the paths tried to suck the flip-flops off my feet on the way there and back. They were both gone when I returned, so I dressed in my cut off LZ shorts and a tee-shirt, cooked up a beef stew LRRP ration and ate it.

At 6:15, Fuk and Bowers came back and we sat around and BS'ed for a while. Then Fuk got his guitar, and I got mine and we worked on trying to figure out the chords to 'Blackbird' by the Beatles. In an hour or so we'd worked out a rendition, (our own), and Bowers even sang a couple verses of it in a surprisingly good tenor voice. Then his buddy, Mark Rojeski, came in and they got out Dougs' chessboard and set it up and started playing. Fuk and I got into a sort of medley of' 'House of the Rising Sun' (not exactly the Animal's version), and a tune I'd never heard before called 'Song For My Father', written, according to Fuk, in the 1930's by a dude named Horace Silver. The chord progressions were very similar and we found ourselves going back and forth between the songs easily with different variations each time. Fuk would just grin wide when a passage would really fall together, and they did more often all the time. We were actually playing some good music, and I was thoroughly enjoying myself. It's so easy when you're playing with a good musician, especially one who enjoys it as much as you.

Doug and Mark even applauded when we hit some especially good licks, which made us feel like we were appreciated.

At 9:45 they had to get ready for duty at the FDC, and after they left, I stripped again and climbed into my bunk. It had started raining again, hard, and I dropped off like a sack of rocks.

22

DOWN IN THE JUNGLE

I heard "Yo, Hudson!" as I walked in the mess hall door at 6:25 A.M. Still half asleep, I didn't react. I was drifting toward the serving line, smelling bacon and hotcakes, when a large, hairy hand descended on my shoulder and a large voice said;

"YO, Hudson, you in there, boah?"

I turned to see Carbone, big and bristly, smiling at me.

The Mess Sgt., originally from Violet, La., was six foot, two hundred pounds, and always seemed to have a two-day growth of black whiskers from his cheekbones to his collarbones. He had a reputation among the enlisted ranks as a pretty up-front NCO who didn't mess with you unless you screwed-up badly. He was probably thirty-five or so.

"Git ya some vittles, boah, but eat-'em-up quick. I wont you at th' RP early so's yew c'n git th' good stuff 'fore it gits picked-over, heah?"

"Sure, Sarge!" I said, trying to brighten up.

After all, this is my first day on the job as 'Ration Driver'. I scarfed down a load of bacon and cakes with a big glass of powdered milk. (Man, I sure miss real, whole milk!) I rinsed my tray and went back to the cook's office, where Carbone explained, in detail, what he wanted in the way of food supplies. He warned me about 'short' cases, lettuce rot, "soft 'maters an' mealy 'taters".

"Them guys'll push anythang own yew if ya let 'em." He pointed out, "Don' let 'em! Pick through everthang an' git th' very-best! An' don' take no argyments, heah?"

I said I understood and he explained how to get to the Ration Point, who was in charge down there and;

"I 'spect yew back heah no latah than ten hunnert ires, 'zat cle-ah?"

'Clear as mud, Sarge!' I wanted to say, but held my thoughts to myself. Instead I said, "Sure, Sarge.", tucked the clipboard under my arm and left.

Daylight was coming on strong when I checked the ¾ out of the motor pool and as I turned onto the little road that ran to the RP, behind the PX, the sun was up on the horizon of the airstrip that abutted the back gates of the Supply Depot

Trucks were already lined up, waiting to get into the loading docks where forklifts and loaders were dumping supplies into their beds. I got in line, three trucks back from the gates, and smoked a cig while I waited and watched the action on the docks and the beautiful sunrise that glistened off the PSP of the runway.

There was a morning mist drifting about, coating every surface with heavy dew that sparkled in the weak rays of the early morn. I day-dreamed about the dew, twinkling in the sun on the clover in our back yard at home, and on the leaves of the willow tree that was back in the corner next to our neighbor, Mrs. Hurst's, apple tree.

The truck in front of me started up and moved, snapping me out of my dream. I looked around as I eased up behind him again. 'Oh, well.' I thought, 'Here, we have dew glistening on the razor wire and chain link fence.'

It took nearly an hour before I finally backed the ¾ in to the dock. I jumped, stiffly, out and handed my REQ. form to the loader on the raised platform, a PFC named Jackson, according to his tag.

"Sgt. Carbone wants me to check everything out before you load, OK?" I yelled over the roar of a 'Deuce' that was pulling away.

"Yeah," he said, "C'Mon with me an' you can check it as I put it on th' lift."

He jumped into the seat of a yellow, gas powered, forklift, started it up and motioned me to stand on the front tines of the fork, which I did. And we were off! He practically burned rubber and whizzed through the door into the warehouse. I was hanging on with white knuckles and got a blurred tour as we flew past racks and racks, and shelves and shelves and pallet upon pallet of goods. You name it, they had it, from Apples to

Zinc sinks. The place was a scrounger's paradise. Visions of future trades and deals were whirling in my head, already.

We screeched to a halt at the canned articles where Jackson, ('Just call me Jax'), stacked on cases of juice, cans of lard, canned veggies, etc. I checked each box and can carefully, and checked it all off on my clipboard. I rejected one box with one end crushed and Jax cheerfully replaced it with another in better shape. He was very efficient at his job and within fifteen minutes, we took off for 'Produce', where there were bins and bins of tomatoes, potatoes, oranges, apples, squash and zucchinis and some stuff, I don't know what it was.

We each grabbed a wire mesh grocery cart and started down the aisles. It was sort of like shopping in a huge supermarket, except you have to imagine four foot by six foot by four-foot deep bins, holding gigantic amounts of veggies. I picked through it carefully, but still, a lot of the stuff was either wilted or crushed. I mentioned this to Jax, and he told me I needed to get here early to get the "Top quality" stuff, before it gets picked-over. I asked how early was 'early'?

"The officers cooks are usually here by seven, and they get the picks, but I'm always here by six, so, come as early as you like." He informed me.

We spent almost an hour in produce, and I got a good load of veggies, but Carbone would have to overlook some of the wilted stuff. I promised myself I'd be here by 6:30 tomorrow and see if I could do better. We drove to several other parts of the warehouse, picking up odds and ends, then back to the dock to load it into the truck.

In conversation as we traveled around, Jax had hinted to me that if I had any 'Special Requisitions', he'd 'see what he could do'. I told him I'd keep that in mind, but seeing as how this was my first day on the job, that I'd better stay with what was on the official sheet.

"The 'Red Ball Express' brings in stuff every day that don't get picked up or needs to be re-routed." He told me, "We got another whole warehouse full, an' some of that stuff's been in there a year or more."

My ears must have perked up and I asked, "What kinda stuff?"

He grinned, "Most anything you can name. Listen, I can tell by th' gleam in your eye, you're gonna need something 'Special', so, keep me in mind when you do, OK?"

234

I thanked him and thought, 'He's obviously a 'scrounger' beyond my experience.' But I DID have my ambitions. I'd have to discuss this with Jim.

At 9:45 I pulled up to the side door of the mess and the cooks helped me unload and store away the provisions. Carbone was a little testy, (That th' best they got?), about the produce, but I informed him of my plan to get there earlier to get the best pick. He liked that.

"Yew might work out, after all, Hudson. We'll see." He smiled, then added, "Don' fergit, I need yew to pick up ice (Pronounced "ass") at 1600. Meantime, I heered yer good at paintin' signs an' stuff."

"Uh... yeah, I guess so." I answered uncertainly.

"Well, I need me some new mess hall signs, yew wanna work own that?"

"Sure." I said

He took me and showed me what he wanted. I measured and told him I'd get right on it, but it might take a couple days.

"Thass fine, boah."

He grinned and slapped me on the back hard enough to propel me out the door. I parked the ¾, scrounged some plywood from some packing crates in the motor pool, and lugged it to my hootch, where I set up in the shade and began lining off the letters for the signs.

The next week passed in a slow flurry of activities. I only picked up rations three days a week and ice every two days. The rest of the time I was painting signs or driving errands for whoever, or painting the serving area wall with a huge Cav patch, and an equally large Unit crest on the wall above the door to the officer/NCO dining room. The Lifers really liked that! It also put me on a 'Good Buddy' status with Carbone.

The rainy season was coming on strong. At first you could expect it to rain at 4:00 every afternoon, last about an hour, then quit. Then it slowly rained a little longer every day until it was raining more than not.

Vietnam is a miserable place at any time, but during the wet season it becomes almost intolerable. Mildewy clothes, muddy boots, skin rashes caused by wet, hot skin all the time. White, wrinkly feet with boot blisters that won't heal. And this was in a rear area! I felt really sorry for the guys out on the LZs and the poor ground-pounders in the 'Boonies'.

"They must be up to their necks in it!" I commented to Jim one evening as the monsoon waged outside our door.

They were. I found out first hand on Tuesday of the next week.

Since I wasn't hauling rations that day I was 'volunteered' again for another sandbag detail. We flew out at 0630 that morning and made a stop at a small outpost with an airstrip called Quan Loi, just north of An Loc in the 'Fishook' area. The Chinook we were on picked up a group of 2/7th grunts there and we were to fly on to LZ SANDY, a new temporary FSB. We didn't know it at the time, of course, but SANDY was set up to supply arty support for 1st CAV troops preparing for the upcoming 'Cambodian Incursion'.

There was a little delay at Quan Loi, while the grunts got themselves assembled on the pad. Our detail, which included Jim and Pagans, Terry Leonard, and a guy from commo whom I'd seen around, but hadn't met 'til now, Rudy Anderson, and me, were allowed to get out and sit on the flight line while we waited. I climbed up on a guard tower and snapped a picture of the crew from above with my little Ansco camera that my Aunt Polly had given me as a going-away present. I waited up there, talking to the day guard, mostly 'cause I could smoke up there, 'til the Infantry Sgt. trooped his guys out and they started loading into the chopper.

We flew out of Quan Loi at 0845, low-leveling over the dense jungle of the 'Fishook'. We'd also picked up a sling-load of 155 rounds and a ¾ ton truck, which now dangled, under the chopper, swinging from a large strap anchored to a beam that stretched across the 4'x 4' floor hatch. The hatch was open in the deck almost directly in front of my sling-seat along the inner wall. I could look straight down at the jungle, two-three hundred feet below, and watch the truck and ammo swing back and forth, back and forth, back and.....well, you get my drift. It made me a little woozy.

Rudy's sitting just forward of me and some infantry guys are to my right. The other three in our group were somewhere back in the bay with the twenty or so grunts. A pallet of equipment is lashed down in the middle of the bay, covered by a tarp.

All conversation is pretty much impossible due to the roar of the twin Turbo-prop engines, the whopping of the blades and the whoosh of the wind coming in through the hatch. You could be heard if you yelled, but basically, nobody bothered. I just stared out the hatch and tried not to puke.

We cruised along, slowly gaining altitude 'til, after fifteen minutes, we were at two thousand feet; nothing but green jungle below. We passed through a pocket of air turbulence that jerked all our necks and the chopper slued sideways momentarily.

Before I could think 'What was that?', there was a loud 'BANG' and the engine noise was suddenly much quieter. We, in the back, looked around at each other and I wondered 'Can this be good?'.

It wasn't!

I looked forward, into the pilot's cabin, in time to see one of the door gunners leave his post at the side bay window and lean into the cabin. Then he turned and ran back to the hatch by my seat, reached out and pulled a big red pin out of the sling anchor on the beam. The one marked 'EMERGENCY'. I watched in awe as the sling loads, truck and all, fell, in slow motion, into the jungle below.

"WHAT'S GOING ON?" I yelled at the crewman. A question that showed on everybody's face right now.

"STRAP IN TIGHT! I THINK WE'RE GOIN' DOWN!"

Then he was gone back up front and he and the other gunner began strapping themselves into jump seats against the bulkhead between the cabin and the bay.

These, of course, were the last words I wanted to hear, because I didn't want them to be the last words I ever heard

Anderson leaned over and hollered.

"DID HE SAY GOIN" DOWN?"

"I THINK SO!" I answered.

I looked around and saw how everyone's faces were pale and I saw a lot of scared looks in the other guy's eyes. Through the floor hatch, sure enough, the treetops were already considerably closer and we were descending, not like a rock, but still damn fast.

The engine noise had dropped off 'til we could hear the pilots shouting orders to the crew. They sounded scared, too, and this did not help my confidence.

The door gunner who'd released the slings, unharnessed again and ran back past us and tugged on the straps holding down the floor cargo. Satisfied that they were secure, he turned and was going to go back to his seat when it must have dawned on him that there were twenty-some guys back here that didn't know what was going on and were scared shitless. He stopped and visibly took a deep breath to calm himself, then said, loud enough for everyone to hear his croaky voice;

"In less than one minute, we're going to hit the jungle!"

He pointed out the hatch downward, like we didn't know which jungle he meant.

"The engines have quit and won't re-start. The only advice I have is, hang on to anything solid you can find. Stay strapped in! It's gonna be rough! If you survive the impact, exit the ship anyway you can and as fast as you can! Th' Captain has already dumped th' fuel, but there's still a chance of fire or explosion."

Finished, he ran forward again and strapped back into his seat.

'Oh great!' I thought, 'If we survive the crash, we'll still probably blow-up.'

I cinched-up my spindly webbing harness as tight as it would go and I noticed everyone else doing the same. I heard some guys cussing, but I also heard some others praying. Next to me, Rudy was repeating, "Oh God, oh God, oh God..." over and over again. I had a sick feeling in the pit of my stomach, not unlike how it feels to top the big hill on a roller coaster. I'm sure a needle could not be inserted into any of our assholes at that moment.

The door gunners had shipped both the M-60s and got them secure when we brushed the first trees. I gulped air and I heard moans all round as a tremendous thumping/screeching, amplified by the metal walls, arose from all around me. The noise stopped for a second, and the ship was still level and flying. I exhaled my last big gulp.

Then we hit the tangle of limbs of the jungle canopy. I heard and saw the Plexiglas of the front windshields implode just as we were engulfed in a dark greenish glow. The helicopter lurched to the left and things started flying around in the cargo bay. I saw a blur of green outside the windows across from where I sat. I was being whipped around like a willow branch in a high wind.

A large tree branch suddenly thrust in through the floor hatch, whipped around the bay and caught several guys on the other side of the plane. Just as suddenly it was gone. Only to be replaced by more limbs, leaves and other stuff being funneled in through the large opening in the floor. All this lethal debris mingled with any loose objects that were lying around in the bay, including somebody's M-16 rifle, which cracked me in the head as it went by. It was like a storm inside the chopper as it careered through dense canopy.

Coherent thought was impossible in the screeching, tearing noise and the lurching, shaking movement, but I somehow knew we were still going a hundred-plus MPH, though I could feel the G-forces as the ship slowed, burrowing into the treetops.

Airborne projectiles were pummeling everybody. I got creamed again by a wooden ammo crate right in the ribs. My flack jacket took most of the lick, though I heard my bones creak and it knocked the wind right out of me. I was gasping anyway, so I hardly noticed, trying to hold on and at the same time dodge the killer junk.

As we ground on deeper into the jungle, the chopper jerked right, then left, the nose came up, and the nose went down, like a toy being shaken by a giant kid. Sometime during this a prop blade broke off, sliced through the fuselage wall to my right, and hit some of the Grunts, knocking them loose from their harnesses. They, in turn became projectiles, flying awkwardly around the bay, banging off the walls and ceiling and other guys.

We hit something really solid, probably a tree trunk, and the cargo load, on the floor, came loose and avalanched forward, as we slowed radically. The door-gunners were both buried in boxes and equipment and bodies of the flying Grunts, some more of who were knocked loose by this jumble of rushing, crushing weight.

I was watching all this as if it was in slow motion. I was dazed from several blows to the head. I'd lost my helmet at some point, but I don't remember when. Anderson kept bashing against me on the left, seemingly trying to break my death-grip I had on a metal wall stud. I became aware of someone yelling "SHIIIIIITTTTT!!!", then realized it was me. I was not alone in this, I think Rudy was harmonizing with me.

After the big jolt we were still moving fast but I'd bet our (Airspeed?) had slowed by half. We had a couple of brief seconds of near silence before we hit the second layer of canopy. This was comprised of mostly leaf and limb debris from the upper layer, but it was no softer. We went over on the right side and I'm hanging from the ceiling by these flimsy seat straps, my arms and legs flailing uncontrollably. Several more

Grunts are loose now, screaming and bashing off everything. I watched helplessly as one of them flew out the floor hatch in front of me and disappeared into the green blur. Seeing this, I somehow managed to get my grip on the wall stud again, (I think I left finger marks in that piece of metal), and held on. Right then, the only thing that scared me more than being on this helicopter, was the thought of falling out of it.

Rudy's hollering "I'm dyin', I'm Dyin'!" now. We're all being beaten senseless by the scrap metal and junk that's winging and dinging around. More tree shit is bursting up through the floor hatch, like a volcano erupting. We must have clipped another trunk obliquely, because the left side of the plane, just forward of me, suddenly bends inward about three feet, blocking my view in that direction. Our descent changed direction to the right in a neck-wrenching jerk, and I caught a glimpse of Terry L. tumbling by on his way forward. I'm snugged up against the bent wall, still hanging onto the wall stud, and Rudy is hanging onto ME! I let go with one hand and tried to push his weight off my already aching ribs, but he wailed in protest.

"DON'T LET GO! MY STRAPS! MY STRAPS!"

I felt my ribs cracking with each impact, but I stopped pushing and held onto him by his pack harness. I realized if I let go he'd fall right out the hole in the floor. Besides, he had a tight grip on a wall stud on the bent-out section, and his weight was anchoring me snugly against the metal bulkhead. We screamed in each other's faces and clutched our handholds as the careening ship jolted through the second layer and into the third.

The bottom layer of canopy was made up of leaf and twig build-up from the two upper layers and was very dense, but I guess, it didn't have the huge, hard, living limb structure of the upper layers, therefore, it 'seemed' softer. Immediately a big 'poof' of dead leaves and sticks blew up from the floor hatch, and again, half reduced our speed. Again, there was an avalanche of bodies and debris past our 'fly on the wall' position and we were almost dislodged by a flying pallet that glanced off Rudy's back before moving on to, I'm sure, cream some other poor bastard up front.

We plowed through for a few seconds, the ship tilting back upright. I happened to be looking down, when I saw clear space out the floor hatch. I saw the ground, way, way on down there.

"Oh, shit! We're still way off the ground!!" I yelled in Rudy's ear. His face swung around, panic in his eyes, and was about to say something, I think, when we hit the ground at about thirty-five MPH, (My guess, later).

The huge helicopter bent in the middle and suddenly the floor came up and hit Rudy's back, slamming him into me even harder.

'Oh God, we're dead!' I thought.

The prevalent sounds for those four long seconds were screams, rending metal, grinding, thumping, crashing and banging.

With a final 'WHANG', we came to an abrupt stop that finished piling almost everything that had been in the rear against the forward bulkhead. My neck was stretched on the final impact and my head bounced off the wall, knocking me silly.

After several hours, (probably two minutes), I woke with a start, and while I tried to get my eyes to focus, I tried to remember what had just happened, and why I seemed to be dangling in mid-air. I blinked and looked around. Rudy is lying below me on the ground showing through the hatch. He's unconscious (or dead, I thought). In the dim, smoky, dusty light, I see a few others, like me, hanging limply from wall harnesses. A few are stirring, or trying to extricate themselves from their straps. That's when I remember. "Fire! Explosion! EXIT SHIP!"

I searched for my harness release, but in my confusion, I couldn't find it. I pulled my M-16 bayonet from its scabbard on my canteen belt and sawed, (Damn! Why don't they sharpen these things!), 'til the webbing gave way and I fell on top of Rudy, who pushed me off and called me a MF. I didn't mind, I was just glad he was alive. One of the Grunts hobbled by and pulled me to my knees.

"C'mon, we gotta get outta here!"

I grabbed Rudy by his tattered flack jacket, pulled him upright, and repeated the invective.

"C'mon, we gotta get outta here!"

I struggled to my feet, my head spinning. I felt like I'd been beat-up with baseball bats all over my body. I pulled the still dazed Rudy up and turned, looking for a way out.

The interior of the ship, in the 'twilight', (But its still morning?), didn't resemble, at all, the way it looked before. The walls and floor were bent at odd angles, and piles of debris, including bodies, were mounded up front. Leaves and sticks were almost knee deep in places. I heard moans from under the piles. Somewhere, somebody was still cursing. I stumbled through the hellish scene, pulling Rudy, to where the left side door gunner's window should be, but found it blocked completely by brush. I looked around for the Grunt, but he wasn't in sight, so there HAD to be a way out. I looked left and where the wall had buckled out there was light coming through a hole torn in the aluminum skin of the aircraft that appeared large enough for a man to get through.

I towed Anderson over, told him I was going out and explained that he was to follow. The hole was low to the floor, so I knelt and rolled out. I fetched up against someone's legs. That someone was Jim, battered and bloody.

"I was just comin' to look for you, seen anyone else?" he said.

Just then Rudy rolled out the hole and 'ooff'ed into my back.

"Well, there's two more. You guy's hurt bad?"

I shook my head, even though I really hadn't checked to see if I was really damaged or not. Among all that general pain, it was hard to tell. Rudy shook his head and managed, "I don' think so."

Jim got me by the arm, pulling.

"Well, then get up an' help get the others out."

Behind Jim was the Grunt Sgt., dripping blood from numerous cuts and scratches, also. He limped past me and stepped over Rudy and, with his bare hands bent a large, jagged piece of metal helicopter skin back out of the way, enlarging the hole, and re-entered the ship.

I stood up and flexed all my limbs, and, though they hurt like hell, they all worked. Amazing! Rudy was up, too, and if I looked half as bad as he did, I must be dead. He was bleeding from hundreds of small cuts on his face and arms. There were green places that would soon be bruises over almost every square inch of his visible skin. His fatigues were tattered and torn and the back of his flack jacket was missing, except for the inner lining. All in all, we ALL looked like plane crash victims.

Jim followed the Sgt., (Blake, I learned later), into the wrecked chopper. Rudy and I stood for a moment looking around and at each other.

"I can't believe we're still alive, can you?" Rudy said, shaking his head.

"Are we?" I wondered.

"I think so. Bein' dead wouldn't hurt this bad."

I looked at my watch. 9:08 A.M. Or was it P.M.? In this gloom it was hard to tell.

"Wow!"

"What?" Rudy asked, picking at something sticking out of his face.

"Eight minutes ago we were flying along, a bunch of dumb, semi-happy fools, an' now…"

"Now we're a buncha fools in th' shit!" Rudy said looking around at the mangled wreckage of our former transportation. Our gaze went to the huge tree trunks, spaced 20 to 30 feet apart, that formed this primordial forest. The ones we'd miraculously managed to miss, mostly, on the way down. And the one we didn't miss in the last second of our flight, around the base of which the nose of our helicopter was wrapped.

"An I DO mean, sheeit!"

The forest floor had very little underbrush, as no light, to speak of, penetrated the solid canopy fifty feet overhead. There were just little sparse bushes and clumps of grass. The forest floor was spongy and soft from eons of compost settling from the giant trees. It smelled like a greenhouse, and was just as hot. The drifting smoke from the wreck, mingled with air so heavy it left a film on your skin. I could tell immediately that nothing would ever dry completely here. Wouldn't be good for wounds, either, I realized.

"We better help out, man," I said, to keep that thought from continuing. "Bound to be a buncha broke-up guys in there." I nodded to the chopper.

"Yeah. OK, c'mon."

He turned and ducked back into the hole in the ship. I followed, stiffly.

We entered a scene of quiet pandemonium. Guys who looked like walking dead themselves were digging out guys who looked REAL dead. They were throwing crates, boxes, and tree limbs around, sometimes exposing a head, a leg, or an arm, some of which were twisted, at odd angles. They'd get a hold of any appendage that looked like it wouldn't pull off and jerk the wounded guy out of the jumble and set him up against the far wall if he was breathing or conscious. The still ones were laid out on the tilted floor back by the hatch where my seat had been. There were ten guys, counting Rudy and me, searching through the rubble. Six guys were sitting against the wall, and so far three guys were laid out, not moving, though I couldn't tell if they were dead, or what.

I moved over by the brush-choked door gunner's window and started to pull at the twisted limbs. I set my boot into the pile and grasped a large limb to pull at and the pile called me a "Son of a Bitch." Turned out I'd stepped right on Terry Leonard's leg. The broken one, I found out in no uncertain terms when I'd extracted him.

"Sorry." I said, miffed. After ALL, I HAD pulled HIM out of the pile, and HE calls me a SUM-BITCH? I dragged him, not very gently, over and propped him against the wall where he continued to cuss under his breath, between winces of pain.

Ten minutes of hard digging later, we'd cleared the bulkhead between the flight deck and the bay, and extracted six more guys, including the door gunners, who'd taken the brunt of the debris face-on. Unbelievably, though they both had stove-in ribs and multiple contusions, they were conscious and actually smiling when we pulled them out. They, I'm sure, knew they were lucky to be alive.

Sgt. Blake peered into the pilot's compartment and yelled for some assistance. We all crowded up, ready to lend a hand.

"Get something to pry with!" he ordered, "A steel bar, crow bar or something!"

He pulled two more Grunts out who had piled up under the dashboard and handed them back. They were pretty broke up but still alive and we laid them out on the floor as gently as we could.

Next came the co-pilot, a Second Looie, who, other than a big gash across his forehead and scratches everywhere else, seemed perfectly fine. The pilot, a Captain, was a different story. He was pinned in his seat by the bent and twisted frame of the cowling and both his legs were crushed. "Probably his pelvis, too." I heard the Grunt medic say after he'd checked him out.

Some metal bars were found and after considerable prying and tugging, the seat mounts were broken, allowing the pilot to be carefully extracted from the cockpit. I couldn't believe he was still conscious and cussing a blue streak under his breath, even as we carried him back and laid him out on the floor. Tough dude!

Sgt. Blake did a head count and came up with twenty-six guys, not counting the officers. Three were missing. I told him about seeing the Grunt fly out through the hatch on the way down and two more were found wandering around, dazed, outside the ship.

Thirty men in all, and only twelve were completely able-bodied. Seven had minor broken appendages or bones. Five had serious breaks or wounds and were down for the count, though conscious. The Captain was the worst wounded. Two guys were unconscious with serious wounds and expected to die and two were dead. One guy was missing and counted as dead.

Thankfully the Medic was among the able-bodied and took charge of dressing the wounds best he could and detailed some Grunts to bag the dead. He set up a crude aid station in the rear cargo bay inside the chopper and attended everyone's wounds according to seriousness.

We all, at Blake's orders, scrounged around for usable equipment and supplies.

"After all, this is still 'Indian-country'," he reminded us, "an' th' VC mighta seen us go down. We'd sure make a prime target out here in his back yard."

A smart-ass in the rear of the group said; "If anybody's out there, Sarge, we prob'ly dropped that there truck on 'im." We all laughed. A little humor goes a long way in situations like these.

We gathered up ammo for the 60s and found most of our rifles and ammo for them. We dug around for our personal stuff, but THE most important thing was water. All in all, we had about four gallons of it, thanks to twenty four canteens and a couple of two quart bladders that were in the chopper's emergency pack. Not a lot, but it'd keep us going for a while. Sgt. Blake immediately commandeered all the water and told us it would be rationed according to need.

The choppers on-board radios were smashed beyond repair, and we were left with two walkie-talkie types that had a range of about a mile in flat country. The Lt. said he'd radioed 'Maydays' all the way down, but had not been acknowledged, so, for all he knew, maybe nobody knew that we were even down.

"Here we are in 'Gookville', in th' jungle, in th' dark!" quoth Rudy.

23

LOST IN PARADISE

The helicopter pilot was our ranking man, of course, but he was wacked-out on morphine. The co-pilot, a butter-bar lieutenant, only had a head wound, but he was a real REMF and didn't have any experience as a ground-pounder. He didn't have the foggiest idea what steps needed to be taken to secure our position and to preserve our lives until we could be rescued. He DID have sense enough to defer to Sgt. Blake and allow him to take care of the details of our impromptu ground operations.

In this, Blake was THE MAN.

By 11:00 A.M. he had every able man, including the Dirty Thirty group, either salvaging equipment or doing a careful recon of the area, or preparing a defensive perimeter for a NDP. For surely, he told us in no uncertain terms, we shouldn't expect to be found and extracted for possibly some time. Maybe days! I, for one, didn't relish the thought of staying out here, our asses flapping in the breeze, as it were. I was certainly not alone in this sentiment. Everyone was bitching and complaining, but he told us to "Clam-up, get to it and DO IT!" unless somebody had a sure-fire solution to our problem.

None of us did, of course, but that didn't stop us from bitching.

Rudy and I found ourselves on the RECON patrol that consisted of eight men. We split up into pairs and each pair went off on each point of the compass about 150 meters, looking for any landmark, clearing, or possible LZ.

"Keep an eye out for gooks, too!" he added, almost as an afterthought.

Some afterthought!

Me and ol' Rudy took the west route and, carrying as much ammo as we could lay our hands on, skulked off into the rather sparse undergrowth, sneaking forward like we'd likely stumble across an NVA division or something.

The 'Fishhook' region, near the Vietnam/Cambodian border, is rough country; not mountainous, but hilly, and covered in a thick growth of jungle and rain forest. This area was, as I said before, virgin forest with 150-200 foot tall trees towering on 3-4 foot diameter trunks.

The lowest limbs, supporting the lower level of canopy, were at least 50 feet up, and, we'd found out the hard way, there were two more layers above that. Therefore, very little light filtered through to us on the ground. We had very little difficulty pushing our way through the foliage, which consisted of scrub trees, clumps of saw grass, and something that looked like Elephant Ear plants. And moss. Lots of moss that made the ground spongy, for which I was grateful, as it allowed us to creep very quietly on our mission. The air was perfectly still, pungent smelling, hot and wet. The mosquitoes were thick and hungry and I spotted leeches on the leaves of the brush, so I told Rudy and we avoided contact with the leaves whenever we could.

'Lotta ways to lose blood out here!' I thought.

Now, I'd been out in the jungle, on firebases, but I'd never been 'Out' in the Jungle. I won't lie. I was scared. But Rudy was scared shitless. He'd only been in-country a month, as a RTO in Phouc Vinh and never figured on being in a real combat situation.

In his nervousness, he was stumbling along beside me, crashing through the bushes like a wild animal. I played the 'Old Hand' part and tried to get him to calm down and exercise noise discipline so the gooks, if there were any, wouldn't know we're coming. It helped calm MY nerves, trying to instruct him in the ways of 'Boonie-walking'. I was somewhat successful, and by the time we were out about the max distance, we were both concentrating and peeling our eyes for anything out of the ordinary. It became so quiet, I felt it was just the two of us in all the world. It was creepy. Really creepy.

We stopped a long way out and just stood still, goggling around at our surroundings. It was all so....foreign to both of us. No sound, save the buzzing of gnats around our ears, and a 'Fuck You' bird in the distance somewhere, screaming his distinctive call, that echoed off the trees at irregular intervals.

Distracted as I was, I couldn't help being struck by the natural beauty of this place. The giant trees soaring up into the brownish green sky above our heads. The vegetation, while not thick, was lush, and sprouted anywhere it could. Some of the larger plants were pallid, almost albino, from lack of light, but sort of glowed, beautiful in their pallidness. Here and there, a weak beam of sunlight found its way through, visible as a laser beam in the thick air. Anywhere it touched the forest floor was a profusion of bright green leaves and even flowers! Huge, pink or white lily-like exotic blooms that, in contrast, made everything in their surroundings drab and colorless. Curious Rudy, eased over to one of the blooms, bent and sniffed. He looked up, his nose wrinkled.

"Damn! Smells like shit'r somethin'!" He whispered.

I had to laugh, and it sounded so loud, in all that quiet.

"Just like a lot of things in this country." I whispered, "Looks good on the outside, but rotten inside."

I'd been following my compass bearing all along. I sure didn't want to get any more lost out here than we already were. I took a piece of white writing paper and stuck it on a high bush limb where it would be visible for a distance, as a reference point, and we moved off north to circle out on a radius of fifty feet or so. It took a half-hour to come back to our starting point, and we hadn't seen anything but bushes. There were definitely no clearings or landmarks. I removed the piece of paper and we sat down to rest a bit and smoke a cigarette.

"God, it sure is beautiful here, I'nt it?" Rudy said, exhaling smoke through his nose and gazing around.

I nodded as I lit up.

"Yeah, beautiful as some of th' snakes they got over here, but they'll still bite you." (Veteran sage wisdom.)

"Shit! Snakes!"

Rudy bounded to his feet, searching the ground around for slithery things. None were apparent, and he settled back down.

"I think snakes may be the least of our problems right now, man." I said, "We need to watch out for the two-legged kind. The ones with guns."

"You seen any gooks since you've been here?" he asked. "In-country, I mean."

"Yeah."

"Like, up close?" awe in his voice.

"Yeah."

"Had to...you know....kill any?"

"Yeah." I said, not proudly.

"Was it...like...hard?"

"No..." I thought a minute, inhaling smoke.

"....the killing was easy. Th' thinking's what's hard."

I said this more harshly than I'd meant.

"Wow, man, I didn't mean...." His voice trailed off.

"I know, man." I soothed him, "I just mean... I'm not some kinda Gung-ho fucker, ya know? I ...guess I just don't want to talk about it, 'specially not now, OK?"

"Sure, OK, man." He nodded. "I guess we got other stuff to concentrate on, right?"

"Right." I said and smiled.

Rudy was young and new. He'd learn a lot while he's over here without my help. He smiled back and we finished our butts in silence.

I reversed our compass heading and we found our way back to the wreck. I reported what we'd seen, (or not seen), to Sgt. Blake and then joined Jim, Rudy and Pagans, sitting by the tilted plane, trying, not very successfully, to soothe Leonard.

Terry, in his usual manner, was cussing the lifers who sent him on this "Fucked-up detail!"

"Sandbags, my ass! They're tryin' to kill me! It's some kinda conspiracy, I'm tellin' you. Oh, them fuckin' fuckers 've fucked me over too many times!", etc, etc.

When all the RECON pairs had come in, it was determined that there were no NVA troops in our vicinity at present, though two of the grunts reported finding an "Old, old" bunker about a hundred yards east, but it showed no signs of occupation since "Jesus left his shoes."

While we were out, besides our walkie-talkies, they'd come up with a PRC-25 radio. The hand-helds worked OK, but the radio had a busted battery, and the spare hadn't been found yet. Rudy, being COM-

249

MO, was put in charge of trying to fix the longer-range PRC-25, but he told the Sgt. if the extra battery couldn't be located, it was hopeless.

Blake grouped us up and had a Pow-Wow. He informed us, sparing no details, the situation we were in. Low on food, low on water, wounded guys that would probably die if we weren't rescued within the next couple days. According to the co-pilot, we were approximately nineteen miles out of Quan Loi and twenty-six miles from our destination. According to the map, the nearest settlement was a hamlet named 'Ba Veng', but it was another ten miles beyond our location, with rough terrain between. We were going to have to wait 'til someone on the ground or a helicopter or plane came by close enough to contact on our little radios. Until then, we'd just have to "Tough it out."

At 4:00 that afternoon, it started raining again. Of course we didn't feel it 'til 4:30, because of the overhead cover, but we HEARD it bust loose at 4:00. We had time to move the wounded and our supplies into the hulk of the chopper before the rain seeped through the canopy and started coming down in 1-quart drops.

Sometimes the water built-up in the leafy cover until the mat couldn't hold the weight, then it'd dump suddenly, three or four gallons, on some hapless soul walking below. Wouldn't have been so bad if you'd had your soap ready. We stayed relatively dry inside the chopper, except for six guys who were sent out on LP around our camp. It was still raining hard about 8:00 that evening when I wrapped myself in my poncho liner and settled against the wall into a restless sleep.

At midnight, I was shaken awake by the Sgt. and told to relieve Private Simms on the LP.

Man, it's really, really dark in the rain forest at night. No light from the moon or stars or anything! Blake used a red-lensed flashlight inside the chopper, but would allow no lights at all outside. I followed him out by holding on to the back of his pistol belt.

"How'm I s'posed to find him, Sarge?" I asked the blackness when we stopped.

"He's a hundred yards out that direction." The dark answered back.

I groped and found his arm so I could tell which th' hell way he was pointing.

250

"What's th' password, Sarge, I don't wanna get shot sneaking up on somebody."

"Candy Cane is th' outgoing, and th' counter is 'Yipes, Stripes', got that?"

"Candy Cane, Yipes Stripes, …uh…yeah, I think so."

I turned to go and he touched my shoulder.

"You'll be relieved at 0400. Listen for this whistle."

He blew a call that was supposed to imitate a night bird.

"That means somebody's coming out, OK?"

"OK, Sarge."

"I just whistled so Simms knows you're coming, now go!"

He aimed me outward and pushed me off into the blackness.

I sort of squat-walked for the first 20 feet, 'til I ran into a sapling tree, cracking my sore knee and making a bunch of noise. Then I decided to go hands-and-knees, with my rifle over my shoulder, creeping along, feeling ahead with my hands.

'Man, I can't see shit!' I thought. It was complete absence of light, like being in a cave. I crawled forward, trying to stay in a straight line and counting my knee paces, trying to judge the distance. (100 yards = 300 feet = 300 12" knee paces, I figured). After 275 knee-paces and two more altercations with bushes, I stopped and stage-whispered "Candy Cane", feeling very stupid. I listened for a minute and whispered again, "CANDY CANE!" Still no answer. I eased forward another ten paces and croaked again, "CANDY CANE!"

This time, somewhere off to my right came, "Yipes, Stripes!"

"Simms?" I whispered, trying to fix his location.

"Yeah, who's that?"

"Hudson, I'm your relief." I crawled in the direction of his disembodied voice and in about ten feet I ran my head into his stomach as he stood looking for me.

"Hey! Watch out, man!" he oofed.

"Sorry, I can't see a thing."

"And you won't," he said "that's why they call it a 'listening post', 'cause you can't see."

Smart dude!

"Well, you heard anything?"

"Just you crashin' in th' bushes, man."

"Anything else?"

"No, but things have been crawlin' over me all night. I don't know what they are, like some kinda crabs 'r somethin'. They don't seem to bite."

Oh, great!

He headed back in and, with some satisfaction, I heard him tangle in a bush and cuss it, trying to get past it. I settled in and started listening. The one real disadvantage an Artilleryman has is 'Artillery Ear'. A constant 'ringing' in your head that, under normal circumstances doesn't bother you, but in that vast silence, it sounded, to me, like an entire army of crickets.

'I don't think I could hear a train over this!' I thought.

I strained my eyes and ears for any sight or sound, but all I saw was black and all I heard was crickets. I was scared and could imagine a VC sneaking up on me, so when the first 'thing' crawled over me I jumped two feet and nearly screamed. Whatever it was it went on and I eventually settled back down until another one went across my hand that was resting on the downed tree I was sitting beside. This time I figured it was time to move. I crawled 'til I felt the end of the log, then went straight out 'til I found a bush about ten feet away. I squatted down and continued my watch from there. Whatever they were, they left me alone the rest of the night.

At 4:00, I was relieved, (and I DO mean relieved), by Jim Lynch. Before I left, I told him to stay away from the log and, of course, he said, "What log?"

I crawled back to the wreck, checked in with Blake, wrapped up in my poncho liner and crashed.

About 8:00 A.M., I woke with a start, feeling like things were crawling on my face. I think I was having a dream that things were crawling on my face, but even after I was fully awake and had lit my first cig, I STILL felt like I was being crawled on.

I reached up with my hand and rubbed my face.

Besides a two-day growth of beard and dirt, I had a hundred little scabs on a hundred little cuts ranging from pinpoint size to a couple inches long. From the crash, I guessed. I hadn't even noticed. My body was racked with pain and my swollen knee didn't want to support me at first, until I flexed it enough to break the crust of dried blood on my pant leg.

I managed to stand and hobbled around the cramped inside of the chopper. The first scene I saw was the wounded; laid out in rows in the rear of the cargo bay. Some were awake and the Medic was helping them eat C's or drink water from a canteen. Most of the others were still, though moans came from under some of the poncho liners. The Medic, a guy named Wilkins, stood and walked past where I was standing.

"How they doin', Doc?"

He dug some more cans of food out of a box and then looked at me.

"Some good, some not so good."

He shook his head. He'd been up all night, I'm sure, and looked like a warmed-over corpse, himself.

"They'll find us today and pull us out of here. Bound to!" I said, hopefully.

He looked at the captain, moaning and twitching under his blanket.

"I sure hope so," he whispered so only I could hear, "this is no place for open wounds."

I knew the Captain was the worst injured. His legs weren't just broken, they were crushed and the skin was split open from knee to crotch like overstuffed sausages. I knew they were wrapped, to keep the bugs off, but his blood had soaked through the gauze and his blanket, and the ever-present flies were buzzing thickly in the confined space.

Mosquitoes were feasting on open sores, making everyone that much more uncomfortable.

Wilkins was right. Anyone with a halfway serious wound wouldn't last long here.

"Yer buddy...uh...Leonard?"

"Yeah?" I answered.

"What's with him, anyway? I thought I'd hafta knock him in th' head t' get him t' let me set his leg. He's a real asshole, ya know?"

Wilkins shook his head, grinning.

"Yeah, he's THAT alright!" I laughed, "A real independent thinker. I don't see him, where is he?"

He thumbed toward the 'door', where gray morning light was filtering in.

"Out there somewhere, thank God, using his rifle as a crutch. Wouldn't sit still, even with th' morphine in him. He's still cussin' them lifers."

I laughed and shook my head, then ducked out through the hole. The scene I was greeted with was like something out of a science fiction movie. Or maybe a Salvador Dali painting.

It was lighter outside, but only by degrees. A heavy fog hung about waist high, blanketing the ground. I felt like I'd walked into a cloud. Other guys were walking around, hunched over like little old men. Their upper bodies appeared to be floating on the mist. Also, suspended in the cloud were heads. I realized it was guys sitting down. One of the heads was Jim, so I shuffled over, trying not to trip on invisible bushes or debris or men.

"Hey, man." I greeted him.

"Hey." He looked up and I saw that his face was a mass of cuts and bruises, too.

"You look like you've been in a cat fight an' lost." I grinned.

He studied my puss for a second.

"You ain't no beauty, either."

"I feel like shit." I moaned.

"Who don't? I feel worse'n I look."

"Whatcha doin'?"

"Cookin' Beanie-weenies."

Even this close, I could see nothing below his shoulders.

"Yeah?"

Sure enough, he bent and brought up a steaming C-rat can and stirred it with his mess spoon.

"Breakfast." He said simply and took a bite.

I got a whiff and realized I was so famished even Beanie-weenies at 8:00 A.M. smelled good. I'd have to go back, get my stuff, and see what kind of selection was left in the ration box.

"Seen Terry?" I asked.

"Little while ago." He mumbled around a bite of beans. He gestured with his spoon.

"He stumped off that-a-way. Got a slat o' crate wood strapped to 'is leg an' walkin' like 'Chester'."

"He's ripped on morphine, I hope he doesn't get lost." I said.

"No chance, man. Terry's th' original Bad Penny, always shows back up."

I nodded, laughed, and went off to get my cooking gear. A few minutes later I was sitting on my helmet next to Jim. Rudy'd joined us and we brewed-up coffee and I had some kind of chicken/gravy thing that I chose not to identify or look at too closely. It was delicious, but only when you're starving.

Rudy looked even crappier than Jim and me with purple and green bruises all over his face, contrasting sharply with his blond hair. His pug nose was crooked, somehow. He also had a splint on the middle finger of his left hand, wrapped in a brown army sock that made him look like he was carrying a potato. I hadn't noticed this yesterday, and said so.

"My finger started turning blue last night an' it swelled up." He explained. "Th' Doc looked at it an' said it's broke. Funny, I didn't even notice, everything else was hurting so bad." He chuckled.

"I'm still worried about Terry." I said, chewing. "He could wander out there an' th' gooks'd get him."

"Nobody'd care." Jim said.

"Sure wouldn't." Rudy agreed. "He's bein' a real prick. Even worse'n usual."

"Well, he's been through a lot, with his leg, an' all." I said. I don't know why I was defending him; he IS a prick.

"Shit, ain't we all." Jim spat.

"'Sides," Rudy said, "he won't get far on one leg an' a rifle."

I finished off my warm cherry Kool-Aid.

"Guess not." I agreed.

After chow, I felt considerably better. Amazing what even bad food will do for you.

In a little while Pagans came over and sat with us and we discussed our predicament. Rudy'd been at the radios since dawn, but there'd been no answer to his calls, so the Sarge had him shut down to conserve the batteries. There didn't appear to be any 'friendlies' on the ground anywhere near us. Hopefully no gooks, either.

255

"Surely they'll be looking for us today." I offered. "We've been gone 24 hours, already."

"We're s'posed to listen-up for planes flyin' close enough to pick up our transmission." Rudy informed us.

"I heard th' Grunts talkin' last night." Jim said. "They said there'd been a lot of VC and NVA activity in this area in the last month an' that we're right on the Ho Chi Minh Trail out of Cambodia into III Corps. They've been movin' a lot of men an' material through here under th' cover of these trees."

"Yeah, they're completely invisible from th' air down here." Pagans said.

"Yeah," I reminded them, "an' so are we."

"There it is!" They all intoned.

"The Doc says the bad wounded gotta get outta here ASAP, or they'll get gangrene from th' climate an' th' bugs," I said, "Th' captain's in real bad shape, I think, the Doc seems worried about him."

Pagans shook his head and looked down.

"Well nobody's going anywhere 'til a plane flies close enough to call on our radio, but they're gonna be looking for us, you can bet on it." he said, hopefully.

"Yeah, man, you bet yer life!" Jim said sadly.

"Well, I hope they come soon," Rudy said, "it's spooky out here."

I sat back and belched, (playing the Hardened Veteran again), and said,

"In this soup (the fog) th' gooks could come in right among us an' we wouldn't know it 'til they jumped up and said, 'Chiu Hoi, mutha-fucka!'"

Rudy looked all round and whispered, "Oh shit!"

Jim and Pagans said, "There it is."

24

RESCUE!

About 2:00 that afternoon, the mist had gone at least. It slowly evaporated as the heat came up. The air was still thick, but you could see through it, anyway. We were all lying around, conserving energy, reading or writing letters home; or just sleeping; recuperating.

I happened to be looking the Sgt.'s way when he sat up straight, cocked his head sideways, listening to something. I started listening, too, but ten or fifteen seconds went by before I heard anything. By that time most of the other guys were up, listening to the wonderful sound of a helicopter engine, getting louder by the second. Some guys started yelling and waving, like, yeah, they were going to hear us from way up there.

Blake was already at the chopper with the radio clutched in his hand. We all shut up and listened as he spoke slowly, deliberately, into the small speaker on the front of the unit.

"ANYONE, I repeat, ANYONE IN LISTENING RANGE.... THIS IS DOWNED HELICOPTER CREW ON GROUND AT ....." he glanced at a note he held in his other hand, "CO-ORDINATES 0086912 DASH 3856, PLEASE ACKNOWLEDGE, OVER!"

I could hear an unbroken hiss from the radio as we all strained to hear. I crossed my fingers. The engine sound was getting closer. After fifteen seconds passed, Blake repeated the call, but there was still no answer. The chopper sounds were going off, now, to the west. Soon it was gone completely. We all slumped in disappointment.

"Shit, I thought for sure he was close enough!" Pagles said in frustration.

Sgt. Blake was standing there, still holding the radio.

257

"Don't worry, men. They're probably searching in a circular pattern, so when they come back next time, they'll be right over us."

The Lt. was there, too, and added, "He's right. They always search in a spiral. I know those pilots, and they won't quit until they find us. Don't worry."

His words were thin encouragement. We all sat back down, but the tension was as thick as the air, as we all strained to hear the sounds of a helicopter at any second.

A half-hour passed and finally, we heard the 'Thump-Thump' coming toward us again, growing louder and louder. Blake had turned the radio off, but had not set it down.

He repeated the call, same as last time, and we all held our breath.

No answer, and the bird was almost right on top of us, judging from the sound.

Rudy was ten feet away and was calling on the other walkie-talkie, on a different frequency. His face lit up, (Purple and green), and he yelled.

"I got 'em on 'Dust-off' freq, Sarge!"

I, at least, breathed a sigh of relief!

Blake spun the dial on his set, the stronger of the two, and we all heard a 'pop' as someone keyed the mike and crackled.

"LAST TRANS, REPEAT PLEASE, OVER."

Blake spoke carefully into the mike and was answered! We all started jumping around, forgetting for a moment our injuries, and slapped backs and hands. He shushed us after a moment so he could hear.

"DOWN CHOPPER, THIS IS GUARDIAN ANGEL, CAN YOU GUIDE US OVER YOUR LOCATION BY SOUND?... OVER." the voice crackled out of the speaker.

"THAT'S A ROG, GUARDIAN ANGEL, YOU ARE PASSING OUR LOC TO THE SOUTH, REPEAT, SOUTH, DO YOU COPY?"

"DOWN CHOPPER, COPY SOUTH, AM SWINGING NORTH NOW, OVER."

We waited a long minute and then the 'whopping' sound was directly overhead and small twigs were raining down from the canopy, though we couldn't see anything but vegetation, we knew the chopper was there and we were elated.

Blake called him and told him to hold that position.

"ROGER, DOWN CHOPPER, I HAVE YOU FIVE BY FIVE, UNDERSTAND AM OVER YOUR POSITION, AM MARKING CO-ORDINATES. THERE IS NO SIGN OF YOUR ENTRY FROM UP HERE. WHAT IS YOUR SIT-REP, OVER."

Blake explained about our wounded and our need for medical supplies immediately and extraction ASAP. The chopper pilot asked us to pop smoke so he could exactly locate us. We popped a green smoke canister and the cloud drifted straight up with no wind to blow it. After a minute, the pilot came back.

"WE DO NOT SEE SMOKE, REPEAT, DO NOT SEE SMOKE, CAN YOU ADVISE US ON THICKNESS OF THE CANOPY, OVER."

The Lt. reached for the radio and the Sgt. handed it over.

"GUARDIAN ANGEL, THIS IS LT. JENKINS, CO-PILOT OF DOWN CHOPPER. THE OVERHEAD IS THREE LAYERS, REPEAT, THREE LAYERS, WITH HEAVY CONCENTRATION OF DEBRIS. CAN YOU SPOT A CLEARING OR LZ WITHIN A CLICK OR TWO OF OUR POSITION, OVER."

Another minute passed and we heard the helicopter swing out and circle, then come back on station.

"THAT'S A NEGATIVE, LT. NO BREAK IN CANOPY ANYWHERE AROUND HERE. OVER."

"GUARDIAN, CAN YOU PULL US OUT OF HERE? OVER."

"GROUND, THAT'S A NEG. I DON'T HAVE EQUIP-MENT FOR JUNGLE EXTRACTION. WILL RETURN TO BASE AND SEND CHINOOK WITH PENETRATOR, BUT WILL BE TOMORROW BEFORE A BIRD CAN BE BROUGHT UP THIS FAR, DO YOU COPY? OVER."

"I COPY, GUARDIAN, ANY CHANCE SOONER? OVER."

"NOT A CHANCE, LT. NEAREST PENETRATOR AT TAY NINH. THEY"LL MAKE AN LOC TONIGHT, AND BE

ON STATION BY 0800 TOMORROW. SORRY FOR DELAY, LT. OVER."

"GUARDIAN, GROUND, DO YOU HAVE ANY MEDI-CAL SUPPLIES ON BOARD YOU CAN DROP US TONIGHT? OVER."

"THAT'S A ROG, LT., HAVE YOUR MEN TAKE SHEL-TER AND I'LL TRY TO DROP IT RIGHT IN YOUR LAP, OVER."

We all got inside the chopper or against a tree trunk and soon there was a crashing sound and a torrent of leaves and limbs, along with a 6 foot long, two foot in diameter tube with rounded ends thudded to the ground some fifty feet north of the wreck.

I heard the Lt. inside the ship acknowledge the rescue package, thank the pilots and sign off.

We all started talking at once. The SLAP-SLAP of the chopper receded, only to be replaced by the slap-slap of our hands on each other's backs as we generally rejoiced.

The LT came out and held up his hands for quiet and we all got control of ourselves.

"Men, we're not out of this, yet,...." He paused, "but there's hope, there's hope."

He waited while we burst into another round of backslapping and laughing, then he continued.

"Now, when Wilkins gets the Med supplies unpacked, I want all of you helping him tend to the wounded." He nodded toward the medic, who along with two of the Grunts, were already unlatching the catches on the emergency canister. "When we've done all we can do for them, then see to yourselves. Get some chow, gather your equipment into a small bundle not more than twenty pounds, max. Then get as much rest as possible, we're gonna need it!"

He turned to Sgt. Blake.

"Looks like we'll be here another night, sergeant," we all groaned at the prospect, "so, same drill as last night for perimeter guards and LPs." He looked around the group again. "Any questions?"

A voice from the group said, "Uh... yessir....uh, what's a...pen-etrator, sir?"

I was wondering the same thing, as, I'm sure were others.

"The 'Jungle Penetrator' is a large weight, attached to a climbing rope, designed to drop through the overhead to allow extraction of personnel on the ground." He recited from a training manual, I'm sure.

"You mean we gotta go back outta here through THAT?" Leonard said, unbelieving, pointing to the canopy.

"Unless you'd rather walk." Blake interjected.

We all laughed as Terry shook his head.

"Hell, no, Sarge, but… ain't it kinda …dangerous?" Terry persisted.

Blake's expression became serious.

"Not as dangerous as trying to walk out of here with as many wounded as able, and a DAMN-SIGHT less dangerous as stayin' here waitin' for th' gooks to find us."

The LT looked at us and, I'm sure, saw the impact of THAT statement on our faces. None of us wanted to be here any longer than necessary.

"Any more questions?"

There were none, so Blake handed out details and we all got to work helping the medic or gathering equipment. He told us that anything that couldn't be carried on our backs would have to be destroyed, along with the chopper wreck. We were told to stack all of the extra supplies and equipment in the belly of the hulk, which we did. Three of the grunts began setting C-4 charges on the piles and around the helicopter fuselage, and running the wires to a central location, for quick hook-up when the time came. I couldn't help thinking, it would be hard to sleep in a helicopter that was wired for self-destruct.

At 1745 we'd done all the preparation we could. All the wounded were re-bandaged in clean dressings and those that needed it, and some, (like Terry), who didn't, got more morphine. All the junk that we'd carefully carted out of the chopper, of course, had to be carried back in and was thrown in piles in the open cargo bay and wired with explosives.

Sgt. Blake then called us all together, including all the wounded that could be helped or carried out, and gave us a textbook lecture on the "M-1802 'Jungle Penetrator'".

He read from, believe it or not, an Army Manual that was included in the emergency pack with the other supplies. He recited:

"Penetrator, Jungle. Uses and application in the field. Consists of an 8"X 30", 200 lb. Artillery projectile, without the explosive charge,"

'Thank God!' I thought.

"Attached to coiled, braided 1 ½" rope, knotted at 36" intervals for climbing, that can be hand-deployed through thick canopy, from a hovering helicopter. The rope, and accompanying cable suspended lift-baskets, are attached to a floor mounted winch system that allows some play for the movement of the rescue vehicle while in hover mode. After extraction is complete, baskets are reeled in and rope and weight are jettisoned."

"Man, I ain't done th' rope-climb since basic." A voice said.

"Hope you was good at it," another Grunt chided, "'cause if you stop in front of ME, you'll get a bayonet up yer ass."

"Hell, that's gotta be a 200 foot climb, man," Terry bitched, "How'm I s'posed t' climb with this broke leg?"

"Everyone that CAN, climbs. Those that can't, go up in the body baskets. It won't be easy either way, but there ain't no other way, so get used to the idea. Clear?"

He went on with special instructions to certain guys, assigned the guard roster, (I wasn't on tonight. Good!), and released the rest of us to "Get your shit together, 'cause tomorrow morning, if some dumb-shit slows things up 'cause he can't find his ass with both hands, THAT dumb-ass is stayin' HERE! Do I make myself CLEAR?" He smiled sweetly.

'Perfectly!' I thought and turned to the chopper, trying to think what else I could part with from my pack. Everybody else was doing the same. Twenty pounds on your back on a vertical climb, feels like forty after the first 50' or so and gets heavier as you go up. At my 115 pounds, my pack equaled 1/6 of my body weight, compared to 1/12 of most of these guys. I still refused to dump my camera, though it weighed two pounds by itself, but figured I could pick up a new shaving/shower kit at the PX and I definitely hoped I wouldn't need my whole 500 rounds of ammo. Also, my canteen and pistol belt could go, but NOT my poncho liners. By the time I was through, I figured I'd have to carry about 12 pounds, not counting my rifle and helmet, which the Sgt. wouldn't let us dispose of.

"You'll NEED that 'pot' on th' way up through those trees, to keep yer dainty heads from gettin' bumped!"

He DID let us DX our flack jackets, so we wouldn't have to heave that 12 lbs. of lead up the rope.

By the time we were all squared away, it was full dark. Blake still wouldn't allow any lights exposed outside the chopper, and it was too damn dark to do anything else. I found me a spot by a tree root, (away from the wired-up chopper), and, wrapped in my mildewy poncho liner, tried to sleep and not think of the hard climb we'd have to endure tomorrow. Tried to concentrate on how great it was to be rescued, at all! But, the way my bones hurt NOW, I wasn't sure how I was going to make it in the morning. If these skinny little arms were gonna pull me up out of this jungle, or not. But, one thing I DID know. I'd go out trying!

Right before I finally drifted off, I realized it hadn't rained all day, so far, and thought, 'Good.'

Around midnight, it rained. Hard.

Sore and wet, I moved into the wired-up chopper. Slept like the...shudder...dead.

25

UP THE MAGIC ROPE

At 5:30 A.M. I was awake. So was most everybody else, due to the raging storm outside. The rain of last night had, as of about 3:30, turned into a full-blown monsoon. Sheltered, as we were, under the layers of foliage, the only effects of the tempest we experienced, was the continual dripping and bucket-splashes of rainwater, and the noise.

We could hear, but not feel, the howling wind that shivered and swayed our leafy ceiling. The movement also shook loose leaves, twigs, chunks of compacted debris and some large limbs, that banged off the metal fuselage, causing us to jump and increasing everyone's irritability. I went out to take a leak and almost got creamed by a hunk of wood six inches in diameter and three feet long. It literally scared the pee out of me. I felt like we were a bunch of cavemen, hunkering in our cave, fearing we had angered our thundering Gods and waiting for retribution.

"They ain't gonna send nobody out in this shit t' rescue our sorry asses." Leonard said, disgusted.

I thought about it for a second and said,

"No, probably not, but it's just as well."

Jim looked at me as if I'd lost my mind.

"Whadda ya mean, 'just as well'? I wanna get MY ass outta here as soon as possible."

"Me, too." I replied, "But the next helicopter I get on is gonna have to be GUARANTEED to fly, an' I ain't flyin' in no monsoon. No Way!"

"I wonder how long monsoons last?" Pagans asked no one in particular.

"Sometimes days, I think." Jim said.

"No shit? Really?" Terry struggled to his feet, (well, foot, really), "Shit!" he muttered and stumped off, leaning heavily on his M-16 cane.

"Hell, I don't know!" Jim retorted defensively, "They're th' Asian equivalent of a hurricane. A huge tropical depression coverin' hundreds of miles. I read that once, somewhere."

"Well, whatever, it's a cinch we're stuck here 'til it blows by an they can get a bird in th' air to come out here an' get us." I peered out the round porthole-like window by where we were sitting. The gloom outside matched the gloom inside.

"Yeah," Rudy said, "We might just as well lay-dog an' not get our bowels in a uproar, we ain't goin' nowhere. Think I'll have some chow."

"Man, I wish you hadn't said that!" Pagans said.

"Said what?" Rudy turned back.

"'Bout yer bowels, man. Now I gotta GO."

We all chuckled, despite our woes, knowing he'd get pretty wet if he went out now.

Rudy went over to the piles of stuff, found an opened C-Rat case, and started going through it. Jim and I joined him. We selected our meals and went over by the door gunners open window, partly to get some air, but mostly 'cause it was far enough away from the wired explosives to keep us from blowing up while we lit our C-4 stoves. I had Beanie-weenies again and Jim and Rudy both had Beef and Potatoes.

I stuck my hand out the window a let the rain wash the bean juice off and I noticed the rainwater was considerably cooler than our canteen water. I held my canteen cup out and let it fill from a steady stream that cascaded from somewhere above, then mixed in the cherry Kool-Aid. I smacked my lips and was about to drink when Jim put out his hand and stopped me.

"You really shouldn't drink that water, man."

"Why not?" I said, "It's just rainwater."

Jim leaned close, said low,

"That Grunt that blew out on th' way down?"

"Un, huh?" I didn't see where this was going.

"Well....he's hangin' up there, somewhere." Jim pointed up. "'Sides, lord knows what else's died up there."

I threw the Kool-Aid out the window.

10:00 A.M. passed with no let-up in the storm.

11:00 A.M.

Noon. Hell, 2:00 P.M. Man, we were really getting antsy.

Finally at 3:00 the wind died down some and the thunder stopped entirely. It may have been my imagination, but I thought the drippage had slowed down a little, too.

4:00 P.M.

5:00 P.M. 'Hell, are we gonna hav'ta stay out here again tonight?'

The Medic and the LT were talking about being worried the Captain wouldn't make it another night out here.

Finally, at 5:30, we heard the Slap-Slap of a chopper coming our way. We all ran out, hollered, and waved 'til the Sgt. told us to shut-up.

The LT got contact on the radio and Blake was running around telling everyone to get their shit and detailing guys to help carry out the wounded. That chopper flew off but within ten minutes another, larger, from the sound, came and hovered over our position. Shortly, a crashing sound was heard from above and an object, the Penetrator itself, came through, bringing with it a cascade of limbs and debris.

It looked like a huge plumb bob and it thudded into the ground pointy end first, imbedding itself half its length in the mossy soil. The yellow knotted rope snaked down and coiled around the weight until it was played out then stood there bobbing and waving like it was alive.

"Cool!" I heard someone say.

"We'll see how cool it is when we're halfway up it." I muttered.

We were all ready to go and were grouping up closer when the Sgt. told us to stand back. Just then we heard the sound of chainsaws starting up in the canopy, and soon, limbs and big hunks of foliage were falling out of the overhead. In less than ten minutes, we got our first look at our 'Guardian Angels'. Two men in rappelling harnesses, carrying big saws, had cut their way down through nearly 75 feet of trees, opening a way up for us. One man slid on down to the ground, while the other stayed just below the opening and guided the first of the body baskets through the narrow opening and let it down to the first man.

"We got ten minutes! Fifteen, max, to get everyone up." He yelled.

We all gathered again at the rope, except for the Medic and his team and the guys detailed to set the charges on the helicopter.

"I want everybody hustling on th' rope, NO DELAYS! Once you start climbing, DON'T STOP, or you stop everyone behind you. DON'T HURRY! It's a long way up and you'll need every bit of strength you got just to make it to the top, so PACE YOURSELVES and DON'T MAKE MISTAKES! It's a long way down, too."

We were listening closely to his instructions, as if our lives depended on them. Of course they DID!

Then he grinned and said.

"OK, first man on th' rope. Going up! First floor, Garden Dept., second floor, Firewood Dept., Third floor, A RIDE OUTTA HERE! LET'S MOVE IT, MEN!"

The first guy started climbing, and scampered up like a monkey on a string. The rescuer let him get to the third knot and started the second man, and so on.

Then it was MY turn and saying a prayer for Charles Atlas-type strength, I pulled myself up, and up, and up. I concentrated on the feet of the guy in front of me, mostly so I wouldn't be tempted to look down. The knots were muddy from the boots of the first guys, so in order to not slip my grip, I'd cling to the rope with my knees and place each hand individually around the knot above, then pull myself up to the next foot knot.

The rope was swaying and going up and down with the motion of the helicopter, hovering somewhere above. The chopper pilot, though, was doing a tremendous job, holding it to three feet or so in either direction, but still as I neared the canopy, I could hear the guys already in the thick branches, cursing and thudding off limbs as big as your waist.

At the twentieth knot, (I was counting them), I was right below the canopy. I paused to let the guy in front untangle his rifle barrel from a vine. I turned mine upside down, hoping to avoid that, and then turned to tell Rudy, who was right beneath me, to do the same.

My eyes were drawn to the ground, some sixty feet below.

Some little, tiny men were rushing around a bent up toy helicopter, (the DEMO crew), and a line of six men were clinging to the rope below me, swaying in the non-wind like ants on a string.

Oh, my stomach felt like I'd eaten a mixture of Jell-O and butterflies.

I figured I'd better concentrate on looking UP, but before I did, I saw the first basket with the Captain and the door gunner with the broken ribs, coming up. The chopper crewman accompanied them with his saw to help ease the basket through the branches. They passed me as I was just ten feet up into the canopy. I got a glimpse of the pilot's face as they went by and I think he was smiling. Either that or he was in pain.

Maybe both!

The chainsawers had done a pretty good job of clearing the main branches out of the way. But the smaller stuff whipped back and raked across your face and hands trying to knock off your helmet (which we all wore with the chin straps tight), or pry your grip loose from the rope. Leaves, dirt and debris rained down on me from the other guys above, blinding me, going in my mouth, down my shirt. My pack or rifle were continually hanging on a branch or limb, and, of course, just then, the chopper would take a dip or rise, and I'd hang on with both arms to keep from being pulled off. I was completely engulfed in green creepers at one point and, except for the yellow rope in front of me, I could see nothing else.

I cleared the first layer and broke out into the nether land between canopies. The top of the first layer looked solid enough to walk on, though I was not tempted. I could see two guys in front of me and Rudy's head and shoulders poking out below.

Another basket emerged from the brown/ green mass, this one carrying Leonard and a banged-up Grunt. I was pulling up another knot as they passed me.

"Hey, Mouse!" Leonard yelled, "Race ya t' th' top! Ha, Ha!"

"Shut up, Terry!" I gasped, straining. In a few seconds, he was gone into the second layer. A few seconds later, so was I.

The second layer was a repeat of the first, but maybe not as thick or dense. A third basket passed going up as I was entering the third level. I noticed a lightening of the ambient light, and that the foliage was greener and brighter than down below.

'Hallelujah!' I thought, too winded to respond aloud, but there was definitely light at the end of the tunnel.

I finally emerged from the treetops into SUNSHINE and blue skies. There was no sign of the storm of this morning. My heart leapt with relief. I gazed happily around 'til I heard a voice from above.

"HEY, MOUSE! HAVIN' FUN YET?"

It was ol' smart-ass Terry, looking down out of the hatch of the Chinook, now only thirty or so feet up. He was grinning and so was I.

"SHUT UP, TERRY!" I yelled, out of breath.

Finally, after an eternity on the rope, I was hauled, unceremoniously, through the belly hatch of the chopper and propped against the wall alongside the rest of the rescuees. We could hardly raise our arms or move our legs, from the muscle cramping caused by the rope climb, but we were, to a man, all smiling, even Terry.

"Nice of you to show up, Mouse!" he smirked.

"Just shut up, Terry." I laughed.

The LT and Blake were the last to be pulled aboard.

The two baskets were lashed down and the 'Penetrator' rope was cut and I watched it drop into the jungle below. Free of its tether to the ground, the chopper hovered up and away about 50 feet. The Lt. had asked the pilot to hang around for a few minutes so he could be sure that the wrecked chopper self-destructed. We'd moved over so as not to be directly over the blast, which, we learned, was not entirely necessary. Sure enough, after a couple minutes, the sound of a huge explosion reached us, but the only indication anything had happened from up on top were a few tendrils of smoke drifting up from small fissures in the endless canopy. Many smaller, secondary blasts followed in quick succession.

"Yep, she's a goner alright!" I said to Rudy, propped against the wall beside me.

"Good riddance!" he spat, "Fucked up plane from th' very beginning."

"That wreck will be there, lost under those trees, 'til th' end of time." I mused as the rescue ship heeled over, headed toward An Loc.

"Better it than US!" Rudy said.

"Fuckin' A!" I smiled.

The group split up on the chopper pad at An Loc. The wounded were immediately loaded into ambulances, and rushed off to a nearby Medical facility. The Grunts were to be picked up by truck and billet at their HQ unit, there. The sun was down as they started loading onto the truck, and Rudy, Jim, Pagles and I walked over and thanked Sgt. Blake for helping get us out of a jam, and we all shook his hand.

He thanked US for our help and co-operation and, smiling a tired smile, wished us luck. He climbed up into the 'Deuce' and waved, as did the other guys in the back, as they drove off.

"Ruins my faith in th' Military Way." I said, watching them go.

"Whadda' ya mean?" Jim asked.

"I mean an E-6 who's a good guy." I answered.

"Knowhatchamean." Jim said, "Don't seem ...natural."

"He's STILL a 'lifer', though." Rudy said.

"Yeah, but there's a place or a time for th' 'lifers' of this world, Rudy. In a situation like th' one we've just been through, if it weren't for 'lifers' like Blake, we'd ALL been up shit creek THEY'RE th' ones with th' experience to know th' right things to do and when to do 'em."

I was waxing pretty philosophical, but hell, my life had just been saved.

"There it is!" Jim and Pagles said simultaneously.

A ¾ picked us up and we spent the night at the same Med station the wounded were taken to. I don't know which one because it was dark when we arrived and dark in the morning, when we left.

Our worst wounds were treated, and, bless 'em, we were allowed to shower and clean up if we wished, and we got new, ill-fitting, but clean, fatigues to wear, and a hot meal, which was leftovers from their mess, but still tasted mighty fine.

Even the cold, powdered milk.

By 2200 that night, we were all tucked in and crashed, big time. Lying in my bunk, right before I conked, I said 'thanks' to God, (or whoever's in charge, up there), for not having ended my story; for allowing my buddies, and me the chance to go on. To what? I certainly didn't know, but I was sure glad for th' chance.

26

PHOUC VINH

We flew back to Phouc Vinh at first light the next morning, on a C-130 cargo plane. Someone must have called ahead, because Ralph was there, in a ¾ ton truck, to pick us up at the airstrip terminal. He informed us we'd almost been given up for dead and was full of questions. We filled him in on the ride back to the unit and he was amazed that we had survived at all. So were we! We all knew how close we'd come to being a statistic, another number chalked-up to the so-called 'Conflict in Southeast Asia'.

I was even glad to see ol' Phouc Vinh again. It was almost a homecoming at HQ. The BC, Capt. Johnson, met us as we were dropped off at the CP, smiled and welcomed us back and told us we'd get the rest of the day off to recuperate, and that chow was waiting for us at the mess. Some of the on-duty guys from S-2 and S-5 came out, waved, and applauded as we walked over to the dining hall. We, appropriately, bowed and waved back like a bunch of celebrities.

At the mess hall, we were greeted by Carbone, himself, all smiles and slapping our backs and calling us 'His Boahs!'. After hours chow was almost unheard of around here, but the big ol' Mess Sgt. deemed us worthy of some "Spatial treatment" after our ordeal. He served us himself, sausage and powdered eggs, coffee, juice and powdered milk, and, best of all, some of his wonderful biscuits, with grape or strawberry jam. Man, that man could do biscuits to rival, even, my Grandma Mary's. Light, golden and huge. A meal in itself. I passed on the entrée and went straight for two of these delights, dripping with butter and jam.

'Oh God,' I thought, 'this is why you let me live!'

The appreciation of small pleasures is magnified in your mind after an experience where you'd almost lost it all. Almost sure you'd never eat a biscuit like this again. Or see your loved one's face. Or the blue sky, even. Yes, I must say, those were the best biscuits I've ever eaten.

During the meal, Sgt. Jackson came in, welcomed us back, and told us to rest up today, for tomorrow our asses would be his and we'd have to go back to work. He also informed us, LZ Sandy managed to get built even without our help, and from now on, transportation to the LZs would be arranged differently. For an 'Air Mobile' E-7, we all knew Jackson hated airplanes, and helicopters in particular, and if he had his druthers, he'd ship us out in trucks, the hundred or more miles, sometimes, between firebases.

This, of course, would take hours to accomplish compared to minutes to do the same thing in a chopper. And, of course, this is the First Cav., 'Air Mobile' Artillery, so, we fly. Jackson still didn't have to like it. I wasn't sure if I liked it either.

"Hey Sarge," I asked around a mouthful of biscuit, "Any idea why our plane...you know...went down?"

I knew, if anyone would know about this, it'd be Jackson.

"I heard th' BC getting' a report from th' co-pilot this morning. I heard him talking about 'massive electrical failure', that killed both engines at once. Then you just fell outta th' sky."

He shook his head as if to say, 'Wouldn't've happened in a truck.'

"Hear anything 'bout th' pilot? How he's doin'?" Jim asked.

"Alive, I think. Shipped him out to the hospital in Tokyo, last night."

"Good...He was a gutsy guy. You should'a heard him cussin' every one o' them fuckin' trees we hit!" Rudy laughed.

We all did. The relief of our return setting in. Jackson laughed, too.

"Oh Rudy," I chided, "You couldn't have heard ANYTHING over your own screaming! 'Oh God! Oh Shit! Oh Fuck!' all th' way down!"

A crowd of about ten or so men, including the First Sgt., I noticed, had gathered to hear the story, laughing along with us.

Rudy turned to me, a shocked look on his face.

"Yeah? An' WHO was that yellin' 'WE'RE DEAD! WE'RE DEAD!' in MY face all th' way down?"

The BS went on like that for quite some time, the crowd picking up details as we unwound, letting it spill out. I got a big laugh when I told 'em about stepping on Terry Leonard's broken leg, and how I was tempted to let him lie there, under all that junk, when he called me a "Sum bitch."

After a while, after the story got told, The crowd drifted back to what they were doing, and we were gathering up our breakfast trays. Sgt. Jackson stood up to leave.

"'Lectrical short." He shook his head, sadly, "Almost killed by a 'lectrical short. Glad you boys made it back!"

Jim smiled, holding his tray.

"Sarge, I'm even glad to see you, too!"

I went straight to the hootch and racked-out until 1500 hours.

When I awoke Fuk and Bowers had a million questions. Fuk said he thought he'd lost his music partner; Doug joked about not wanting to have to learn to play my guitar just to keep the crazy Hawaiian happy. They were genuinely glad to see me. I reiterated the story for them.

"Sometimes it takes a lot to kill a 'Mouse'." I told them.

I took a long time in the shower, the warm water easing the pain in sore muscles and strained joints. I checked myself out in the mirror over the sink, tip-toeing to see I even had bruises on my butt. Green and blue. All my normally exposed skin and even some not-exposed areas had cuts and scratches, some of which had festered. My Mom, in her wisdom, had made sure I had a bottle of Merthiolate in my shaving kit, to kill 'them foreign germs.' I spent a while setting myself on fire and painting myself orange 'til I looked like I was wearing war paint. If THAT doesn't kill the li'l germ-suckers, nothin' will!

I had chow in the mess hall, sitting with Rudy and Jim. Before it was over, it became a repeat of this morning, and we had to go over the whole bit again for those who, for one reason or another, hadn't got th' poop. We each added a little more of our own perspective to the tale, and all the guys were enthralled. Nothing this exciting had happened around HQ battery, since TET of '68, and none of these guys had been here then. I noticed the First Sgt. listening again from his table in the NCO room, and as we were finishing up, he stood and walked over.

"Glad yew boahs've made it back, year?"

We were all, I think, surprised at the sincerity in his voice, and the small smile on his normally dour face.

"Thanks, Top…uh… glad t' BE back." I managed.

Everyone nodded his thanks and the big man moved on out the door. Right outside, he jumped in someone's shit for something and bulled the two hapless individuals away down the street.

"Wow!" Jim said, awestruck. "He was almost…I don't know… human there for a minute!"

"Yeah!" Rudy said, similarly bewildered, "He…. Smiled!"

After dinner, we adjourned to Jim 'n Ralph's hootch. We sat in th' wooden chairs on the roof, drinking cold cokes and snarfing M&Ms from the PX. Mmm, mmm. The good life.

Fuk came down with both guitars and we sat around making up goofy lyrics to the tune 'Run Through The Jungle', by Credence Clearwater. The song was basically about crashing in a helicopter, but also somehow involved Jane Fonda, LBJ, and Nixon.

We laughed 'til we cried.

At 9:30, when Fuk went off to work, I went back to the hootch, packed the guitars in their protective wall locker, stripped and lay out on my bunk, read about a page of my book and fell into a deep, dreamless sleep.

Friday morning, being a regular ration day, I was up and at the DP, (Distribution Point) at 0-dark-30. Jax had been right about that 'early bird getting the worm', thing. I was there at seven or before, and the pick of the good stuff was mine. Juicier, ripe tomatoes, un-crushed produce, highly prized, hard to obtain seasonings. All the stuff the officer's mess usually grabs before the regular loading hours start at 8:00, much to the delight of Carbone.

The Sgt. was thrilled when I showed up the next morning with a new fuel oil tank for the kitchen range, to replace the old, leaky one that had to be drained every night, to keep it from leaking out the equally precious oil. I'd swung a deal with Jax for some empty wooden ammo crates, (a mere truckload), of which we, being right next door to the main supply, a 105 unit, had plenty. They'd been burning them in a pit until I convinced their man on that detail, to give them to me instead, in exchange for some LRRP rations, which I managed to swipe a good supply of at the DP.

"Everybody needs ammo crates." Jax said, "If you c'n supply me with enough crates, we'll do some tradin'!"

And we did. I also got two long bolts of vinyl coated, bright red cloth, which I knew Carbone was wanting for the mess hall curtains and tablecloths. I also got a wood screen door for my hootch, which, after much modification, including some radical carving with a dull bayonet ('I'm gonna sharpen that sucker someday!'), still fit like a four fingered glove. Still, it kept out all but the smallest bugs.

Days went by in regular routine. I picked up rations, ran errands, painted names, slogans or unit crests on some officers jeeps from other units, at the request of our BC, and worked more deals with Jax and another guy, an E-5 named Smitty, at the PX.

I managed to round up six OD green coolers to transport hot food out to the LZs. I got a thirty foot, green cargo parachute for the NCOs so they could throw a big cookout under it's spreading cover, the smell of their barbecue steaks driving the enlisted men crazy. Of course, WE weren't invited. We were all glad when it got rained out in the middle, and they carried their party indoors.

The 'Rainy Season' was full swing now and rarely did a day go by that it didn't pour at least once for an hour or two, creating miniature Colorado Rivers in the ruts in the red mud of the streets.

I pulled guard duty again and spent another night staring into the dark, wet night. I got Day Guard, in Tower November, a couple days later, which was a dick-job. I sat all day watching the gook traffic, mostly Lambrettas and motor bikes, on the Dong Xuai road outside the perimeter, and, it seemed like, dodging shells from the 105 unit, that fired out over the tower all day long. Talk about shell-shocked!

I also drew 'Shit Burning' detail, where you pull out the cut-down drums of diesel and, well, you know, from the latrines, drag them off on a piece of PSP behind a jeep, hopefully downwind, and set fire to them. A lousy job, but a quiet one, as nobody comes around while you're doing it. I got some reading done.

Terry Leonard came back, wearing a walking cast, and playing 'Combat Veteran' to the max. He got a Purple Heart for his broken leg and you'd have thought he was John Wayne's brother.

He and Weitzel and Ralph and several others were pretty much regulars down at the 'Old Bunker' every night, smoking dope and horsing around. Rudy, Fuk and I went on occasion, but none of us wanted to get a rep as a 'Pothead', so we held it to a minimum. I just wanted to maintain my 'Low Profile'.

Ralph told me one day that the other guys kinda thought I was standoffish, or 'too straight'. I told him I liked the guys, and the 'Smoking Ritual' brought us together and formed a bond, I guess you could call it, between all of us.

"I just don't want th' hassle, ya know?"

I explained that I wasn't, like, moralizing, or anything, just ....cautious.

"I don't want th' Lifers watchin' me all th' time, tryin' to catch me AT somethin', ya know? I just wanna be like a mouse, small and unnoticed."

Ralph nodded.

"There it is, man. I understand, an' so will everybody else."

Relationships being pretty loose among us 'Lower Echelon' cannon fodder, they all DID understand. They knew I wasn't a Rat or an aspiring Lifer or anything, so anything else I did was OK.

The end of March, we had more rain than not, and sometimes it was torrential, coming down in sheets.

Rudy and I had taken a 'Deuce' to the airstrip to pick up some heavy, wooden crates one dreary day, and were on our way back, on the open section of road out between the chopper pads, when it turned really ugly.

The wind suddenly picked up to near hurricane force, driving the rain straight into us with the force of pebbles being thrown. I could hardly see, but kept on driving, slowly, through the gale. I was afraid if I stopped, we'd be picked up and carried away, truck and all.

The wipers couldn't begin to keep up with the amount of water being blasted against the glass. The canvas top on the cab was popping and snapping in the pressure of the wind forcing wet spray around all the windows and doorframes, getting us wet, but we hardly noticed. I barely discerned the right-hand turn in the road in time, and cranked the wheels around and made the turn. This brought the wind broadside on my side of the truck.

With a couple of loud snaps and a tearing sound, the canvas over the bed gave way and flew off, carrying the wood frames with it. Rudy hollered "Jesus!" and looked at me with eyes big as saucers. The whole truck is rocking over to the right and, still moving, I'm fighting the steering wheel with every ounce of strength I have.

"If we can make it around the next curve," I yelled over the howl, "we'll be back at the battery!"

I really couldn't see much past the hood of the truck. The rain was now horizontal, the canvas top snapping like gunshots. I DID see the curve to the left ahead and laboriously pulled the wheel around, but the truck didn't turn! The wheels were cut hard over, but the force of wind on the side of the body wouldn't allow the lumbering vehicle to turn into it. We slid forward into the ditch and came to a rocking halt at a fifteen-degree angle away from the wind, which was still doing its best to topple us over.

"I guess we'll just sit it out here!" I yelled at Rudy and shut off the engine. "I can't turn it into the wind!"

I could tell he didn't like it but resigned himself with a nod.

We huddled in the swaying cab as the rain, if anything, worsened, and was blowing in through every crack in the frame of the cab, soaking us like we were standing outside. Soon my teeth were chattering, and I realized I was shivering with cold. I looked over, and so was Rudy.

That's when I heard 'The Noise'.

A big 'KA-THUMP' sound, somewhere off to our left.

Loud enough to be heard over the shriek of the wind and the hail of bullets, (or maybe it WAS hail), pelting the steel body with a continuous roar.

Rudy's mouth formed a perfect 'O' and he said, his voice trembling,

"What was THAT?"

"I don't KNOW!" I trembled back.

There it was again! 'KA-THUMP!!' Closer, it seemed, and I thought I felt the ground shake, just a little.

We both peered into the maelstrom, like we'd see something. Nothing but maelstrom to be seen.

Again! 'KA-THUMP!!' Closer!

'KA-THUMP!! KA-THUMP!!!' Louder still, the ground really shaking now!

Rudy's eyes were huge, now, and I'm sure mine were too, as something HUGE and blacker than the storm blotted out the light from the front windshield, was there for a second, then, with an almost deafening 'KA-THUMP', was gone again.

"W-What th' FUCK?" we yelled in unison.

Whatever it was, it KA-THUMP'ed its way away to the right. We heard a couple of big crashes over that way before the sounds were absorbed into the general noise of the storm.

We sat out another half-hour of debris banging off the truck, causing us to jump with fright. The whole time, the truck was threatening to overturn, but never quite did. Every time I thought we were going on over, it'd settle back and rock crazily some more.

Finally, as quickly as it had come, it quit. Quiet so loud it made your ears ring!

"Jesus! I've heard of 'Frog Drowners' before, but, MAN!" Rudy exclaimed.

I had to laugh, I'd never heard of 'Frog Drowners' before and the image struck me funny.

"We almost get our asses blown away, an' you sit there laughing?" he said, incredulously.

"I can't help it, man, you're TOO goofy!" I think I might've been in shock or something, but I was feeling pretty goofy then, too.

Rudy tentatively opened his door, tested the air and climbed out onto the running board.

"Hey Mouse, it's quit, but you gotta SEE this shit, man!"

"See WHAT shit?" I said and climbed out and up into the now open bed of the truck It became apparent what 'shit' he meant. The shit that was all over everywhere!

We seemed to be in a vast wasteland of bits and pieces of stuff from who knew where. Papers plastered into the barbed wire fences that lined the road. Boxes of wood and cardboard tumbled around like a bored kids blocks. Off away to our right lay two completely smashed Huey helicopters, smoking in their revetments in the middle of an open field, surrounded by crumpled metal wads and big corrugated sheets, bent into surreal shapes. Tent canvas flapped in the breeze, caught on some kind of outcropping behind us. The sky was still blue-gray, shedding eerie light on this scene of devastation.

"Now THAT'S what I call a Monsoon's monsoon, mon!" Rudy laughed, glad, as I was, it was over.

I noticed some more smoke over across the wide field with the two crushed choppers. It was coming from a group of low buildings that had obviously been hit by that KA-THUMP thing that had just missed us.

We both climbed up high on the front rail of the truck bed for a better view. We saw large gashes in the PSP and the ground, marking a trail from our left to within feet of the front of the 'Deuce' and on off to the right across the field, over the choppers and to the cluster of buildings about an eighth of a mile away. Whatever it was, it had been big! And heavy! But what th' hell was it?

We strained our eyes and finally Rudy said,

"A motor pool tent!"

"A what?" I asked, peering at the tangled mess.

"Like's in our motor pool, man. Big canvas an' steel tent! Round top so it sorta rolled with th' wind. Might even BE ours!" he said.

"I'll be damned!" I said, now picking out the shape of the huge, Quonset hut- shaped end protruding, and partially collapsed, from the wall and roof of another building.

We goggled around a bit more, then I said we should be getting back to the unit before they declare us dead again. We jumped in and I started up, backed out into the sloppy road and spun all ten wheels in the muck. I made the curve left with hardly any effort this time and we roared the final quarter mile to the familiar red gates and turned in.

Things at HQ had obviously not been any better than where we'd been. Debris was everywhere. The tin roof of the Commo hootch was peeled back, exposing somebody's Grateful Dead poster hanging in tatters from an inside wall. That and the overturned water tower were the worst of the damage I could see, but, damn, the place was a mess.

We drove to the motor pool and I was relieved to see that our motor tent was still intact, except for the flooding. A foot of water stood inside and around the tent and Sgt. Holly was sloshing around inside, retrieving tools and equipment from the water.

I parked the 'Deuce' and we got out and helped Holly straighten up as the water level slowly subsided.

I heard Rudy comment to Holly during this.

"It's weird enough over here without being killed by a big tent!"

'Shit, Rudy, you're goofy!' I thought.

27

APRIL 1ST, 1970
Fools Day

Jim, wiping his hands on a greasy rag, walked over to where I was grinding the starter on the ¾ ton Ration truck. The engine turned-over but wouldn't start.

I was getting pissed because I was already late for my ration run and ice pick-up, and I'd wanted to get it done before it rained again.

"Shit! Piece o' junk!" I slammed my hand against the dash, making all the gauges jump, and my hand hurt, but not helping start the engine one bit.

"Probably just wet from th' flood, man. It'll dry out by this afternoon." Jim said, then sniggered, "If it don't rain again."

"Well, o' course it's gonna rain again…. in about an hour, looks like!"

I jumped down from the running board into the gravelly goop of the parking area. We'd all resigned ourselves to wet feet and I hardly noticed the water squishing between my toes anymore.

"Still take a coupl'a hours to dry it out in th' shop." Jim said.

"Crap! It's gonna be a Fool Day, alright!"

"If we weren't fools," Jim said, astute for 7:00 in the morning, "we wouldn't be HERE, now would we?"

I wasn't aware then, how foolish I could be. I'd find out in a bit.

We managed to start one of the Chrysler 'Deuce and a half' trucks and I borrowed it to make my ration run. I blew a blue cloud of exhaust smoke as I muscled the big 'Six-by-six' out the gate. I never knew why they called it that. It had two sets of dual wheels on each side in the rear, and the two front wheels. That'd make it a five-by-five, wouldn't it?

Anyway, I made my ration run, as usual, and was back in the unit by 0930. It still had not rained. I was glad for it but my luck ran out halfway to the Ice Point. A slow drizzle started; a gentle, straight down kind of shower. What we called a 'Soaker' back home.

The guys at the PX ice plant loaded me up with six 100 lb. blocks, bedded in straw, as usual, to keep it from melting and help protect it from being busted up on the rough roads of the base. I drove back to the 'Dirty Thirty' and it looked like my luck had changed. It stopped raining as I backed up to the mess hall door.

'Great!' I thought, 'I'll get this stuff unloaded an' hide out at the motor pool th' rest of the day.'

How wrong I was.

The problem with using the 'Deuce', was the height of the bed. The steel edge of the floor was a good four feet off the ground, and it took one guy up in the truck handing down to another guy on the ground to off-load stuff. One of the cooks climbed up and started sliding the 8" x 10" x 36" blocks down to the edge, where I'd take them onto my shoulder and transfer it to another cook, standing in the propped-open door, who'd hand it on to the next guy who'd put it in the cooler.

I was handing-on the third block when the cook in the truck misjudged his timing and slid the next block down before I had completed the transfer. I heard it slithering on the wet steel and turned to see it teetering on the edge. I stumbled three steps back as it fell, reaching my right hand out to catch it.

This is where the foolish part comes.

I KNEW I wouldn't be able to stop that 100-lb. chunk of ice from smashing on the concrete step below. I KNEW I was off balance and should not have put my hand in harms way. But I DID anyway. Needless to say, the ice never even slowed down and my poor hand was between it and the concrete. 'Between a block and a hard place.' I'd hear for the next several days.

I heard 'CRUNCH' and I saw stars!

The ice block didn't even break, but my hand did!

I yelled and cussed. I jerked my hand back and it looked weird. The normally straight bones on the back were pressing up at odd angles under the thin skin, which was already red from internal bleeding. I jumped around and waved my arm wildly, like I wanted to fling the offending thing, and the searing pain, away from me, cursing the cook, the truck, and the Army in general. This hurt so bad, I stopped and settled for clamping my mashed metacarpus between my thighs. I grunted and felt like crying.

Carbone came running out yelling "What th' fuck!"

This had all happened so fast, I don't think any of the others knew what had just happened. The cook up in the truck pointed at me and said, "I don't know, Sarge."

He came over to me, hunched over with my hand between my legs. I allowed him to pull it out and as soon as he saw it he shouted,

"GAWD! Yer hand's broke!"

All I could manage right now was,

"No shit, no shit, no shit, no SHIT!"

Carbone took me over to the Aid Station (conveniently located right across from the mess hall), where Doc Phillips (who was not a doctor, but a Medic), shot me up with something that made me not care if I was on fire. The Doc felt my hand (which I'm sure hurt like hell, but....), wrapped it in gauze about four inches thick. He told Carbone to go tell the First Sgt. I needed to go to 15th Med for x-rays, and that he'd drive me down to Bien Hoa himself. Carbone rushed out and the Doc told me if I needed anything from my hootch, to go get it and to be back in ten minutes.

I answered, "Hunh?"

The trip to Bien Hoa was a blur. Not only from the speed that the Medic drove, which seemed considerable, but also from the drugs pumping through my veins. My hand throbbed through the induced haze the whole way.

At the hospital, I remember being led into a dark room, where I was obviously X-rayed. Then to an exam room where a doctor, (real one this time), read the prints and did some amount of crunching and popping on my hand, which stood my hair on end, even with the drugs. He finished up by wrapping my palm and lower fingers in cloth, uncomfortably tight, and slathered the wrap with quick-drying plaster, to form a cast that felt like it weighed about twenty pounds.

He then proceeded to fill out a card and handed it to me. I tried to take it, out of habit, with my broken paw. It fluttered to the floor. He picked it up and pressed it into my left hand, dangling uselessly at my side.

"This is your 'Profile Card.'" He explained, slowly, as if to a retard, "You'll be on light duty for three weeks, or at the judgement of your Medic, longer if necessary."

I nodded, dumbly.

"Try not to bang the hand around, or move it for a week or so, until the bones begin to knit, OK?"

I nodded again, he could be sure of THAT!

"When it's ....comfortable, try and use it to keep flexibility in your fingers, understand?"

He seemed so...sincere, it made me want to cry again, but I staved it off by nodding emphatically.

Outside, Doc Phillips was leaning against the truck, smoking and waiting for my return as I was ushered out the front door. A Spec-4 clerk was leading me, as I tended to drift off on my own. I was clutching my little paper bag, containing my card and a bottle of painkillers, to my chest like a kid with his lunch bag on the first day of school. I was still wacked-out on the morphine, so they urged me into the passenger seat, where I sat, dreamily trying to ignore the pain, while they talked a minute, outside. Then Doc climbed in beside me and started the engine.

"How's it feel, now, Hudson?"

"Hurts like hell!"

He nodded.

"Looks like hell, too!" I carefully held my purplish-blue fingers up for inspection.

He shuddered. "Damn right, it does." He said as he saw the swelling and discoloration.

He put the truck in gear and eased out of the parking area onto the main road and soon we were back on the 'highway' north toward Phouc Vinh. The afternoon had cleared and the sun shone down on the rice fields and countryside flashing past my window. I found that if I concentrated on the scenery, I could block out my throbbing hand for minutes at a time.

The Doc surprised me by lighting a joint and passing it over to me.

"A little more 'pain killer' won't hurt." He said, smiling.

"What th' hell." I figured, and took it. I took a deep drag that made my eyes water, but the THC immediately enhanced the buzz left over from the morphine and as I exhaled, I sighed.

"Oh, wow!"

I had another hit before I passed it back and I was back in the land of the living dead. He took it and hung it in his mouth while he inserted a cassette into his tape player, on the bench seat between us.

Crosby, Stills and Nash filled the cab with 'Ventura Highway'.

I sat back and watched Vietnam go by with all its variations of color and drabness. Aside from my hand, everything was 'cool'.

About 5:00 we came to the Song Be bridge. The Cowboys and Pepsi-girls had their motor bikes lined up under the trees on the Phouc Vinh side. Doc slowed the truck.

"Wanna check it out?" he inquired.

"Sure, why not." I was game for anything, in my mental state.

We pulled in and parked in the long afternoon shade, next to a jeep with 1st CAV, 2/7 markings. We were immediately swarmed with four 'Cowboys', selling dope, Pepsi, cigarettes and their 'sisters'. All #1 virgins, of course.

We declined the dope, (since we were already stoned), but I went for a luke-warm Pepsi. We went over and sat under a tree while the 'Cowboys' talked-up the assets (no pun intended) of their 'sisters'.

Two of the girls were off in the bushes, entertaining the occupants of the jeep. The other two sidled up to us, touching, smiling, and smelling of PX perfume. Generally making themselves available.

The Cowboy who concentrated on me had a 'Used Car Salesman' pitch. He said I could do anything I wanted with his 'sister' (except kick her tires) for 500 P. Even without the hard sell, his female companion was very pretty.

Somewhere between age twelve and thirty, she was a compact 4' 3" tall and weighed less than 80 lbs. She had shining long black hair, to her waist, and deep, dark eyes that flashed in conjunction with her white, white teeth when she smiled. And she smiled a lot! She was wearing a modified version of the Ao Dai dress, except, instead of pants, her mini skirt was higher than mid-thigh. From my vantagepoint, on the ground, I was enjoying a vista of sculpted legs that went right up to heaven.

Money exchanged hands and Doc went off down a small dirt path toward the river, while I was led into a small clearing where she laid down a blanket and took off her clothes.

I don't know if I was just stoned, or whether she WAS the most beautiful thing I'd ever seen. Anyway, all too soon it was over. (About five minutes). My beautiful apparition dressed as quickly as she'd undressed and with a "You fini!", she was gone, leaving me limp and smiling, dressing much slower than she had. Fumbling with my fly buttons with my left hand and easing my hand cast into my shirt I realized that I hadn't given my wounded appendage a thought for over ten minutes.

'Ah, the medical powers of 'Luv'.' I thought.

When I got back to the roadside, three girls and all four Cowboys were flocking around another jeep that had just pulled in, chattering their spiels. Doc was nowhere in sight, so I wandered down the path to the river. The walk through the woods was pleasant, but I missed the chirping of the birds, and the chatter of squirrels, so prevalent in nature walks back home. I wondered why there were no cute woodland creatures in the forests of Vietnam.

'Anything that don't bite back, gets eaten.' I guessed.

I heard them squealing before I came out onto a shelf of gravely beach at the riverside next to the concrete bridge support. Doc and his little cutie were cavorting in the brown water. She, riding his shoulders, her wet, naked body gleaming in the dying sun, was flinging her arms, trying to throw him off balance. He, trying to hold onto her legs and grab her tits at the same time.

I laughed at this spectacle, but was embarrassed for intruding, so I turned and walked back up the hill to the truck, where I smoked a cig and finished my, now warm, Pepsi. My girl, named Li, (or Lee), of course, came over and took my empty bottle for the deposit, I suppose, and we chatted in our pidgin-English.

"GI, you like fuckee?" she said, casually, like she'd asked me if I liked cookies.

What could I say?

"Well…SURE!"

"You come back, make more fuckee, OK?"

I tried to be suave, appealing.

"Well...SURE!"

She giggled a distinctive 'little girl' sound, daintily covering her mouth with her fingers. "You bring friends?" she turned to walk away.

"Well...uh....SURE!"

I heard her tinkling laugh as she walked back to the group, and soon she was leading another GI, a big country-boy type, off into the woods.

I watched them go with a sinking feeling in my stomach.

'What a waste!' I thought, 'A beautiful girl like that in the States, would be flirting and dating, looking for the 'right' man to have kids with, to raise a family. Instead, because of where she was born, because of this fucking WAR, she's a roadside whore at th' damn Song Be bridge.'

The morphine and the pot were wearing off, my hand was throbbing viciously and I was depressed as hell by the time the Doc came back. He jumped into the truck, humming and smiling and started the engine before he noticed me, huddled in the corner by the door massaging my right forearm with my left hand, and frowning.

"What's'a matter? Didn't you get laid?" He asked as we pulled out onto the road.

I didn't answer, immersed in my own dark thoughts.

He shrugged and drove us back to the base.

I spent that evening, and all the next day wallowing in self-pity. I couldn't play my guitar, I couldn't write, hell, I couldn't hardly scratch my ass with my left hand. I was a mess, both physically and mentally. I snapped at anyone that came near, so everyone, even Terry Leonard, gave me wide berth. I felt like I'd given the world a chance and the world had shit on me. Oh, Woe!

Finally, on the third day, out of sheer boredom, I volunteered for something. (Stupid, stupid, stupid! The first rule of the Army is: NEVER VOLUNTEER!)

But, foolish as it seems, I did!

'Greenline Detail'.

Laying barbed wire. Setting trip flares. Stringing tin cans on the strands of wire as 'rattlers'. No real heavy work. Just routine repair and upgrade. The two other guys on the job, Rudy A and Nick Nickerson, could do all the stake-driving and stuff, I figured, And I'd hold the end of the wire while they strung it out and stuff. I could, maybe tie-on cans. Anything that'd get me outside doing something!

Off we go, to the 'Killing Zone'.

The morning's cool. Only 85°, or so. It rained last night, so it's muddy between the short patches of grass that grows among the lethal strands and booby traps. But the sky is a clear blue, the humidity has dropped off for a change and it promises to be a fair day to work. Out in the open. Soaking up rays.

We drove the mess hall truck, loaded with coiled barbed wire and a couple iron stakes, gloves, bailing wire and cutters and a sledge-hammer. There were two cases of WP (white phosphorus) grenades, to be used as trip-flare traps and a bunch of tin cans from the mess hall. We parked behind bunker #42, gathered what we could carry, and Nick, being the 'ranking' Spec.-4, led off into the bunkers 'front yard'.

We were following a map, supplied by the First Sgt., that showed the way through the maze of wire, trip-traps (both phosphorus AND frag), Claymore mines and pressure mines. With this map, you suppos-edly couldn't go wrong. I hoped so! I was following in Rudy's footsteps, as he was stepping right where Nick was walking, slowly through the rows, constantly consulting the page of directions, pausing frequently, checking distances.

We picked our way through to the outermost strand of con-certina wire and located the spot where the neighboring farmers water buffalo had plowed out a whole string of wire during his meandering, one recent afternoon. The poor bull, we understood, had suffered mortal wounds and the loss of a foreleg, due to an unfortunate encounter with one of the many frag-traps available in this part of the perimeter.

Drawn by the sound of the explosion, I had watched briefly from beside the EM latrine, as the enraged Papa-san threw up his fists in an-ger, shouting unintelligible curses from out beyond the wire barrier to the guys manning #42. But they just shrugged and hollered back for him to go away. He eventually did, only to return an hour later with another water buffalo to drag off the carcass of the first one. It took him more than an hour to untangle the animal from the wire. Several of us went down to the 'old bunker' for an elevated view of the proceedings, and were making bets on how long it would take for him to blow himself up on another trap. We were amazed, and actually a little scared, when he hooked up the pulling animal and dragged the carcass away across the field, without setting off a single flare.

"Like, maybe he knew where they were all the time!" Jim muttered, next to me.

When we arrived at the scene, that day, we found that the farmer hadn't hauled ALL the carcass away. There was a rotting haunch and some unidentifiable chunks of cow lying around. Blood, dried black now, was spattered everywhere for yards. Flies, of course, were thick on the putrid smelling meat. So much for a pleasant morning's work.

"EEWWW! Man, That's gross!" Rudy wrinkled his nose, as did we all.

Rudy and Nick drove the new stakes and by 12:30 we'd strung the new wire and set three new trip-flares in that section. We'd tried to be careful not to step in the gore, but Nick finally did, raising a thick cloud of flies that buzzed us and bit us until we finished our work and moved away.

We had some more trip-flares to set in the inner string, so we worked our way back in and were glad when the flies didn't follow. We already had a system down for setting the traps, so we got busy.

A flare-trap consists of a WP or frag grenade, with the pin out but firing handle still on, inserted into a tin can that's wired tightly to a stake or tree. The can holds the lever in place while a wire is attached to the grenade on one end, pulled taut, and secured to another stake or tree on the other end. The theory is: someone (hopefully an enemy) will hit or stumble across the almost invisible wire, pulling the grenade from the can, releasing the lever, causing an explosion or flare to go off. This will give said enemy's position away to the brave and noble (but sneaky) men of bunker #42.

Since it took two good hands to tie on the cans, Nick did that. Ditto for running the trip wire, so Rudy took care of that, and attaching the wire to the grenade. That left me to unzip the flares themselves from their little cardboard packing tubes. Easy enough. I'd pull out the gray 4 inch long cylinder with its handle and pin, squeeze the handle in a bit so it could be inserted into the can on the post. Also easy. I'd then insert the flare two thirds into the can and let the handle out 'til it made contact with the inner sides of the can, effectively holding the grenade in place.

Cinch! I'd then pull the pin and Rudy would attach the wire and gently push the flare all the way into the can.

I'd just removed the second grenade from its tube, stood, and was walking over to where Nick was putting the finishing twists on the baling wire can-holder. The flare was clutched in my left hand, fingers firmly holding the lever. The pin was in. I heard a 'tink' sound and looked down in time to see, to my horror, the little metal cap, the one that holds the firing hammer down, break off from the whole lever and fly off, letting the hammer go, right before my unbelieving eyes. I heard the 'pop' and then the sizzle sound as the timer mechanism fired, right there in my hand!

My first thought was 'OH SHIT!! FOUR SECONDS! I GOT FOUR SECONDS!!!'

I didn't have time to throw it, so I rolled it off my palm into the wire between Nick and the still unsuspecting Rudy. I only got so far as "FIRE IN TH' H...." when the flare went off.

I was closest to it (three feet) and was instantly blinded by the flash. I felt a blast of white/orange heat wash over me and smelled and felt my mustache, nose hairs, eyebrows, arm hairs and head hair crinkle and burn away.

"OH SHIT THISISIT!!" I yelled and fell backward into a strand of barbed wire, luckily not setting off any more traps.

I heard Rudy yell "HEY!!" and Nick holler "What th' fu...!!" But I could see nothing but a pinkish white opaque world. I started screaming bloody hell and felt hands pulling at me, yanking me out of the slashing wire and dragging me a short distance, out of the circle of heat into the cool, cool air.

Nick obviously poured his canteen over my head, putting out my smoldering hair, and washing out my eyes. The cold water was almost as big a shock as the heat had been, and it shut me up, but at least now I could see a little.

Nick was kneeling next to me, and through a blur I could see the scared look on his face. I heard Rudy hollering "Is he OK? Is he OK?" I looked over and he was still trapped on the other side of the sputtering grenade, unable to get past in the narrow aisles between the strands for the intense heat. He didn't seem to be hurt, thank God, just scared.

"I don't know," Nick yelled back, "he's pretty cooked!"

"I think I'm OK." I managed, "I can see now. A little."

Nick hollered to Rudy, "He says he's OK."

To me he said "Think you can get up? We'll take you in if you can get up."

I tried to stand, using my forgotten right hand for support, and fell back with a grunt. Then I tried to stand using my left hand and even worse pain flooded over me, making me nauseous.

I fell back with another grunt and stared through my miasma at my left hand. I'd been so concerned about my vision, I'd failed to notice that all the skin on my left palm was blackened and burned. Crisp like overcooked bacon. Talk about nauseous.

The flare finally burned out and Rudy rushed to my side. Between the two of them, they practically carried me out of the KZ and put me between them on the seat of the truck and Nick drove like a bat outta hell to the Aid Station.

Doc Phillips said, "Not you again?" when they carried me in. Rudy told him what had happened and he swung into action, powdering my hand in case some of the phosphorus had gotten into the wound. Then he gently swabbed my hand with PK burn ointment from a big green tube. Then he wrapped several layers of gauze loosely around my palm and secured it with tape.

He gave me some more pain pills and told me that was all he could do. I had second degree burns on my hand and a glorified supersunburn on my face and arms. Not to mention, no facial hair. My mustache, which I'd cultivated for nine months, was gone, along with my eyebrows and lashes. My ball cap had protected my head hair except for the very front, which was singed ragged.

"It'll hurt like hell." He told me, "but barring infection, it'll heal within a month."

Rudy and Nick were relieved that I wasn't going to die, and told me so. I thanked them and apologized for almost killing them. I explained that it wasn't my fault; that the grenade was faulty, but I'm not sure if they believed me or figured I was the biggest klutz to come along in a while. At the time, I really didn't care. I just wanted to go someplace and lie down, curl into a ball, and sleep the next two months away.

Doc helped me to my hootch and he and Fuk helped me undress and get into bed, where I stayed, except for latrine breaks, for the next three days.

The Doc came to see me the second day. He swabbed my burns and changed the gauze. My unwrapped hand looked like a piece of meat and I nearly got sick, though Doc Phillips said it looked better, to him. To me, it looked like I'd be deformed for life.

He told me to come in and let him see me every day to swab the wounds. That way the scabs would stay soft and would reduce scarring. I told him I would, but the third day, I just couldn't bring myself to going out, stumbling around, on my pain drugs, both hands bandaged up like …I don't know… some kind of… invalid or something.

Hell no! I'd stay right here in my little world, sipping water from a canteen with a plastic straw, (courtesy of the Doc), eating a candy bar now and then, and block-out the rest of Vietnam with the new 'Chicago Silver' album in my headphones. Volume UP! My mood was black and I did not want to be disturbed.

Next day, Bowers and Fuk MADE me get up. They said I was stinking up the hootch.

"At least get up an' clean your stinky ass up, man." Fuk said, wrinkling his nose.

I resisted, but they pulled me down from my bunk.

"How'n hell am I supposed to even wash with no hands." I said, disgusted.

"Well, I ain't washin' you, but you sure gotta get washed, some-how, or you sleepin' outside." Fuk, backed up by Bowers, insisted.

"We'll figure out a way." Doug said, and they did.

They used the plastic bags that my tape-player instructions came in, two of them, inserted over my hands and secured with elastic blous-ing-bands above the wrists. This sealed my wounds off from getting wet and allowed me to cup a bar of soap in my right hand and suds up most of my offending parts. I just had to be careful not to drop the soap or it took a while to slide it against the wall and squish it back up onto my cast. I found this out quickly.

Drying off was another trick, involving getting the towel between my teeth, letting it hang down and rubbing it around with my forearms.

Not really effective, but adequate. To get my back, I held the towel in my teeth, draped it over one shoulder, and rubbed against the wall.

Tooth brushing was out. I had to settle for chewing some toothpaste, squeezed out against the metal sink edge, swishing and spitting. Ineffective, except for the minty taste.

Hair combing? Forget it. Just have to dry as it stands.

I managed to get my skivvy shorts on by throwing them on the floor, hooking my toes in the leg holes and raising my legs so they slid up (or down, as the case may be), followed by a lot of wiggling. Luckily, all army clothes were too large for me, especially skivvy-shorts.

'Life is gonna be a pain!'

Pain is right! My right hand settled into a dull ache, but the left one, the burn, hurt like well, fire! For a full eight days. Every day I'd go in and the Doc would clean, powder and change my wraps, and he gave me some tips on how to exist in a bandaged state.

I learned to carry a tongue depressor in my shirt pocket. This six-inch, slender piece of wood, inserted into an ace bandage wrapped around my cast, allowed me to turn book pages, pry open screen doors and scratch; great achievements, to me. This same method could be used for spoons, forks or toothbrushes, too.

Going to the latrine was a whole different story, which I won't go into here, except to say it gives you a whole new appreciation for opposable thumbs.

I could smoke if I could find someone to light it for me.

I wasn't comfortable, but I could exist.

Two weeks later I'd become a local 'Pain in the ass' around the battery. With nothing to do, I'd wander around watching everyone else work, and being stoned on pain pills, I got in the way a lot and annoyed everyone until they shooed me away. I'd hitch rides, sometimes, down to the PX or to the airstrip to watch the planes come and go. I read all my books. I couldn't write or play my guitar. I'd hangout at the motor pool 'til Sgt. Holly'd run me off, then I'd wander over to the 'old bunker' in the bamboo patch and smoke dope with the 'Heads'.

Life was mundane, and so was I.

I had way too much time to think. By the time my burn scabs started coming off and I got the hard cast off my right hand replaced with an ace bandage, I'd worked myself down into a deep, 'I don't give a shit' kind of a depression.

A lot of people didn't like me.

"I don't give a shit!"

I'd let my hygiene go. I'd walk around in daylight wearing T-shirts, baggy, un-bloused pants and my 'Ho Chi Minh Racing Slicks' shower sandals. I stank.

"I don't give a shit!"

Of course this brought the 'Lifers' down on me, but with my 'profile', and the fact that I was 'convalescent', there wasn't much they could MAKE me do.

"I mean, what're they gonna do? Send me t' Vietnam?"

I'd become an ASSHOLE! I admit it, but I couldn't help it.

In the third week of April, I was holed-up in my bunk when Tabaranza came in and told me someone wanted to see me in the CP.

"ASAP!" he said.

"What for?"

"Beats me," he shrugged, "Big-time officer. Says he gotta see you. Better clean up a little 'fore you go."

"Screw 'im." I retorted, "He can take me like I am. HE wants t' see ME, I don't wanna see HIM."

"Suit yourself," he said, leaving, "but make it quick, th' man seemed pretty upset."

"Yeah, yeah. I'm comin'."

I climbed down, slipped on my shower shoes, and followed Henry to the CP.

I entered and the First Sgt. was sitting at the front desk. With a tilt of his head he indicated I should go on into his office. He shrugged.

'Oh, oh.'

I walked through the inner door and a large man, a Major, I could see as he stood to greet me, said: "Hudson? PFC Hudson, from Lexington, Ky?"

I gulped, expecting bad news.

"Yessir."

He told me to close the door and have a seat. He indicated the chair in front of the desk. I did and sat down, a sinking feeling in the pit of my stomach. He sat across from me and I noticed his collar tabs. A chaplain?

'Oh, oh.'

He folded his arms on the desk and leaned toward me.

"How long since you wrote home, son?"

I had to think a minute. What's THIS about?

"'Bout a month or so, sir, I think."

I'd last written about a week before I broke my hand. I generally sent a letter once a week, but lately I'd been so...absorbed... I hadn't given it a thought.

He looked at me intently.

"I have received a communication from the First Cavalry Head Chaplain, in the 'States, that HE has been contacted by your mother, a Mrs. ..." he consulted a note in his hand, "Bonnie Hudson, in Lexington. She said she had not heard from you since mid-March and wishes to find out what has happened to you. Is that your mother's name?"

"Uh...yessir, that's my Mom."

"Is there a problem?" he asked, concerned, "Something I can help with?"

He looked so sincere.

I held up my bandaged hands.

"Maybe you can write a letter for me, sir?"

His smile widened. Now he understood.

"I'd be glad to, son."

I was incredulous.

"Sir... you mean MY Mom called the big Chaplain, and stirred everybody up to find out why I hadn't written?"

"I'm sure your mother is concerned for your well-being, Hudson, and your letters are very important to her. As, I'm sure, hers are to you."

"Uh...yessir, they are." I stammered.

"Are there any other problems?" he asked, "Other than the, uh, injuries?"

"Well... not really, sir." I said, 'I've been kinda...down, I guess, 'cause I can't even brush my own teeth, an' stuff. But it don't mean nothin', I mean, I'm OK, sir."

He looked at me and my slightly, shall we say, disheveled, appearance.

"It looks like you need to pull yourself up, above your own hardships, and face the responsibility to the ones, back home, who love and support you. Take THEIR needs into consideration, even while your own needs are seemingly great. Your letters are the only link you have to your lifeblood. Your Mom wants to hear from you, son, OK? And your mother is a very…forceful…person, according to my communiqué."

I smiled at this, first time in a month.

"You don't know th' half of it, sir."

He laughed, and I did, too.

"I'll write your Mom and tell her I've talked with you, and you seem as well as the situation will allow. I won't mention your injuries. That'll be up to you in your OWN letter that you'll dictate to whomever you can get to write it, tonight. Is that understood?

"Yes sir!" I said, "I'll get my Mom off your back, sir."

He laughed.

"Thank you, Hudson. That'll be all."

I stood, gave a bandaged salute, and walked out past a wondering Tabaranza and First Sgt. I left them wondering and laughed out loud, all the way back to my hootch.

28

APRIL 27, 1970

Yesterday afternoon, the Doc told me I could leave the bandages off my right hand, and to try and use it some, to increase the flexibility. My left was looking pretty good, too, but I still had to protect the new, pink skin of my palm with two wraps of gauze. The fingers of that hand, too, were free and healed enough to use.

"Hallelujah!"

I'd gotten Fuk to write my letters for me and, coming back to reality, I'd gotten myself more 'squared-away' in my attitude. I cleaned up my act enough to keep the officers and NCOs from looking at me with distaste.

Last night, I tried to play guitar, down at Jim's, with Fuk and a guy from Echo battery named Corey. My hands weren't quite up to it, so I let Corey play it. And, man, did he play it! He and Fuk played some wild solos and we sang and strummed 'til the wee hours.

Corey was just passing through, going back out to the firebase after a two week R&R in Bangkok. He was a chatty guy, nervous as a cat. Short in both respects: 5'5" tall, and "72 days and a wake-up". He had haystack blond hair and large, always scared looking, cornflower blue eyes. As I said, he played a hell of a guitar, and told us his R&R stories about getting laid and throwing money away like confetti.

I saw him this morning right before chow, getting into the S-2 jeep for the ride to the chopper to take him back out to LZ SANDY, (the one we didn't quite make it to). I walked over and told him I'd enjoyed the music last night, and wished him luck. He dapped me, (gently, 'cause of my hand) and told me to look him up if I'm ever out at E battery.

"I don't plan on any more time in th' field, if I can help it, but who knows." I laughed, and waved as they drove off. He flashed those blue eyes and 'Peace-signed' me.

In the mess hall, Jim, Ralph, Jack Pagans, Nickerson and Leonard were sitting at one of the rear tables, next to the NCO area door. They were talking to Sgt. Holly and Sgt., Jackson, sitting at their own table in the other room.

"When d'ya think it's gonna come off, Sgt. Jackson? Are WE gonna hafta go?" Jim was asking as I came in.

I picked up a tray, a bowl and a spoon, a mini-box of Frosted Flakes, two packs of sugar and a glass of milk and went to sit down.

"Week or so, I think," Jackson answered, " but soon, and yeah, we'll go, bet on it!"

I sat next to Nickerson and asked, "Go where?"

Jim looked at me and said, "Cambodia, man!"

"Yeah?" I asked, "What for?"

"Gooks, man." Ralph said from across the table.

"They say th' Big Gook Base Camp is over there, less'n a hundred fifty miles away." Nick informed me.

"Yeah, COSVN. Th' main NVA an' VC trainin' camp for all of II an' III corp."

Sgt. Jackson had finished and walked over carrying his tray.

"In th' past, whenever we made it a little too hot for 'em, they just 'dee-dee-mau'ed' across th' damn border, where we couldn't go." He told the group. "They got R&R centers an' everything over there in th' 'Fishook' area, an' th' 'Parrots Beak'."

"But if we can't go over there...?" Pagans started.

"Th' Gooks've been mixin' it up over THERE, too." Jackson said, "Attackin' cities an' villages, an' not stayin' in their jungle strongholds. Th' US has made a deal with ol' Sihanook, or whoever's in charge over there. Th' Cambo's want help kickin' th' Gooks OUT, an' WE just wanna kick th' Gooks ASSES, so, looks like we'll be goin' in, real quick, now."

Wow! This was pretty exciting news! We'd all griped about not being able to take the fight TO the Gooks. How we could whip 'em if we could flush 'em out and make 'em stand and fight. Now it looked like the US was going on the offensive again for the first time since early '67, and if we could surprise 'em over there, thinking they were safe, we'd...

"Kick their ASSES!" Leonard, his foot still in a cast and propped on a chair, said, after Jackson left.

"You couldn't kick a baby's ass with that rock on your foot, Terry." Jim said, standing and gathering his tray.

We all laughed and Pagans and Nick got up to leave, too.

"Jackson said he thought it might end th' war." Pagans said, hopefully.

"Bullshit!" Jim spat, "This war won't end 'til they run outta Gooks. An' they'll NEVER run outta Gooks. They got a endless supply of 'em up north, there, in Hanoi."

'Too true!' I thought.

The other guys cleaned up and left. I was finishing my cereal and Sgt., Holly was still back there sipping his coffee. We were the only ones in the building. The kitchen crew and Carbone were all outside, smoking and BS-ing by the side door.

I was getting ready to spoon-up the last bite of my breakfast, when, to my surprise, the bowl came up to meet me! The soggy, cold flakes and the little bit of milk went into my eyes and nose and the bowl clanged off my forehead. Before I had time to think about that, my table and chair, and me, were tossed five or six feet into the doorway to the NCO section, where I landed, HARD, under the overturned table.

My ears were ringing, and as I crawled out, wondering 'What th' hell?' I stood up and wiped the milk out of my eyes.

The first thing I saw was that the dining hall was a total shambles. Tables were thrown over, chairs and benches broken. Carbone's new red vinyl curtains, (he'd sewed 'em himself) hanging askew. Food from the serving line was splattered everywhere.

Sgt. Holly stepped through from the other room, over the table blocking the door.

"What th' hell was THAT?"

"I don't know!" I said, looking toward the kitchen. Or should I say where the kitchen had BEEN.

Now there was a hole. I realized, through a haze of smoke, I was looking outside at the still standing, burned remains of the old washhouse. The rear wall of the mess hall was gone!

"Whatever it was, it hit th' kitchen." I said lamely.

Carbone had picked himself up from the road outside, and burst through the screen door, which was now hanging on one hinge. He was followed by two of the cook's crew who stood, transfixed, as Holly and I were, and as Carbone was for a moment, goggling at the instantaneous destruction of a building.

The big Mess Sgt. was the first to react.

"WALL FUUCK!!"

His scream snapped Holly and me out of our trances.

"THEM DAMN YANKEE GOOKS DONE GONE AN' DONE IT AGAIN!!"

Holly and I edged to the other side door as the big hairy Sgt. got wound up and started picking up broken chairs and throwing them at anything left undamaged in the room. All the while, screaming about if he ever got a "holt" on some gooks and how he'd "slaved" to keep "Biscuits on them pore broke tables!" and on and on.

Outside, the smell of cordite and burned food was strong. A thin pall of smoke hung over the area. Holly and I walked around to the remains of the rear of the building, now broken timbers and shredded sheet metal. Sgt. Jackson was already there, digging around in the debris, picking up shards of shrapnel.

"Yo, Jackson." Holly said as we walked up.

The Survey Sgt. nodded to us engrossed in his examination of the blast.

"What was it Sarge? Mortar?" I asked, picking up a still hot jagged piece of metal with some gray paint still on the smooth side that was imbedded in the ground next to my foot.

"Too big for a mortar..." He answered, concentrating on a twisted piece of casing, "...gotta be a rocket. 122 I'd say."

He meant the Chinese/Communist 122 mm, launcher-fired rockets the Gooks seemed to have an abundant supply of, but rarely ever fired around here during the day. Their launching mechanism had to be set up for firing, highly visible from the air and subject to attack, until broken down again, for reuse, after firing.

"Gooks 're sure getting' balls." Holly commented.

122s For Breakfast

Just then the 105s next door fired out an answering volley and we stopped and watched for the result. We couldn't see the impact zone, about a half-mile out, but we heard the six rounds plow-in. There was a continuous rumble, like many truckloads of rocks being dumped simultaneously, and a small haze of smoke drifting up into the sky, out there.

While a small crowd formed to view the 'mayhem of the day', I walked back to my hootch and changed into a clean shirt, grabbed my little camera and went back and snapped some pictures of what a rocket the size of a round, wooden fence post can do.

Things settled down, with the exception of Carbone, who cussed the rest of the day, as he and his cook detail cleaned up the mess in the mess. I was caught by the 1ˢᵗ Sgt. and informed, since I was 'back on duty', (I guess the Doc ratted-me-out), and since Tabaranza was a 'Single Digit Midget', with only days 'til DEROS, I'd be assigned as the BC's driver. I was to report to him ASAP to drive him to Tay Ninh City.

I got my field gear and met Capt. Johnson at the CP at 0830. We drove out past Carbone and his crew tossing twisted sheet metal out the back of the mess hall.

The BC had a little map, which he clipped to the dashboard. It showed the route we would take marked in red pen, for the nearly six hour trip to Tay Ninh.

We went south on Hwy. 19 and instead of taking the turn-off for Bien Hoa, we continued on straight 'til we reached Hwy 13. We turned left, toward a large town named Thu Dau Mot, which we passed through and eventually took a secondary road to the right. We followed this road about thirty miles to its intersection with Hwy. 22, which ran through a smaller town, with an attending Army base, named Cu Chi. We stopped for chow at the 'B' battery compound at Cu Chi, and The Captain spent a half-hour talking to their BC.

I spent the time eating a cold C-Rat in the jeep, and talking to a Spec.-4 named Parsons, the Battery Clerk, there. I asked him how it was, there, in Cu Chi.

"Pretty cool." He said, "'cept th' dang gooks keep....appearin'... like, out o' nowhere, 'round here."

I looked around, half expecting to see VC.

"Whadd'ya mean...appearin'?"

"Like, one minute they're not there, an' next minute they are."

"INSIDE th' base?"

"Yeah, with grenades or satchel charges. They blow some shit up, then just...... disappear." He had a mystified look.

"A lot?"

"Here lately." He nodded.

We, of course, found out, after the war, the whole Cu Chi area was undermined with VC tunnel systems, allowing the gooks access to almost any part of that base. I was glad I never had to stay there for any length of time.

We exited Cu Chi, (not soon enough for me), northeast on Hwy. 22 and passed through another large town called Trang Bang, then through Go' Dau where we turned onto another secondary road and headed north. We zipped through a series of small hamlets with names like Bong Trang and Long My. Right past Long My, we were stopped by an 11th Armored Cav 'Duster' track, with it's dual 20mm cannon, mounted in the turret. It was parked sideways in the road, blocking both sides.

The Sgt. E-5, in charge of the roadblock, informed us that there had been some action on the road, up ahead, and we'd have to wait until the road had been 'cleared'. We sat around and soon two more trucks had come up and, told the situation, pulled in behind us to wait.

At 2:30, the Sgt. told us to follow him, in convoy, and he'd escort us to Tay Ninh. I was first in line, behind the 'Duster' and found out the TRUE meaning behind that name.

Finally, about 3:30, we pulled up at the south gates to the city We'd been looking, but had seen no evidence of fighting along the road-in, but next to the gate itself, was a pile of at least twelve VC bodies, guarded by a group of beat-up looking ARVN Rangers. The corpses were buzzing with flies and already stinking in the heat.

Not wanting to hang around, I quickly passed the track, waving thanks to the Sgt. and drove across town toward the Army base, dodging the bike and scooter traffic along the way in the bustling city.

Exotic, (and some NOT so exotic), smells assailed our nostrils in this foreign place. Cooking, Nouc Mam sauce, sewers, animals and the 'Great Unwashed' populace all combined to form a heady aroma that I only experienced in Vietnam. No American city, no matter how stinky, ever smells like that.

At one turn, on a side street, I caught a glimpse of the Steam Baths and had to grin to myself, remembering the last time I'd been here. I decided, if I had a chance, I'd see if Lee or Li, was still working, and get a rubdown. Chances are!

Once on the base, I drove to the same place where we'd 'stood-down', months before. (It seemed like years). 'A' Battery compound. We pulled up at their CP and Capt. Johnson told me we'd be spending the night, and that he wouldn't need me, or the jeep, 'til 0800 in the morning. I could see the battery clerk for quarters.

I had the whole night to myself!

'Ahhh! Steam bath, here I come!', ran through my head.

"Stay on base, Hudson, the city's off limits." The BC told me as if reading my mind. "Any questions?"

"No sir. I've been here before. I'll find something to do." I said, disappointed.

I arranged for my quarters and dumped my combat gear. It was too early for chow, so I jumped back into the jeep and drove to the PX and shopped for some candy, a toothbrush and paste, and some cigs. Then I just drove around base for a while, killing time and checking things out.

Even if I hadn't heard the scuttlebutt about the 'Cambodian' thing, I'd have known something was up. The camp, which seemed so sleepy and uninvolved before, was now abuzz with activity. Trucks were roaring everywhere. Places that were totally empty during my last visit were now crammed with men and materials, trucks, tracks and troops. An almost steady stream of Chinook choppers was bringing in more.

Tay Ninh is located, conveniently, halfway between the 'Fishook' and 'Parrots Beak' areas of the Cambodian border where it juts abruptly into Vietnam.

The NVA were reputed to have strongholds in both locations, so, it stands to reason if the US were to launch an offensive against these places, Tay Ninh would be the logical 'jumping-off' place for the invading troops. It showed in the anticipatory attitudes in the soldiers I met, and in the general 'hustle and bustle' of an army, preparing for a 'Big Push'.

At 1700 hours, I drove back into the compound, parked, and locked the jeep next to my hootch. I walked to the mess hall and had 'A' battery's version of 'Mystery Meat'. Carbone has a 'way' with mystery meat. Makes it almost edible. 'A' Battery's cook obviously had no such 'way'. The food was greasy and cool, but, being hungry, I choked it down while observing the other diners. I didn't recognize anyone.

After chow, I walked down to the Ranger Battalion, and, sure enough, they were still serving beer and the 8:00 movie was to be, you guessed it, 'Green Berets' with the 'Duke', himself. (It wasn't QUITE so scary, this time.)

There were a bunch of guys there, and we all got a little rowdy, yelling jeers and comments at parts of the movie. The projectionist finally got fed-up and shut off the machine just as the 'Gooks' were about to attack the camp. We all moaned and complained.

"If you guys can't shut-up and watch this movie, I can put the OTHER flick on. What'll it be? 'Green Beanies' or 'Shitty Shitty Bang Bang,'" he yelled over the general bitching.

Of course, we moaned that much louder, but pretty much in unison, we yelled,

"GREEN BEANIES!"

He started the flick again, and soon, we were right back, jokin' and jerkin' around, but we had a grand time, making fun of the 'Big Hero', who none of us would follow into a bar, much less, combat!

The beers made me sleepy, so I left before the picture was over. I knew how it ended. I walked slowly back to the compound under the black sky, filled with bright stars, but no moon. I was thinking, contemplating my future.

I was getting 'Short'! 40 days an' a wake-up 'til I could go home! I was thinking about the seven months I'd have left in my hitch when I got back. Stateside Duty? What did I know about the Regular Army in the States? Nothin'! It'd be Bullshit and more Bullshit! I knew THAT much.

I wasn't looking forward to it, but what were the alternatives? Stay here?

Hell, I didn't relish THAT thought, either.

Life in the 'Stateside Army'?

I'd probably end up in some podunk unit on some podunk base in Podunk, Nebraska, where all they do is polish boots and kiss asses. I hadn't polished a boot OR kissed an ass in so long, I didn't think I could, anymore.

I couldn't believe it! I was considering extending my tour!

I'd heard, if you came away from Vietnam with 150 days or less left in your hitch, they'd let you out on what is called an 'Early Drop'!

OUT as in OUT! Of the Army! No stateside duty, no active or inactive Reserve duty. Nothin'! Just OUT!

THAT part I liked.

It was just the thought of an extra two months in this hellhole.

The Evil I KNOW, versus the Evil I don't know.

The thought kept running around in my mind.

By the time I reached my hootch, (for the night), I'd made up my mind, ('I should be shot for this!'), to extend. As soon as we got back to

HQ, by damn, I'd sign the papers and stay 'til the 10th of August and, by damn, get my Early Drop. I wanted it THAT badly!

The three 'A' battery guys, whose hootch this was, were home when I walked in.

I said "Hi." And introduced myself and told them I'd only be there for the night.

They were three 'Gun Bunnies' from their # 3 gun. Their names were Jack, Randy and a guy called 'Fireball'. They had a card game going on a footlocker, pulled out to the middle of the room. The overhead light bulb, shaded by the conical metal cover, cast light on the cards and left everything else in shadow. A haze of cigarette smoke hung in the air, drifting through the beam of light like fog.

"You from headquarters?" The one called Randy asked.

"Yeah."

"Know anything 'bout th' shit comin' down 'round here?"

"Uh…no…not really." I answered.

"We heard we're gonna invade Cambodia, 'sat right?"

Randy didn't seem overly bright.

"Y'all know as much as I do." I said, watching Randy raise the pot holding only a pair of twos. "I heard th' ARVNs and 1st CAV are gonna help th' Cambos kick th' NVA outta their country."

'Fireball' was obviously cleaning house, judging from the pile of money in front of him on the table. It was 'Dealers Choice', and they were playing something called 'High Chicago'.

"Know when?" Fireball asked, studying his hand and laying two cards, facedown, on the green box.

"No, but soon, I think."

"We heard May first." Randy said, slapping down another raise, still the lonely twos in his spread.

"Really?" I said, "That's only a couple days off!"

"Yeah, that's what all th' action's all about." Randy continued, "They musta shipped in a whole division, last couple o' weeks. AW SHIT!"

Randy's poor li'l twos, and Jacks three nines did not equal 'Fireballs' three queens, and, with a huge grin appearing under his bushy mustache, he raked in the rather large pot.

Jack threw down his cards. "Armored CAV, too. I saw 'Dusters' and gun-tracks, parked by the airstrip, this afternoon."

"Shit, that cleans me out." Randy slapped down his cards in disgust. "I'm out."

"Me, too!" Jack said, rising and stretching.

"How 'bout you, Hudson, feelin' lucky tonight?" Fireball, asked, hopefully.

"I haven't felt lucky since January sixth of last year." I laughed, "I'm gonna rack-out an' get some down-time. Gotta six hour drive back to Phouc Vinh tomorrow."

I pulled my poncho liner from my ruck, spread it on the bare upper berth mattress, and climbed up. I laid my rifle and ammo bandoleer on a crossbeam, unlaced my boots and set them next to the ammo. I wadded up my flack jacket for a pillow and lay back, thinking. The other guys were milling around, getting ready for bed, also.

"Did any of y'all know anyone who extended his tour to get the 'Early Drop'?" I asked nobody in particular.

They all came to an abrupt stop.

"Hell, no!" Fireball said, incredulously.

"You'd hav'ta be crazy!" Jack said.

"Yer, kiddin', right?" Randy said.

I rolled over, facing the wall.

"Yeah, heh, heh, I was just kiddin'. Just wonderin', that's all." I said, inwardly embarrassed.

After lights-out, I lay awake for another hour, deliberating in my mind my decision to extend.

Was I crazy? Would it be a terrible mistake?

Who knows?

Aside from a little 'Grievous Personal Injury', and the occasional rocket in the mess hall, things had not been too bad, lately. I knew, by this time, what things were all about in th' 'Nam. What I DIDN'T know was what all sorta shit would be waiting for me in the States.

I swung back and forth, 'til I dropped off into a troubled sleep. I dreamed of big, mean Drill Sergeants, yelling at me to polish my boots and brass. I could even, in my dream, smell their foul breath in my face as they harassed me all night.

When morning finally came, my first thought was, 'Hell, I'm gonna DO IT!'

My mind was made up! I'd extend! Hell or high water, I'd stay where I felt I had a modicum of control over my fate. I just hoped it would not be the fuck-up of all time.

0800 found me in the jeep, parked outside the CP. Fifteen minutes later, Captain J. came out, jumped into the vehicle and without even a "Good morning" said, "Let's go!"

We followed the Engineer 'Road Sweep' crew back down the unpaved road south 'til we met Hwy. 22. They turned right and we went left. We saw nothing unusual the whole way back until we crossed the Song Be Bridge. An MP was standing in the road, holding his hand out, palm forward, signaling for us to stop. I pulled adjacent to him and the Captain asked him what was up.

"Booby-trap, sir." He informed us. "Deuce an' a half, blown to shit, along with th' driver."

"How'd it happen?" I asked.

"Command-detonated, from those trees over there."

He pointed to the approximate spot where I'd gotten laid so recently.

"Poor driver, pulled in to get some ass, an' when he stepped outta th' truck it went up. From th' damage an' th' size of th' crater, I'd say it was at least a 155 round. Maybe a 175. Buried right where he parked. According to the assistant driver, who got out alive, he just stepped down off th' running board and vaporized. We ain't found none of him yet, anyway. Blew th' whole truck up in th' air an' it landed on its side, there, 'bout ten feet over."

The still-smoking hulk was laying half on, half off the road, almost in the same spot where the Doc and I had parked, that sunny afternoon. I repressed a shudder, knowing it could easily have been us.

The MP jeep was parked a short distance away, the other MP was tending to an injured but conscious man leaning against the front wheel. Even at a distance of 50' I could see the whites of the guys eyes, as he continually peered, fearfully, around the area, pointing, occasionally, with a shaking hand with a burned-down cig between his fingers.

"Are you two MPs alone here?" The Captain asked.

"Yessir, but not for long. We been here 'bout ten minutes, but there's a squad of 2/7 Grunts comin' from Phouc Vinh, should be here any time now."

"Do you need assistance, or can we proceed?" The BC asked.

"No sir, we'll handle it. Y'all go on your way, but keep yer eyes peeled for trouble. This may be an isolated incident, or not. We don't know."

He stepped back and waved us on past the still smoldering wreck. As we rounded the still somewhat intact front end of the truck, we were afforded a view of the crater beyond. The MP wasn't just joking about the size of the hole.

"Good God, Hudson, the hole's at least ten feet across!" The captain said, astounded.

"An' looks 'bout seven or eight deep, sir." I said with an unrepressed shudder.

Johnson sat back in his seat.

"Let's go, Hudson, and don't slow down 'til we reach Phouc Vinh!"

"I wasn't aimin' to, sir!" I said, meaning it.

I slammed the jeep into gear and blasted off northward, wasting no time. We passed an APC, going the other way within three miles.

"Must be th' Grunts," I commented, "going down to look for 'Victor Chuck'".

"Useless!" The BC grunted. "Those VC are miles away, by now. Back in Phouc Vinh, or somewhere setting up another booby-trap. If I stayed in Vietnam ten tours, I'd never begin to fathom the way they think, or act. Their dedication to their cause is admirable, but their tactics are brutal to the extreme."

"But extremely effective, sir." I commented.

"True, Hudson. Very True. It's just, they're so...devious about it. Won't just come out and fight, like we wish they would. They strike and hide, strike and hide. Plays hell with our brand of warfare."

"They're sneaky, alright, sir. They look like kids in costume. Most GIs can't take 'em seriously 'til th' li'l gook blows their ass away. I've never been able to tell who's an enemy an' who's not."

"An army disguised as civilians, Hudson." The Captain shook his head as I drove through the gate into Phouc Vinh base.

29

CONVOYS

Phouc Vinh was rockin' an' rollin' with activity that last day of April and the first days of May.

A 10,000 man force, comprised of 1st CAV, 11th Armored CAV, and ARVN Regulars had crossed the border into Cambodia on the first of May, obviously catching the VC and NVA flatfooted in their strongholds in the 'Fishhook' and 'Parrots Beak' areas of III Corp.

This huge incursion, supported by our 'Air Mobile' artillery and air strikes, was met by stiff resistance in both areas, but especially in the 'Parrots Beak', where the NVA fought to hold their ground. The 'Fishhook', while not deserted, had more sporadic fighting as the ground troops routed whole armies into flight, before the determined allied troops. Huge caches of arms and matériel were being reported found by marauding US and ARVN companies.

In the first days of the incursion, several sandbag details were sent out from HQ to fill bags for 'C, D, and E' batteries, as they moved from LZ to LZ, firing support for the troops as they swept into Cambodia. I had a week left on my 'Profile Card', so I wasn't sent on these missions. Instead, Rudy and I were assigned a five ton truck and sent to An Loc, in a convoy of thirty trucks, to await orders.

An Loc, a medium sized town, with its accompanying Army base, was about ninety miles north on Highway 13, a nice, paved road through increasingly hilly and jungle-covered countryside. The weather was dry and hot, but with the windshields up and the breeze blowing, and the cassette player blaring BS&T and Chicago tapes, we had a pleasant three-hour drive to a compound alongside the airstrip on the sprawling base.

We arrived at 1130 and got our position in the line of some fifty other parked trucks. There were temporary tents set up for officer/NCO quarters and services, but we driver teams would be living in our trucks for the next several days.

"Pretty cool," Rudy said, "like Gypsies."

And 'like Gypsies' we lived. Eating LRRP rations, (thank goodness I had a supply of them, most guys had to eat C-rats), washing our socks and bathing in our helmets, and sleeping on the hard benches under the canvas cover in the truck bed.

Next morning, we were called out at 0600, given an hour to eat and get ourselves together, then told to form up in convoy on the road. We wolfed a quick breakfast and, in order to get a front position in line, we threw our stuff in a pile in the back and moved the truck out to the road. I didn't want to be first in line, in case of attack, but I didn't want to be choking on the dust from fifty trucks in front of me, either. We got seventh position back, which was acceptable, to me.

On The Road Again

At 0730, we moved out to a wave of the arm and a "YO-O-O!!" from the commander of the 'Duster' that was our lead vehicle. We moved out smartly, west, on an 'improved' road, meaning it was dirt, but had been oiled and compacted. Bumpy, but the dust was held to a minimum. Sixty miles later, we came to a place called Ka Tum, where we were joined by another 'Duster' and two 'Ducks', funny looking, amphibious armored vehicles that, to me, looked like big steel Corvettes with tractor tires and fifty caliber machine guns. These were to be our escorts into Cambodia. We left Ka Tum on a recently plowed out, definitely unimprovedroad, (more trail, than road, really), northward, across the border.

The terrain was increasingly rough. Mountains and valleys buried in thick jungle. No wonder 'Charlie' felt safe up here. You could hide a city in here.

And they DID!

Our destination was a huge clearing, beneath double canopy, well cleared and trodden, with bamboo buildings connected by gravel or wooden walkways, bunker complexes, and trenchworks. I half-expected to see NVA or VC soldiers walking around or training in the large, log-benched amphitheater. Instead, GIs were dragging crates, canisters, sacks of rice, and all manner of stuff to a pile in the floor of the amphitheater, or to another pile over by one of the main buildings. The trucks were being backed up to the latter pile, and a loading crew of ten men were making short work of stuffing each bed as full as it would go. After a short wait, our truck was loaded and we were instructed to pull back out onto the trail and park, which we did. We had plenty of time, while the other 43 trucks waited their turn, so we got out and walked around, checking out how the 'other half' lives.

We saw rows of barracks-like buildings, made of bamboo, with a lot of the previous tenant's belongings still in evidence. Half-eaten plates of food still on tables, piles of hastily-thrown clothing on bunks and floors, magazines, open and placed face-down, as if the reader had just marked his place while he went off to get a 'cold one'. Spooky!

There was a 'Jungle Gym' style obstacle course, a swimming pool, (pond, really), metal warehouse buildings, bunkers and tunnels everywhere. All wired for electricity and phones, just like a city. It looked as if the enemy had just left and I even felt a chair seat, expecting it to still be warm.

"God, it's spooky 'round here!" I whispered.

"You sure th' gooks ain't just out to lunch, 'r somethin'?" Rudy whispered back.

"Don't know, but let's don't hang around, OK?"

We'd been warned not to be poking around in the buildings in case of booby-traps, and I, for one, didn't have to be told twice. We walked back to the truck and waited, smoked and tried to suppress our uneasy feelings.

By 3:00, all the trucks were loaded, and we headed out, back the way we came. I was almost glad to be back in Vietnam. I'd gotten a real fidgety feeling, across the border in the deep jungle of Cambodia. Rudy, too.

"Where'd all th' gooks go?" he wondered.

"Probably out here along th' road, waitin' for us." I said it jokingly, to scare Rudy, but it kinda scared me, too. We made sure our rifles and ammo were handy in the cab, and Rudy about wore his eyes out, peering into the almost impenetrable forest alongside the road.

We hit Ka Tum again, but passed on through, taking a road south through Tan Chau and numerous small villages and emerged into wide plains of rice fields, away from the mountains and jungles. It felt good to be able to see in all directions, and I finally began to relax.

Late in the afternoon, we came within sight of a large mountain, rearing up from the plain. I pointed it out to Rudy.

"Hey, man, that looks like Nui Ba Ra. See th' beacon light on top?"

"Yeah? So what?" Rudy asked.

"We must be near Tay Ninh City."

Sure enough, after another mile, we spotted its sister mountain, Nui Ba Dinh, and a half-hour later, we were passing under the painted pagoda gates of Tay Ninh.

We were off-loading until 7:30, at a marshalling yard, and ended up in a line of parked trucks in an open field, next to a chopper pad, eating LRRPs at 8:30 with an 11th AC 'Duster' crew, that was parked next to us.

Wild guys, those 'Tankers', which is what they call themselves.

Each track is a unit unto itself. Usually commanded by an E-5 or 6, they are so mobile, they rarely come into contact with 'Lifers'.

They had a tendency toward the eccentric, both in clothing, (Flip-flops, cut-off jeans, no shirts), and manner, (dope smoking, fighting, clowning around). I, personally, believed their brains were scrambled from the noise level in those rolling junkyards they rode around in.

We had a regular party that evening, in the back of my truck. Someone produced a beat-up guitar and we took turns strumming and singing. We got high, we joked and laughed and BS'd 'til after midnight, when I left and passed out across the bench seat in the cab. I don't know how long they went on, but Rudy was really rough, when, at 0700, I shook him awake in his bedroll on the bench in the bed of the truck.

We had a quick breakfast and I drove to the POL and topped off the tanks with diesel. We were back in line again at 0800, to head north for another load.

We passed through Ka Tum, again, but this time we took another trail, west for a while, then bearing around to the north. Later we found out, part of that trail was the infamous 'Ho Chi Minh Trail'. VC Highway. We crossed streams and small rivers on well-engineered wooden bridges, and in some places, the road was wide enough to pass two trucks, easily.

We eventually came to another Cadre area, or training facility, and again, our truck was stuffed to the gills with equipment and matériel. While there, we watched as engineers wired explosives to buildings and piles of supplies. Anything not hauled away would be destroyed. I couldn't see how the NVA could function, after losing all this, obviously valuable, equipment. But, of course, they DID.

This time, my truck was filled with arms and ammunition. SKSs and AK-47s, new, still in crates. Chi-com 51 cal. Anti-aircraft machine-guns. Some mortars and rocket launchers, with rounds and rockets, and a half million rounds of small arms ammo.

"Make a merry blaze, if we get hit!" Rudy commented as we watched the lethal shit get loaded into the truck.

"Hope we don't get hit." My lame comment.

We were escorted, safely, back down to Tay Ninh that evening, and off-loaded by eight o'clock, but not before Rudy and I both scarfed a new SKS and two boxes of ammo, as souvenirs. We stowed them under the bench seat, in front, along with our other valuables.

We had a repeat party in the parking area that night, with even more guys, but it didn't last as long, or seem as merry. All the driving, loading and unloading, plus all the tension was taking its toll on us and we were exhausted. Stories were being told, of the ground action taking place in the combat areas.

First CAV and the ARVNs had hit it pretty lucky in the 'Fishhook' area. They had met pockets of resistance, men left behind as a stopgap against the invasion, but the main groups of NVA, in their usual fashion, had vanished into the dense jungle. They left behind a trove of arms and equipment, which we were in the process of hauling out or destroying, but so far, the body counts were not near what had been expected.

25th Infantry, however, operating in the 'Parrots Beak', had not been so fortunate. They'd walked straight into the shit and were advancing under heavy opposition, taking many casualties, but exacting a heavy body count of enemy dead. The NVA units down there, had chosen to stand and fight instead of vanishing, and were paying the price for facing highly motivated (and pissed-off), American troops.

About 10:00, a guy standing on a bunker adjacent to our truck-park, yelled for us to come and look. Rudy, several other guys and I, climbed up and immediately saw what he meant. The dark purple sky, clear as a bell, had bright flashes of lightning, but no thunder, on the western horizon.

"Hey! Why we got lightnin' on a clear night, but no thunder?" some guy said.

"Ain't lightnin', dummy, that's a 'Arclight'." Another said.

"Arclight? What th' hell's a Arclight?"

"B-52s, man. They're 'Carpet-bombing th' 'Beak' tonight." The guy who'd called us over, said.

"Those flashes are bombs?" I asked.

"Yeah, big ones. 500 and 1000 pounders."

"If we're close enough to see 'em, shouldn't we hear 'em, too?"

"We will. Eventually. Hell, that's twenty, thirty miles away. Takes a while for th' shock waves t' get here." He explained.

It was an awesome spectacle that continued for a half-hour, and before the flashes quit, true to his word, the rumbling began. An almost continuous sound combined with a slight trembling of the earth that went on almost fifteen minutes after the flashes stopped.

"Wow, man, if it's that loud HERE, I can't imagine what it must be like THERE!" one voice in the dark said.

"I heard, if you're within a quarter mile of a 500 pounder, it'll jelly your brain." Another voice said.

"If yer within a quarter mile of a 1000 pounder, it'll blow yer eyeballs out."

"Wow!" several voices, including mine, said simultaneously.

After that, I went and slept in the cab of the truck again. I think I felt the rumbling again several times during the night. Between that and the almost constant out-going 175 and 8" artillery, I didn't sleep well that night. At dawn, tired from tossing and turning on the lumpy seat, I stumbled out and splashed water on my face at the water trailer.

I smelled food and my stomach made sounds like a mini-arclight. I followed my nose and found that a temporary mess hall had been set up among the 'Lifer' tents and I was told it was open to all, so I went in and ate powdered eggs, powdered milk, powdered biscuits and, hell, powdered bacon, I guess.

'This shit makes C-rats taste good.' I thought, fuzzily.

0800, we were on our way north again, driving practically blind in the dust of the trucks in front. This convoy was the largest one yet, and I hadn't been on the ball enough to get a good spot in line, so we breathed dirt for three hours. There were at least 100 trucks, including 20 ton semi's and 20 ton 'Load King' hopper trucks, and I was about 70th in line. I couldn't help but think what a great target we made, running up and down the same roads every day at the same times.

Sure enough, a little past Tan Chau, the convoy came to a halt. I climbed out onto the front fender to see what was going on but the dust obscured everything past three trucks in front of us.

Shortly, a 'Duster' came squeezing past on the narrow road and I recognized the E-5 commander in the turret as Smitty, the guy we'd partied with.

"Hey, dude! What's th' holdup?" I yelled as he went by.

"Mines, man. Took out a truck up front. Got some guys dead. Keep your eyes peeled for snipers 'n shit, could be a trap!"

I was glad I wasn't the only one worried about how this would be a great opportunity to blow up a bunch'a trucks, and ME with 'em.

Rudy and I, and the other drivers, also, I saw, made sure our weapons were handy and ready while we waited for the road to be cleared and the crater filled, so we could continue. Finally, a half-hour later, we moved out and soon passed a blown-out 'Deuce' bent almost in half, lying on its side by the road, smoke still drifting out of the burnt-out cab.

"Shit!" Rudy said.

My sentiments, exactly.

Despite this, no more aggression was directed at us and we drove on into Ka Tum.

Today, we turned right, onto the road we'd used to come from An Loc, and after fifteen miles, turned left onto a freshly dug road that took us into an even more scary looking part of Cambodia. After ten slow-moving miles through the thickest jungle I'd seen yet, we came to a halt at a small group of about six bunkers. The engineers had obviously just cleared the area around the bunkers.

"Why in hell'd they bring so many trucks for this little-bitty buncha bunkers?" Rudy wondered.

I wondered, too.

We were so far back in the line it was a full three hours before we got up to the loading area, which, by this time was stacked high in matériel.

"Where'd all THAT shit come from?" I wondered.

Just then a damn FORKLIFT came rumbling up out of one of the bunker entrances, loaded with another huge stack of boxes.

Rudy and I just looked at each other and shrugged.

I maneuvered into position and the loading crew stood back as another forklift brought up a big pallet of what looked to me like 155 mm. artillery projectiles and plunked it down in my truck and used the tines to push it back into the bed against the front wall.

"Where'd all this stuff come from?" I asked a loader who was standing nearby.

"Under ground, man. They got tunnels like you wouldn't believe. Go for miles an' miles!"

The forklift clanged another pallet of 'Joes' into the truck, then another, then another until we were loaded solid with the huge, green bullets.

"Wonder where they got all th' 155 rounds?" I said, conversationally.

"Beats me, Jack." He said, "But we got enough of 'em to fill your truck an' several more, too."

Now fully loaded, I pulled away and took my position behind the line of trucks parked, aiming back along the road we came in on. It would still be some time before all the vehicles were fully laden, so Rudy and I got out and walked around, looking into the bunker houses. They really weren't houses at all, but coverings for tunnel entrances that sloped down about twenty feet below ground and leveled out in a 15'X15' tunnel that stretched out of sight from ground level.

We were squatting down, trying to see up the tunnel when a Spec-6 with a clipboard in his hands came out of a hidden opening in the wall at the bottom of the ramp and walked up toward us.

"What-all's down there?" I asked as he nodded to us.

"Not much, now. This one's just about cleared."

"You think it'd be alright if we took a look?" Rudy asked.

I wasn't too fond of THAT idea.

He looked at us like we might be a little nuts.

"Uh…sure…I guess so. It doesn't seem to be booby-trapped or anything, but don't go far, guys. This thing goes on for miles, with all kinda branches. If you got lost, it'd be DAYS before you found your way out. OK?"

"Sure, OK!" Rudy was excited.

I also thought that Rudy WAS a little bit nuts, but, hey….

"Uh…Thomas?" I read his nametag.

"Yeah?"

"We're from 1/30th Arty, in that five ton over there?" I pointed, "If we're not here when it's time to leave, could you maybe remember…. you know….where we went?"

He brightened.

"Oh, sure! But, no shit, be careful. I almost got lost after the first three turns, first time down."

"Thanks a lot, man."

"Oh, and…." He smiled, "we're still not REALLY sure th' gooks aren't still down there."

"Oh, REALLY thanks a lot, man!" I said, a chill followed the yellow streak down my back.

"He's bullshittin' us, man!" Rudy laughed.

Rudy COULD laugh, he wasn't so short he could walk under a snake. I said so.

Thomas laughed, too.

"Well, yeah, I was, really, but….what do I know? I just write things down, I'm no tunnel expert."

"Long as you can remember where we went if we come up missing, OK?"

"Yeah, OK, guys, listen. That little branch you saw me come out of, right at the bottom, on the left?" we nodded, "That's pretty interesting. There's some posters on th' walls and stuff, and you don't havta go very far, OK?"

He seemed apologetic for BS-ing us.

"Sure, OK, thanks, man, C'mon, Mouse, lets go!" Rudy was still hot on this.

On the way down the long ramp, the temperature dropped twenty degrees but the ever-present humidity made the air dank, earthy-smelling. I gripped my rifle tight. I didn't lock and load, but I wanted to. I DID check to make sure my magazine was in tight and the selector switch was on 'FULL'.

Rudy did, also, I noticed.

At the bottom, cleverly concealed by a slight ridge in the rough wall was a narrow opening, wide and tall enough for a small man.

I was not going to have a problem going through, but Rudy?

Rudy was only about an inch taller than me, but out-weighed me by near 70 lbs.

I, of course had to go first, so, if necessary, I could shove him back OUT.

I had to hold my weapon at my side, and sli-i-i-de in two feet to a not-very rounded right-hand turn. I poked my head around the bend, no shit, expecting to see ol' Charlie, ready to blow my brains out, but there was only another bare dirt wall three feet beyond and another curve, this time to the left. Light was coming from around the bend

Good! That was when I realized, my rifle was on the wrong side of me, in my right hand, away from any potential enemy. No way could I pass it, front or back to point it at anyone.

"Shit!" I mumbled, my voice muffled by the close quarters.

Rudy, grunting into the opening behind me, heard me.

"What?"

"Nothin', man, just a couple of turns." I said, "You makin' it?"

"Yeah, but it's rippin' th' buttons off my shirt!"

I had to laugh, but when I did, I hit my head on the wall, showering dirt down my collar.

"Shit!"

"What?"

"Nothin', c'mon!"

I squeezed around the turn to the next corner and peeped around, again feeling a frisson of fear down my back. Rudy sucked it in and came around the first bend behind me.

The tight tunnel opened out into a 10' X 10' X 30' room with a rounded ceiling. Walls, floor and ceiling were red dirt, but had been troweled with mud to a sort of red stucco finish. A single bare bulb illuminated the space. It was suspended from the ceiling by a wire that ran across from another door opening in the far wall. There was nothing in the room, except several sets of footprints in the scuffed-up dirt on the floor.

Rudy slithered out of the hole behind me as I bent and studied the marks.

"Jeez, those gooks must be TINY!" his voice boomed in the small space and he cringed.

"They're big enough to leave tracks." I whispered, "Look."

He squatted down beside me and peered at the confusion of prints in the dust.

"There's a couple o' sets of jungle boot tracks," he said, quieter this time, "but what are those?" He pointed to the many other prints. "They look like tire tracks."

"Ho Chi Minh Racin' slicks, man." I whispered

His eyes got round.

"Ya mean, like, Gooks?"

"Who else you know wears 'Slicks', dummy."

"Well, these tracks don't look very old."

"No they don't," I agreed, "but they all seem to be headed..." I pointed down the next tunnel, "...that way."

He stood up.

"Well let 'em stay down there," he said, "this place gives me th' willies. C'mon, lets get outta here."

His enthusiasm had waned considerably, but I'd come this far, I wanted to see more than just one bare room.

"Naw! YOU'RE th' one wanted to see th' tunnel, so lets see th' tunnel."

I took his arm and pulled him to the entry of the other hallway. About thirty feet down that way, I could discern another wider space, with a bit of light coming from above.

"You first, this time." I pushed him into the door. It was wider, but not much taller than the first tunnel.

"OK, OK." He grumped and ducked his head and walked slowly into the dark opening.

The room at the end was dark, and at first appeared to be a dead end, with no exits at floor level, but looking up, I could see some light coming out of a two foot by two foot square opening in the upper right-hand corner of the back wall. A full ten feet off the floor.

"How th' hell do ya get up there?" Rudy said.

I felt the walls in that corner, and sure enough, there were hand and foot holes that dug into the stucco surface, almost invisible in the gloom.

"Like this." I said and climbed up and looked into another short crawling-size shaft with a brightly-lit room beyond.

I pulled myself into the small tunnel, crawled ten feet, and came out into a room thirty feet on a side with a ten-foot ceiling that was supported at intervals by steel posts. This room, lit by four light bulbs, was not empty.

It looked like a classroom. Wooden benches were arranged in even rows facing a chalkboard on the wall, situated behind a bamboo podium. A large portrait of ol' Ho, himself, was hung to the left of the blackboard, and the other walls were festooned with posters, all depicting Vietnamese people, some in uniform, some not, raising either fists, weapons or garden tools. They all seemed to have the same recurring theme of 'Rising up' or 'Claiming Victory', and all the poster faces had the same expression, somewhere between a scream and a grin. All their eyes seemed to burn with righteousness. We couldn't read the words, but it wasn't necessary, 'the message' was clear from the pictures.

We walked around, looking at the papers, written in Vietnamese that were on the lectern. The pamphlets, picturing more heroic looking gooks, were scattered on the benches and the floor. The North Vietnamese brand cigarette butts crushed into the dirt. One busted gook sandal lay in one of the four other dark doorways that led into the room from who-knows-where.

"Man, this is getting really creepy." Rudy whispered "It looks like they JUST left."

"IF they left." I said, about half-jokingly.

Rudy gripped his rifle tighter.

"Shit, don't say that. C'mon, Mouse, lets get th' fuck outta here, while we can still find our way back."

"Some adventurer!" I chided him "Let's at least get us a souvenir for our trouble."

I took several of the pamphlets and Rudy pulled down one of the colorful posters, folded it and stuffed it into his pocket. I wanted the picture of Ho, but he was too big, in his frame, to go out easily the way we came, so I left him hanging.

We retraced our path, wasting no time, and were soon back at ground level. The hot sun on my face felt good.

After another hour and a half of sitting, smoking and waiting, all the trucks were finally on line and we started our engines in preparation to move out. The big Chrysler of mine, started hard and ran ragged, belching blue smoke, but we chugged out onto the trail with the rest, with me pumping the pedal and adjusting the choke, trying to make the beast run smoothly. About five miles farther on, it just quit.

I was completely blocking the path, so the entire convoy halted, until Rudy, me, and a couple of volunteer mechanics found the problem. A clogged fuel separator. The part that takes the impurities out of the diesel, before it goes to the engine.

I'd topped-off the tanks again this morning, and had obviously gotten some fuel contaminated with water, which had collected in the glass jug attached, for that purpose, to the filter body. I unscrewed the jug and dumped it, blew out the filter with compressed air from my on-board compressor, screwed the jug back, and voila, it started up and we were off again.

We made the main highway before the engine started coughing and belching again. I dropped out over to the side and was in the process of dumping the separator again when the escort 'Duck' pulled alongside and asked if we needed help. I told him no, that we'd have it going again in a minute, and we'd just jump back into line. He said "OK" and drove on.

We got moving again and got in line, but the truck was still not running smoothly. We managed to keep up with the 30-MPH convoy for another 20 miles before she died again! Clunk! I coasted to the side and found the jug completely full of muddy looking water.

"This stuff must be half water!" I commented.

I was surprised it would run at all, but run she did for another twenty miles. Then another twenty miles and dump. Another twenty miles and dump. Each time falling a little farther back in the line of trucks.

By a quarter to seven that night, we were within ten miles of Tay Ninh and she pooped-out again. It was getting onto dusk, and the convoy was speeding up in anticipation of getting back into the safe base. The last truck in the line passed as we were raising the hood and the rear point 'Duster' stopped alongside and asked us what the problem was. I told them we'd be running again in about two minutes. They went on and hollered for us to catch up.

With the motor chugging, now, we regained the road and, even with the pedal to the floor, we could get no more than thirty MPH. I started playing with the controls and found, with the choke half closed, the engine gained a little power. Forty MPH. Forty-two MPH. Forty-five MPH! All right! The main convoy was a dust cloud in the distance, but by damn, we're moving!

I was still playing with the controls and in the near twilight, I almost missed a rather sharp right-hand curve. I had to wrench the wheel over hard, and when I did, the driver's side front tire blew with a bang. I saw the split rim fly off into the air as the truck axle and brake drum dug into the dry dirt of the road.

The huge speeding machine, momentum carrying it on, began to settle down on the left, making a scrunching-screeching noise. As we slid along, I had no control and the truck continued to tip to the left, then the rear wheels let go and the rear end started coming around. Then we ran out of road as we went off the edge of the curve.

Still going a good thirty five-MPH, the thundering behemoth rolled completely onto her side. MY side. Suddenly I had a mouthful, a face full of water, gushing in through the tilted up windshield as if someone had directed a fire hose at me. I briefly heard Rudy begin to scream "AW SHIII….." and I was completely submerged. We'd gone off into a rice paddy, filled with stinking, slimy water and we were now sliding on our side on the slippery mud bottom. I felt a crushing weight, (Rudy), pinning me and holding me under water. I guess I'd been screaming too, because I had practically no air in my lungs, and what little I DID have was being crushed out of me by Rudy's big butt.

We slid on another fifty feet before coming to a jerking halt. Stopped now, the truck's weight caused it to settle six, eight more inches into the bottom muck.

Desperate for air I pushed against the anchoring weight on me and just managed to get my face above the surface and gulped air (and mud) and started choking. Adrenalin pumped into my veins and with a mighty heave, I popped Rudy out through the windshield hole and managed to sit up with my head above water, breathing heavily. I was vaguely aware of Rudy splashing around out by the hood, so I pulled myself up and using my foot against the steering wheel, I propelled myself out through the windshield frame. I landed on Rudy's back, just as he was starting to get up, knocking him back into the grayish-green muck, and I followed him under.

In a very few seconds, both our heads popped up out of the muck, spitting and spewing. I wiped the slime out of my eyes and saw a lump of brown shit sticking up in front of me. Then I realized it was Rudy's head as his gloppy hands came up and wiped his eyes. We stared at each other in the waning light, the whites of our eyes the only thing betraying that we were human. Then his mud split open, revealing white teeth, and he started laughing.

"Jeez, Mouse, you look like a turd!" he guffawed.

His laughter was contagious and I couldn't help myself.

"You look pretty shitty yourself!" I managed.

We busted-up and snorted a full minute, sitting there in the water that had the consistency of mucus. Finally, I got a mouthful again and spit it out, getting my breath.

"Well, we're up to our necks in it, again." I said.

This, of course, set us off again and, still laughing our butts off, we struggled to stand up in the slippery slime. Not too successfully, at first, I slipped and went under again, causing Rudy to laugh that much harder, which caused him to slip and go under, too.

At last, upright, we held onto each other for support and sloshed our way around the overturned cab and, even in the near darkness, I could see the whole disgusting scene.

"Wow, man!" Rudy chuckled, "You get your license at Sears, 'r what?"

The truck, looking for all the world, like some dead prehistoric monster, lay on its side, half submerged in the water. The load, some six hundred 155-mm arty rounds, was strewn from the edge of the road, across the paddy, to our feet. Most of the rounds were under water, but a few were poking up out of the slop and there were a couple of mounds of them visible, back closer to the road.

"Whatta' we gonna do now?" Rudy wanted to know.

"Well, I'M getting' my stuff and getting' out of this paddy an' back up on the road."

I sloshed back around the cab and Rudy followed. I leaned in through the windshield and found my flashlight, still clipped to the dash, and using it, I managed to find all our stuff, which I handed out to Rudy, who stacked it on the side of the hood. Everything was wet, including Rudy's tape player.

"Bummer, man!"

Our M-16s and the SKSs were inundated, but we poured the water out of the barrels and dried them, best we could, and they'd be fine. Our rucksacks were a soggy mess, but everything in mine was funky, anyway, so, what the hey. We carried our gear and waded ashore and plunked down on the dry dirt, mud clinging to our clothes and oozing out the drain holes of our boots. It was full dark by now.

"Think they'll come back for us?" Rudy wondered.

"Sure they will!" I said, sure at that time.

"Think we oughta like...start walkin', 'r somethin'?"

"No." I said, "I'd think they'd want us to stay with th' truck, ya know? Guard th' load, keep it from getting' ripped-off."

"Yeah, like we're gonna hold off a buncha gooks wanna steal 'bout a million pounds of explosives." Rudy said sarcastically.

"Well, I still think we'd better stay here, an' when they come back for us, THEN we'll decide about th' load. OK?"

"OK." Rudy said, unenthusiastically.

Out there, on the road, in the dark, the silence was deafening.

We sat on our packs, back-to-back, loaded rifles in our hands, imagining things creeping up on us from all sides. Our cigs were soggy, Rudy's dope was wet, and he'd lost his favorite cherry bowl in the mud, anyway, so there wasn't much to do except sit and worry and wait. Time dragged on.

8:30....9:30, and still no sign of a rescue.

"I think they've forgotten us!" Rudy said, anger in his voice.

I had to agree.

"Looks like we're gonna be out here all night."

I know I was scared, and Rudy, too. But where were we gonna go? Tay Ninh is still ten miles away, with nothing between but more of the same. The nearest ville, is ten miles the other way. We were exposed, on an open road surrounded by rice paddies. The nearest tree line, a quarter-mile away, wasn't even discernable in the black night.

"Hey!" Rudy whispered, a little later. He was facing toward Tay Ninh.

"What?"

"I think I saw somethin'."

I spun around, not wanting to see anything, and I didn't.

"Gooks?" I said, hair raising on my neck.

"Don't think." He whispered, "A light 'r somethin', down th' road a ways. Don't see it now."

We both strained our eyes for a minute.

"There!" he said, excited.

I saw it, too!

"Yeah, it's a light, alright." I stood and watched a small, bouncing light appeared to be coming toward us on the road.

"Gooks don't use lights, do they?"

"Don't think so," I answered, "but I ain't gonna be out HERE when it shows up, even if I gotta jump back in th' paddy."

I gathered my stuff and was preparing to do just that. Rudy followed my example. The thought of re-entering that swamp was bad, but it was the only place we had to hide if it was an enemy, and better wet than dead, I figured.

Rudy was in, up to his knees. I was ankle-deep. I stopped and peered down the road again. The light was nearer, now, and coming fast. Then I thought I heard the rumble of an engine.

"Wait a second, man." I held his arm and we looked harder, and listened.

Now the sound was the unmistakable rumble of a tracked vehicle.

"Gooks don't got tanks, do they?"

"Not 'round here, they don't!" I replied.

"Then...."

"YEAH!"

We sloshed back up onto the hardpack and were waving our arms as an APC materialized behind its dim blackout lights. It stopped beside us in a cloud of dust.

"Y'all got a broke down truck?" a voice from the darkness above said.

"You might say that!" I answered, "It's over there," I pointed uselessly in the blackness, "in th' rice paddy."

"How th' hell'd it get THERE?" the E-5 said as he leapt down from the fender.

"Tire blew an' we slid in." I answered, "Dumped our load in th' water, too."

"Yew Boahs OK?" the Sgt. drawled.

"Yeah, just funky!" Rudy laughed.

"Sure ARE! I smelled y'all 'fore I saw ya!" The APC Sgt. joked. Or maybe it wasn't a joke, we DID smell like dead things.

"We cain't do nothin' 'bout th' load, tonight, I guess, so y'all boahs git own in an' we'll git y'all back t' Tay Ninh. They missed y'all at th' marshallin' yard an' sent us out t' find ya!"

"Glad y'all did!" Rudy aped his drawl and tried to shake his hand, but he jerked back like we had the plague.

"Don' go gittin' all huggy, boahs, jes' git own in." he laughed, "an' open them ventilator flaps, back there, too. Y'all STANK!"

Gratefully, we opened the rear door, and threw our gear in and took seats on the benches along the walls inside. We left the rear door open on the ride in, the stench in the enclosed area was too much for US, too.

We rolled into Tay Ninh City at 11:30 P.M., and since we no longer had a truck to sleep in, we were given cots in a tent reserved for E-5 and up. We stripped off our crusty clothing and boots outside and were given buckets of water to try and kill the swampy smell. After sloshing off head to foot, I used another bucket to rinse out my uniform and boots, which I hung out to drip-dry on a tent rope. The CQ at the marshalling yard provided some towels and some clean (but huge) skivvies which we wore to bed, finally, about 1:00 A.M. I wrapped up in the scratchy wool army blanket that was on the cot, and was immediately asleep.

Next morning, wearing stiff, damp, but somewhat cleaner fatigues, (still a little smelly, too), I went to the temporary CP at the yard and informed them that our truck and load were still out along the road.

We were loaned a truck and given a 'Duster' escort out to the site. We arrived at 0930 and found the truck, looking forlorn, sunk in the mud, but the artillery rounds were gone. We found a few, but, somehow, in less than ten hours, the gooks had hauled off over ten thousand pounds of ordinance. On bicycles! Sandal prints and bike tire tracks marked the entire area. They even took the time to strip the truck of anything useful that they could carry.

"Oh, well," I commented, "we took it from them up north, they just took it back, I guess."

We spent the rest of the morning trying to pull, cajole, drag or otherwise extricate the truck from the mud, to no avail. Even with chains hooked to both the loaner five-ton AND the Track, (with its two souped-up Cadillac engines), we were only able to move it about twenty feet. Unable to pull it close enough to the road to get the proper angle to right it up onto its wheels, the track driver radioed back to Tay Ninh for a tank retriever, that was there accompanying 11th AC.

The tank retriever, a huge 16 wheeled tow truck with both winch and boom, arrived at 1:30 and within 20 minutes, had our truck upright on the road, dripping mud and kneeling down on the drivers side on the broken wheel.

Rudy, the tow truck driver, and I inspected the undercarriage and steering gear for damage. Other than being coated in crud and probably severely out of alignment, it all looked OK so we jacked it up and installed the muddy spare wheel, which mercifully, was on the submerged side of the truck so the gooks didn't steal it. We sloshed out the seat and floorboard with 5-gallon jerry cans of water we'd brought for that purpose and while that dried, we dumped the fuel separator, and all the remaining contaminated fuel from the tanks. Then we put in the two 5 gallon cans of good diesel we'd brought. After about twelve tries, the engine finally caught, belched smoke for a few minutes then settled into a normal idle.

At 3:15, with Rudy driving the loaner and me in our truck, we followed the 'Duster' and tow truck back to Tay Ninh.

Another convoy had gone out that morning, but we'd, of course, missed it. In fact, it had passed us on the way out as we were struggling with the truck. About thirty trucks and tracks, were barreling north to the border.

When I checked back in at the CP, I was told to go on back to Phouc Vinh. So at 4:00, tanks topped off with fresh fuel, we headed back along the road through Cu Chi. We looped around through Thu Dau Mot and then north to Phouc Vinh. The truck drove OK except for a shimmy in the steering. I had to hold it to keep it from drifting to the left. Rudy spent the whole drive trying to dry-out and fix his tape player and grousing. At a little after 9:00, we pulled into our motor pool and shut the engine off.

"Jeez, what a trip!" Rudy said, gathering his stuff.

"No shit!" I replied "You hungry?"

"Hell yeah! We ain't eaten all day an' I'm starved."

We'd, of course, missed chow so after stowing our gear in our hootches, we went to Jim and Ralph's hootch to bum some LRRPs.

Jim was full of questions. Ralph, too, so while we snarfed down our beef stew, we filled then in on our adventures. They were suitably impressed when we told them about hauling out the NVA caches and the trips into Cambodia, and about exploring the tunnel system. I whipped out the pamphlet, now somewhat dry, and they studied it like they could read Vietnamese.

Rudy told them about the truck wreck, still blaming it on my driving skills. I countered with the fact that if I hadn't controlled the skid, we'd have flipped upside-down and drowned for sure.

"Sounds like you didn't leave much for th' gooks, up there!" Jim commented.

"Except a whole truck-load of arty rounds." Rudy said, elbowing me.

"Yeah, they took them back, alright." I admitted.

Things had not been quiet in Papa Victor, either, while we had been gone. Sandbag details had gone out daily to the LZs, filling bags for the day, then coming 'home' for the night. Jim and Ralph had been to LZ East, a new firebase, and to LZ Sandy, in the last two days. They said both places were 'Flaky', with lots of Gook activity in both areas. But so far, neither base had been attacked.

"Only a matter o' time, though." Ralph professed.

Poop was, the NVA, caught flatfooted in their strongholds, had bugged-out in several directions and were unable to re-group for any large action. First Cav and the ARVNs had really shook them up and had inflicted some impressive casualty numbers, as well as disrupting their whole supply chain. Good news was hard to come by in Vietnam, but to us, this was really excellent news, and we celebrated by smoking a bowl and clinking coke cans in a mock toast to "Ho Chi Minh, may he live forever in this country, after we go home!"

At 11:00 I realized I had yet to report-in at the CP, so Rudy left for the shower and bed, and I walked over and told Terry Leonard, the CQ that night, that we were back.

He wrote us down in the log, then started asking questions. I waved him off, pleading exhaustion, and promised to tell him the whole story tomorrow.

"God, Mouse! You stink!" he noticed.

"No shit, Sherlock. I'm hittin' th' shower, an' then I'm gonna sleep for two days."

"No you ain't." He said looking at the roster.

"Whatta you mean?" I asked.

"You got ration-duty tomorrow an' ol' Rudy's on for a sandbag detail to 'C' battery, leavin' at 0800. Better get some sleep. While you can."

"Well, shit!" I spat, and left.

At the shower, Rudy was finishing up and looked, clean, like another person entirely. I informed him about the detail tomorrow and he went away cussing the army and all therein. The shower was cold, but wonderful.

I hated that Rudy was going out to the LZ tomorrow, but hell, I was glad it wasn't me. My hands were almost entirely healed, now, but damned if I'd let-on. I sure didn't relish the thought of going out to the 'Boonies' again. I'd do almost anything not to go.

'Too short!' I thought.

Then I remembered my plans to extend my tour.

'I'll think about that tomorrow.'

30

CAMBODIA AGAIN

Three days went by. In the light of day, I thought differently about my extension plans. I wavered back-and-forth, stay-or-go, go-or-stay? I asked some of the guys.

Generally, the opinion was: "You gotta be nuts! GO!"

I knew I had to make up my mind soon, as you had to submit your paperwork, according to 'Clark th' Clerk', at least fourteen days prior to your DEROS date. That means, sometime this week or next.

I performed my ration-duties by rote, wrapped up in my dilemma, until May seventh, when I was scheduled for a 'pioneer detail', cutting a new LZ in Cambodia. Place called Evans. I bitched, of course, that I was too 'short', but to no avail.

0800 in the morning, I was on a chopper, with ten other guys, on our way back into Cambodia.

Myself, Rudy, Lynch, Leonard, Weitzel, a black guy called 'Brother B', a new guy named Dunkelberger (Dunk for short), Bowers friend Rojeski, and some guys from Commo I didn't know, carried our packs and weapons, as well as the 'pioneer equipment'.

This consisted of chainsaws, gas cans, axes, wedges and sledge hammers, shovels, rakes and all manner of implements of destruction. Our orders were to help an engineer unit clear a hilltop for a temporary LZ/firebase.

At 0920, we circled in on one of many hilltop knobs that stuck up hither and yon, from a primeval forest of Teak and other hardwood trees. They set us down in a small cleared area right on top. Considerable activity was already in progress. A small bull-dozer was knocking down the smaller trees that grew on the thin soil of the knob. Surveyors were laying out lines for bunkers or buildings and a big E-7 engineer sergeant immediately jumped us and sent us out to the tree line. We were told to start cutting trees to widen the kill-zone.

I was given a chainsaw and I proceeded to hack away at the clumpy underbrush that dotted the hillside above the tree line.

After a bit of this, I was sweating like a pig and I needed to pee. I shut down my saw and set it on a rock and walked down to the trees looking for a likely bush.

I entered the cool shade under the trees, humming a vague tune and unbuttoning my fly as I rounded one of the huge Teak trunks. My eyes were still adjusting from the bright sunlight and just as I was ready to 'whip it out', I thought I caught a slight movement in the grassy clumps at the base of the tree.

Momentum carried me for another step as, hand-in-fly, I peered into the gloom.

'What IS that?' I thought. 'A vine? A coil of thick rope?'

Nope!

The 'vine' rose up to the height of my nearly exposed man-hood and quivered there for the full second it took for me to think 'SNAAAAAKE!' It was a biiiig cobra. It's hood started extending to it's defensive form, I saw it's tongue flick twice, sniffing the intruder's scent, and I saw it's beady, black eyes blink.

When he, or she, opened it's eyes after that blink, it must have wondered, 'What was THAT?'

During that quick blink, I had jumped backwards, I estimate, ten feet and landed running in reverse, pissing down my leg as I went. (I'm grateful that I went for a #1 and not a #2).

I bumped into Jim and waved my free arm, (the one not still stuck in my fly), and yelled "SNAAAAAKE!"

Jim looked at me, looked down at my hand in my pants, and started laughing.

"That ain't no snake, man," he guffawed, "just a li'l bitty ol' worm!"

I suddenly realized what I must look like and jerked my hand out of my fly.

"No, man! BIIIG SNAAAAAKE!" I pointed to the tree, thirty feet away. "THERE!" I was gasping for breath.

We took our rifles and checked it out, but the snake had vamoosed, leaving not a trace.

Jim said it must have been my imagination, or "wishful thinking", he accused, laughing his ass off.

Huffy, I told him I'd never pissed on myself from imagination before.

"You weren't never this 'short' before, neither." He laughed.

True!

We worked two hours cutting out undergrowth around the bases of some huge Teak trees, piling the debris in the KZ for burning as we went. That done, we had a line of thirty-some trees, with trunks in excess of four feet in diameter, left standing, tall, majestic and hard.

Hard as concrete.

We found, after many bone-shattering blows, that axes were almost totally useless against these behemoths. All we were doing was skinning the bark off and hardly nicking the smooth, brown wood underneath. The edges of the axes went dull after just four or five chops, then just bounced off without leaving even a dent.

Chainsaws weren't much better. You'd cut in scarcely an inch or two and the chain-teeth would just round off and quit cutting. We each carried four extra chains, but it would take forty chains to get through just one tree trunk.

'No wonder...' I thought, breathing heavily after grinding down my second chain, '....it takes days for those lumber-gooks to cut a tree like this!'

Unable to make any progress against these 'rock-trees', we consulted the engineer Sgt., who was directing in some sling loads of supplies. He considered a minute, then asked if any of us had any experience with explosives. Turns out Dunkelberger, (Dunk for short), is some kinda expert. So he consults with the Sgt. and soon we're headed back out to the trees carrying boxes of C-4 Plastique, (same as in the Claymore mines, except packed in blocks, wrapped in oiled paper), and 250 foot rolls of 'Detonation Cord'.

Dunk held a short class on the procedure, and soon we were wrapping each tree with Det Cord and packing the white, rope like winds (Four times around each tree should be enough, Dunk said), with a healthy pack of gray, putty-like C-4. We strung the cord between each

334

of the trees, in hopes they would all blow at the same time. We joked about what a show this was going to make. We had NO IDEA!

We fell back to the center of the nearly cleared knob, waited while Dunk and Sgt. wired the charges, and word went out that there was to be a 'Big Boom'. Ten minutes later, when all personnel were gathered out of the blast zone, the Sgt. yelled "FIRE IN TH' HOLE!!" and clicked the clacker, sending an electrical charge down the wire, which blew a blasting cap that set off the Det Cord, which blew the C-4.

That whole quadrant of the future firebase, disappeared in a cloud of dirt, smoke and flying debris. KA-BOOM!!! All thirty trees blew at once, jumping into the air ten, twenty feet, then crashing down into the huge cloud of smoke.

Some fell outward, into the forest, knocking over other trees, some fell inward, across the brush piled in the KZ. The earth shook, almost knocking everyone down, and dust rose up beneath our feet. Most of us had our ears covered, but the blast was strong, the concussion made my eyes bulge out for a second. Even us hardened artillery guys had ringing in our ears.

Clearing LZ in Cambodia

335

We'd obviously used a bit more explosive than was necessary, but the mission was accomplished. We'd seen the tree tops totter and fall and everyone cheered, especially us 'Pioneers'. We were glad we wouldn't have to chop those mothers down.

However, as the dust settled, and the smoke drifted away, somewhat, the cheering died-off. Tall gouts of flame were erupting from the brush piles inside the LZ and also from the forest around us. It didn't take long for us to realize we'd set a major forest fire!

The sergeants started bellowing orders and people started scurrying around, moving piles of supplies and equipment out of the path of the fire. It didn't help that the wind, at about ten-fifteen MPH was blowing directly across the clearing from the hottest part of the inferno, now raging just outside our perimeter. The fires in the brush in the KZ were not as big, but they were just as hot and much closer. Glowing embers began drifting down around us, setting anything they touched afire, be it a pile of equipment or a man's hair or clothes.

We had very little water available. In fact, all the water we had was in our canteens, the water trailer having yet to be sent out from the rear. The Sgt. organized parties of shovelers and sent them out busily extinguishing burning mounds of matériel, burning bushes and grass all around our, for the moment, still safe clear area. We all wet our towels and draped them across our heads and shoulders against the shower of blazing debris, but we all got burns on our arms and hands as we worked feverishly, securing our supplies or putting out the fires that sprang up among us. At 60 feet, the fires in the forest and KZ were hot enough to toast bread, and everyone was getting singed hair, mustaches, and burn holes in our fatigues.

More than an hour of intense fire-fighting ensued until, by 2:00, we'd gained enough ground to feel fairly safe inside our clearing, though the fire still raged in the forest around us. In fact, it had spread until it was ALL around us. We'd shoveled dirt on the burning piles until it died down enough for the 'dozer to push it out and down the hill into the burning forest, where it was rapidly consumed by the inferno among the trees. I got a break about 3:00 and got Rudy to snap a picture of me, perched atop a stack of artillery powder canisters, in the middle of a forest fire. Ah, Macho Me!

Keeping a close eye on the fires, we went back to our original task of building this LZ. Two of the bunker holes got dug and we were set to filling sandbags for the walls. Smoke-inhalation was our main worry, until the fires upwind of us finally burned down at about 5:00, we were all choking and gagging, even with wet cloths tied over our faces to filter out the acrid fumes.

At 1930, choppers bearing a company of Grunts, whose job it would be to guard the LZ tonight, came in, dropped their loads, and flew out with a bunch of 'Tired Puppies', in Terry Leonard's vernacular, eager to get back to the relative safety of Phouc Vinh. As we lifted up above the blackened KZ, I commented to Rudy, "We might've fucked-up usin' too much C-4, but we sure created one helluva kill-zone around THAT LZ!"

Sitting on Ammo in a Forest Fire

He nodded and we looked down in time to see that the entire western side of the mountain had burned to a point almost a half mile from the perimeter of LZ Evans. Then we were rising into the cold, clear air of early evening, high above the endless reaches of the Cambodian jungle.

We all smelled like a house-fire, but, man, that air smelled Good!

There were no bunker parties that night. Everyone was too exhausted. I racked-out at 9:30 after showering and eating, then dreamed all night that I was back in the barracks at Ft. Knox, KY. The building was on fire, but the drill Sgt. wouldn't let us put it out until I'd put a spit-shine on this huge pair of boots. The fire was getting hotter and kept melting the polish off the toes of those big boots, but the big Sgt. just stood behind me, yelling for me to finish-up so we could get out, or we'd all burn-up.

I woke up sweating at 0500 and lay there thinking until 0630.

When I walked out that morning, I'd made up my mind. After a bowl of cereal in the mess hall, I went straight to the CP and told Clark to give me the forms for an extension of tour.

After he recovered from the shock, he dug in one of those big, green file cabinets and came up with the proper papers. I sat down right there and filled them out, not wanting to delay for fear of changing my mind again. With a large sigh, I signed it and handed it back to the still incredulous clerk.

"You sure, Mouse?"

"Hell no." I muttered, "But file 'em ASAP, 'fore I can change my mind, OK?"

"OK, man," he shook his head sadly, "I'll turn 'em in this morning."

'SHORT-TIMERS FEVER.'

It affects everyone, regardless of rank.

You get 'Short', down to less than thirty days left in-country. You get paranoid. You feel put-upon if confronted with details that, earlier in your tour, you'd have accepted without a thought. Time drags by at a snails pace and there's nothing you can do to speed it up. Just thirty more squares to X-out on your calendar. You think, "Please, please, I've been through enough, already!" You feel the odds are against you, now that you've made it through 335 days over here without getting killed. You may feel, and justifiably so, that the 'Lifers' are plotting ways to GET you killed before your tour runs out. You just wanna be left alone. You just wanna go HOME!

I was feeling like that. Only, NOW, I wasn't 'Short' anymore.

I'd gone from 28 days, to 88 days left, in the stroke of a pen. How low can you go! I felt better, having made my decision. But, MAN, 88 more days of this crap! All this went through my head as I walked down to the motor pool that clear, deceptively beautiful morning.

I was unassigned today, due to our late arrival back in battery last night, so I planned to spend my time hiding in the pool, away from harm and 'Lifers', washing the dried muck off the 'Deuce'. It'd stood there for two days with the reeking paddy-mud still caked on the driver's side and undercarriage.

I hooked a hose to the NON POTABLE water trailer in the motor pool and, using a bucket and long-handled brush, worked at removing the crusty, stinky mess from all the cracks, bends and folds of the big truck. I managed to work-up a major sweat, but by 1330, it looked more like a vehicle than a mud pie.

I'd had all morning to think, as I worked. I'd decided to become as 'invisible' as possible. I assumed since I was no longer 'Short', I'd be eligible for LZ details, which I wished to avoid like the plague. I'd be as unavailable as I could be. I'd hide. I'd accept shitty details, no matter how mundane, as long as it didn't involve flying out to a firebase.

I spent the next week, running my ration job, mornings and afternoons. Dodging 'Lifers' and hiding is not easy. I took on any mission that took me out of the compound, or, preferably, off base. I spent some time at the Song Be Bridge, which was back in business again. I drove to Long Binh twice to pick up stuff at the Service Battery, there. Generally, I tried to just stay out of everyone's way.

During this period, Sgt. Holly and some of the enlisted men hatched the idea for an EM club. A sort of bar, lounge, kinda thing where E-5 and below could relax, drink beer, listen to music. That sort of thing. Holly pitched the idea to the BC and got local approval and official approval from DIVARTY, the next day. It was a GO.

Problem was materials.

Foundation and floor? No sweat! Holly had a friend at 8th Eng. who said, if we did the excavation, he'd supply enough concrete for a 18' X 25' slab. Three days later, with everyone pitching-in between details or after work in the evenings, we had a level spot dug and formed-up north of the shower shack, across the road from the motor pool gate. On the fourth day, a concrete truck arrived and Holly personally supervised the pouring and finishing of the slurry.

Then came the walls. Again, no sweat. I used my trading contacts and procured several truckloads of empty 105 ammo crates. These, in the usual manner, were filled with dirt and nailed together, one atop the other, to form the walls. These cost us some used jeep parts and a rusty 500 gallon water tank that had lain, unused, behind the motor pool tent since anyone could remember.

OK. Now for a roof. Different story.

Plywood, timbers, and PSP were almost unobtainable.

Tarps and sandbags could be gotten from our own supply room, but the heavy materials were as hard to find as gold.

Sgt. Holly, Jim, Ralph and I, in a late-night meeting at the motor pool, decided, we'd have to get the stuff through our usual procurement procedure. We'd steal it from somebody else.

A couple nights later, Rudy, Ralph and I were just cruising in a 'Deuce' around the perimeter road after dark. We 'happened' past a bunker construction site where there were a number of these 8" X 8" X 20' beams, lying in a stack. When we got back to our unit, we were surprised to find that six of those beams, (luckily, JUST the number we needed for our project), seemed to have been 'magnetically' attracted to the metal bed of our truck. They had just 'jumped in' as we drove past, we told a laughing Sgt. Holly.

The plywood took some planning. I cased-out the 8th Eng. yard and found their 'Sheet Barn', where they kept the plywood for their concrete forms and such. An open-sided facility, it stood back at the rear of the compound, about thirty feet from the rear fence, a six foot high chain link affair with posts twelve feet apart and a single strand of barbed wire across the top to discourage invaders. We were not that easily discouraged.

That night, I spent three hours staked-out, across the perimeter road which ran along their fence line, in a clump of bushes watching the guard rotation within the compound. Their guard system was very lax. A walking guard seemed to make a round about every hour, back there, and spent the rest of the time in a sentry shack by their front gate. The back of the target building was completely out of sight of the sentry shack. Before walking back to my unit, I checked the depth of the drainage trench that ran between the fence and the road.

Back at headquarters, around 1:00 A.M., I rounded up my fellow companions-in-crime: Rudy, Jim and Ralph. They were game when I'd explained my plan, so off we went in the dead of night on 'Operation Swipe th' Wood'. (Jim's turn of phrase.)

We drove without lights, which was no easy task on this moonless night. We arrived at the spot I'd picked out earlier, and parked the truck behind a stand of trees across the road from our objective and waited. Right on time, at two o'clock, the guard strolled by the back of the shed and then rounded the corner out of sight.

"Perfect!" I whispered in the dark cab.

We gave the sentry a few minutes to get back to his shack, then leapt into action, so to speak. Jim, being the tallest, took the set of bolt cutters we'd brought from the motor pool and slunk across the road like a commando. He was followed by an equally slinky Rudy, and between the two of them, managed in less than five minutes to cut the fence at one post and roll it back to the next post. This left an opening twelve feet wide in the fence, through which I promptly backed our truck, carefully negotiating the shallow ditch by the road.

'Wouldn't do to get stuck at this point!' I thought as I made it through the fence and backed straight up to the open side of the building. There, right inside in a bin were stacked numerous sheets of ¾ inch plywood. I lowered the tailgate and Jim and Rudy got up into the bin and started selecting sheets.

Rudy jumped back down. Jim shuffled us the sheets, one at a time, and we slid them, as quietly as possible, into the truck. Jim picked carefully through the stack. These were used concrete forms and some were pretty rough, but finally we had our quota of fifteen sheets.

Loaded, I pulled the truck away, back out through the fence and, while I parked in the trees across the road, they pulled the fence back together and used baling wire to re-fasten the two ends together. Jim, standing on Rudy's back, twisted the coiled barbed wire together at the top and, badda-bing, badda-boom, except for some mashed grass in the ditch by the road, you couldn't even tell anything had ever happened. The two commandos scrambled back across the road and had just settled on the seat in the dark cab next to me.

"Look." I said.

The guard, a tad early on his round, sauntered around the corner of the building and walked past the spot where we'd been parked less than five minutes ago. Even had he been more observant nothing seemed out of place and he walked leisurely on his round, totally unaware that he'd just been ripped off.

"Whew!" Jim whispered, "That was close!"

"Sure was!" I answered.

"Wow, man. It's just like 'Mission Impossible', on TV." Rudy quipped.

"Yeah," Grinned Jim, "th' good-guys always get away."

We all had a good laugh, though quietly.

"Well," I said seriously, "We're on a roll an' it's a nice, dark night. What say we finish our 'Midnight-Requisition' run and go on and get some PSP?"

"Where?" They asked.

"I know just th' place!" I smiled and punched the starter button. The engine caught and, still without lights, I drove off around the deserted perimeter road.

Five minutes later, I pulled up on the side of the road next to a wide-open field on the left, the greenline on the right. We were smack in the middle, between two of the widespread guard bunkers. At this point, in the dark, we couldn't be seen by anyone more than thirty feet away.

From up in the bed, I had a good view of the road, both directions, as it curved away around the base in case a vehicle came along. I knew this was highly unlikely at 3:00 A.M., unless it was the Sgt. of the Guard, and his jeep had blackout lights that could be seen for a quarter mile. No sweat.

My cohorts joined me standing in the bed.

"OK, Mr. Thief," Jim asked "what're we doin' here?"

"Observe!" I said. With a sweeping motion of my arm I pointed to the open field.

About twenty feet on the other side of two little strands of concertina wire was a virtual sea of PSP. It extended at least 100 feet to our left and right, and out of sight to the horizon.

"Man!" Rudy exclaimed, "That's th' runway from the airstrip! You crazy?"

"Yeah, man." Jim exclaimed, "You can't just go rippin' up th' runway. They might need that!"

"We ain't gonna take it ALL!" I laughed, "All we need is about fourteen sheets. We can take 'em off th' edge an' nobody'll ever notice. Besides, if those pilots need every foot of that steel t' get airborne, they're not very good pilots. Now, y'all get yer butts over there and unhook fourteen o' them panels an' stack 'em by th' fence on these blocks." I handed them three 4" X 4" x 2' chunks of scrap wood I'd thrown into the truck back at the unit.

"I'll be gone about fifteen minutes, be ready when I get back. OK"

"Well, OK." They agreed, reluctantly.

"What'll we do if somebody comes along, I mean...?" Rudy asked.

"Just lay down flat out there. Be th' dirt. Pretend yer a sapper." I kidded them, "Nobody without a spotlight will see you in this darkness. Now, go on. I'll be back soon. Be ready!"

I drove back and parked the 'Deuce' in the motor pool. It was about 3:30 and except for a lone helicopter winding up in the distance, everything was dead quiet and dark as hells' basement.

I walked on up the line of parked trucks and found what I'd spotted that morning as I tried to figure a way to filch fourteen 2'x14' steel panels, all weighing in excess of 150 lbs. The Tank-Retriever belonged to the 175-8" Self-Propelled Arty unit across the road. Due to lack of space in their compound, it was parked in our pool. I'd even surreptitiously checked to be sure that it was gassed-up. It was.

'I'm not stealin' it,' I rationalized, 'I'm just borrowin'.'

I started 'er up and the engine seemed to thunder in the dark quiet. I waited and looked around for several minutes, but no lights came on, no voices raised. Carefully, without lights, I eased the giant truck out of it's spot and idled it out of the compound onto the main road. I'd never driven anything so huge, or with more knobs and levers in the cab. I figured out which one of the small forest of levers sticking up out of the floor was the gearshift. It had fifteen speeds, (I think), but I only used five of them traversing the road back to the airstrip. I was going for

343

slow and quiet. I passed no other vehicles and saw very few signs of life in the seven-minute drive.

Rudy and Jim had just clunked the last metal plank on the stack when they heard the sound of my truck. They were 'Being the Dirt' out by the pad when I pulled up alongside the fence and stage-whispered, "I'm Baaack!"

I'd also noticed, this morning, there were several long lengths of heavy chain in the back. I jumped out, handed Jim one of them, and told him to loop it around both ends of the stack and leave some slack in the middle.

They handled the chain and I backed the truck into position so the rear hoist-boom was over the wire. With the truck idling, Jim and I figured out how to operate the winch and hydraulic lift and soon we had the 1500 lbs., or so, stack of steel suspended five feet off the ground. I checked the chains and they seemed secure, so we jumped back into the cab and I started off.

Jim and Rudy had been surprised when they saw me drive up, but Jim had immediately figured out my plan, and it'd gone off well. We celebrated and high-fived each other on the short drive back to the unit.

"Just like 'Mission Fuckin' Impossible'" Rudy kept saying.

0410 in the morning I rumbled quietly through the Dirty Thirty gate.

"Oh, fuck!" Jim said.

"What?"

"There's Carbone!" he pointed to the lighted door of the mess hall.

I forgot how early the cooks start in the morning, and the big Sgt., drawn by the sound of our engine, had stepped out to see who was out driving through the unit this early in the morning.

"Shit!" I spat. I didn't know if he'd rat-us-out or not, but he is a 'Lifer'.

He waved us down. I pulled up and he looked at the Retriever. Then he looked at us in the cab. Then he looked back and saw the swinging stack of metal sheets hanging back there. He scratched his head for a second, then sort of smiled. He walked around to my window.

"I didn't see nothin'." He said and grinned.

I grinned back.

"Thanks, Sarge."

"No big thang." He replied, "But yer own ration-duty in..." He looked at his watch, "three ayers. Don' be late, now, heah?"

"No problem, Sarge, I'll be early."

"Bet ya will."

He shook his head smiling, as I rumbled on down and into the motor pool where we dropped the load behind the tent and I parked the truck back in its spot.

By May 27th, our EM Club was taking shape. The walls were up, the roof on and we were down to the decorating and painting. I made more trades for 8' projectile crates that were broken-up and used for building the bar, benches, paneling, a couple booths and doors. I'd worked some deals with Jax, down at the Ration Point, and obtained some Formica top tables and some wooden chairs, six bar stools and an old, but working Fedder's air conditioner. The A/C unit was quickly installed in the wall next to the bar and we were the only air-cooled spot in the whole unit, besides the FDC bunker.

All the wood fixtures, including the walls, were scorched with blowtorches to highlight the grain, sanded then varnished to a high gloss. This lent a 'homey' knotty pine, neighborhood bar atmosphere to our little club. It sort of reminded me of the old Green Lantern Restaurant, on Seventh Street in Lexington, where my Dad had been a regular and they'd taken my sister and me, as children, for a rare 'evening out'.

We didn't have a jukebox, but a Sony stereo tape player and amp/receiver was donated by somebody, so we could have 'Tunes'. Also donated were war souvenirs for hanging on the walls. NVA helmets and a flag, a broken AK-47, a pair of crossed sabers of unknown origin. The 'Lifers' were placated when I painted a big 'Dirty Thirty' insignia on one side of the wall behind the bar, and a big yellow Cav patch on the other. The middle space was reserved for a big poster of Raquel Welch, decked out in her '1000000 years BC' furs. She sure filled-out those skins a lot better'n those animals ever did! Other Pop and Psychedelic posters hung around the place in strategic locations. I donated my big, camouflage cargo parachute that was nailed up as a ceiling covering.

A big beer-cooler icebox came from Carbone and was installed behind the bar. Someone came up with some rattan rugs for the floor.

All this came together fairly easily, but we were awaiting the 'Crowning Touch'.

Pagans, who was from Milwaukee, had a cousin, also a Veteran, who dealt in pool tables. He'd collected $600 from any interested parties, me included, and had ordered a Regulation-size, used Bally table, with a one-piece slate. His cousin couldn't promise WHEN the table would be delivered, just that it WOULD.

Meantime, we could drink and relax in our own club, which, according to regulations, was off-limits to anyone above the rank of E-5, without specific invitation.

Holly, of course, it being his idea in the first place, and it wouldn't have ever happened without his pull with the NCOs, was nominated the 'Official' bartender. He accepted this honor with a grin on our opening-night on June 3rd and popped open and served the first 'brewski' to Terry Leopold, who ceremoniously swilled it in about three seconds, to the wild applause of a crowd of thirty five guys. The stereo was cranked up with 'Temptations Greatest Hits' and we were in business.

June 6th, my original DEROS date, also my birthday, we were jerked back to reality. A barrage of mortars, eighteen in all, came in on our quadrant of the base, causing considerable damage, but no deaths, to my knowledge. One round hit right next to the NCO latrine, blowing shrap-holes in the side wall, but, luckily no one was in residence at the time.

Another round landed not ten feet outside my hootch door, but failed to go off. When I poked my head out after the attack, I saw this weird thing sticking up out of the ground. On closer inspection, I realized it was a bomb, and ran and got Sgt. Jackson, who, accompanied by the First Sgt., came and pronounced it a 'Bomb and probably dangerous.'

(Well, no shit!)

They decided to wait until morning to defuse it, when it was light, and told us to stay away. No problem there. I lay awake all night, though, waiting for it to go off any second. It didn't.

Next morning, Jackson was back. I peeked out and saw him using very scientific equipment on the shell. He was poking it with a stick! I didn't know the procedure for disarming a mortar round, but I didn't think that was it. I ducked back inside and donned my helmet and flack-jacket. I stuck my head out one more time to snap a quick picture of 'Fools in Action', then crawled under my bunk 'til they'd taken it away for disposal at an ordnance yard.

The morning of June 8th, Clark found me in the motor pool and informed me I'd 'volunteered' to drive a truck for 2/19th Arty, the 105 unit next door. Apparently, I'd been 'loaned-out' to them for a couple of days to go on what they called 'Hip-shots'.

"What th' hell's a 'Hip-Shot'"?

"You'll be driving a ¾ with a gun-crew in th' bed and one of their 105s hung on th' back." Clark informed me, "They've got some S&D units out looking for those gooks who dropped those mortars th' other night. Th' Grunts're working up around Dong Xuai an' they're just a little out of 105 range, so 2/19 is sending three guns out on th' road, following-up to fire support if th' squads need it."

"I got it. Like, drop th' guns and 'shoot from th' hip'."

"Right!" he nodded.

"Sounds flaky." I said.

"Probably not." He assured me, "I don't think you'll get more'n fifteen, twenty miles from Phouc Vinh. You'll have to stay out tonight, so take your field gear and three days rations and lots of ammo."

"We gotta stay out on th' road tonight?" I said, incredulously. Nobody wanted to be out there after dark, especially after the mortar thing the other night. Especially not ME!

"Guess so," he continued, "But you'll have a 'Duster' escort, so it oughta' be OK."

"Easy for YOU to say." I mumbled, then to him:

"When?"

"Soon as you get your stuff and get over to their CP."

So an hour later, at 1000 hrs. I'm bumping out the north gate of PV in an old Dodge 'Power Wagon' ¾, loaded with supplies and Gun-Bunnies, a 105 bouncing along behind like a good dog. We headed north, toward Dong Xuai. The day was bright and sunny and promised to be a scorcher.

Our convoy consisted of three trucks pulling guns, one ¾ carrying ammo, a command jeep carrying the radio and first Lt. Jones, the 'Honcho', and his driver, and our 'Duster' escort, following behind. I was the first truck behind the lead jeep and our speed settled at twenty MPH for ten miles 'til we got our first fire-mission.

Rice paddies on either side of the road, we had to just drop the guns right there in the roadway and fire the mission. Luckily, we'd encountered hardly any traffic on the highway, so far this morning, and no one came along as the crews set-up the little 'pop-guns', as we 155 'Cannon-Cockers' called 'em, and prepared to fire.

These guys were good though, they had their pieces 'laid' (sighted on a certain azimuth) and ready to load in two minutes, twelve seconds, according to Lt. Jones and his silver Rolex watch.

The 'One-oh-Deuce' (M102 Howitzer) is a relatively simple piece of equipment to operate. Being less than half the weight of its big brother, the 155mm gun, the 102 is maneuvered easily by a four-man crew. It's wheels do not have to be jacked-up off the ground to fire, and its rounds have a brass casing that holds the powder and, like a big bullet, has a detonator built into the bottom. The whole round is a sixty-pound package, handily and quickly handled by any burly Saxon-mothers' son who is adept at shoving things into holes.

While the crews did their thing, I wandered over to the big PRC-25 radio, mounted on the side of the jeep with a tall whip antenna waving above. Lt. Jones driver, a Spec.- 4 named Jones, also, was listening with headsets to the radio traffic and writing down numbers on a spiral pad. These, I knew, would be the co-ordinates for the location the FO, (forward-observer), wanted the rounds to impact on, or at least near-to, so as to catch 'Charlie' with his 'jammies' down and send him to see his ancestors.

I listened as he relayed the deflections and quadrants to the Gunners on each piece, who were positioned less than twenty feet away. They were poised, ready, and quickly made their adjustments, rammed a round, each, and slammed the breaches closed.

"NUMBER THREE.... FIRE MARKER !" the #2 Jones yelled.

The #3 Gunner yelled,

"FIRE IN TH" HO..BANG!!!!"

The little cannon had a 'crack' sound, higher-pitched than the throaty BOOM of the 155. A gray smoke-ring followed the round's trajectory for thirty or forty feet, then dispersed into the air, leaving a slight haze. The air reeked of Cordite, and I thought 'Well shit.'

We all, of course, had our ears plugged with our fingers or, rarely, real earplugs, and that lessened the effects of the concussion, but it still bulged your eyes and left a ringing sound, louder than the usual subliminal cricket chirps present in the hearing of all artillerymen.

"BATTERY READY...." #2 Jones called, listening to one earpiece of the headset, finger in the other ear.

#3 gun immediately ejected the spent brass shell by flinging open the breechblock. Another round already cut and fused, was loaded and the block clanged shut.

Lt. Jones was struggling to see his Rolex, with his fingers in both ears.

Five seconds passed.

Ten.

"BATTERY...FIRE FOR EFFECT!" #2 Jones spat.

"B-B-BAM!" The guns fired almost simultaneously.

A cloud of smoke drifted back across us.

The smell made me kind of queasy.

'I don't know if I'm just paranoid, or maybe this shit really does make me sick.' I thought.

I walked back by my truck, which was a little more up-wind, and leaned against the front bumper, looking at the lack of scenery, while they popped off two more rounds on different co-ordinates, swabbed their tubes, and waited to hear if they'd be needed again.

Ten minutes went by. The morning was proving to be as hot as I'd expected. There, literally, was not a cloud in the sky, other than the man-made kind, which drifted off lazily across the flat rice paddies 'til it dispersed in a haze.

The ever-present 'Stripe' flies were buzzing around in the still, quiet, sun-splashed road. The only sound was the gun-bunnies, slapping at the flies, whose bites felt like a lit cigarette burn, and when you slap at them, they jump up six inches so you slap yourself, but not him. The moment you raise your hand to see if you've squashed him, he jumps back down on the same spot and bites you again. So you slap yourself again, but not him, over and over 'til it really gets to some guys. Me included. I ended up crawling under the front bumper, where there was the only shade for miles, and the bugs seemed to lose track of me and went on to attack one of the other poor saps who happened to occupy this particular part of Hell.

Finally, #2 Jones called "Cease Fire!" and unplugged the headset and turned down the volume and the squelch on the radio, leaving a small hiss as the crews, almost without a word spoken, wiped off their pieces and prepped them for portage. Five minutes later, we're on our way again.

We drove about another mile before the lead jeep turned left, onto a barely-discernable, dirt track, just ruts, really, that led back into some long straight rows of skinny, tall rubber trees.

"We're headed into th' Plantation." I heard one of the guys in the back, say.

"Sure, we is!" this guy named 'Bull' said. "We been heah be-fo, man. 'member? 'Las time th' gooks wuz thick as them daymn flies back yonder."

Some of the guys laughed, but maybe a little nervously.

I didn't know if he was called Bull because of his size, (He was a big man), or for his obvious ability to scare FNGs.

"When was that?" I asked.

I figured any information was better than none, which is exactly what I knew about this area. I'd heard the rumors, of course. The V/C supposedly had tunnel complexes in among the rows of trees and in 1968, during the 'TET Offensive'. Hundreds of NVA and V/C had emerged from this section of the huge plantation, and completely overran the outpost at Dong Xuai, killing a lot of ARVNs and holding the town for days, until they were evicted by the 2/9 Infantry out of Phouc Vinh.

"We wuz in heah las' month," Bull said. "This heah th' Michelin Plantation, man."

He smiled as he realized that two guys, FNGs from their clean, green uniforms, were soaking it up like sun. He directed his attention on them. I listened as I drove. He continued.

"We came in heah, man, an' th' gooks wuz a-jumpin' ever'where. These heah trees? They runs alla way ovah t' th' daymn Song BE ribber. Ain't nuthin' in heah but trees an' gooks, trees an' gooks, man!"

"Aw, there ain't no gooks in here, man." A PFC retorted

"Yeah!" the other FNG said, "Where'd they hide? There ain't no undergrowth or jungle t' hide behind."

He gestured at the barren, slightly hilly terrain under the spreading canopy of the trees.

Bull smiled knowingly.

"Tunnels, man! Hunnerts o' tunnels. All ovah th' daymn place."

He paused for that to sink into their poor, unschooled, FNG brains.

"An'.... FULLA GOOKS!" he finished, screaming the last two words and causing both boys to flinch back, their eyes round.

He and several others laughed their butts off at this. I had to chuckle a little, too.

"Anyway," he wasn't about finished yet and continued.

"Some whurs in heah, they's a big V/C ville. Name'o Ca Ma, 'r somethin'. It's own this othah li'l ribber. Gooks bringin' rockets an' shit down from this big ol' lake, nawth o' heah. Bringin' 'em down in them sam-pan boats, at nighttime."

He paused and lit a cigarette. The FNGs, fully absorbed now, held their breath.

"Anyway..." he continued, "they brings this shit down an' supplies th' local 'Victor Chucks' an' THEY blow th' shit outta' places 'round heah."

I looked back to my driving and saw that we were approaching a small village of thatched huts with a sprinkling of tin roofs, farther down the road. There were approximately twenty-five of these on either side of the road that went straight through town. Dogs, chickens and a couple of pigs were around the huts and in the street as we entered, slowing to ten MPH.

I was even with the door of the first hootch on the right before I noticed a little girl, standing mostly in shadow inside the poor-looking shack. She watched us go by with a frown on her face. Just as we were almost past, a hand reached out of the darkness behind her, grabbed her shoulder and pulled her back into the gloom.

"Real friendly place." I mumbled to no one in particular.

No other human was in sight. It gave me the willies, driving through this seemingly empty town. Knowing the population was just behind these flimsy walls. I imagined them, hunkering back there, holding RPGs or AK-47s, waiting for the strategic time to attack. Wipe out the 'Imperialists'. Namely, ME.

'I'm STILL too short, for this!' I thought.

"Shit," I heard one of the 'Bunnies' say under his breath, "this place is SPOOKY."

We picked up speed as we neared the other side of town. I, for one, was eager to be gone from this place.

"Why'nt we liven this heah place up a li'l." I heard Bull say in the back.

I turned my head in time to see him throw something out the side of the truck. Whatever it was, it went sailing through the open door of a grass hut. Second from the last in the village. At first I thought he'd lobbed a grenade, and held my breath, waiting for the explosion.

"ARE YOU NUTS?" I finally managed.

Before he could answer, a green cloud erupted from the doors and windows of the hut and I, with a sigh of relief, realized it had been a smoke grenade, not a frag. The huts inhabitants, two mama-sans and four kids came scrambling out the door into the small yard, coughing and rubbing their eyes and coated, head to foot with the bright green powder from the smoke. Both adults raised their fists in the air and cursed us and the other trucks that were now rolling past.

Bull and a couple of his buddies thought this was hilarious and made fun of their plight, cracking wise about 'Green Gooks' and such. The other three, including the Gunner and the two FNGs, just looked angry and embarrassed.

"Shit, Bull, you doofus!" Their gunner, a corporal named Timson, yelled and stood up and faced off with the smart-ass gun-bunny.

"What'd you go an' do THAT for?"

"Awww, fuck, Tommy. I's jus' havin' a li'l fun!" Bull said, but backing down since Timson was an inch taller than him and had at least twenty-five pounds on him.

"Yeah, yeah, you dumbass." Timson advanced until his face was three inches from the other mans. "One o' these days you're gonna get us blown away with your happy horseshit. Now, siddown an' shaddup, an' that goes for all o' you!"

"And if those gooks back there weren't V/C before, they are NOW." I added over my shoulder. "If any more of you wiseasses has any more ideas 'bout throwin' any ordnance outta this truck, I'll personally help your Gunner kick your ass an' you'll be ridin' back on th' howitzer th' rest of th' way."

"Yeah? You an' whose fuckin' army?" Bull started up toward the front, but Timson anticipated the move and kicked him square in the seat of the pants as he passed.

"I SAID, siddown an' shaddup, stupidshit. Th' driver's right! We don't need t' make any more enemies out here. We'll be bivouackin' somewhere tonight within a couple clicks of that ville, an they know it. And, we'll hav'ta pass back through again t' get back t' th' main road, so, COOL IT! HEAR?"

Bull gave me a blazing stare, which I returned, but said, "Yeah, yeah, Tommy." and backed-off.

The convoy was now beyond the village and the lead jeep pulled to the left and signaled me to pull alongside.

"Is there some kind of disturbance, back here, Hudson?" The LT shouted across the gap between the two vehicles.

"Uh, small one, sir, but we got it under control, I think." I answered.

The jeep dropped back even with the bed.

"Corporal Timson? I expect you to keep tight reigns on your crew. The very last thing we need out here is somebody, especially YOU, Twick," he eyed Bull who tried to shrink down on the bench, "making trouble among the people. We will be stopping overnight within walking distance of Ca Ma. You WILL NOT ASK FOR TROUBLE. Is that clear?"

"Perfectly, sir!" Timson answered, "Don't worry, there'll be no more bullshit."

"See that there isn't!" The LT said and his jeep sped up and retook the lead position.

With the Lt. now out of earshot, Bull, (Twick? I thought.), mumbled.

"Well, gee whiz, fellas. I's jus tryin' t' make th' li'l fuckers easier t' see at night, bein' all green lack that!" He chuckled again, but he was the only one, now.

Timson leaned up close behind me and said, "We try to ignore him, Hudson, after all, he IS an ignoramus."

That got a general laugh from all but Bull.

I had a good idea which personality trait Bull was named after.

We crossed a small river on a rusty steel bridge and drove on through the vast, seemingly unending rows of trees. Rubber trees. Tall, spindly-looking because of their foliage being fifty feet up on a bare trunk that was only 1½ feet in diameter at the base. Their bark looked like stained, white paper, split horizontally occasionally. Puncture scars were evident all around their bases where the rubber/sap had been si-phoned off for years. They were planted in rows, straight as if laid-out by a surveyor, twenty-five feet apart and the same distance between the rows. Surface roots were running outward from each tree in the reddish-brown soil, mixing with the root system of the next tree, allowing very little undergrowth to survive.

I could see a great distance down the rank and file of forest as it seemed to 'march' past my truck. The vertical white trunks, combined with the straight, black shadows and the movement of our progress, played tricks with my eyes and caused a sort of 'hypnosis' that I had to shake-off every few minutes. The road changed directions a couple of times, causing the shadow-slashes to swing suddenly to a new angle and it was, like, "Whoa!'. I felt like the trees had moved and we'd kept on straight. Weird!

A half-hour later we came out onto a plain that looked about a mile wide, very flat with sawgrass nearly five feet high. The track we were following wasn't paved but was hard-packed and relatively smooth. The grass grew right up to the edges of the road, leaving only a twelve-foot furrow through a sea of waving green.

Approximately halfway across the expanse, there was a wide spot in the road and the Lt. waved for us to stop. He got out and gave instructions for the guns to be set-up, and then we'd break for chow until a mission was called. Hungry, everybody hopped to it.

Being 'Driver', I had nothing to do with loading, unloading, or setting or firing of the guns. I was 'Just a Driver'. If the truck needed moving or maneuvering, that was my job. If the truck was parked, then so was the driver. Tony and Russo, the other two drivers and I joined the Track crew and watched the proceedings perched on the fender of the 'Duster'.

The 11th AC guys, looking for all the world like military gypsies with their bandanas and various forms of cut-off clothing, lounged on their vehicle during these breaks, trying to look 'BAD'. They did it well. Everything about them was intimidating, but after I got to know them better, they were just another bunch of guys, mostly draftees, like me.

Their 'Commander', an E-5 named Wilcox, was the only RA and he was big and mean looking; an ex-biker from Modesto, Calif. But in conversation he was polite and intelligent and we had a discussion on the merits of bombing the harbors at Haiphong and whether Johnson was dragging the war out for purely political reasons or for the real benefit of the South Vietnamese people.

After the guns were set-up, we cooked our C-rats and in the middle of eating them, a mission came in on the radio. I munched my Chicken A La King LRRP ration and watched the crews work. Ten rounds were fired, southward, back the way from which we'd come. I wondered about that.

'Not good, maybe.' I worried in my mind.

After the mission and after eating their left-over cold C's, the gun-bunnies bitched as the Lt. called,

"Saddle up!"

We turned the trucks around, hooked up the guns and drove a quarter mile back south, stopped and popped ten more rounds on almost the same azimuth as before.

At 5:30, #1 Jones saddled us up, turned us around again and we drove back to the spot we'd occupied earlier. This was to be our NDP, (Night Defensive Position), and I was not a happy camper.

"Man, we're kinda out here flappin' in th' breeze." I commented to 'Li'l Andy', the track driver, who was 6' and 200 lbs. A three-quarter moon was rising on one side of our clearing as the sun set on the other.

"This grass could hide an army." I continued, indicating the waves of growth surrounding us.

"Lousy position, a'right." Andy said, blowing smoke out his nose. His Brooklyn accent thick as the evening air.

"But whatcha gonna do, huh?" He shook his head sadly. "Don' mean nuthin', no ways. Ya either get t'rough dis 'r ya don't. Nuttin' ya do over here don' mean nuttin'."

He paused and I said, "There it is!"

"I mean, ya c'n fight 'r ya c'n hide. Ya c'n be th' best Goddamn soldier in th' whole army, 'r ya can be a fuck-up. It don' matta. When yer numbah is UP it's UP. That's IT! Don' mean nuttin'."

I thought about this for a while.

"It don't mean nothin' over here, man," I said, "But when I get home, I think I'm gonna be surprised how important all this is gonna seem."

"Yeah…" he said, thoughtfully, "could be."

"It'll mean we did our THING, man. The TOUR, and a little more. I'm no patriot. Hell, I think patriotism's a dead issue, these days, but I'm not ashamed of anything I've done over here, so far. I feel like I've served God an' country, an all that. If I survive this shit-hole, by damn it BETTER mean something! Especially to those, so called, 'Patriots' that sent me over here. They owe me!"

He turned and looked at me appraisingly.

"Fuckin' A, man, Fuckin' A!"

31

STARRY, STARRY NIGHT

When it was good and dark, about 9:30, the Lt. called us together in a group next to the jeep. Everyone except the gun captains and 'Duster' crew, were on guard detail, either LPs, or walking guard. I was on LP.

My partner for the four-hour stint, was a mousey little guy, about my size, named Randy Trotter. He was from Stringtown, Ohio, I found out later. I also found out about his sisters abortion, his Aunt who smoked dope, his Daddy's drinking, hell, how many times he'd jerked-off in his life. He wouldn't shut up! Whispering, whispering, all night!

I reminded him, several times, that this was a 'Listening Post', not a 'talking post', and he'd stop for maybe five minutes. Then:

"Hey, Hudson, you ever see a cow chase a man into a pond? Well I did!" Then he'd start into another harangue about 'Uncle Charlie' or some such shit.

'JEEZ!'

Finally, in the wee hours, he wound-down and all was quiet except the occasional 'Fuck You' bird with his plaintive "Fuck-yewww! Fuck-yewww!" off in the distant, blacker-than-black tree line at the edge of our clearing.

It wasn't as dark, here in our clearing, as it is in the jungle. The moon shown down on us with a silvery light that allowed full visibility for at least 200 yards around. And the STARS! I don't think I'd ever seen so many. I was reminded of a night back home, shortly before I was drafted. Two buddies and I, stretched out on our backs in a back pasture on Calumet Farm, sharing a pint of Cherry Vodka and a jug of grapefruit juice. YUK! The sky, then, had been a dark blue dome with stars scattered from horizon to horizon. It was like that, tonight.

I stared at the glittering points dreamily for a while until I remembered where I was.

Gookland! And only a mile or so away from a village full of pissed-off green gooks!

I thought about how visible WE were, sitting out here in the moonlight. It didn't take a Rocket Scientist to figure out that a mortar tube in the tree line could take us out with one walk down the road. I nervously sat out the rest of the guard tour, but all was peaceful. At 2:00 A.M. we were relieved and I gratefully climbed onto the truck seat and crashed.

At 0630, somebody came by and banged on the truck door.

"GET UP! GET UP! GET UP!"

I raised up and looked at the retreating figure in the morning mist. I saw it was #2 Jones.

"Whassup?"

"Movin' out at 0700. Get yer chow an' get ready!"

I fell out of the cab, grumbling, splashed canteen water on my face and, since there was no time, I settled for some dry chocolate cake from a can, washed down with warm cherry Kool-Aid. No sooner had I finished this repast and lit a morning cig, than the LT barked.

"SADDLE UP!"

The trucks were loaded and the guns hooked-up and we headed off north again. This time we went all the way to the other side of the clearing and entered another section of the Plantation.

Trees and shadows.

About a half mile in we veered left on a smaller track, bumpy and rough, and bounced along at fifteen MPH for a while with the sun at our backs. Suddenly the lead jeep honked its horn and sped up to forty MPH, the Lt. waving us on. We bounced high on the rutted surface and raised a mini dust storm behind us.

We came to a clearing among the trees and the jeep skidded to a stop and #1 Jones jumped out.

"FIRE MISSION!" he yelled.

We slid to a stop in our own cloud and the crews dropped trails and had a round in the air within six minutes. Not bad for a bunch of dumb 'Bunnies'. We fired three rounds for effect, saddled-up and took off again, winding, twisting and turning through the all-alike rows of trees, 'til I was completely confused in our direction. I hoped the LT knew where we were.

Finally, mid-morning, we were in an area where there had never been a road and we pulled to what must have been the edge of the Plantation. The guns were set up in the dappled shade of the tree line, facing out on a wide, grassy valley. We waited. We cooked up some lunch and waited some more.

At about 3:00 P.M., we finally got a fire-mission and the guns fired-up all but ten rounds in the ammo truck We were then told to saddle-up for Phouc Vinh.

'Fine with me!' I thought as the crews hustled to load and hook-up.

As we drove off, Timson, sitting up front with me, said, "I hope th' Lt. knows how t' get us outta here. I've been lost since this morning."

"Me too." I admitted.

We jounced along, eastward for a couple of miles and came out on a paved highway, where we turned right, or south. The pavement seemed velvety smooth, after the beating we'd given the vehicles inside the Plantation. We zoomed along at forty MPH and the breeze was wonderful in the late afternoon heat.

We came to Dong Xuai from the opposite direction as before, and pulled up in front of a yellow, stucco, French-colonial building with an ARVN flag hanging limp from it's pole in the round space in the middle of the circular drive. I noticed as we stopped, my brakes were grabbing on the front, causing me to jerk to a halt.

The Jones Boys jumped out and walked inside and while we waited, I crawled under the front end and checked the brake hoses and drums. Everything LOOKED OK but I noticed that the drums were very hot to the touch. Of course, what WASN'T in this weather? I checked the master cylinder, and the fluid level was all right, so I figured it must have been a fluke, or something.

Fifteen minutes later, back on the road, we were barreling along at forty, headed for PV. I noticed that the engine seemed to be straining to maintain the speed. Soon, I had to down-gear to third to keep up speed and it was getting worse, it seemed. A few minutes later, I smelled a rank, burning smell and tendrils of smoke came from under the front fenders. The engine was whining, trying to push the resisting vehicle forward. My speed dropped to twenty and the lead jeep, unawares, pulled away until I honked my horn to alert him to my problem. I pulled over to the side and the jeep reversed back to us.

When the #1 Jones came up, I was on my back under the front bumper trying to determine what the problem was.

"What's up, Hudson?" The Lt. wanted to know.

"Hell if I know, Lt. OW!" I said, burning my fingers on a red-hot brake drum.

"Looks like th' front brakes are locked up, sir."

I stood up and dusted myself off.

"The engine's been pulling hard ever since Dong Xuai. Looks like th' brakes finally welded shut."

Lt. Jones, who, actually, was only two years older than me, but whose responsibility was for the entire mission, said, "Well shit!" and stood there thinking for a moment.

"Timson?" he said, reaching a decision.

"You and your crew hang your gun on my jeep, take your personal belongings and disperse among the other trucks."

He turned back to me, as they jumped down and went about moving the cannon.

"Hudson. We're only five miles from PV. You'll stay with your vehicle, while the convoy proceeds. I'll send help out to you as soon as we get back to base. It's..."

He consulted his watch.

"...1845. It'll be dark by 2200. A maintenance vehicle should be here no later than, say... 7:45. Understand? DO NOT leave your vehicle unattended."

I knew he was just following the 'Book' on this, doing his job, but damn, I didn't want to stay out here alone again! Too short! I told him so, in those words.

He sympathized, but insisted I stay with the damn truck (in those words). He DID assign a man to stay out with me. Guess who? Ol' 'Ramblin' Randy' from Stringtown.

"Oh, great!"

Before the last vehicle had pulled around me and gone on, Randy started.

"Wellll, Hudson. Just you and me, I guess."

'This guy's too dumb to be scared.' I thought.

"Lemme tell you 'bout th' time me'n my uncle Josh went out t' my Granny's house? Way over in Columbus…BLAH, BLAH, BLAH!"

While he rambled, I was thinking. Hard!

'There's gotta be a way.'

After a few minutes, it came to me. I dug out the tool bag from under the seat, took a wrench and crawled under the truck. It was pretty desperate, but I knew I'd be crazy from Randy's yackin' long before they came back to tow me. Besides, I really wouldn't be leaving the vehicle. Just, maybe a few pieces of it. Ol' Randy watched me, but never skipped a beat in his monologue.

I had checked the rear brakes and they were OK. I removed the front-wheel driveshaft, pulled it out and tossed it into the weeds. I put the tool bag back and wiped my hands on a rag.

"Hey, Randy!" I interrupted him just as he and his uncle were, I think, tipping cows in some Ohio field.

"UH…yeah?"

"Shut up an' get in," I motioned to the truck, "we're outta here!"

"But, I thought you said the brakes was locked an' we was stuck out here?"

"They ARE, but WE aren't. Just shut-up an' get in!"

I ran to the driver's side and climbed in. I wasn't sure that this'd work, but I sure hoped so, so I wouldn't have to kill my first US soldier. He got in the other side and I started the engine, holding the clutch pedal to the floor.

I let the engine cool itself for a moment, and idle-out smoothly.

"Whatcha gonna do, Hudson? Did'ja fix it?"

"Not exactly." I said as I eased the clutch in. "But I did this once in a fifty-one Pontiac that didn't have near the horsepower this truck has, and it worked."

I didn't tell him I'd only had fifty feet to go in the old 'Poncho' and it was in the snow.

Now we had five MILES. On dirt.

As the clutch caught, the engine, pushing against the locked wheels bogged down and died. Shit!

'Low Range!' I thought and restarted the engine.

I jammed the transfer case lever into 'Four-Wheel-Low' and let out the clutch again.

This time, with the lower gear ratios, the engine bogged down some, but we started moving!

Slow, but moving!

I didn't pull up onto the pavement, thinking the dirt of the shoulder would be easier on the tires as the two front wheels slid like skis with the rear set driving them forward. We plowed two grooves in the dirt about two inches deep, but by damn, we're moving! I quick-shifted into second-low gear and we achieved five MPH. I had to physically fight the steering wheel, to keep us aimed straight, but it was getting dark quick, due to some clouds on the horizon, and I was determined to get this hunk-o-junk to Papa Victor, no matter what. Sooner the better!

"One hour to Phouc Vinh!" I smiled.

"Wellll…sheeit!" almost speechless for 'Ramblin' Randy'.

I concentrated on steering and not hitting anything that might stop or slow us down. Randy got back onto his cow-tipping story. That was one long, long hour.

The right front tire blew first, mainly because I'd ground it into the edge of the pavement a couple of times, avoiding obstacles on the left. This made it want to drag to the right, and it took all my strength to hold us on course. In the third mile, the left one went with a BANG and a puff of dust. The steering evened out again and our speed slowed to four MPH, but we were still skiing along, trailing a burning smell that I hoped was just the tires. The temp gauge on the dash was running hot, but not in the red zone, yet.

'These engines were built for abuse, and this one's getting it today.' I thought.

We were now skidding along on flat tires, fairly smoothly, considering, but I knew it wouldn't last. Another mile and the right tire ripped completely off the rim and ka-thumped under the rear wheel and out the back. The steel wheel rim actually slid easier than the rubber tire had, and now I was forced to fight the steering to the right. My arms felt like I'd been wrestling gorillas, but we had less than a mile to go. It was 7:30 and almost dark and still no sign of the promised tow-truck.

The left tire finally shredded down to the rim but didn't come off. Now we're sliding on steel. In the near darkness, I begin seeing flashes of light reflecting off foliage on my side of the truck. I think the poor truck must be on fire and lean out to see, but it's just sparks from rocks striking the steel of the rims. No fire just yet, but the engine is getting really hot, now. The gauge is registering in the red zone and the hot oil smell is rising up from under the hood in waves. I figure a quarter mile to go. It's true dark.

At last, we're on the straight stretch that leads to the PV north gate. I eased the vehicle up onto the pavement accompanied by loud screeching and flashing sparks. With the reduced resistance of the asphalt, our speed increased to eight MPH and at 7:45, engine steaming and the one remaining tire smoking, and much to the amusement of the MPs, I crept the Dodge through the gates and pulled to the side and stopped.

I breathed a sigh of relief.

Randy of course was still yakking and going on, but I had tuned him out a half-hour ago and I just waved him off, got out, and leaned against the side of the truck. My arms were shaking as I tried to light a cig. I had to brace my Zippo with both hands to get it to the end of my cigarette.

The MPs, four of them, gathered around, inspecting the ground down wheel rims and asking me questions, checking us out.

Before I had time to answer, #2 Jones, in the Lt.'s jeep, followed by a wrecker, drove up and stopped when they spotted their vehicle parked inside the gate. They swung in, parked ahead of me, and got out. He inspected the truck, noting I'm sure the smoking tire, ruined rims and the smoke and steam rising from under the hood. He walked over to me, a half angry-half surprised look on his face.

"Looks like we won't have to go out for you, after all."

"Where there's a will, there's a way." I said grinning.

"You'll be hearing from Lt. Jones about this damage to our truck." He said, sort of threatening.

"Hell, I don't care." I said, "I'm not stayin' out there for any reason. I'm too Short and truck parts are too cheap!"

He got my drift, laughed a little, and offered me a ride back to my unit. The wrecker pulling the Dodge followed us. I was dismissed at their CP, cut through the fence by our commo shack and found Clark, feet up, in our CP reading a book.

"Hey, Mouse, decide to come back?" he asked, putting down his novel and reaching for the logbook.

"Yeah."

"How was it? Th' Hip-shoot, I mean."

"Not bad if you like camping out under th' stars." I replied, "an' drivin' like 'Dodge-em' cars all over hell-n-back."

"Anything happening out there?"

He wrote me down as 'returned' in the book.

I filled him in on the trip, finishing with how I destroyed the truck. He got a big yuk out of that!

He told me a lot of shit had been happening "up north", meaning the 'Fishhook'.

"Delta battery at LZ Sandy got hit hard last night and took some casualties, but I don't know how many." He informed me. "An' 'E' battery came off LZ East to LZ Ike and got 'Sapper' probed, but they held 'em off an' scored nine V/C KIA. No US wounded."

I thought about Scotty and T.C. and the guys I knew in 'D' battery, and hoped they were OK.

"What's happenin' 'round here?" I asked.

"Well… we got a sandbag detail goin' out to LZ South tomorrow, but you're not on it."

"Thank God!" I breathed.

"We got a new XO. A Major Payne."

He caught the amused look on my face.

"An' from all indications he's a…."

"Major Pain?" I finished for him.

"You got it! Can you believe?"

"Yeah, I can believe!" We both laughed

"And, we got a new First Sgt." he said, a smile playing at his lips.

Anderson had rotated a week ago and Sgt. Ambrose, an E-8, had been filling in until a replacement came.

"Yeah?"

"Yeah, an' guess who?" his smile widened.

I just stood there, looking puzzled.

"Who's your favorite First Sgt. of all time?"

I thought for a second until realization dawned.

"Oh, no. You don't mean...." I said, horrified.

"That's right, 'ol Puke-face himself." He laughed, either at the name or the look on my face.

Wilson!

"You mean nobody's shot him yet?"

"Not yet. Maybe you'll get your chance, now."

It ran through my mind that my life could be hell, from now on, if that man sees me. I'll have to really become invisible, now. It won't be easy, for nearly two months, but I swore I'd stay out of his way, if at all possible.

"Oh, an' Weitzel got his 612 discharge! He's leavin' out tomorrow!"

"So he finally convinced 'em he's crazy? What'd he do?"

"I heard he called Sgt. Major Toms a 'Fat, stupid little man' to his face an' ol' Tom's almost had a coronary."

"Jeez, he really IS nuts." I exclaimed.

"That he is!" We both laughed again.

"I left your mail on your bunk." He said putting his feet back up, "There's a big manila Dept. of the Army envelop in with it."

"Oh Shit. I always get nervous when one of those has my name on it."

"Probably somethin' to do with your extension." He assured me.

"Or my discharge papers." I joked, "Good, I'll leave with Jon-Jon in th' morning."

"Sure! An' I'm th' Pope. Bless you, son."

He waved a benedictory hand toward me, I waved a finger at him and left.

The KP crew was cleaning up in the mess hall, so I knew better than to try to get any supper there. I walked around the building toward the hootch and heard a big hoopla coming from the new EM club.

Curious, I walked down and a real party was in progress, with Weitzel as the guest of honor. He was the center of attention, as usual, and nobody noticed me at the door. I watched for a few minutes and then left.

I was feeling 'drove hard an' put away wet'!

I needed some food, a shower, and a bed, in that order.

I'd seen Fuk at a table at the club, so I knew the hootch would be empty. This suited me fine. After ol' Ramblin' Randy, a little solitude and quiet was just what I needed. In the room, I stripped to skivvies, set up my stove, started boiling water for my LRRPS and cocoa, and checked my mail.

A letter from Mom, attached to a 'goodie box'.

'Oh boy! Maybe some cookies.' I thought.

And that damn big Army envelope! My name, unit, and 'Official' stamped in red on the front. I picked it up with a sinking feeling in the pit of my stomach.

'Bad news!' I thought, 'These things are always bad news.'

I peeled the seal loose and pulled out a set of orders.

"Oh shit." I mumbled to myself and started de-ciphering the 'Army-ese'.

A minute later, I realized I was reading Promotion Papers.

"Well!" I said, brightening, "I'll be damned. I'm a Spec.-5!"

I certainly hadn't expected to be promoted again so soon.

'What th' hell, I AM an Extendee.' I thought. 'Doing more than my prescribed time in this stink-hole of a country. They owe me!' I smiled.

Feeling considerably better, I slipped the papers back into the envelope, and grabbed my 'goodie box'. I tore open Moms letter and, sitting in the circle of the reading light at the desk, I read as I tore into the box. This was the first 'Care Package' I'd received since April. I was pretty sure Mom was sending them, but I assumed they were getting lost or destroyed in the APO system, though I HAD been getting letters.

She sent her love. ('I love you, too, Mom.') Said her back was better. Was walking around, now, but couldn't sit. She had to get better so she could resume cooking duties at home, before my Dads cooking poisoned them both. Ha! Wanted to know what I was up to, did I get the last box she'd sent in May. (See I KNEW she'd sent 'em, I just never got 'em.) She hoped I'd enjoy what she sent and urged me to share with my buddies.

"Th' hell I will." I said as I looked in the box.

She sent me a whole, precooked canned ham!

A big chunk of sharp Cheddar cheese!

There were two...things..., looked like wrapping-paper tubes, the ends sealed up with masking tape, packed carefully in the bottom. One was filled with Ritz crackers, the other, with Oreo cookies!

"Man, a feast!" I said to no one there, "Bless you, Mom!"

And a carton of Larks! No more dried-out PX Marlboros!

I mixed my instant cocoa and spent nearly an hour eating ham and cheese on crackers 'til I was gorged. Oreos for desert!

'Man, life is sweet.'

I lit up a Lark, and started a letter home. I thanked her for the goodies. I gave her a brief, very sanitized version of my last week's activities. (To keep her from worrying, I very seldom told her the truth.). She was upset over my extension. I wrote that I wouldn't have done it if I were in any danger. That driving rations for the mess hall was the 'safest job in the Army', and for her not to worry. I told her about my new promotion, and I knew she and Dad would be proud. Dad, especially, since I now equaled his rank it had taken four years to earn during WWII. I finished up with my love, told them to take care of themselves, and that I'd be seeing them in August. I sealed the letter, and by that time I was too ragged-out for a shower, so I hid my ham and cracker leavings and other goodies, and crawled into my bunk and crashed. I didn't even hear Fuk come in, much later.

At a little before dawn, the next morning, I woke with a start. I had the feeling someone, or something, had touched me on the leg. I was flat on my back in the upper bunk, poncho liner pulled up to my chest. My head was turned outward, so, in the dim light coming in through the door, I could've seen anyone standing there.

No one was there.

Puzzled, and still half-asleep, I lay still, trying to figure out what had disturbed me.

Then I felt movement, down by my feet.

'What th'....'

Whatever it was, it was pretty heavy, and it was coming up, slowly, between my legs, on top of the covers. It was at my knees, now.

Now wide-awake, I was thinking furiously.

By the time it reached my crotch, I figured I didn't have time for subtlety.

367

My left arm was at my side, on top of the light cover. I pressed down on that side as I grasped the sheet with my right hand that was underneath on the other side. I was very careful not to move my legs.

Whatever it was, I could now tell it had four feet as it was standing on my stomach. I didn't breathe.

In one movement, I yanked hard on the poncho liner with my right hand, pulling it taut. At the same time I rolled left and brought my right arm up, catapulting my invader out into the air. Thank goodness I had neglected to pull my mosquito net down last night, or this would not have been possible. I saw, in the dim light, a form with writhing legs, go sailing across the gap and into the darkness where Fuk's bed was.

I heard a thump.

Two, three seconds passed in absolute quiet.

I heard two more thumps in quick succession, then a blood-curdling shriek.

Raised on my left elbow, I heard grunts, squeals and all sorts of commotion over there and then, feet slapping the concrete floor. In the weak gleam of dawn-light, I saw the silhouette of Fuk and a big rat, running, side-by-side, out the door, the screen door slapping back, and then quiet again.

After the shock wore off, I almost fell out of bed laughing!

A few moments later, Fuk came back in, flipped on the light, grabbed the broom from the corner and advanced, warily, on his bunk, swinging his weapon back and forth. I was laughing so hard, I couldn't tell him that the rat had escaped at the same time he did and his brave display with the broom cracked me up even more.

He danced around, brandishing the broom, peering into the still dark corners of the bunk. He was on his knees, trying to see into the darkness underneath, when I finally managed,

"It's gone, man!"

He looked up at me with the roundest eyes I think I've ever seen on a man.

Between guffaws, I explained how he and the rat had left together and that it was the funniest thing I'd ever seen.

"Funny, my royal ass!" He panted, "That thing went straight for my throat, man!"

I laughed some more, now sitting on the side of my elevated bed.

"Musta been rabid, 'r something to attack a man in 'is bunk, like that! It was like it just FLEW at me!"

I laughed some more, figuring MY part in the rats flight had better remain a secret. At least for the time being, or I could become a broom-casualty. I'd let him assume it was the RATS idea to attack him.

Finally, Fuk, being the good-natured dude he was, was laughing, too. We both broke up again when I described their side-by-side flight out the door and his expression when he came back, ready to do battle.

"I think HE was more scared than you were, man!" I said, trying to catch my breath.

He ruffled through his covers, making sure nothing else had crawled in, also, then lay back down.

"Now that I'm on day-shift at th' FDC," he said, "I'm having a hard time sleeping at night. Did'ja hear about Weitzel?"

I nodded.

"Well, we partied 'til about 1:30 this morning, and I still didn't get to sleep 'til about 3:00, so I'm rackin' as long as possible."

It was only 5:30, but I was wide-awake, now, so I promised to guard Fuk from any more rat attacks, and got up. I gathered my shower kit, wrapped myself in my towel, slipped into my shower-shoes and headed out into the first light to wash the two-day funk off my body.

As I came up to the shower-shack, Weitzel himself was just coming out.

"You're up early, man!" I said in greeting.

"I'm outta heah today, man. Got my papers!"

"Yeah, I heard! Congrats, man. We're gonna miss you, around here. I think." I said, kiddingly.

"Hey, Mouse. Yer a good dude. Do me a favor?"

"Uhh...sure, Jon Jon, what?"

"Take my dogs, man." He said, meaning the two mongrel dogs he'd somehow managed to adopt and keep for the last two months. "I can't just turn 'em loose. Th' Gooks'll eat 'em an' th' Lifers'll shoot 'em."

"Well' hell....I don't know." I hesitated.

369

I liked his dogs, two females named Rags and Poopie, and all, but I was pretty short now, too, and didn't need that kind of responsibility right now. I told him so.

Jon-Jon, Rags and Buddy

"Aw, c'mon, man." He almost pleaded, "Yer th' only guy I'd trust t' take care o' my pups, man, or at least find 'em a safe home, so's they don't get 'et. Whatcha say?"

I knew Jon Jon wouldn't, normally, plead for you to throw water on him, if he was on fire, so he was really sincere about this. I knew he loved those dogs.

"Well, OK, man." I conceded, "Bring 'em up here, before you leave, an' I'll take 'em."

"Wow, thanks, Mouse!" he dapped me, fist-down, fist-up. "I knew you'd come through. Th' kids'll take care o' you, too, man."

He always called them 'Th' Kids'.

I had an idea!

"Hey, John, c'mon over here an' let me get a picture of you in your pink towel, to remember you by." I took his arm.

We were both dressed in towels and flip-flops, but, of course, his was big and pink, as was his style of craziness.

I got Fuk up again, complaining, but he used my Ansco and got, I hoped, a good shot of me and Jon Jon Weitzel, from south Chicago, crazy man and dog-lover, framed by a Vietnamese sunrise, on the day that HE left and I became a dog owner.

At 0730, he brought 'The Kids'. In my hootch, he squatted down and explained to the panting, wagging pair, that I was to be their new 'Daddy', and they both panted some more. I got down and let them lick my hand, (not my face, I knew all too well where those tongues had been.) They only panted more, but they must've understood, 'cause after he hugged them both one last time and we dapped our good-byes and he left, Rags and Poopie stayed with me, with hardly a whimper, and followed me around the rest of the day.

The dogs were of a breed known as 'Gook Dog'. Small, Cocker Spaniel sized, spotted dogs, with tails that curled back over the rump, and wagged furiously. Poopie was black and white and Rags was yellow-blond and white. They both had flop-ears, except one of Rags', which stood up proud, giving her an attentive look all the time, like she was listening to every word you said.

She probably was, but if she did, she chose to ignore any bit of advice I'd give them. Those dogs did what they chose, most of the time, but would hang with you on the merest promise of a bowl of food that evening. They were friendly to everyone except Lifers, whom they'd growl at, but loyal only to the man that dishes up the cold beef stew C-rats in their bowls at suppertime.

Poopie was renowned as a rat-killer, extraordinaire, so Fuk was extremely glad to have her sleep right next to his bunk. She had little, black beady eyes that glittered with an undiminishing excitement with life, and a face that showed every expression people show. She loved to be held, but was a respectful dog, following along two or three paces behind, checking out all that I encountered.

Not Rags. She was the party-girl, always dancing circles around me or tugging at my pants leg.

She had a bad pants leg habit. Hardly anyone was safe from her gnawing, pulling on any pants leg in range. She drew the line at officers and NCOs, thank goodness, but almost all the enlisted personnel had chew marks on the right leg of their fatigues. Only the right leg, though, curiously.

Fuk came up with the theory that if Rags doesn't like a guy, she'd chew his left leg, but she must've liked everyone. She was so sweet, though, that nobody minded, other than minor irritation when she interfered with a job, playing. She'd quit, if you'd tell her "NO!" and swoosh your hand at her, not hitting her, and she'd leave you alone for the rest of the day, choosing other victims 'til they swooshed her. By the end of the day, she'd have just about chewed everyone around. Next morning, she'd start the whole thing again, starting with me when I slipped my pants on.

They rode quietly in my truck, heads hanging out the passenger window, ears blowing up straight in the wind. They'd sit quietly in the cab while I was loading rations, and were obedient when I used my 'Lifer Voice' on them.

"Git down NOW, boah, 'r y'all'll git BUSTED! HEAR?"

They'd cower like a boot-camp private.

They were good dogs, though, a week later they ran afoul of Carbone for scavenging behind the mess hall and got reported. First Sgt. Wilson came to me and told me, in no uncertain terms, to keep a tight rein on the animals or else. I mentioned that the NCO's dog, T.I., ate regularly at the back door of the mess hall, and Carbone, himself, fed her.

"Tha's different!" he replied, "She's a NCO dog. She got priv'lidge!"

"So your dog outranks my dogs?" I had to ask, forever the smart-ass.

He gave me a burning look.

"Tha's right! An' don' you forget it!"

I started to ask if the dogs should be wearing rank insignia, but Wilson, I knew, still held that little puke thing against me, so I just said,

"OK, Top, I'll try and keep 'em under control."

"You betta, 'r I'll shoot 'em, myself!" he said, hatefully.

I burned HIM with a look and got in his face.

"If you're threatening those dogs," I said quietly, "you're threatening every enlisted man in the unit. They all love those dogs. You'd do well to make sure NOTHING ever happens to them, or you'll make about fifty instant enemies around here, and I won't be the least of 'em."

"Is that a threat?" he stepped back a pace.

"No, it's a promise." I said and stared him down.

He turned and left without another word. I knew I was courting disaster, messing with that man, but I'd be damned if I'd let him harm my dogs.

I reported to the mess hall the next morning as usual, and found out I'd been replaced as ration driver by one of the cooks, named 'Brisket', for his small pot-belly. Carbone told me he was sorry, but I'd been gone too much and too long on other details.

This was true, but, somehow, I sensed the hand of Sgt. Wilson in this. Deep down, I figured he was trying to root me out of my gravy job and leave me open for more hazardous duties, like LZ details and such. I wasn't far wrong.

For the next week I pulled details like burning the S-2's classified documents at the burn pit at the rear of the compound, picking up odds and ends at the airstrip, and driving Capt. Johnson, who was a really nice guy for a captain, around on his appointments. I felt like I was skating on thin ice.

I drew perimeter guard one night. Ralph, a new guy named Dietz and I were stationed on Tower November for the night. All was quiet until about 3:00 A.M., when Bunker #42 reported movement in their wire at their 11 o'clock position.

We checked it from our elevated position and, sure enough, something WAS moving around out there, just beyond the wire. Something as big as a man. It didn't seem very intent on hiding, but in the brush and high grass, we couldn't tell what it was, so, naturally, we assumed it was 'Charlie' and reported it to the Sgt. of the Guard.

The SOG, a new guy, himself, got so excited he flipped his jeep over onto its side behind the bunker when he pulled in at high speed. We all chuckled, as soon as we determined he was OK and he ran into #42 and checked the 'movement' through their Starlight Scope. He couldn't determine what the shape was either, so we heard him, over the radio, call for 'lume rounds from the 2/19th Arty.

Within minutes, the silvery light of the flare rounds drifting on their parachutes lighted the entire segment of the green-line. I focused my powerful binoculars on the object and it was an anteater. A fucking aardvark! I radioed my report to #42, told the SOG that he didn't seem to be armed, and was moving off to our left, now, toward #43. The new Sgt. 'rogered' my report, and shortly, we saw him and three of the bunker inmates come out and rock the jeep back onto its wheels and he drove off.

The rest of the night, the radio 'BS' involved anteater jokes and comments like "My uncle was the only aunt-eater I ever knew." Or, "Don't let th' anteaters sneak up an' French-kiss you, they'll suck out yer tiny li'l brain!" Anyway, the aardvark got away and wasn't seen again.

In the morning, when I climbed down from the tower, there was Poopie, waiting for me, jumping and running circles in her usual, excited, dog greeting. I don't know how long she'd been there, or, for that matter, how she knew where I was. Both dogs had been sleeping on the floor while Fuk strummed his guitar last night when I left, but there she was, panting and smiling, so glad to see me.

The ¾-ton guard truck pulled up in a cloud of dust, to pick us up after guard, and DAMN! Poopie, in her near-frenzy, somehow got in the way and the front tire knocked her down and passed completely over her. She let out a loud yelp, then lay there, half under the running board, whimpering.

Scared shitless, I gently pulled her out, expecting the worst. She wasn't bleeding, but her eyes were wild and her tongue was lolling out into the dust on the road. I ran my hands over her, carefully checking for broken bones. Her hip felt strange and spongy, and as I talked softly to her as I probed, she tried once to get up but her hind legs didn't work and she flopped back down with another sharp, pain-filled, yelp.

The truck driver was beside himself with remorse, almost in tears. He helped us get the hapless animal onto a folded poncho and onto the truck seat. I got in beside her while Ralph and Dietz climbed in the back and we screeched away and flew back to the compound to the aid-station.

Ralph got the 'Doc' out of a sound sleep while Deitz and I carried Poopie in and lay her gently on the examining table. She 'yiked' at every movement but lay quietly, breathing hard, on the table. The Doc came in and got a concerned look on his face when he saw who his patient was. Phillips loved Poopie as much as anyone.

"I'm not a veterinarian!" he lamented, "Hell, I'm not even a doctor!"

"You're all we got, Doc." I said, pleading, near tears, myself. "See if you can do something for her!"

He started with a reduced dosage of morphine, to help with the pain. I explained what had happened and my observations as he went over the little furry thing with gentle, but probing hands. She snapped at him, half-heartedly, when he felt down along her flank where I told him I'd felt the 'spongy' bone.

After a couple minutes, he looked up at me.

"Well, there's no bleeding… and she hasn't lost bowel or bladder control, so that's a good sign."

I could tell he was trying to be reassuring.

"But, something in here," he pointed to her right flank, "either her hip, pelvis or back, is broken, Mouse. I can't tell which without an X-ray."

"What'm I gonna do, Doc?"

"Well, I could….. uh….. put her….uh….down."

"NO!"

I'd unconsciously grabbed his arm to steady myself and squeezed 'til he winced.

"OK, OK!" He pried my fingers off. "We'll think of something."

"Any chance of it healing on its own?" I asked, grasping at straws.

"Possible, but not likely." He answered, "If the bone's broken and separated, it'll need to be set, which I know nothing about on dogs. Plus, there's the issue of keeping her immobilized. In a cast, would be best, and I don't have the facilities, here, to do a body cast on a dog, or a person."

"But there's gotta be somethin' we can do!" I said, desperation in my voice.

"Hey, Doc," Ralph interjected, "Don't they have guard dogs and scout dogs in th' Army? I seen 'em down in Bien Hoa. They got a whole Scout Dog unit, down there, man. They gotta have a place where they take care o' wounded 'r sick dogs."

Doc brightened. He snapped his fingers and slapped ol' Ralph on the back.

"You're right, man. They DO." Doc said, "Tell you what. You take her to your hootch, keep her quiet, and I'll make some phone calls from the CP and see if I can find out anything, OK?"

"OK, Doc. But hurry, man, I don't know what I'd do if she...you know...."

"We'll do our best for her, Mouse, the best we can, OK? Now go on and let me get busy."

I gathered up my wounded pooch, using my flack jacket for a sort of brace to keep her from drooping over my arms, and carried her like I was walking on eggs, back to my room. I put her down as carefully as I could, cooing reassurances, but she yelped again as I laid her on Bowers bunk and she looked at me with fear rolling her eyes.

Ralph had come along from the aid station and we stood, looking at Poopie, in her misery, whimpering and shivering. I got my poncho liner, folded it and covered her to keep her warm. Ralph patted my shoulder and told me not to worry. I thanked him for helping and for his suggestion about the scout dogs.

"Ain't nothin'." He said, "Got a Blue Heeler at home, myself. I'd do most anythin' for that dog, too, so I know how you're feelin' right now." He smiled and left.

It was just 0700, but the word spread fast and within a half-hour, guys were coming, tentatively, to the door and whispering inquiries about the dogs condition. Some, like Terry Leonard, supposedly big, tough, soldiers had the beginnings of tears in their eyes. It impacted on me, how much influence a small dog can have on us, supposedly superior humans. I fidgeted around the hootch, but invariably ended up sitting on the side of the bed, stroking her ears and trying to comfort her, 'til it got too much for me and I'd have to go off and fidget some more.

A little before 0800, Doc Phillips came running in, and, out of breath, told me had all the arrangements made. He'd gone through eight buddies before he got in touch with a Captain at 4th Vet. Med in Bien Hoa, the Scout Dog unit.

"That's great, Doc!" I said, pumping his hand like a well pump. "Can I borrow your truck to drive 'er down there? I got th' next twenty four hours off, 'cause I had guard last night. I can have her down there in…"

"Won't need to, Mouse," he interrupted, "There's a chopper winding up, right now, on the Echo of the 82nd pad, next door. They said they'll fly you right to the place."

"Wow!" I said, amazed, "Just like 'Med-Evac'."

"Actually, it IS a Med-Evac chopper. They'll drop you off on their way to 15th Med, but you'll have to find your own way back. Better saddle-up and get on over there, they're waiting."

He clapped me on the shoulder and I smiled my thanks.

I didn't want to have to deal with a rifle and ammo with the dog, so I strapped on my Army .45, in it's shoulder holster, that I'd acquired from a DEROS-ing 2/19th gun-bunny last month, slammed on my helmet, carefully gathered up Poopie and took off.

Several guys saw me as I dashed across the compound and wished me luck and to "take care of th' Kid!" I yelled back thanks and that I WOULD, as I cut through the motor pool fence to the chopper pad on the other side. There, waiting for us was a LOH, (Loach), helicopter, a big Red Cross emblazoned on its side, it's blades swirling the early morning dust. The co-pilot was standing alongside, waving for me to hurry, and helped my wounded passenger and I into the rear compartment. I strapped in on one of the fold-down jump seats, but didn't think that would be good for the dog, so I placed her between my feet on the floor. Thirty seconds later, we were high above the green-line of Phouc Vinh, in the cold morning upper air, heading south in a beeline for Bien Hoa.

The sun had risen enough above the horizon to cast long misty shadows across the flat plains far below. My spirits had risen enough to have hope that I could help save this poor little animals life. In the short two weeks since I'd taken over their care, the two dogs had become like part of me. If something happened to one of them, something would go out of me, something irreplaceable. I was, at that moment, more scared for that little dog than I'd ever been for myself during all the shit that had happened during my tour. And that was saying something, 'cause I'd been plenty scared at times.

The rear compartment was separated from the cockpit by a bulkhead, so it was just me and the pooch, both of us shivering in the cold rushing air coming in the open doors. As we approached Bien Hoa, the pilot hung an abrupt right bank and the chopper tilted over until the ground was straight down out the right door. I was fearful Poopie would slide out the down door, and held onto her with my feet, while bracing myself with my hands. I needn't have worried, as the centrifugal G-forces of the turn plastered the dog to the floor. I could see her whimpering, even though I couldn't hear her. I wondered what was going through her drugged, pain-fearful head.

The bottom dropped out of our flight and we bumped down on a PSP pad near some low, white buildings. I immediately saw a sign by a gate that said, '4ᵗʰ Vet. Med'. I unstrapped and jumped out and gathered the dog in my arms. I stepped over by the pilot's door and yelled thanks. He smiled from behind his mirrored glasses, reached out and scratched Poopie's ears and wished me luck.

I turned and ran as smoothly as I could away from the prop-wash as the pilot wound up again and took off, clattering into the distance. I squatted down, put the dog across my knees, and checked her to see if she'd been harmed by the flight, or if I needed to do anything. (Though I didn't know what I could have done.) She seemed no different, so I gathered her again and headed for the gate.

A sign, reading CP, on the first building, beckoned to me and I shouldered in through the wooden screen door, which slapped shut behind me. At the sound, a Spec. 4 spun and looked, first at me, then at the bundle in my arms. He nodded.

"Wait one." He said and went through a curtained doorway and I heard him address someone in the other room. Mumblings were exchanged and then a Captain Blaine, according to his nametag, came in. He took a cursory look at Poopie and told me to follow him. We exited and he went to the right, around to another, larger white building and we entered there through a wooden, paneled door.

Inside was a combination examining room, surgery and kennel. Wire cages lined one wall, but only German Shepherds occupied two of them, obviously, judging from their bandages recovering from some sort of mishaps. Another wall was a chemistry analysis set-up with Bunsen burners and all. In the middle was an examining table, its stainless steel top gleaming in the bright light from the overhead array of bulbs. He instructed me to put the dog down on the table.

"I understand you have a…bit of an unusual patient for us?" he smiled.

Blaine was a tall, medium built, handsome man in his mid-thirties. He wore black framed glasses and his quick smile immediately calmed me. I liked him just as quickly, because his smile showed real concern, true caring.

"Uh… yessir," I stammered, "Her name's Poopie an' she got hit by a truck, an' everybody loves her an' we gotta do somethin real quick or she's gonna…." It all poured out of me and he had to stop me with a raised palm.

"All right, all right, Hudson?" he read my nametag.

"Yessir."

"Just have a seat over there," He indicated a chair by the door, "and let me have a look."

"If you don't mind, sir, I'm too nervous to sit, do you mind if I watch, 'r I can help if you need…."

He chuckled, a low mirthful sound that took my anxiety down a couple of notches. He held up his palm again to interrupt.

"No, no, Hudson, that won't be necessary, just stand there and watch. Now…. Let me see."

He bent over, adjusted his glasses, and started probing with the gentlest fingers I'd ever seen. I shifted from foot to foot as he "Mmhmmmmed" and "ahahed" for about five minutes, seeing things about the dog I knew were totally invisible to me.

Finally, he straightened, and looked into my eyes.

"Without X-rays, I can't tell for sure, but it appears her pelvis is broken right about….here."

He pointed to the spongy area I'd felt earlier. It was now a little swollen, I noticed.

"C-can you save her, sir?" I said, my voice breaking.

"Well…." He rubbed his chin in thought.

My heart was beating fast, in fear that he'd say no.

"We're not supposed to treat indigenous animals, of course," he continued. "but you say this is your company mascot?"

"Yessir!" I nodded emphatically, "Everybody loves Poopie except for...." I almost said Lifers, "Uh....people who don't like anything."

He chuckled that warm laugh again.

"Well, the Army's obviously been feeding her, and she DOES fill a need for your company's morale, so I guess we can do something for her."

I couldn't help myself, I grabbed his hand and started pumping it.

"Oh, thank you, sir, you just don't know...."

He gently dislodged his hand and said, "Yes, yes I do, Hudson. We'll do the best we can, but you'll have to leave her here for at least a week, maybe longer. OK?"

"Sure, sir, whatever it takes. I'll PAY for the treatment, if it's necessary, anything, just so she can get taken care of and get well." I gushed, relieved.

"That won't be necessary, Hudson. I can tell you're a real dog-lover, so just go back to your unit and try to relax, we'll do the very best we can for her. Leave your name and unit designation with the clerk on the way out and as soon as she is ready, you'll be contacted and you can come pick her up. Try not to worry."

After leaving instructions on how to reach me at the CP, I walked out into the blazing mid-morning sun. The heat swept over me and I half-swooned. Now that my tension had been eased, and I had time to think, I realized that, except for a two hour catnap last night, between guard shifts, I'd had no rest since night before last. I also had not eaten since last night and I was getting weak from hunger and fatigue. I also realized, I had no way to get back to PV.

"The Artillery never walks."

That's just one of the many Bullshit Mottos they have in the Army.

"An Army travels on its stomach." Is another.

I was DEFINITELY traveling on my hot, tired feet.

There was mainly local civilian traffic on the four-lane highway between Bien Hoa and Long Binh. Trucks, busses, cars and motorcycles. The trucks were all loaded and wouldn't stop for a hitchhiker. I didn't want to get on the bus with the thousand kids, the screaming mama-sans and their livestock. The motorbikes were all zipping through traffic and around the other vehicles, causing near collisions, like they were suicidal.

I walked on the dusty shoulder, breathing the heady aroma of diesel fuel and burning shit. The hot sun, now almost directly overhead, had melted the tar surface on the road. The vehicles going by sounded like pulling the backing off contact paper as their tires rolled on the sticky surface. I'd started out walking on the smooth edge of the pave-ment, but when my boots started sticking to it, I stepped down into the dirt along the side. Then the tar on my soles accumulated about a pound, each, of dry dirt and I had to stop and scrape my boots with a stick.

'Man, I hate this country.'

A walking tour through a section of Long Binh City where the tourist attractions seemed to be poverty stricken homes, run-down aban-doned buildings and the occasional bomb or rocket-damaged area, one of which was still smoking. The exotic sights were just depressing, today.

It took until noon to get onto the base at Long Binh, where I quickly thumbed a ride in a jeep to the Air Force BX. I needed food! A cheeseburger and a chocolate shake were just the ticket (not to mention the air-conditioning!)

Refreshed, I stepped back outside and the heat slapped me again. I felt better now, but man! I hiked a couple of blocks until I thumbed on another jeep and got a ride right to the 1/30th Service Battery. I waited there for an hour to catch a ride in the back of a Deuce on the way to An Loc. They dropped me in Tuong Hoa, where the road split. They continued on north on Hwy. 13.

I waited at the crossroads for thirty minutes and caught a ride, on another Deuce, into Phouc Vinh. I had to hike across the base and arrived at HQ, sweaty and dragging, a little after five. I went straight to my hootch, but not before being stopped by five guys wanting to know about Poopie. They were relieved at my report and I told them to spread the news and that I didn't want to be bothered for at least four hours, please. I needed some sleep.

Rags was waiting outside my screen door for her nightly beef stew and a good leg-chew. I greeted her and told her not to worry about her little buddy. She was, of course, more interested in the beef stew.

Afterwards, she settled on the rattan rug between the bunks curled up and went to sleep. Good Idea!

Fukijima was out someplace, so, in the quiet hootch, in the dying sunset-light, I died until 9:00, when I was awakened by my stomach. The burger and shake were gone. I got up, snarfed a LRRP beef stew, (Rags got some, too.), and a warm coke, walked to the shower and scrubbed the two-day funk off, dressed in fatigues and flip-flops at the hootch, and went to the EM club. Rags went off on one of her night missions.

The pool table had arrived! Nick and Pagans were busy uncrating it and setting it up in the back third of the room. The mood was high and so were the twenty-some guys there. They all had heard the poop on Poopie, but had to come slap my back and ask particulars, anyway. I sat at the bar, had a cold coke, and told them about the trip down and back and that the little dog was in good hands and would be back soon.

Clark came in about 10:00, and after inquiring about Poopie, ruined my short good mood by informing me that I was scheduled for a sandbag detail, in the morning at 0800 to a new LZ called Becky.

Crap!

I could see Sgt. Wilson written all over this. He'd seen that I lost my cushy ration job so he could send me out on crappy details, where I'd have a better chance of getting killed.

"I know it's true, but what can I do?" an old song on the stereo mocked me.

Pissed-off and still dead-tired, I went back to the hootch and crashed, only to dream all night about Poopie being run over and squished by an enormous tire, and I had to bury her in a hole I'd dug to fill a million sandbags. It was a bad night and I woke up still tired.

32

'BECKY'

By 0830, June 12th, five other dejected souls and myself were in-flight in a Chinook. We were headed, roughly, northwest over the dense jungle region known as the 'Iron Triangle'.

We hovered, briefly over LZ South, to hook up two slings of supplies, then went due west about thirty miles and let down into a clearing in the trees. The only clearing visible for miles, I noted with some discomfort. This observation did not escape my fellow travelers, either.

"This is LZ Becky? It's just a li'l hole in th' jungle." said Harry Depp, a new-guy PFC, who was seated next to me.

"What's th' LZ stand for?" someone quipped from behind me, "Little Zit? I've had pimples bigger'n this."

The LZ WAS small! Probably not more than 250 feet across from tree line to tree line, and crammed full. Echo Battery, late of LZ South, had split-battery and three of their 155s were here, set up in temporary berm-pits on the north side. I spotted a six-tube mortar platoon of ARVNs and six 105s of the 2/19th lining the south perimeter. There were, maybe two platoons of ARVN infantry in fighting positions around the LZ.

'Not many men, in a big ol' jungle.' I thought.

We'd been told that the, so-called, LZ was only a temporary installation. Placed there to act as a fire-support base for the 1st Cav and ARVN units operating in 'Area 353', wherever that was. The Grunts were in the process of 'bottling-up' an NVA division that had been routed up in Cambodia, and Becky would also act as a jumping-off place for those units. I was sure ready to 'Jump-Off'!

As we hovered-in and dropped the slings, I got a good overhead view of the set-up. I didn't like what I saw. The guns were too close together, there wasn't adequate protection for the men, as far as bunkers and trench-works were concerned, and the Kill-Zone, around the perimeter, was way too narrow. The actual tree line came to within twenty-five feet of the gun pits, in places, and there was only a measly four strands of concertina wire around the defensive ring. I don't know if it was a premonition, or what, but I immediately mentally labeled this place a 'Death Trap.'

It was a colorful death trap, though. The trees were very green, the earth was very red and our moods were very black as we landed and exited the ship into the dust cloud.

We stood in our group, holding our weapons and shovels, while the dust settled. There was me, Jim Lynch, Ralph, 'Brother B', (from HQ supply), and the two new guys, Harry Depp and Freddy Fulks. It was 1000 hrs and hot as blazes. Already the sweat was running down my back, and I hadn't even moved yet.

The 1/30th gun-chiefs were expecting us, ran over, and set us to building powder bunkers in the three pits. At one o'clock, these were finished, and after a very short lunch break, we were instructed to beef-up the perimeter berm walls. The surrounding trees shielded us from any breeze, and the temperature was near 130°, so we were eating salt tabs like candy and sweating out water by the gallon.

Two choppers had come in since we'd arrived. One bearing more supplies and another carrying an ARVN Ranger company, that immediately saddled-up and moved out into the jungle to the north. At 3:00, a third chopper hovered in and started to descend. We stopped our digging for a minute to shield ourselves from the prop-blast. When the bird was about 75 feet off the ground, over the thump of the rotating blades, I thought I heard a strange ratcheting sound. It seemed to be coming from out in the jungle to the north.

Someone yelled, "LOOK!"

The hovering helicopter suddenly dipped and the engine stuttered and started to smoke. I could see little pieces of things floating down below it, like chaff in the wind. The choppers engines increased power, still stuttering, and flew off southward, trailing a smudge of smoke.

All work had stopped on the LZ as we watched the bird out of sight and sound. Then the silence was so acute, I could hear flies buzzing in the still, hot air. All at once, everybody's talking and yelling.

"Jeez, whut wuz thayat?"

"Did'ja hear that?"

"Yow! That chopper almost bought it, man!"

Then all the Lifers started giving orders at once, getting the ARVNs awake, in case of an attack. We were told to get down and lock and load, like we weren't already. Then one of the 105s fired a marking round. I looked over there and saw that they were at a high trajectory, meaning their targets were very close. Judging from their angle of fire, I guessed it to be inside a half mile.

'Somewhere, less than a half-mile from here, there're some guys who'd love to kill me.' I thought right before the 105's first six-gun salvo. A few seconds later, the "karruuump,ump,ummpp!" of the rounds landing, probably a quarter mile to the north. Close enough that, after the crashes of the rounds, we could hear trees falling over. Close.

'It won't be easy, though.' I smiled inwardly, despite my nervousness. It sounded like pure Hell out there.

They fired two more salvos, spreading the impacts over a quarter mile square area. In between, we listened to more foliage disintegrating.

Then the Howitzers fell silent and the mortars started popping rounds into the same area.

"Thunk, thunk, thunk..........BAWAM! WAM!! WAM!!!!"

We could now see the smoke, above the trees, from the target area.

We could also see the flashes of the impacting ordnance, reflected on the undersides of the smoke clouds. Close.

"Fire for effect, boys!" I said, without looking, to a guy next to me on the berm.

"Fuckin' A, Mouse!" He replied.

I turned to a familiar voice. It was Corey, the guitar player.

"Hey, wow, man!" I exclaimed.

His white teeth flashed under his little, blond mustache. His pale blue eyes and shock of unruly blond hair gleamed, dirtily, in the sun.

"I was just jokin' when I told you t' come up and visit me, man."

385

We 'Dapped 'n Slapped'.

"Yeah, well, next time you're just gonna havt'a come an' see ME, 'cause you live in a pretty bad neighborhood, here." I laughed, glad to see him.

The mortars stopped, and we were waiting, I guess, for the other shoe to drop.

"What th' Hell are you doin' out here, in th' pure boonies, man?" He asked.

I told him about the 'shit-bag' details.

"Sucks, man."

I told him how short I was.

"REALLY sucks, man."

He told me that he's a gunny on this gun, and has been for eleven months, three days, ten hours....he looked at his watch....and thirty eight minutes.

He's even shorter than I am.

"Really, really sucks, man." I commiserated.

Jim came over, recognized Corey, Dapped him, and we lit cigarettes and discussed the situation.

Corey had heard that an NVA 'supported division' was in the woods, somewhere north of here, being pursued by our Grunts and the ARVNs, (better known as the 'De-fenders o' De-mocrazy').

Evidently, the Gooks wanted out of Cambodia and to get back into Vietnam.

"And they're comin' through these very woods. Ain't WE lucky."

Freddy Fulks, sitting nearby, heard this last comment and scooted over. I think he was afraid to stand up.

"Are we...like, safe, man?" his voice shook, "I mean... they won't attack US...will they?"

Corey shook his head, snorted a laugh.

"I think you could call LZ Becky a lotta things, but 'SAFE' ain't one of 'em."

I 'Roger-ed' that, falling into my 'Seasoned Veteran' pose. I told him not to worry, that you could only die once, and besides, it don't mean nothin'.

Jim and Corey both said, "There it is."

Fulks just looked confused.

He hadn't learned, yet, what that means.

It means don't complain about things you have no control over.

It means if something bad happens, it's not your fault. You didn't volunteer for this shit.

It means, if your number's up, it's up. You've, really, got no choice.

It's a reflection of how it was in civilian life, where you generally controlled your own destiny. In Vietnam your fate can be decided by some starched-shirt REMF in an air-cooled office in Saigon. As long as you're in the Army, whatever you do, whatever happens, "It Don't Mean Nothin'."

Our conversation was cut off by the sound of small-arms fire out in the jungle a ways off but not far. Then there were a series of small blasts that could have been grenades or B-40 rockets. Then the 'Dirty Thirty' got their first fire-mission.

Corey ran off to the gun and their gun-captain, a Spec-4 named Winston, told us to get back to shoveling, unless told otherwise.

We shoveled and filled and built walls, our rifles nearby, casting glances at the wall of trees out there, hoping to not see anything.

At 4:30, an ARVN patrol unit came back into the LZ. They looked kinda shot-up and were carrying two wounded (or dead).

Scuttlebutt flew around the LZ faster than a stripe-fly.

They'd supposedly staked out a trail just north of the LZ and had caught an NVA squad of eight men, carrying rocket tubes and rice ball rations. The ambush went off and they scored four bodies, recovered and destroyed most of the supplies.

That was the good news.

The bad news was the trail showed signs of heavy, recent use, including truck tracks. They'd later heard movement on the same trail and scouted it out. They'd seen a "large body of men', walking "Brazenly" down the trail toward the "vastly out-numbered" ARVN force. They'd called in the 155-fire mission, on that group of soldiers, while they retreated. The fire, they reported, had been very effective, landing amongst the enemy ranks, killing many and causing the rest to disperse into the surrounding jungle.

"I think there's a lotta Dinks out there." Ralph said, during a pause between bags.

"I think you're right." I answered.

At 5:30, a Huey gun-ship flew over and drew fire from two different .51 caliber AA guns. One east of the LZ, one west.

We watched the show from the ground, as the mortars waited until the gun-ship hosed down a suspected gun-site, then, with direction from the chopper, they pumped round after round into the trees, blowing up many trees, but no enemy AA. Two minutes after the mortars stopped, both the .51s opened up again, this time hitting the chopper, which was still circling, looking for, but finding no targets. The helicopter ended up being the target, and had to go off-station with a smoking engine. As soon as the chopper chugged away, the 105s fired off on the last reported enemy locations and blew up a lot more jungle. We heard no more machinegun-fire after that.

"Did we get 'em?" Fulks asked me.

"Who knows?" I answered, getting back to my shoveling, "But don't bet on it."

At 6:00, another Huey, a 'Slick', (meaning with no guns), this time came over, escorted by a Cobra gun-ship. The Cobra, probably the 'Baddest' chopper in the Army, was equipped with 40mm rockets, twin 5.56 mini-guns and automatic 'Blooper'. (40mm grenade-launcher that shoots the same rounds as the M-79.)

The Slick drew fire from three sites, this time. East, west and north. The Huey took evasive action as the Cobra began strafing runs on first one position, then another. Unfortunately, he couldn't silence all three at once and the Slick and the Cobra started taking hits. We watched, fascinated, as the Slick first lost half its power, due to a bullet in the engine, then we watched pieces fly and fall off it as the pilots plexiglas windows and wind screen imploded.

The stricken ship angled tail up and sputtered away above the trees to our south, out of sight. The, now wounded, gun-ship took off south, too, following the Slick.

The sandbag detail had been told to get ready to bug out as soon as that chopper landed. It had been our ride home. We were left standing in the center of the LZ, cursing and looking forlorn, holding our rifles and shovels.

Uncertain what we should do now, we drifted over beside the FDC shack, and I caught an E-6, actually, the NCOIC for the base, and asked him if there was a chance of our getting off Becky tonight.

Considering the two near-shoot-downs of incoming aircraft, we were told, the chance was mighty slim that anyone would be going anywhere.

"Hell, the choppers won't come anywhere near here, s'long as those 51s are out there." He finished and turned to a Lt. who'd just ducked out of the bunker.

The guys started bitching and discussing among themselves. The Sgt. and Lt. stepped away, talking. I listened.

I heard the Lt. say we'd get no 'Fast Movers', (bombers and strafing jets), until morning, when they could ID the 'Friendlies' in the area.

The Sgt. said we'd be pretty much on our own, out here tonight.

The young Lt. nodded.

"That's right, Sarge, we're going to get a minimum amount of air cover, due to the distances involved, and we've only got the other three 155 guns of E battery, on LZ South, with range enough to fire support missions for our location."

As they walked out of earshot, their conversation mingled with the mumbling of the group behind me. But not before I heard the Sgt. say something about "surrounded" and "9th NVA Division".

'Does that mean we've got THEM surrounded?' I thought.

'Or that they've got US surrounded?'

I figured I might not want to know and turned back just as Lynch was saying;

"...an' I SURE don't like bein' stuck out here with ol' Marvin," he gestured toward the ARVN Rangers who were now taking up fighting positions around the perimeter, 'as MY protection. It'd take two o' them li'l fuckers t' whip one o' theses damn mosquitoes we got out here." He slapped his neck, looked at the smear of bright red blood on his fingers.

"MEDIC!" he chuckled, "I'm wounded!"

The group laughed, but there was a feeling of fear among us.

I didn't know what their fears were. Mine was the 'Chicken Little' Syndrome.

One day a piece of the sky falls on you and ends your world.

From my limited experience in combat, the guys I'd seen get killed had been done-in by 'random fire'. Not a well-aimed bullet from a determined enemy soldier.

Fulks, the new guy, was really shaking, scared shitless.

Depp, his FNG buddy, wasn't.

"Least we got us a whole company of 'em, an' their mortars. They don't look like such pussies t' me," he whispered as two Rangers walked by, carrying an M-60 between them, bandoleers slung over their shoulders.

"Bull-shit!" Brother 'B' said, standing and facing the group.

"Ain't NO mo' chicken-shit soldier than ol' Marvin."

Both the FNGs looked to 'B' like he was about to reveal a real 'Truth' about combat, like he was a serious veteran. I knew ol' 'B' had spent his entire tour so far, consisting of two months or so, in the supply room at HQ in Papa Victor. The Brother swelled at the attention.

"Sheeit! Take more'n a buncha li'l bitty gooks t' take down this heah nigga!"

He paused to make sure he had the new-guys full attention, then continued.

"Bad dudes in my 'hood back in Dee-troit tryin' t' get me fa yeahs. Nebba Happen, GI!" he boasted, "Don' know 'bout you dudes, but I'm a Bad Mo-Fucka an' betta NOBODY fuck wit' me!"

I could see that Ralph, who made no secret of the fact that he, being from the south, was a tiny bit racist, but didn't like Bro 'B' on general principals, was just about to say something that would start a situation, so I intervened.

"OK! OK! We're gonna be stuck here at least tonight. Probably tomorrow, too, so I think we should split up in twos and join the gun crews. Help out anyway we can."

"Yeah, that way we get to hide behind some o' those walls we built today." Jim said, helpfully.

The others nodded.

"Alright…uh…I guess just choose-up partners and, Jim, you go to #1. Ralph, you got #2 an' I'll take #3."

Jim took Fulks, Ralph got Depp, and I ended up with 'B'.

They took off for their respective guns and 'B' and I walked over toward Winston to volunteer.

"What th' hell's the 'B' stand for anyway?" I asked, conversationally, curious.

"Bad!" his reply

'Oh, great!' I thought.

Winston was more than glad for any help he got. He sent 'B' to the M-60 bunker on the berm, but since I had boo-koo experience on the guns, I'd be the 'Powder Monkey' and cut the charges, or help with the loaders if necessary.

Corey was the AG on this gun. One of the reasons I'd chosen it. So I'd know SOMEBODY. He greeted me with a dap and a smile.

"Guess you'll be visitin' a while longer'n you thought."

"Looks like it!" I smiled back.

It was getting dark now, so I asked Corey if they had any extra rations, since we'd only come prepared for noon chow.

"Sure, man, somewhere."

We walked to the powder bunker that I'd personally built that morning, and rooted through a pile of supplies and he came up with a case of Cs. We squatted next to our packs and cooked-up on C-4 stoves. We ate, sipped warm Kool-Aid and talked 'til full dark.

He told me he was sorry I'd had to stay out tonight, but was glad for the help.

"We've only had five-man crews for the last month," he said, chewing spag. w/ mt. Sce.

"An' with 'Vietnamization', we ain't gettin' any replacements."

"So you just grab th' first guys that happen by." I kidded.

"Yeah." He laughed, "We're also known as th' 'Friendly Thirty.'"

"Good friends in a BAD neighborhood."

"Somethin' like that."

"Anyway," he continued his thought, "guess when I ETS, next month, the crew'll be down to four." He shook his head. "How they gonna run a gun with just four guys?"

"Well, you c'n forget ME takin' your place," I said seriously, "I'm goin' home, too!"

He said it jokingly, but his eyes were serious.

"We gotta get off LZ Becky, first."

There it was.

At 2230, Winston told us to "Do our thang" and we did. Prepping for all-night fire-missions everybody had their jobs like on all the other LZs I'd been on. I knew to crack open the powder cans, pre-cut some #1s and #2s, since I assumed most of the rounds would be for short range, and uncrate some fuses and line them up for quick access. Corey and I fused three rounds and stacked them on the ready rack, one WP and two HE.

Then we waited.

Most guys, myself included, were too keyed-up to relax. I walked over to the M-60 bunker to say Hi to 'B'. I ducked into the small space and there was 'B', feet up on the window sill next to the barrel of the, still-unloaded machine gun, leaning back against the blastwall like he didn't have a care in the world. He greeted me.

"YO, Holmes, 'sappenin?"

I wondered, 'Hmmmm.'

"Hey, 'B', think maybe you oughta load that baby up?" I gestured to the useless gun.

"Hey, yeah, man." He said and scrambled to get up like it hadn't occurred to him.

Then he looked at me with bloodshot eyes and said, like it was his idea all along.

"We oughta load this heah baby up, so's we c'n kill us some gook muthafuckas."

He fumbled with the ammo belt in the can, pulled it up twisted and tried to jam the first bullet in the string into the feed slot on the side of the gun. It wouldn't go in, of course, so he tried holding the bullet in the slot and pulling the charging handle.

'He's fried on something!' angrily shot through my mind.

Exasperated, I grabbed the belt from his fumbling hands. Since the charging handle was already back, I unclipped the breech cover, raised it and snapped the third round into the slot, leaving two hanging out the ejection port. I slapped the cover back into its catch, released the charging handle, and locked it forward. I checked to make sure the safety lever was forward and then I turned on him.

I got in his face.

"I've nearly been killed by gooks," I began in a low voice, "I've nearly been killed by my own mistakes," I paused, breathing hard. "But, damn if I'll get killed by some ignorant, strung-out fool, who doesn't have enough sense to see that his own ass is showing!" Loudly!

Stoned and confused, he actually looked back to see if his pants were falling down.

"Jeez!" I cried, "You're fucked-up on somethin, aren't you!"

He grinned, but not for long.

I was on him like white on rice.

Maintaining my cool, as much as possible, I told him what a low sucker he'd be if he let down someone who was depending on him, especially ME, if the shit really does come down tonight.

"Get your shit together, man. YOUR life may depend on bein' able to just think."

He backed off, probably assuming that, since I was on a tour extension, I was probably dangerously insane. Just then, I WAS.

Did he have a rifle?

"Yeah."

"Ammo for it?"

"Uh...yeah!" he pulled out one mag.

"That all?"

"Uh...yeah."

"Jeez!" I had to hunt up some more M-16 mags for him and help him load 'em.

During this, he seemed almost apologetic, for 'B'.

"You c'n sure be a li'l lifer prick, when you wanna be."

I looked up from the ammo can where I was helping him load HIS magazines. I glared at him.

He held up his palms. Smiled.

"I'm just tryin' to help you save my ass." I commented.

By the time I left, he seemed alert. I hoped it would last.

The night had settled on us like a cloud...of mosquitoes. They were feasting on us and even the greasy GI repellant wouldn't keep 'em off. The air was stuffy and humid and the LZ was completely quiet. I swear, the only sound was the slapping of the guys killing bugs.

I was reading another MacDonald book by the dim red light of my flashlight in the powder bunker. It was a little after eleven. I heard an engine running. A truck engine.

'Who th' hell's drivin' th' truck around, this time of night?' I wondered. I stood up, tucked my book in my leg pocket and went out to see. I ran into Corey and Winston.

"Who th' hell's...." I began.

"SHHH!" it was Winston. "Listen up."

I stood there quiet. It was very dark, but my night-vision was well developed, now, and I saw several guys standing near, with their ears cocked, as mine were, to the north.

A low gas-engine rumble was coming, not from inside the base, as I'd assumed, but from out in the jungle. 'Not far off.' I listened closely and realized it was not just one truck. 'Three? Four?' I could even hear them grinding as they shifted gears.

"It's that trail th' ARVNs hit this afternoon." Winston said, finally.

"Man, th' Gooks really got balls t' be runnin' up and down th' roads this close to an LZ!" I said to Corey, standing there, beside me.

"It don't take a lotta balls, if they know they out-number us." He said, lighting a cig.

I fished one out, too, and we walked over, sat down and leaned against the dirt berm. We smoked and listened to the sounds in the jungle.

"Whadda ya think?" I said, after a few minutes.

"Well..." Corey began, "I think they know we're here, our strength an' all, an' they're just tryin' to get past us."

"Like, they'll leave US alone if we don't bother them."

"Somethin' like that."

Some more minutes passed, and the engines were still passing out there at a good pace, right to left of our position.

"Hope you're right." I said.

Corey got up and started walking back to the gun. I watched him go. Halfway there, I saw his silhouette outlined, as with a flashbulb. There was a series of huge crashes in the jungle. I saw Corey's head snap around and then he fell to the ground. I thought maybe he was hit and started up to go get him when he low-crawled back to me at the wall. The flashes of the continuing string of explosions lighted his eyes.

"Shit! It must be an AA, man."

"A what?" I asked as the booms suddenly ceased.

"Auto-ambush! Th' ARVNs must'a set one on th' trail today, an' th' gooks just set it off."

We sat there, a full five minutes, waiting for something else to happen, but the night was still again. No trucks. No explosions. Just bug-slapping.

'Quiet as a tomb.' I thought with a shiver.

"Boomp…boomp…boomp…boomp", small sounds from out east in the trees. A sound I knew all too well.

"WE GOT INCOMING!" I yelled and Corey and I ran as one to the nearest cover. The gun trails. We crawled under just as the first mortar rounds impacted on the other side of the clearing, then started 'walking' toward us across the LZ.

"Carrump! CarrUMP! CARRRUMP! CARRUMP!!!!" They came. The fourth one blew dirt over our berm from inside the LZ.

I was squeezed under the left trail of the Howitzer, with Corey. I could see Winston, alone under the right, his arms over his head, lying face down. After every explosion, I heard him yell.

"SHIT!"

After the last one.

"SHIIIT!"

A few dead silent seconds passed then the 105s opened up with a six-gun salvo, then into a fire-for-effect pattern. They pumped out thirty rounds in less than three minutes, east to west on pre-arranged co-ordinates along that trail. I thought I heard some secondary explosions among the cacophony of sounds.

Illumination rounds went up all around the LZ, and in the silvery light, I jumped up and headed for the powder bunker, through drifting, acrid smoke. Thinking as I ran, I decided to check on Bro 'B', in the 60 bunker. I dodged over there, stuck my head in, and saw the whites of his eyes in the reflected light. He didn't look stoned, now, just scared.

"You OK?"

He nodded.

"Seen anything out there?" I asked, indicating the trees.

"Hell no! I ain't stickin' MY head out that hole t' get it shot off!"

"Shit!" I mumbled to myself, and stuck my head up and scoped the flickering shadows out at the tree line. I didn't see anything that presented itself as a target, just flickering shadows. I ducked back down.

"Look, 'B'," I said trying to be reasonable, "YOU'RE th' one has to let us know if th' gooks decide t' come in on us." He just looked more scared. "Get yer shit together, man!"

He didn't say anything, so I punched him, hard, on the shoulder. I knew it hurt and he turned and glared at me.

"That's right!" I said, "Get pissed!" and punched him again.

I thought he was going to punch me back, but he didn't.

"GET PISSED!" I repeated. "Act like this is th' ol' neighborhood, back in DEE-troit. Some punks'r gonna try'n come in here an' take over. They'll take yer girls, yer cars, yer houses, everything! You gonna let 'em?"

He thought a minute.

"YOU GONNA LET 'EM?" I yelled in his face.

"HELL NO!" he yelled back.

"GET PISSED! STAY PISSED AN' GET EVEN!" I rocked him with another shot to the shoulder.

He DID punch me back, that time, but mostly connected with my flack jacket.

"Now we're even!" he said and smiled a little.

"PISSED?"

"HELL YEAH!"

"GOOD!" I backed out and went to the 'Monkey Shack'.

Winston had just called 'Fire-mission'.

He called the deflection and quadrant and Corey spun the ranging wheels to their settings.

"Hudson! Charge one and make it snappy!"

I grabbed a pre-cut, ran, and handed off to Corey who stuffed it in the breech, behind the first WP round.

Winston slammed the block and I thought the gun had gone off prematurely. A huge blast lifted me off my feet and threw me headlong, sprawling in the dirt. I felt dirt peppering my back and I thought I heard the "PINGS" of shrap hitting the metal of the gun. I raised up on one elbow and looked back, but the gun was there, still intact, and Corey, Winston and Graham, one of the loaders were picking themselves up from the ground, also. A mortar or rocket had landed between our pit and #2, but we were still undamaged. Winston and Corey recovered and the Gun-Chief hollered "FIRE IN TH' HOLE!" and pulled the lanyard. Our first round went out with a flash, a crash, and a cloud of silver smoke.

We kept on firing. Three, four, five, six rounds, as did the other guns, as fast as we could load 'em and adjust. In the huge volume of sound, I really could not differentiate between incoming and outgoing, but during my frenzied running back and forth, I caught glimpses of sparky explosions all over the base. During one run I saw the distinctive red streak of a B-40 RPG coming in to a 105 pit on the other side of the clearing. I also saw red tracers of either an M-60 or M-16's over there.

"WE GOT GOOKS IN THE WIRE ON TH' ARVN SIDE!" I yelled at Winston as I handed another charge to Corey. The Gun-Chief got on the Landline and talked a few minutes, then turned to us.

"Lower th' tube down. Zero degrees."

'Oh, oh!' I thought as the barrel came slowly down to level trajectory.

Winston called "CHARGE TWO! ROUND 'BEEHIVE!'"

I'd heard about 'Beehive' rounds in AIT. They had a thin-casing shell, filled with tens of thousands of little, sharp nails. When fired, the projectile spins out of the barrel, arms after a very few revolutions and explodes thirty or forty feet out and the nails are deployed in a spread pattern covering an area, sometimes as large as a football field. It was strictly an anti-personnel weapon: the modern equivalent of 'Chain-Shot'. I'd never seen one fired, and had never hoped to.

'Guess I'll see one tonight!' I thought as I cut the charge.

I got back in time to see the round, with its distinctive blue band painted on it, rammed into the breech. The gun was charged and fired after Winston yelled, "BEEHIVE!!"

On level trajectory, the round going out creates suction that pulls dust and smoke out, also. The gun belched and the shell went off almost immediately, thirty feet out above our barbed wire barrier.

The flash temporarily blinded me, and the smoke obliterated the tree line, but after a minute, the area cleared and I saw, through drifting tendrils, utter devastation. Smaller trees were knocked down. Trees still standing were stripped of their bark. Foliage hung in tatters, debris still drifting down. The entire line of growth for a width of fifty feet had moved back at least five feet.

"WOW!"

The round had passed directly over the M-60 bunker at a height of maybe five feet. Right after the round had exploded, Brother 'B' popped out of the bunker and ran, unarmed and wild-eyed, toward the rear opening in our berm.

The two loaders, Graham and 'Jonesy', caught him by both arms and held him while he struggled a moment.

"Where you goin', man?" Graham asked, grinning.

'B' looked around, like he'd just become aware of all of us.

"SHIIT!" he stammered, "I t-thought y'all had b-b-blowed-up!"

"Naw, man. We still here." Jonesy said.

"An' we still gonna need YO ass in that bunker, on that 60, pro-tectin' OUR asses from those trees out there!"

They shoved him back the way he'd come and he hang-dogged back into the bunker.

"Thanks, guys." I said, passing them on my way for another charge.

We fired three more 'Beehives', and ceased firing. The incoming had stopped and eventually, the outgoing fire all petered-out. We all stood around, sweating and breathing hard for a couple minutes.

I heard someone moaning over by #2 gun, to our left. Then somebody hollered "Medic!" over there and the moaning got softer, then stopped. Some ARVNs were running around, over across the LZ, jab-bering. Otherwise, things were disturbingly silent.

Winston broke the interlude and told Corey and the loaders to "police-up." He told me to check on my "friend" in the 60 bunker.

'B' was staring fixedly out the gun-port, when I ducked in. He was squeezing the grips on the 60 with, (can you say "white-knuckles" on a black guy?) He jumped and bumped his helmet on the PSP when I touched his arm.

"You OK. 'B'?"

"Huh?" his face looked slack, pale.

"You OK?" I repeated.

"Uh...yeah...guess." Tension seemed to deflate him as it drained out and he drooped.

"Still pissed?" I said joking, trying to make him feel better.

He looked at me, questioningly, then smiled.

"Uh... yeah, I did."

At first I didn't catch it, but then I did.

'Probably when that first 'Beehive' went off.' I thought.

"It's OK, now, for the time-being." I said, changing the subject, "But you stay here, OK?" He nodded and I felt like I was talking to a small child.

"Keep a sharp eye on those trees out there, and if anything moves, shoot it, OK?"

He nodded again and said OK in a weak voice.

I walked through the still-drifting smoke to the powder bunker, threw out the empty canisters, lined up fresh ones, and cracked the seals. I unboxed more fuses and lined them up on their sandbag shelf. Inside the small, cramped room, the smell of my own sweat, mixed with the 'bug-juice' was overpowering.

I wondered if it was 'Fear' that I smelled. They say dogs can smell fear on a man.

'Take a mighty big fear to make a man smell it.' I thought.

'Hell, I've been so scared, I oughta stink to high heaven', I thought again. Strangely, I was calm now. Not 'at ease', of course, but not jumping around, shaking and moaning. I chuckled to myself.

"If I'd had TIME, I coulda shook an' moaned."

Then I thought about ol' 'B' and the look on his face as he ran from the bunker after the first 'Beehive.' It struck me funny. Then I thought about Winston, yelling "Shit" over and over. I wanted to bust out laughing, right there in a powder bunker, in the middle of a flaky LZ in Vietnam.

"I'm goin' NUTS!" I said to myself and realized I was talking to myself.

"I need to get outta here an' get some air!" I said.

"You sure DO!" I answered.

I shook my head as the urge to chuckle came over me again. I stepped up out of the recessed bunker and walked around the gun-pit to ease the stiffness in my back. I realized my legs were wobbly and I'd been hyperventilating 'til my face was numb. Then I noticed everybody else. They were "Zombie Walking" too. Eyes red-rimmed, cigs dangling out of clenched lips. Arms at their sides stiff shouldered. I wondered if I looked that bad.

'Probably.'

I looked at my watch, tapped at the scratched-up crystal, held it to my ear to check if it was running. It said it was only 12:30 A.M.!

'Gotta be wrong!' I thought. It seemed like the attack had gone on for many hours, but the "Timex keeps on Ticking" as the man says, and it had only been less than a full hour.

'Time may fly when you're havin' fun,' I thought, 'but it sure creeps in combat.'

We finally settled down and relaxed a bit after the adrenaline wore-off. We finished squaring-away and I went and sat by the 60 bunker, smoked cigs and talked to 'B'. He'd regained some of his composure and was almost arrogant again.

"You ain't took no more o' that stuff, have you?" I asked him, meaning what he'd been high on before.

"Fuck no, man." He replied, earnestly, "This SHO ain't no place t' be fucked-up."

"There it is!" I smiled and we sat, looking at the dilapidated tree line in the pop-flare light.

They hit us again at 4:00A.M a little more aggressively, this time, with mortars, 107 rockets and B-40s. The ARVNS got some small-arms fire on their perimeter and during the fray, I spotted red and green tracers, flying around over there.

We fired HE airbursts, this time, timed to explode out over the tree line, showering anyone below with hot, deadly shrapnel.

The #2 gun took two B-40 hits on the berm. One just missed their M-60 gunner, the other deflected and air-burst behind their gun, killing their gun-captain and a loader. I could see, by craning my neck, their bodies, lying still where they'd fallen. I saw Depp take a round to the gun and Fulks coming behind with a charge cut.

'Poor FNGs,' I thought, 'what an intro to Vietnam THEY'RE getting tonight.'

We kept up the airbursts, but, soon, the pace of the battle increased when the M-60 on #2 opened up, spraying the tree line straight out with red tracers.

"GOOKS IN TH' WIRE!" a voice shouted, "WE GOT GOOKS IN TH' WIRE!!"

I looked out across the KZ and saw four VC, wearing loin cloths and coolie hats, carrying four satchel charges each, emerge from the foliage and bound over the outer strand of wire, dodging tracers like football players eluding a tackle. One of them took two steps after landing and went down. He writhed on the ground for a moment, then went up in a flash of light and smoke. One of his own charges had gone off, it looked like. The concussion knocked the other three off their feet and two became entangled in the wire. They struggled furiously to free themselves, but soon became easy targets for the 60 gunner on #2.

The last gook had been blown completely over the middle strand of wire. He jumped up and was coming on strong. He must have gotten disoriented, because, now, instead of running toward #2, he was coming, obliquely, straight at our berm. At ME! He easily jumped the next to the last strand of concertina. I see, in the pale silvery light of the flares, he's waving some kind of big knife over his head, and though I can't hear him over the noise, I can see his mouth opening and closing, screaming gook curses, I'm sure.

He looks fierce, insane. His big, curved hat, tied to his head with a string, was flapping in the breeze of his passage.

I'm thinking, 'Oh, shit!'

All this registered as I grabbed up my M-16, flipped off the safety, and emptied an entire twenty round mag at him, in three and five round bursts. He didn't even slow down.

Hard to miss, even a moving target, at thirty-five or forty feet with an automatic weapon. I'd even seen little red blooms of blood appear on his naked chest, but he never faltered. He leapt the final strand of wire, staggered slightly, then came right at me, now less than twenty-five feet away, still waving that big-ass knife. He had, in his other hand, now, the detonator handle on one of his satchel-charges. He's planning to blow up anything in his way...namely ME.

I'd taped my magazines end-to-end, for quick change. I'd ejected the empty and was struggling to insert the full one, while keeping my eye on the running VC.

I was thinking, 'I'm not gonna make it, I'm not gonna make....'

His head exploded with a red and white flash and his conical hat flew up ten feet, drifted down and hit the earth a full five seconds after it's owner did. He skidded from his own momentum to within ten feet of the berm between us.

"Oh, Jeez!" I muttered.

I stared, unbelievingly at the headless corpse, twitching in the dirt. The big knife was still clutched in his right hand, the satchel charge handle in the other.

I finally looked to my right and saw Corey, his M-79 'Blooper' still raised and smoking. He lowered it and smiled a wide smile under those 'deer-in-the-headlights' eyes of his. I tried to smile back, but I'm sure it was more of a death-rictus, than a smile. Every muscle of my body was frozen. It took a real effort of will to lower my own weapon and take a breath.

We stood like that for interminable seconds, until the noise of battle jarred us back to reality. We still had gooks in the wire. I looked back out there and was surprised to see that the #2 machine gunner had gotten four more of them, and they were all laying in uncomfortable positions, in and between the strands of wire. The only visible enemy, now, were dead.

It suddenly occurred to me to wonder why Brother 'B' hadn't fired his M-60.

'Easy shot, at that range.' I thought. But then I was called back for more charges and we resumed firing into the trees of our AO. Ten minutes later, the attack was apparently called off out there, and the incoming stopped and, soon, the outgoing halted, too, leaving a smoky quiet in its wake.

As the flares sputtered out, I realized the sky was lightening in the east with the dawn.

"Here comes th' sun, dood-n-doo-doo, here comes th' sun, an' I say, it's alright."

George Harrison must have written that song just for this moment. I hummed it 'til sun-up.

The sun was up, but before we saw it over the trees, the dead, three U.S. and six ARVN, were brought to the center of the LZ and covered with ponchos. One of the Americans had a buddy, kneeling over him, stroking his face and crying. He had to be physically pulled away so the body could be covered.

We walked around, viewing the night's destruction. We didn't have many actual structures, on Becky, but the ones we had, the FDC, the various supply and logistics bunkers, all showed some sign of damage. Blown-in walls, collapsed roofs, burned, blasted sandbags. #2 gun had a huge hole in it's berm from the B-40, exposing the Howitzer to the green-line. One of the ARVN 105s took a direct hit on the gun and was out of commission, along with its entire crew. We looked like we'd been hit hard. We had, but we were still here, for what THAT's worth.

'Yeah, still here.' I thought 'But, hopefully, not for long.'

I figured, surely, they'd find a way to pull this whole rotten she-bang out of here, today, surely. This was not a good place. This was a BAD place and we needed--Hell, we DESERVED--to get out of here ASAP. If they couldn't see that, hell, they were fools.

At 10:00 A.M., Sgt. Wiles, the NCOIC, sent a detail out into the wire to police-up the dead gooks, about fifteen of them, and another detail to repair the holes in our wire. They'd no sooner gotten out into the open area, than they took a casualty from a sniper in the woods. I caught it out the corner of my eye and ear. A small pop out in the trees, and one of the ARVN's on the body detail, went down and didn't move. His buddies scrambled back to the berms for cover, leaving their comrade lying in the dirt, maybe dead, maybe not. Turns out he WAS dead, but still…

Every time someone presented a target, they got popped at from anywhere around our perimeter. We all had to duck-walk or low-crawl, wherever we went the rest of the day, or get plinked like a shooting gallery chicken. This did not improve anyone's attitude.

As the day came on and we got more organized, word went around that the big pullout was to be this afternoon. They were going to try to lift us out under cover of 'Fast Movers' and Cobra's. Soon after 1:00, Sgt. Wiles called all gun-captains, the infantry platoon leaders, and the ARVN cadre together in the CP/ FDC. They came out, twenty minutes later, bitching and cussing. Seems Wiles had been told that air-support from the Air Force was nearly impossible at this time due to some unspecified SNAFU. Therefore, the chopper pilots refused to come in here because of the heavy ground fire. We were going to have to stick it out another night. Winston told us and shrugged.

"Stick it out?" Bro 'B' repeated, "Stick it out?"

He was, understandably, flabbergasted.

"I think we done 'Stuck it Out' 'nuff, 'round heah, you mean, they gonna leave us out heah as…gook bait, 'r sumpin….Jus' so's they don' get no holes in they airplanes?"

"Well…yeah, I guess that's 'bout it." Winston shrugged again. "We get one supply drop, late today, an' that's it 'til tomorrow."

This news made my stomach fall out. It hit everybody hard, but ol' 'B' was livid. He couldn't even speak for a minute. He turned around and stalked off, muttering,

"Evah man fer hisse'f! It's evah man fer his-own-se'f."

We got several fire-support-missions, that afternoon, for units working somewhere out there. We had to brave the snipers to man the guns, but the snipers seemed to have retreated from the heat of the sun and left us be until suppertime, when we were eating and distracted and complacent enough to be up walking around again. Then he pinged off a couple more rounds among us, not hitting anyone, but scaring the pure shit outta some ARVN officer when he shot the clipboard out of his hand.

"This ain't no place for clipboards, no way!" Graham commented when we heard.

At 1600, a Med-Evac 'Slick' flew over and attempted to land to pick up the dead. They were forced to evade and retreat by two .51s out in the jungle, but not before they pushed out a load of supplies, in big slings, that crashed to the ground in the center of the LZ. That was our supply drop, but we still had our dead and they were starting to stink, from the daylong exposure to the heat. The Gook bodies were also hanging out there in the wire all day. They'd turned a sick blue-gray color and swelled to twice their original size. Corey and I wrapped up the 'Headless Gook' this morning before the snipers started, and I'd retrieved the 'Big-ass Knife', (a Cambodian Machete, according to Winston), and his curved Coolie hat, (complete with the hole in the back from the M-79), as souvenirs.

After chow, as the sun was setting, Corey, 'B', Jonesy, Graham, Winston and I were sitting around on powder cans, smoking and talking. Corey started humming to himself, something by Santana. Evil Ways, I think. Soon Jonesy, sitting next to him, joined in on the 'Bab-y', part. Soon we were all humming or singing the words and even Bro 'B' was clapping his hands to the rhythm. I thought we sounded pretty good, even without instruments, and even with Winston's gravelly baritone.

It made us feel better, I guess knowing we had each other, even just to sing with. They started into "When a man loves a woman," by Percy Sledge, roughly working the harmonies, and I leaned back against the dirt berm, listening, and soon fell asleep.

It started at midnight.

The first indication that anything was going on was one lonesome pop-flare went up on the ARVN side of the LZ. The light from that woke me up from a dream where I was back on LZ Ike, in my first ground-attack, way back...when? I was instantly alert, wide-awake, but reality seemed to be just an extension of the dream. Same flare-light, same dirt, guys running around manning the guns, same sick-stomach feeling. Is it fear or is it th' C-rats?

I got up and joined Corey and Winston between the gun trails. We stood, waited, and listened. There were only the underlying sounds of men going around doing their things, and the sputtering of the flare overhead.

"Boomp! Boomp! Boomp! Boomp! Boomp!" from out there.

We all immediately hit the dirt. Winston, still holding his field phone to his ear. I started low crawling for the powder bunker. The first mortars came in at the center of the clearing and, in the flashes I saw Jonesy and Graham, low crawling, also, to their positions at the ready-rack. Behind me, Winston called "Fire Mission!"

I rolled through the door and down the two steps and struggled to my feet as I heard him call, "Charge one! Round; Beehive! Fuse, time!"

'Oh, shit!' I thought, 'Here we go again!'

The incoming mortars were continuous, walking all over the LZ. There'd been no outgoing fire, yet. I cut the charge bag, held it in my hand and peeped out the door. Flashes of explosions were all around. I saw Winston, at the gun, waving to me to come on, so I screwed-up my nerve and ran, full-tilt, and handed-off to Corey, then ran back to the bunker. I was just about to duck in, when, from somewhere, no, several somewhere's, the sound of bugles, (Bugles?), arose from the jungle around us. The notes of a strange "CHARGE" signal, I guess, echoed around the mortar blasts, and gave me shivers.

I'd never heard the gooks use bugles before, but I immediately knew the implications. It meant NVA Regulars. Trained soldiers. Not VC. And lots of them.

'Oh, shit! This is gonna be bad!'

The rattling of small arms fire erupted on the other side of the LZ. The three 155s fired in unison, their smoke blotting out our entire side of the perimeter in the light of our mortar flares that were going up rapidly. Winston called for another charge one and I delivered.

"Here we go again, Mouse!" Corey yelled as I handed off.

I nodded, too scared to speak. I ran back to the bunker.

I stopped at the door and looked out to the tree line where the smoke was just clearing. In the flickering flare-light, emerging from the shredded jungle, were men in dark green uniforms carrying weapons. They marched, I swear, crouch-marched, in a row toward our outer strand of wire. Behind the first line of men, a second line was emerging from the trees, and they, too, started inward toward us, crouching and walking, like they had all the time in the world. I was just thinking 'What a stupid way to attack an LZ!' when all three 155s fired out again, their Beehives exploding out over the wire.

Before the smoke socked-in again, I saw both lines of men blur. Some fell where they had stood. Others were picked up and flung back, bouncing off tree trunks or disappearing into the foliage. Some looked like they were disintegrating, with pieces and parts of them just flying off, blood spraying.

'Good God!' I thought. Then the smoke covered everything again.

Winston called for another round and charge and pulled me back from the carnage. I realized that the incoming had stopped.

'That's a good sign, maybe.' I thought.

It wasn't.

That meant it was time for the 'Human Wave' assault to begin.

We'd all heard the term 'Human Wave' in training. We'd seen it in innumerable war-movies over the years. Nothing can prepare you for the real thing.

Bugles sounded again and, on my way for another charge, I saw, through dense smoke, a pure hoard of men run, this time, not walk, from the trees toward our wire. The gun went off behind me, the other two following suit seconds later. Their Beehives erupted over the wire, sending millions of nails to meet the enemy, their smoke clouding the massacre.

I simply could not believe these NVA. How could they get these men to do that? Get them to run head-on into obviously superior fire-power. Even after viewing the result of the last assault. After all, they're jumping over and stepping on their dead brethren.

'I could never do that!' I thought, 'Nobody could MAKE me do that! I don't have the balls.' I was simply astounded. Shocked.

About this time, I went into a 'working trance', where you do everything automatically, without thought, hoping to just do it well enough so you can keep on doing it. If you can keep-on, you're still alive. I cut many charges and ran back and forth supplying powder to the insatiable Howitzer. I did notice a lot of red and green tracers flying around, some close, some not. Also, red B-40 streaks, flashes of explosions, showers of dirt that came out of nowhere. It all blended into an intense light show that surrounded me. I was nearly deafened by the intensity of sounds. Still, I carried powder, because it was what I HAD to do. What I was trained to do. Time was nothing. There was no time, just NOW.

At one point during that period, as I arrived back outside the bunker, I saw a group of NVA, four in all, running between our berm and #2 toward the middle of the LZ. I grabbed up my rifle and fired at them with no discernable effect. They didn't fire back. Hell, they didn't even look at me, they just ran on.

'You can't even SHOOT th' li'l sum-bitches!' I thought.

Sometime later, we were told to cease fire for a group of Cobra gun-ships that came in and worked our perimeter with mini-guns and rockets. We lay low as the 5.56 minis blasted a stream of red death into the wire, right outside our pits. The rockets blew shrapnel that pinged off the metal shields of our guns and thudded into the sandbags of our bunkers. It seemed they were just as likely to kill us as the enemy, they were so close, but I found myself cheering and yelling "Get th' li'l fuck-ers! Kill 'em! 'kill 'em all.", as the black birds swooped out of the dark sky spewing red streams of bullets and yellow rocket streaks.

At some point, I think right after I fired at the group of NVA, I saw some ARVNs set up an M-60 machine gun between our pit and #2. They began firing out toward the trees. I looked to see what they were firing at, but saw nothing but dead bodies out there. There was nothing moving, nothing alive.

But something was alive out there. The 'Human Wave' had been abandoned, but we still got three more mortar attacks, of six to eight rounds each, blowing holes in our existence until about 2:00, then all went quiet.

There were some men moaning. An occasional rifle-pop. A cou-ple of screams out in the jungle. Some far off yelling in Vietnamese, theirs or ours, I didn't know. Ringing in my ears.

Our clearing was completely filled with smoke, which, with no wind, wouldn't drift away, but dissipated slowly to a blue-gray haze. Il-lume rounds were still going up every two minutes, the flares drifting overhead, so it wasn't dark, but shadows would move inside pockets of drifting smoke, or people would appear suddenly as if from nowhere, giving me a start. Making me jump. I gazed, scratchy-eyed, around at the aftermath. What I could see of the Green-line was full of bodies in all conditions and positions. I shivered for the hundredth time that night.

Inside the LZ was not much better. Some bodies were laying around and calls for medics rang out frequently. The living didn't look much better than the dead. We were all walking around, hunched over from fatigue and strain, mouths hanging open, dazed stares from red-rimmed eyes. Most of us were operating on survival-instinct, only. I jumped when Corey appeared beside me and handed me one of his cigarettes, a Pall Mall, and lit it for me along with his own. We didn't say anything. Just stared.

After a brief rest, Winston had us policing-up, organizing, pre-paring. We got two hours of respite and they hit us again.

The first mortar round hit right at the rear opening of our berm, zinging shrapnel off the rear of the gun and thudding into the sandbags and dirt of our pit. It also thudded into Jonesy, who was huddled down next to the gun-trail. I saw him flip over the trail, blood splattering from his head and chest. The blood seemed very red in the silvery flare light. He hung, over the metal appendage, with his hands and feet touching the ground, his dripping head hanging down and his butt in the air. Winston, who'd been outside the right trail, crawled under and pulled Jonesy down, but I could tell it was too late. He was dead.

The mortars came down like raindrops for a half-hour, augmented by 107mm and 122mm rockets. I thought, 'Now they're going to try to blow us all to hell.' Then they stopped and we heard the ghostly bugles, again. They echoed through the trees, all around us, it seemed. Winston and Corey pulled Jonesy over by the powder bunker and covered him with a poncho.

I'd already pre-cut a bunch of charge ones and was not surprised when Winston called "Beehive" as soon as he got back in position. On my way to the gun with the powder, I heard someone off to my left holler.

"HERE THEY COME!"

Running back, I looked and saw another wave of NVA soldiers coming out of the jungle. They, too, seemed oblivious to our weapons' power, until we nailed 'em, literally, with a Beehive. Again the enemy line shredded, fell back, only to be replaced by more, even before the smoke cleared.

"GUN-SHIPS!" I heard Winston yell, almost hysterically, "HA, HA! WE GOT GUN-SHIPS COMIN' IN. LOAD UP THE NEXT ROUND AN' WE'LL FINISH OFF WHATEVER THEY MISS!"

I ran the charge to the gun and handed it to Corey just as Graham was lugging the next round over. I then ran back to the bunker and dove inside, anticipating the air strike. I hunkered down in there, and heard the choppers coming in over by the 105s.

Then the world came apart. There was a huge flash, just outside my door. I felt the air rush out, then slam back with a force that knocked the sandbag walls over onto me. I was buried under bags and dirt and the partially collapsed PSP roof. I must have been unconscious for a time.

When I came to, I was pinned against the stack of metal powder canisters. I wiggled and slowly freed myself and crawled from the wreckage into an unrecognizable scene. There was no gun and no one around. Confused, I looked around me for something I could identify. There was Jonesy's body, now flung up onto the berm, his covering gone. He was even more torn-up than he'd been when he died. But it WAS Jonesy, so I HAD to be in the right place. I just couldn't fathom where the gun, and Winston, and Corey, and Graham had gone. I realized that, where the gun had BEEN, was now a huge crater, three feet deep and six feet across. The dirt in the hole was still smoking and hot.

I wondered if the gun had miss-fired and blown up?

Then I spied something sticking up outside the front of the berm wall. I crept around the crater and craned my neck to see that, indeed, it was the gun, barrel-down, sort of on it's side. What I'd seen was the left trail sticking up. The one still smeared with Jonesy's blood. The other trail was mangled and partially under the front of the carriage. The back of the gun was blistered and blackened, the breechblock hanging open by one hinge. Now I saw the marks it had made as it jumped the berm wall. Big chunks were torn out of the fortification. What I didn't see were people.

I was aware of the battle, still raging all around me, but it seemed to be everywhere but in my gun-pit. I was in a small oasis of calm, in a desert-storm of activity.

Then I thought about Brother 'B'. He'd been in the now collapsed M-60 bunker. I edged over to the fallen-down wall and started pushing sandbags and steel plate out of the way.

'B'? I called softly, as I dug. No answer.

Finally, I found the machine gun itself, lying on its side, under the heap. Unloaded.

But no 'B'.

I found his M-16 and ammo, and his helmet, but no 'B'.

I wondered about this, briefly, but before I could draw any conclusions I saw much activity on the front of #2's berm. About ten or more NVA were laying on the outside of the wall, firing their rifles into the pit. Red and green tracers were flying all about.

From training, or maybe just on instinct, I grabbed the overturned M-60, dug out the ammo belt can, loaded the machine gun, propped it on the top of the wall on it's bi-pod, and opened up on the gooks on #2, who were completely exposed to my fire. I blasted away on full-auto, like I was going to melt the barrel down. Over there, bodies started flying in all directions. A couple of them tried to turn their fire on me, and DID manage a few shots my way, but I just kept on firing 'til

I'd mowed 'em all down; even the two that cut and ran back toward the jungle trying to escape. I cut one of them nearly in half, the other flew nearly ten feet and landed like only a dead man can land. I ceased firing, the barrel of the gun glowing red.

I'd lost my helmet, so I picked up 'B's, with the "Black Power Fist" magic-markered on its cover, settled it on my head. I picked up his rifle and ammo, and crawled back to the powder bunker. I found a corner and squeezed into it, my back to the sandbag wall. From here I could see the Cobras working on the other side of the perimeter. #2 gun was silent, but #1 was still blasting away at the perimeter. They must have run out of Beehives, and were now firing airbursts of HE at the trees. The 105s were still popping away whenever the gun-ships weren't hosing down their tree line.

Here in the blasted-out #3 pit; there was no activity at all. I figured they thought we were all dead and concentrated on other targets. Suited me! I'd had enough.

After a little while, out the corner of my eye, I saw movement by the supply pile next to the bunker I was in. The cover tarp raised up at one corner then flopped back, exposing a hand and arm. Someone was crawling out. I figured it had to be a gook, so I raised Bro 'B's rifle and was about to shoot when I saw nubby hair and two white eyes in a black face emerge.

'Brother 'B'' I thought, 'So that's where you went!'

I almost shot him anyway.

I guessed that was what he meant by "Ever man Fer His-own-se'f."

He crawled the rest of the way out and peered around, not seeing me in my darkened corner of the wrecked bunker. I was about to say something when several men, including Lynch, Ralph, Depp and Fulks, ran into the pit and fell to the ground, pulling 'B' with them. Suddenly #2 gun exploded with a loud "BLAM" and I was able to see the gun raise up and the stainless steel tube split lengthways into three sections. I knew that they'd 'Spiked' it. Destroyed it on purpose. #1 went just seconds after #2. Same thing.

I crawled out while the dirt was still raining down. They all had their heads covered and didn't see me 'til I was right there.

"What's goin' on?" I asked Lynch.

He was surprised to see me. They all were. Especially 'B', who eyed his helmet on my head. He glared at me. I glared back. Somehow, he knew that I knew. But, right now, I didn't care.

Lynch was out of breath, but managed to tell the story.

"Gooks took over #1, but we booby-trapped it an' dee-deed to #2. It was damaged so we spiked it an' came over here." He looked around as if to say "Where's your gun?"

I used my thumb and indicated, "Out there."

"Oh…" shock on his face, "You OK?"

"Yeah, me an' 'B' 'r OK. How 'bout you-all?"

"Fulks got nicked," He answered and Freddy held up a bleeding forearm wrapped in a green T-shirt, "an' ol' Ralph got knocked in th' head by a gook rifle butt, but that gook didn't know how hard Ralph's head is, an' Ralph got 'im."

"Twisted 'is li'l head off!" Ralph smiled.

I could see it.

"So, what now?"

"First light, we're gettin' outta here." He answered.

I gasped. "What? How?"

"Don't know! But word came 'round to be ready t' bug-out at dawn."

"We're s'posed t' bring all our weapons over by th' CP," Ralph filled in while Jim got his breath, "an' stack 'em t' be destroyed. They're sendin' a shit-load o' choppers t' take us out when th' sun gets up."

I wanted to cheer, but I was too tapped-out. I settled for a smile and an "awright!"

I squinted at my watch in the flare-light. Coming on six o'clock. Be getting light by six-thirty. An hour? Two? We're still under attack. Hell, there're probably gooks running around inside the LZ, right now.

"What about th' gooks?" I said, " They're not gonna just let 'em come in here an' take us away."

As if to accent my words, a wild burst of firing erupted somewhere and an explosion flashed over by the 105s. Two Cobras had worked around to our quadrant and proceeded to blast the tree line and KZ outside the pit with rockets and red streams of mini-gun fire. We all hugged the ground by the collapsed bunker until he moved down past #1 pit. The rockets sounded like bass drum/ cymbal crashes, shaking your chest with each impact. The mini-guns spewed M-16 ammo by the thousands in seconds and sounded like buzz saws.

The whole sandbag detail was here, plus some guys from the other two guns, totaling ten in all. One of the gun-bunnies was a Sgt. E-5. We sat up with our backs to the remains of the powder bunker wall and the Sgt. took charge. Only five of us were armed. I had 'B's rifle, mine being buried in the bunker, and damn if he was gonna get it back. We had the, still hot, M-60. I dug into the berm-bunker and came up with Corey's M-79 and some HE rounds.

The Sgt. Watkins by name, told us he thought the gooks had "shot their wad". But he put Fulks and Depp on look-out on the berm wall, assigned a PFC Bunny to go to the CP and get th' poop, and, to my delight, put 'B' on the berm with the M-60, facing the jungle. 'B' almost turned white, but took the gun, mumbling, and got in place.

After the choppers got through working-out the entire perimeter, the incoming fell off to nothing and the out-going petered down to sporadic pops. Watkins ventured to stand up and when he wasn't immediately gunned-down, Jim, Ralph and I followed suit.

The sky was taking on a gray wash and the stars, seen through the holes in the smoke haze, were disappearing. Dawn. At last. There were still four mortar-flares up, casting their ghostly light on a scene of devastation. I shuddered.

Jim said "Jeez-us!"

The LZ, while never much to start with, was now a sea of smoking holes and mounds. The row of poncho-covered bodies from yesterday and last night had been laid-out in the center of the LZ. They'd obviously taken at least one direct hit and were now strewn around, mingling with more recent bodies of, from what I could see, both U.S. AND NVA soldiers. I didn't count, but there were many. Some were moving, groaning, most were not.

Live guys were emerging, seemingly from the ground itself. Staring around in the same disbelief that, I'm sure, was stamped on all our faces at that moment

Watkins and one of his Bunnies pulled Jonesy's body down from the wall and covered it with a scrap of tarp. I had to turn away.

Jim and I walked over to where 'B' was staring out over the berm. We caught him praying, I think, as we came up, but he jumped when he heard us and stopped, but continued staring out. A look on his face similar to all the other faces I'd see that morning. The look in a deer's eye, at the moment it realizes something has a bead on him. The startled knowledge that, though you're still alive, your life will end at any moment.

Though I wasn't aware, I'm sure I wore the same expression.

Jim and I leaned on the wall and looked out. The KZ was literally strewn with blown-up, ripped asunder, ruptured, leaking, NVA soldiers, in all kinds of positions. From the tree line up to and against the berm wall we were on. Hundreds? Maybe. Seeing and believing were almost beyond my capacity, then, much less counting.

"We...killed....boo-coo...gooks....man!" Jim said, awed.

'B' still didn't say anything, probably still praying.

I gazed around at the destruction inside the LZ.

"But they kicked our asses, man."

"Yeah, but we kicked 'em right back, harder!" Jim said, a mad gleam in his eye. (or was that a reflection of a flare?) "We kicked 'em back an' WE'RE still alive an' THEY'RE all DEAD!" He waved out at the bodies. "DEAD!"

I put my hand on his shoulder. He was trembling.

"I'm, personally, in favor of STAYING alive," I said, slowly, enunciating my words, "so we can't flip-out, now, man! We've got this far! They're comin' t' get us, soon, (I hoped), 'nother hour?"

Jim's face quivered, like he could cry.

"'Nother hour?"

"I sure hope so, man." I did! Fervently.

Watkins voice, over by the bunker, intervened as he told us to gather anything that the enemy could use and throw it into the powder bunker. Including the M-60. We all ran around, as did everyone on the base, gathering stuff and stacking piles for destruction. Four American guys came around, loaded with Claymores and commo-wire, and strung-up charges on the bunker and the piles of equipment. All this took almost an hour, and by that time, it was almost full-daylight. We watched as the 105s, the four remaining ones, were spiked, one at a time.

'They better come quick', I thought, as the last one blew. "Cause now we got no protection.'

At 0715, the first wave of gun-ships came in and laid more waste to our perimeter. They came in fours. Two working both sides at once, and the other two flying cover, above, and spotting targets. In twenty minutes of continuous firing from three waves of choppers, I couldn't imagine anything being alive, out there. Then, for good measure, two F-4 Phantoms swooped in at treetop and Napalmed the jungle right out from our pit. Even at a quarter-mile, we could feel the heat and the air-rush from the blaze of flaming hell created by the bombs.

Just as the jelly was burning off from that, the choppers were back, this time laying down covering fire for a line of twelve slicks that flared-in to a clear spot by the CP, two at a time, and started loading wounded guys. The worst cases were put on the first two, and within thirty seconds, they were back in flight, heading east, out over the trees. Two more landed before the dust from the first settled.

Watkins told us to grab our socks an' get ready. We didn't need telling.

There were at least a hundred and fifty guys, ARVNs and American, alike, jockeying to board the birds, but there was very little pushing or arguing. There were no flight crews, to allow more passenger space, and each crew chief, the only man aboard, besides the pilots, crammed as many guys into the fuselage as possible. I wondered that the bird could lift off the ground they were so packed.

My crowd ended up on chopper #11. I was clinging to a web strap, seated on the edge of the doorway, feet dangling in space. I had a huge rush of fear as we took off and the bird had trouble carrying the fourteen or so guys crammed into its belly. I was mostly afraid of falling out, at this stage of the game, and being killed in the fall. I shouldn't have worried, because you could not have pried my fingers loose from that strap with pliers.

#12 lifted off right behind us, carrying the last of the group, including the guys who'd set the timers on the detonators for the scuttling-charges on the equipment. Before we'd even cleared the tree line, the first piles went up on the ground. The blasts were muffled by the noise of the choppers, but made for a spectacle from my perch. Geysers of dirt and junk flew up, nearly as high as we were.

Another spectacle caught my eye. 150 feet below, in the shredded trees, NVA soldiers were running, full tilt, toward the LZ. A lot of them. I couldn't imagine how they had survived all the shit we'd thrown at them, but they must've, and now, the LZ was theirs.

"Screw 'em!" I yelled at an ARVN, pressed up against my side, as the chopper gained speed and altitude. "They can have it!"

My last glimpse of the clearing called LZ Becky, was NVA soldiers running among the piles of dirt we'd so recently occupied, jumping up-and-down, waving their weapons. Then all the rest of the scuttling-charges went off. All the extra black-powder, all the ammo, mines, cannon rounds, kerosene, gasoline. All of it went up in one huge blast. The smoke obscured the whole clearing.

"We just killed Boo-Coo MORE gooks!" I yelled to nobody, everybody.

Then we were in the air, flying full-tilt for Tay Ninh City.

The sun had never looked brighter; the air clearer, cleaner, colder.

I shivered from the cold, crisp wind, but also, from the release of fear. The elation of having come through it. I'm still breathing this wonderful air being forced up my nostrils by this delicious wind.

When we were about two miles away from Becky, I was still looking back when a huge blast erupted on the site of our recent departure. From our height of 2000 feet, even with the haze of distance, I could see the shock-wave ring out across the treetops.

'Damn!' I thought.

There was another! Another! Another! Shock waves like pebbles tossed into a pond, joining and mingling. Still, they came, many at once and in pairs and singles. Mushrooms of smoke rising from the distant jungle.

I grabbed an arm to my right and pulled it down and I pointed.

"They 'Nuked' 'em!" I yelled.

The man whose arm I had, the crew chief, turns-out, clinging in the door gunners empty perch, said: "Nah! Th' Air Force Arc-lighted 'em!"

Then I could hear the thumps of the 500 and 1000 pound bombs, exploding in the distance. Then the delayed shocks hit our bird and it jumped and rocked as if in severe turbulence. #12 bird, the only one I had sight of behind us, rocked also, bouncing in the reverberations of destruction. Some of the other guys had seen it, too, and they were all yelling "Fuckin' A!", waving their fists in the air, grinning.

33

POOPIE RETURNS

Me and Poopie

We landed at a marshalling area in Tay Ninh and our group was picked up by an 'E' battery 'Deuce', and taken to the 1/30 area. We were questioned by two captains, singly and in a group, as to what we saw and the circumstances of the loss of three Howitzers, (Cannon ain't cheap, ya know!), and other valuable equipment. This 'debriefing' left me with an uneasy feeling. Like, the Army's looking for someone to blame for this, and maybe they'd pick US.

'Bullshit! No Way!' I reasoned.

The debriefing was mercifully short, and by 10:00 we were being fed in 'E' battery's mess. I had a big ham sandwich and a Coke that filled the hole in me, but not the empty space. The six of us from HQ, the sandbag detail, were issued blankets and pillows and assigned a small GP tent, erected next to their CP. It had six folding cots, screening on two sides and a single electric light bulb suspended from the peak of the ceiling. It was hot in there from the mid-morning sun, but by 1100, we were all asleep, or on the way.

I slept until 0800 the next morning. Either I hadn't dreamed, or I didn't remember. I was glad. Their Battery Clerk, a PFC named Ridley, woke us and told us that chow was being held for us at the mess hall, but we'd have to be there by 0830 or they'd throw it out. Jim, Fulks and I, the late sleepers, climbed back into our crusty fatigues, unshaved, unwashed and funky. We hurried to the mess. We hadn't eaten since yesterday morning and, I don't know about them, but I was starved. We joined Ralph, Depp and 'B' at a table where they were already wolfing down lukewarm eggs, sausage, toast and grits. We ate like field hands.

Afterwards, we were sitting, smoking cigs and talking, reservedly, about the attack and the aftermath. A Sgt. E-5 came into the dining hall and asked for me. I nodded and waved him over.

He looked rather embarrassed and stammered when he spoke. "I…uh….know you're not an….official member of…uh…the 'E' battery crew, but….uh….we don't HAVE any body else that w-was…. you know….on the #3 gun…so…"

"So, what?" I said, perplexed.

"The guns…the Howitzers, are being recovered this morning. They're being hooked-in here at ten thirty, along with any other…uh… salvageable equipment."

"So?" I asked, not liking this.

"Well….we've been ordered to have one member of each gun crew on-site to…. ID each piece." He said in a rush to finish.

Now I was really confused.

"ID a Howitzer?" I spluttered, "Hell, it's a big gun. It's green. Looks just like any other big gun. How'm I s'posed to…"

He stopped me with a shrug.

419

"Beats me, Hudson, but they want someone there to certify which gun is which. There'll be a paper you'll havta sign, but that's it."

I shrugged to the other guys, stubbed out my cig, stood and walked out with the Sgt. to a jeep parked by the CP. The E-5 gunner from #2, Watkins, was there, along with a Spec-4, who had been the AG on #1. They acknowledged me as I nodded. We waited a few minutes and were joined by a Second Lt. Dean, whom I remembered as the American base commander on LZ Becky. We all climbed into the jeep and the Sgt. drove us out the gate and turned right. Packed in the rear, the three of us had to hold onto the already-hot metal of the jeep sides for support. We headed back toward the marshalling area where we'd arrived yesterday.

During the drive, the Lt., who was not much older than me, maybe twenty five, explained that, after the Arc-Light on the LZ and mopping-up by the ARVN infantry, the area had been declared clear of enemy by 5:30 yesterday afternoon. All salvageable equipment, including the Howitzers, was being recovered, and was to be hooked-in here. He just needed us to verify which gun was which.

"What's th' big deal, Lt." I asked, "Who cares? They're all three totaled, I can tell you that, right now."

He turned the rest of the way around in his seat, draping his arm over the back.

"Yes, I know, Hudson, but I think there's going to be an investigation to determine if anyone was at fault for the loss and…"

He didn't get to finish, as Watkins interrupted.

"Fault? Hell, th' idiots who put us out there in th' first place! THAT'S whose fault it is! We were lucky t' get outta there alive, surely they can't hold us responsible for damaged equipment?"

The Lt. held up both hands, palms out.

"No, no!" he assured us, "That's not the point! We're not blaming YOU! I think everyone knows we did what had to be done in a bad situation. I'm going to try to make sure there are some 'Lessons-learned', here. I'm sure you all are aware that that LZ should never have been placed there, too far for support fire from other LZs and too distant for sustained air-cover."

We all nodded, enthusiastically.

"You mean you're going to try to nail some big Brass, for getting our guys killed out there, sir?" Watkins asked.

"Possibly, Watkins. I want to make sure someone realizes mistakes were made, and that they're never made again." Dean said, earnestly.

"Amen!"

At the marshalling yard, we sat around in the hot sun for an hour, smoking and talking very little. I, for one, dreaded this task. I'd hoped never to see that piece-of-shit Howitzer again. To me, it symbolized the loss of some buddies, to whom, even though I only knew them for a short time, I'd gotten very close, especially to Corey. I couldn't help thinking back to that night in Phouc Vinh when Fuk, Corey and I were playing guitar and singing. How animated he'd been, with his big grin and pale-pale scared eyes.

'Guess we won't get together, again, to 'play some tunes'.' I thought.

My reflections were cut short by the thump of heavy helicopters and shortly, three big Chinooks hovered in, each with a wrecked gun slung underneath. The guns were set down about 40 feet apart, on the hot PSP.

The #2 gun landed first, right in front of our group. It seemed fairly intact, except for the splayed barrel and broken breechblock.

"Wow" Watkins said, "What a bore-plug and some C-4 can do!"

We all marveled at the 2 ½" thick, bearing steel tube, split into thirds for two thirds of its ten foot length. The recoil tubes and springs were bent radically, the breech block hung by one bent hinge-pin.

#1 came down to our left and thunked over at a crazy angle due to a missing carriage wheel. One of its trails was bent under the other. Its tube was also split and peeled back, flower-like at the end.

I had no trouble ID-ing the #3 gun. It was the only one with an intact tube, but the rear of the gun was smashed and blackened, its trails both mangled, the breech and receiver crooked. Both tires were shredded and great hunks of ¾ inch thick armor plate were torn out of the blast shields, which were bent forward, away from the blast. All this I saw as the chopper dropped its sling and clattered away. The gun sat, tube up in the shimmering heat, rear end about thirty feet away from us.

It looked, for all the world, like some huge, dead beast. As we drew nearer it even smelled dead. First the Lt., then me, then the Sgt., rounded the splayed-out left trail.

"My God!" The Lt. whispered, then wretched.

The entire rear carriage, and around the breech, was splotched with dried, brown blood. Lodged in every crevice were pieces of meat, clumps of hair and green cloth. Flies had either hitched a ride for the flight, or had already found this mess.

I puked where I stood.

The Lt. stepped back about ten paces and heaved, turned around and heaved again. The Sgt. took a quick look, and distracted himself by crossing over and holding the Lt.'s arm while the officer lost his guts.

I turned away and walked stiffly about ten feet, spitting, fumbling for a cigarette. I could still smell it, so I walked another ten feet, lit my cig, and breathed the smoke deeply, and blew it out through my nose hoping to kill that smell.

Lt. Dean came over, took my arm gently, and walked me over to the jeep. I looked at him and he looked pale. I felt pale. My legs were wobbly. He fished under the passenger seat and pulled out a canteen. He swished his mouth out with the water and spit, then handed me the canteen. I'd just thrown up a lot of liquid, but my mouth was dry and the warm water felt great. I dragged that cigarette hard again. The Sgt. waved the other guys away from #3.

"Y'all wanna get sick? Go on, then."

None of 'em did.

"Jeez, Sir. I didn't think a 122 rocket could DO that." I said, just to say something.

He shook his head.

"Can't." He looked like he was glad to have something else to think about besides that gore on the gun. "To lift a 14,600 pound gun completely out of its pit, it'd have to be a 'Trash-can'."

"What's a 'Trash-can', Lt." Watkins asked.

The 'looie' looked up, thinking.

"440 millimeter rocket. Range: about a mile. Usually fired from truck mounted launchers. Explosive power of a 175 or eight-inch shell."

I could tell he was rattling off these statistics to divert his mind, as I was by listening to him intently.

"Jeez," I mumbled as what he said sunk in, killed by a 'Trashcan'.

The Sgt., his stomach as strong as his curiosity, had wandered back over, braved the flies, and briefly examined the gun between the trails. He came back quickly, his face ashen.

"Hudson, you were on #3, right?" He said, queasily.

I nodded.

"Do you know if they had a round rammed when the...you know...?"

The question caught me by surprise and I had to think a minute.

"I remember having handed the charge to Corey, turning, seeing Graham humping the 'joe in his arms toward the gun, then I was back in the powder bunker and...."

"So, he might've had time to ram the round before the...uh...explosion?"

I nodded "He might've. Why?"

"I bent over and looked up the tube, sir," he addressed the Lt., "an' it's dark in there. Something's in the tube. Probably that round."

Lt. dean reached back into the jeep and brought out a walkie-talkie radio. He called-in for an ordnance-disposal crew and we waited fifteen more minutes in the hot sun until they arrived.

It was a four-man team in a ¾ truck. They reported to the Lt. and he explained the situation. The E-7 in charge asked me if I knew what type round was loaded. I tried to picture Graham, running by, with a round in his arms, in slow motion. I didn't notice the round he was humping, I noticed the expression on his face. Grinning...or grimacing. I couldn't tell which, much less the type of round he was carrying. I shook my head.

"We'd been shooting 'Bee-Hives', earlier, then switched to HE's, then some more 'BEE...hell, I don't know. Could be either one."

The E-7 turned to Dean.

"Sir, 'Bee-Hives' can take special considerations. They only take five revs to arm and they're sensitive to impacts, so, I'm gonna havta ask y'all to back off, over there." He indicated a revetment wall about a hundred feet away, "An' me'n the boys here'll take care of it, OK, Sir?"

We sat on the edges of the skin-blisteringly-hot jeep, and the Sgt. drove us the 100 feet to the 10-foot high sandbag wall. The Lt. and the Sgt. stayed in the jeep, while Watkins, Taylor and I edged over against the wall to take advantage of the last foot of leftover morning shade. A good soldier will always look for a cooler place, like a cat will always seek a warm spot.

The OD guys had donned their padded suits and helmets with thick visors. Two of them pulled out a big metal box with a hinged lid, on big casters. They pushed it over to the gun. We'd failed to warn them of the, uh, mess, so we watched from a distance, as they went through the gags, before finally getting the box positioned beneath the breech.

The other two men had erected a stepladder under the muzzle and were assembling an aluminum ramrod, in sections, with a padded end. One man climbed the ladder, inserted the pad into the tube, and eased it down until it stopped, about four feet in. I heard something about "not much resistance" and he pushed the rod slowly in. From our vantagepoint, we couldn't see the round come out, but, what we saw was weird.

The two guys back by the box both recoiled, jumped back three feet, really, and backed off hurriedly, one on hands and knees. The Lt. jumped from the jeep and ran that way. We followed, unable to fathom what th' hell?

We arrived to see the two men, helmets torn off, retching in almost the same spot we'd sullied, earlier.

The Lt. was between the trails, I was outside the left one. We both peered, cautiously, into the padded interior of the box. There in the bottom, looking out. Not a 'Bee-hive' OR an HE. Corey's face! Or at least part of it. A blood-caked tuft of bright hair at the top, half a forehead, one bright blue eye, still scared-looking, a cheek and his nose. Remnants of teeth were visible at the bottom.

I felt dizzy. I turned and lost any remnant of that nice breakfast I'd had this morning. I also lost any dignity I might have had. I fell on my knees in my puke and sobbed. I didn't see what the Lt. did, but he was pretty freaked-out when he ran around and took my arm and pulled me to my feet. He and the Sgt. pulled Taylor and I, who'd been good buddies with Corey and was sobbing, too, away toward the jeep. Suddenly, it was clear in my mind.

I'd just handed off the #1 charge to Corey. Graham was bringing the next round. They'd just fired the previous round. I pictured it in my head. Corey, as I'd seen him doing for two days, pulling the primer cartridge from the breech block, flinging open the lock lever and pulling the gate open, then, bending over. Bending over and looking up the tube to make sure it's clear! That's when it happened. He went up the tube.

"Oh, Jesus."

My knees almost went again, but I caught myself on the red-hot fender of the jeep. The burn jolted me to sensibility.

'He couldn't have known...' I thought. 'You're just here; then you're not. Gone?'

I was aware the Lt. was talking to me.

"You were lucky, Hudson." I heard the end of it.

"Uh...yessir....I know."

"You were in the powder bunker?" he asked.

"Yessir, collapsed in on me; had to dig out. By that time, the gun was gone. Just a big...hole."

"BIG hole, I'd imagine."

'He's trying to keep me talking' I thought, 'keep me from shocking-out. Am I? Probably. Just listen to him, maybe he knows.'

"Hudson?" He got my attention again, "There was another man on #3 survived, a PFC Biggerstaff. Where was he? How did he make it? I believe he was with the HQ group, too, wasn't he?"

'Biggerstaff?' I thought, ' No wonder he calls himself Brother 'B'.'

"He was...assigned...to the M-60 bunker, sir. Behind a blast-wall."

I didn't want to create trouble for 'B'. He'd followed his own instincts. Thank God we didn't NEED him during the attack. He couldn't have stopped a 'Trash-can'.

"I...uh...didn't see 'B', uh, Biggerstaff, until much later, Lt. When the men were gathering before spiking the other guns. I guess the wall fell on him, too, and he had to dig out."

He gave me a strange look.

"Watkins, from #2, reported that during the fight, as we were being over-run, his pit was attacked by a group of twelve or more NVA, firing rifles at the crew. He said someone, from #3 pit opened up with

425

an M-60, at close range, and killed most of them and drove off the rest. Essentially, saving the gun and the men on her. He told me he couldn't see the mans face, but he was wearing a helmet with a black power fist on the front."

"Yessir, 'B' was on the M-60. That's his helmet."

He gave me an even stranger look.

"But you're wearing the helmet. What gives, Hudson."

I'd forgotten.

"Uh…I found it during the fight. Lost mine, so I …put it on."

He cocked his head and looked at me sideways.

"If that's the way it is, OK. But I want you," he included the group gathered round, "and you guys, too, to know that I think every man on Becky did a helluva job. A lot of good men didn't make it, but they, we, faced huge odds and fought with dedication and a ferocity that makes me proud to have been there with you."

His speech caused a welling in my chest, and affected the others, too. I could tell.

"Thank you, sir," I said after a moment, "But I was scared shitless, th' whole time."

This admission brought a small laugh among the somber group.

The Lt., too.

"So was I, Hudson, so was I."

We signed our papers on his clipboard and they drove us back to 'E' battery and dropped us off at the CP.

We made the four-hour trip back to Phouc Vinh that afternoon in a 'Deuce.' There wasn't much talk about our ordeal. There were some questions, of course, about ID-ing the Howitzer, but I sidestepped them, saying it was just a formality. No big deal.

I sat, my back against the wood rail across the front of the bed, my legs stretched out on the side bench. I watched the scenery go by without really seeing it, my thoughts turned inward. The events of the last couple days kept re-running, in snatches, through my brain like a badly spliced movie. Landing and filling bags, the guys smiling, working. The Attacks. The 'Headless Gook', (while he still had his head), waving the big knife that was safely wrapped in my poncho liner in my pack. The panic I felt as I tried to insert the new magazine in my rifle. The rage/fear on his face right before it exploded. The smile on Corey's face, as he stood there holding the smoking M-79.

'He saved my life!' I realized. 'I never thanked him.' I knew it wouldn't have helped anything, but it still made me feel shitty.

I could see the look on 'B's face, running from the bunker.

Watkins, as he tried to explain our situation.

Snatches of helicopters, swooping low, raining death.

NVA soldiers, leaping the wire. NVA soldiers, falling before my machine gun.

A smoking hole in the ground.

A wrecked gun.

Corey's face.

A hand shook me awake.

I'd been asleep.

"Mouse!" it was Jim. "We're here, man, wake up."

I was the last to climb down from the truck, in front of the HQ CP.

The six of us stood in a loose line, facing our reception committee.

The BC, Capt. Johnson, the First Sgt., Clark and several others were there to greet us. Carbone and his cooks stepped out the mess hall door and waved. Capt. Johnson welcomed us back and congratulated us for doing a fine job and returning safely.

During the Captains speech, I was looking around. They all looked so...clean. Neat. Pressed.

We were so...filthy. We stank with fear, smoke, dirt, blood, puke. It all wafted from us like heat waves off the pavement. We were swaying on our feet. Exhausted.

The captain dismissed us and told us we got an R&R day, tomorrow, to rest up.

'I could use a month!' I thought, 'Or fifty-four days.'

At the hootch, Fuk greeted me with a dap, but quickly stood back.

"Man...you stink!" he wrinkled his nose.

I wafted my armpits at him so he could enjoy it all the more. "You would, too."

"Was it fucked-up, Mouse?"

"To th' max."

"We heard some shit."

"Not by half, you didn't."

I told him about the attacks, and Corey and the other guys. He let me ramble for a half-hour, nodding and reacting, but not saying much. It poured out of me like my breakfast, this morning.

Finally, I wound down. He was sitting, cross-legged on the floor in front of me, visibly shaken by my account. He shook his head, sadly.

"Poor little Corey, man. He was a good li'l dude, an' he only had, what? Two weeks left, man. You sure it was him? Up in th'....you know?"

I nodded my head.

"Shit!"

He stood up, patted my shoulder and left without another word.

I cleaned up. (Man, did THAT feel good!) I ate LURPs at Jim and Ralph's. Ralph was already wasted on his 'drug-du jour', so Jim and I went over to the new EM club, where all the guys welcomed us back and bought us beers. I let Jim answer all the questions while I sipped my rare beer and watched Nick and Pagans clean up on a couple guys from 2/19th, on the new pool table.

Doc Phillips came in, saw me, grinned and came over.

"Mouse! I'm glad you're back!"

I thanked him.

"I got a call today, from 4th MED, Poopie's OK!"

"Poopie?" I just realized, guiltily, that I hadn't given that poor little dog a thought since I'd been gone.

"She's OK?"

"Yeah, man, they called today. They pinned her hip, an' she's already up and hobbling around. If you weren't back by tomorrow, I was gonna go get her myself, but since you're back..."

He couldn't finish because I grabbed his shoulders and shook.

"She's OK? You sure?"

"Sure, I'm sure. You can use the MED truck, 'slong as you're back by 1500 hours."

I almost kissed him. He peeled my hands off and I bought HIM a beer.

I kept mumbling "Poop's OK, Poop's OK". Then I realized that I hadn't seen Rags, either, since I'd been back. Doc told me she'd run off the night after I left, had been gone a night and a day, and had come back with a buddy, a black and white mongrel who was immediately taken in and named, appropriately, Buddy. They had taken up with Rudy and were sleeping in his hootch.

"So, Poop's OK and Rags has a boyfriend?" I was truly elated. I ordered two more beers and we toasted the dogs. Everybody there joined in.

When I left, a little loopy from three beers, I went by Rudys', petted Rags and met Buddy. Rags looked good, like she'd cleaned up her act. Maybe to attract a boyfriend, I figured. Buddy was a large puppy, really. Black and white with long droopy ears, a big muzzle and sad brown eyes. He looked, I swear to God, like a St. Bernard except for the curly, gook-dog tail that wagged incessantly. If the size of his feet were any indication, he'd grow up to be the size of a St. Bernard. As it was, he'd nearly knock you over rubbing against your legs for attention.

Rudy was really pleased to have the dogs live with him. He'd made 'em special little beds, and everything. I told him it was OK, and I'd still have Poopie. I told him the news about Poop's recovery and he was all smiles, too.

The beers were knocking me out, so I left and walked back to my hootch. I was still depressed, but excited, too. I'd lost some Human buddies, but my Dog buddies were all doing all right. It was a kind of renewal of hope, for me. I went to sleep, passed-out, really, with a picture of Poopie, bounding through the high grass, chasing her tail, in my mind.

Fuk shook me awake at 0700, and it took me a minute to figure out why I'd had him wake me so early. I quickly showered again, (because I could), jumped into some clean fatigues, grabbed chow and showed up at the Aid Station at 0750. Doc told me to take the truck and I drove off into the muggy morning heat singing along with my tape player to Otis Reading and Carla Thomas, King and Queen album. The drive was like an outing on a sunny day back home on the country roads of Fayette County. Except for the little people in the pointy hats. In a little over two hours, I was in Bien Hoa.

I had no trouble finding 4th MED again. Captain Blaine, himself, took me back to the pens, and there she was. Poopie jumped up and dug at the wire cage until the door was opened and, with eyes sparkling with recognition, she tried to jump into my arms. Her legs were still weak, and she almost fell, but I scooped her up in mid-air and hugged her to me, trying to be gentle on the shaved area on her hip where the long, clean incision was visible, held shut by stitches. She licked my face and yapped, uncontrollably.

Dr. Blaine scratched her ears and told me what a good pooch she'd been. She hadn't even bitten him, though she DID growl at all the sergeants. Typical. Her pelvis had been broken, but it was a clean break, and pinned very easily with a stainless steel rod. As I carried her out to the reception area, he explained that the stitches were self-dissolving and all we had to do was make sure she kept it clean, (Poopie, clean? Hah!), and he had some antibiotic pills for her to take twice a day for two weeks.

I think I embarrassed the Captain with my effusive thanks. I offered to pay for the treatment, (I'd brought $200 in MPC with me), but, he refused and told me to just take care of her. He thought she was a very special pup, too, and he was going to miss her. For a Captain, Blaine was a pretty special guy to whom I will forever be indebted.

On the road back, Poops couldn't jump around much, but contented herself by alternately licking my hand, sunning on the seat, or letting her ears flap up straight in the wind. She barked, gaily, at every Vietnamese along the way, as if to say, 'See, I'm Special'! Every once in a while, she'd yelp from the lingering pain, but she never let it abate the pure pleasure of us being reunited. I cracked-up at her antics and felt better than I had in months.

I got back to Phouc Vinh at 2:00, after a short lunch break at Di-An, where Poopie was a major attraction to two USO girls, who cooed over us, (or HER, anyway), and served us both steak and French fries and a small dose of heaven.

At the unit, I took her directly to my hootch and installed her in her box where, tired and full of USO steak, she promptly conked-out. I spent the rest of the afternoon reading and fending off well wishers who just wanted to hug her. I had to explain that she wasn't 'huggable', yet. They settled for a look into the box and sighed like little old ladies looking at a baby. The dog woke up a couple of times and wagged her tail, (though I think it hurt her to wag), and panted at some of the guys and ate-up the attention. Early evening, she made quite a splash when she got up on her own, and walked gingerly, outside and took a dump, to the applause of about ten men, watching and smiling and saying "Alright!"

The next several days I pulled odd details, like tilling a new section of Green-line in a five-ton truck, towing a brace of tiller discs 16 ft. wide along a ¾ mile by ¼ mile wide area of old rice paddy.

I drew guard duty on Tower November, one day, and even got to take the dog up with me. I mostly read to her all day.

I made a run to Dong Xuai with Rudy to deliver a crate of something. All three dogs had a grand time, barking at gooks.

I got loaned-out, two consecutive days, to the 11th Armored Cav, to drive a 'Duster'. I'd never driven a vehicle with more than one motor. The 'Duster' had TWO. Big Cadillacs, one for each tank-like track. Steering was done by foot-brake pedals, left and right, and speed / forward and reverse by twin joysticks. The farther you pushed these sticks, forward or reverse, the faster you went, up to 45 MPH, and at that speed, even a hard-packed road will rattle every tooth in your head.

I also found out why Tankers wear helmets. I spent two days ricocheting off the radio on one side and a defunct air conditioner on the other.

We spent most of the time running up and down non-existing roads in the Plantation. Every once in a while, we'd pull-up and blow the crap out of some vegetation about a quarter mile away. I never knew if they had actual targets, or just liked to blow up trees and bushes.

During this time, Poopie had recovered remarkably. In fact, she only limped, now, when she knew you were watching, trying to get some more sympathy. She caught a big ol' rat, two weeks, to the day, after her surgery. Good dog.

Rags was pregnant. Buddy, the Daddy. Bad dogs. All we need, around here, is a bunch of puppies. Oh, well, life goes on. Keep ol' Buddy away from Poopie, though.

To the positive, though, Rags had cleaned her act up, being an expectant mommy, I guess, to the point where 'Rags' was not an appropriate name for her any more, Rudy said. He renamed her 'Foxy Lady'.

On June 23, Rudy and I took a 'Deuce', to Long Binh to pick up two crates for the Command Sgt. Major, at the Service battery, there. After they were loaded, I noticed the shipping tags on the huge, rough-oak crates. It was from a furniture company in Washington, D.C., addressed to our CSM.

The surprising thing was the contents.

"A four-poster Bed?" Rudy gasped.

"A WALNUT four-poster Bed!" I read.

"Box springs and Posturepedic mattress!" Rudy read off a tag on the other crate.

We were both highly disgusted.

"Here we are, sleepin' on one-inch thick cotton mattresses, on plywood, when we're LUCKY. An' here's this ol' Fart, in a FOUR-POSTER BED?" Rudy was incensed.

We drove out of Long Binh, on a slightly rain-slick highway. We were cracking hard, on the CSM and his feather bed.

"Why's an ol' hard-ass like HIM need such a soft bed?" and such.

We crested a small hill, following an ARVN jeep down the other side. The rain shower had stopped, but the wind was still gusting across the road. I saw the driver's hat blow off out the side of the jeep and land on the pavement. We were only going twenty-five MPH, so I had no trouble stopping, about fifty feet back, while he stopped and jumped out to retrieve his cap.

A few spatters of fresh rain hit the windshield and I was turning my head to say something to Rudy. Suddenly, the steering wheel, itself, flew up and hit me in the cheek, making me see little birdies. I turned to look at the angry wheel, and it hit me again! In the mouth. As the wheel retreated, I saw one of my teeth, flying in slow motion, glancing off the windshield glass, heading for the floor. The wheel rose up and smote me a third time and everything went red, then black.

I woke up, sitting on the ground, leaning against the rear wheel of the truck. Rudy was calling "Mouse! Moouuse?" as he flicked water on my face, from a canteen. Another face, one I didn't know, with a small black mustache, a booney-cap and the palest skin I'd ever seen, was peering, looking sick, over Rudy's shoulder.

"Is 'e dead?" the face said, voice trembling.

"Nah! Just knocked-out. He's comin' around." This from Rudy.

I got both eyes open, saw double, blinked, re-focused, saw Rudy sit back on his heels, chug on the canteen. The other guy straightened up, wiped sweat, or rain, off his face.

"Man," The stranger breathed, "I thought I'd killed 'im."

I shook my head and bells went off, I saw double again and my jaw felt loose like it wasn't attached.

"Oh, shit!"

I reached up and felt my chin. Hurt! Pulled my hand away and looked. Fresh blood. My blood, thick, on my hand, fingers. Nearly fainted.

"Tooth!"

I remembered the white missile, bouncing off the glass.

With my tongue, I traced the line of teeth, exploring the gap where my lower front tooth used to be. Blood taste. Spit to the side, painfully, felt the tear in my lower lip as I poked my tongue through it.

Rudy said "EWWW!" and the stranger got paler, if that was possible.

Rudy took my towel and gently dabbed at my face, but it hurt so badly, I made him stop.

"Buh-whut hobbin?" I asked through balloon lips. I took the towel and gingerly wiped my mouth.

"I di'nt see ya!" the stranger piped up, immediately, "An' you were right there! Then... BAM!"

I looked at him, confused by this gibberish. Rudy translated.

"HIS truck hit OUR truck."

"Hibbs? HI' OUBBS?" lips not working.

Rudy helped me wobble to my feet, turned me around.

The cab of our 'Deuce', was imbedded in a stand of bamboo. The rear, the bed, the part sticking out, was bent double. The rear wheels, where I'd been sitting, were at least three feet forward of where they should have been. The metal bed, made of ¾ inch thick armor plate, was bent into an upside-down "U". The Sgt. Majors' bed was splinters, strewn across the road, mattress cotton and springs sticking out from a burst crate lodged between the back of the cab and the, now, vertical bed-floor.

I groaned, swayed.

Rudy caught me, turned me back around and set me back down.

Looking back out and down the road, I saw a huge, Red Ball Express twenty-ton semi, sitting, jack-knifed on the road, fifty feet away. No sign of the gook in the jeep.

"He grabbed his hat an' ran!" Rudy informed me, "Good thing, too! If I'd got hold of him, he'd have a busted-up mouth, too."

The Red Ball driver had a radio in his truck and had already called for the MPs, who showed up quickly, being only three miles from Long Binh.

They took a report and roughly dressed my wounds, which were throbbing to beat hell. One of the MPs helped me search for my lost tooth. I unearthed it among the sandbags on the floor over by where Rudy'd been sitting.

Rudy was virtually unscathed, having only some bruises and small cuts, so he elected to stay with the truck and wait for the tow vehicles. The MPs insisted I go on with them, up the road to Thu Dau Mot, where there was a US aid station with a dentist. Rudy helped me gather my stuff and as I climbed into the back of the MP jeep I told Rudy I'd find my own way back to Phouc Vinh.

"And tell the Sgt. Major, I'm just REAL sorry 'bout his bed, an' all."

He laughed and said he would and we were off, down the road about three miles to the home of the 'Phu Loi Prison', Thu Dau Mot.

There was a small American compound, there. A tiny airstrip, a couple chopper pads and about twelve buildings of the wood-slat/sandbag type, one of which housed a Medical unit that had emergency dental capability. I waited while the clerk hunted up someone to look at my wounds

Soon I was examined by a doctor, Captain grade, who after a quick look said I'd need an oral surgeon. He went out and returned with a Major Sapp, the dentist. Sapp cleaned me up and stitched my lip and was starting on my gums when I stopped him and mumbled through the multiple Novocaine shots that I'd saved the tooth.

"Can y' but id bag in?"

It took several tries before I made him understand that I wanted him to try to replace the loose tooth that I had wrapped in a dirty piece of wet cloth. I showed him. He was skeptical, but said he'd try.

He shot me up with a few more needles of painkiller, which numbed me to the eyebrows. Then, with the tooth gripped in a pair of pliers, proceeded to drive my jaw down to my waist, attempting to jam the thing back into place. No luck. It didn't hurt, particularly, but I feared he was going to break my jaw and I was just about to stop him when he gave it up.

"The line of teeth," he explained, "were re-arranged so much by the impact that now there's no room for the tooth to fit back in."

He also told me that the gap would close itself, over time, and then he proceeded to stitch my gum and put a small packing in the socket, to keep it from going dry. My face, even numb, felt like it had been stepped on by an elephant. I could hardly talk. My tongue tended to dangle out one side or another and had to be pushed back in with my finger. Once back outside, I found that, as much as I craved a cigarette, there was just no way I could form my lips around the filter to take a drag. Bummer! I'd have to settle for huffing around the butt, drawing smoke in, and coughing on almost every drag.

I found the company clerk and managed to make him understand that I had no transport back to my unit at Phouc Vinh. He said THEY had no way to get me there, but suggested I try the MP station and directed me there. At the Police shack, the MPs were equally as helpful, saying THEY couldn't take me back, either. Their advice was:

"Get back onto Hwy. 13, a mile east down the road, and thumb a ride on a vehicle headed north."

So at 3:00 P.M., I hiked out the gate and down the little road a mile in the sweltering heat. I was woozy from the wreck and the novocaine and the heat waves radiating up from the pavement made the world swim before my eyes.

I ditched my flack jacket early. Twelve pounds of dead weight. Too hot to wear it. It's gone.

The steel pot was next. I thought it was frying my brain. It's gone. I had my ball cap and I slipped that on.

My cigs kept falling out of my mouth.

435

The sweat, rolling off me, stung my eyes. Rudy'd used my towel to sop up the blood, back at the wreck, so I took off my T-shirt and wrapped it around my head. It helped some.

After the first half-hour, I started noticing other little hurts that, before, had been overshadowed by the mouth wounds. The bruised shoulder, the aching ribs, the scrapes on my neck and the back of my left hand. I also had an unexplainable bump on the back of my head that I found when I put on my cap and my right kneecap was sore. My face was numb, but it felt…itchy….tight…. like the skin was stretched, and the sweat burned my cuts, too.

All in all, I was pretty miserable.

But the best was yet to come.

At the intersection with Hwy 13, was the actual village of Thu Dau Mot. I turned right and walked straight through town, drawing stares and odd looks from the Viets I passed. At the time, I felt like they were sizing me up for the kill. But probably, they were just aghast at the sight of this guy, walking around with caked blood all over his uniform, a hamburger-mouth, twice its normal size, and a crazy, drugged look in his eye, and a T-shirt wrapped around his head.

I DID stop, at the outer edge of town and bought a warm Pepsi from a girl who was selling them out of a wire basket on her motor bike. The syrupy liquid not only bathed my dry mouth and throat, but the sugar and caffeine bouyed-up my nearly spent energy. My mouth still wouldn't seal around the mouth of the bottle, and I dribbled, so I had to look up and pour it into my mouth, being careful not to over-fill, and had to nearly chug-a-lug it. But it was GOOD!

A mile past the village, and the only vehicle to pass me was a Mama-san on a bicycle, and she was going south. I knew this stretch of road and knew that the right-turn-off to PV was about a mile farther on past the town of Tuong Hoa. It was a long mile. At Tuong Hoa, a ¾ driver stopped and picked me up and took me as far as the turn-off. The wind, during the short ride, helped dry my sweat and the canvas seat never felt so good. He dropped me off and continued on north to An Loc. I turned onto the smaller road and started walking, again. It was after 5:00 now.

The road to Phouc Vinh had no highway number, but it was oil-paved and in good condition and dotted with small villages the whole sixty-some miles to my base. The black tarmac reflected the heat of the sun, which was now getting low in the sky. I knew that in two hours it would be getting dark.

'What'm I DOIN' out here?' I thought.

The novocaine gradually wore off as the evening wore on. My head felt like an over-ripe melon that someone stuck knives into, from time to time, at different angles. My jaw throbbed and pulsed and I could hear my heartbeat in my ears.

By seven-thirty, it was twilight and I was too worried to collapse, and stumbled along. I'd covered nearly nine miles from the turn-off and still the only traffic had been motorbikes and the occasional ox-cart. I knew, if someone didn't pick me up soon, I'd be in deep shit. I'd either fall down along the road and die of hunger, thirst, and mortal wounds, or, the gooks'd get me. I'd passed through the hamlet of Tan Hiep and drawn some strange looks. I'm sure they didn't see many lone GIs, walking at dusk, beat-up and bloody, through their village. Or maybe they DID? Who knows.

This stretch of road was deserted rice paddies on both sides for as far as you could see. Which wasn't far in the last light of day. There was almost nowhere to hide, except the paddy water.

'No way! Kill me first.'

A small copse of bamboo, growing on the edge of this one paddy, near the edge of the road, wouldn't be quite dry, but if I hunkered down, in the dark, I didn't think I could be readily seen from the road, and I'd have the water at my back. I wiggled in among the 2-3 foot stalks, my feet sinking two inches into the muck. Foul smelling water seeped into my socks, and I disturbed about a million mosquitoes that buzzed around my head as I squatted among the reeds. I pulled my T-shirt down over my head and peeped out an armhole and put my cap on over the neck-hole on top. I cradled my rifle and bandoleer in my lap, and rolled down my sleeves and tucked my hands into the opposing sleeve. Occasionally, an aggressive bug would bite through the rip-stop material of my jungle fatigues, but mostly, I was spared a blood transfusion in reverse.

'Man, can I get much lower than this?'

In severe pain, dirty, bloody, squatting in mud, being attacked by bugs, hiding in th' weeds, it's still damn hot, scared and out of cigarettes.

'Any lower's gotta be dead.'

Fifteen minutes later, my legs, after walking, what, maybe ten miles, were cramping and numb at the same time.

'I can't just squat here all night.' I decided, but what else could I do.

I stood up, painfully, in place and shifted my weight back and forth, trying to get blood flowing into my extremities. It seemed to be working, but my ears started roaring. I didn't want to shake my sore head, so I poked them with my fingers, and it stopped. I pulled my fingers out and it started again, louder.

Now, groggily, I realized it wasn't my ears, it's a jeep!

'It's coming!' I slopped out of the bamboo, scattering about a million buzzing bugs, to the edge of the road, which was barely discernable in the darkness.

'Going south, but who cares!' I was desperate, 'I'll throw myself in front of it, if I have to!'

Finally, it rounded the curve ahead, and I saw the tiny slits of its blackout lights.

'He's really moving!'

I stepped out, waving my arms frantically, yelling.

He saw me at the last minute and swerved, hitting the brakes, and barely missed me as I was standing nearly in the middle of the road. He slid to a halt twenty feet past, and I heard him call me a "Stupid Sum-bitch!" but I didn't care! I loved him!

I stumbled to the passenger side of the jeep and hung on and croaked:

Thank you! Thank you! Thank you!

Which came out:

"Honk-oo! Honk-oo! Honk-oo!"

"Mouse?" A flashlight snapped on.

"Hunh, hunh."

It was Rudy!

"Jeez! You look like shit!"

"Hanx." I slowly collapsed on the seat. "Oo ook wunnavul!"

"When you didn't show up, an' Clark hadn't heard anything, I got him to call Phu Loi an' th' MPs said you'd left on foot, so I borrowed this jeep an' came lookin'. Jeez, you look worse'n you did this mornin'!"

I looked over at his face in the dim glow of the flashlight.

"Gan be jus go hobe?"

He acted surprised, like it hadn't occurred to him.

"Oh! Sure!" he smiled and snapped off the light.

He swung the jeep around in the road and took off like a bat outta hell.

"You just sit back an' relax, an' let ol' Rude do th' drivin', for a change."

It hurt for me to talk, so I bummed one of his Camels and smoked it while he rattled on through the dark night. I don't remember finishing or throwing that cigarette out. My next recollection is Rudy and Clark hauling me into the Aid Station and good ol' Doc cleaning me up and putting gauze on my mouth and giving me some wonderful pills, then I don't remember anything else. They must've carried me over and put me in bed, 'cause that's where I woke up, next morning.

With the biggest hangover I ever had without drinking.

I lay perfectly still for a long time after I was awake, assessing what might hurt and what won't. The hurts far outweighed the won'ts.

I was trying to summon the nerve to try actual movement when I felt hot breath on my cheek. Bad breath! Followed by a snuffling sound. I carefully moved my head to the right.

Two black eyes, under pointy lop-ears, a wet, black nose, and a pink tongue.

POOPIE!

It came out "OOBAH!" but she knew what I meant and licked my face above the gauze wrapping and, I believe, she actually smiled.

Though it hurt, to the max, I smiled, too.

She pawed at my arm, bouncing up and down on her hind legs on the floor, and barked for me to get up and feed her. That's what it was all about. FOOD! But I took it as an inspiration. This little animal loves me and it's my privilege to take care of her. She was so brave during her injuries, and she expects me to be just as tough as she was.

I creaked up out of the bunk. If not for that little black and white dog, I might've remained there for the next forty-six days.

34

BUSTED

The next week, thanks to Doc Phillips, I was put on light duty to let my face heal. I spent most of the time in the battery compound. I painted some signs for the latrines. They read:

EM (For ours)

<OFFICERS * NCO> (For theirs, like they got confused all the time.)

I spent a lot of energy just dodging Sgt. Wilson.

I volunteered to Sgt. Holly and stayed in the motor pool two afternoons greasing trucks in the shade under the wooden grease-rack. The days were hot and Poopie and I really appreciated the cool darkness of the pit.

Nights were spent at the EM club. Sgt. Holly asked Fuk and me to bring our guitars and several times we had an impromptu sing-along which we all enjoyed. Mostly, though, I just sipped Cokes and watched as Nickerson and Pagans cleaned-up on the pool table.

Everyone in the 'Dirty Thirty' had learned, some the hard way, not to challenge either of these guys at pool, for money. You'd just lose it. Still, every night there was a steady stream of guys from other units, coming in to lose THEIR money. Our 'Resident Sharks' nearly always won.

One night, though, a light-skinned black guy from E-82nd took Nick for over $300 in three games of Rotation. Nick said, later, he'd just had a bad night, but I thought he'd just met-up with one of his own kind.

Another night, a big 'Home-grown' guy, named Burt something, lost a few too many times to Pagans, got pissed, broke a hard-to-replace

440

cue stick, then jumped onto the pool table and cracked the one-piece slate across the break-end of the table. All Hell broke loose!

Jack Pagans, no small guy, himself, roared and grabbed Burt, who I think knew he'd just screwed-up badly, around both legs and toppled him off the green and onto the floor. Four other guys grabbed him and physically picked him up. Burt was kicking and screaming, but each time he'd knock someone down, somebody else would jump in and with a highly pissed Pagans leading the way, they carried him out and across the road. Behind the latrine, they tossed the hapless Burt into the 'Tangle-foot' wire that bordered the road.

Burt was really drunk, but the barbed wire rows, strung a foot off the ground, grabbed him and held him, struggling and cutting himself up, until, sobered considerably, he begged us to help him. It took four guys to extricate the shredded man from the barricade and lift him out. He apologized to everyone, but was forever banned from the 'Dirty Thirty' Club.

After that, even with two wooden crates stacked under it with shims, the pool table was never quite flat, again. You could hear the ball pass the crack and sometimes it would veer a little as it jumped the tiny void. Nick and Jack, being true 'Pros', after a little practice, learned to use this to their advantage, skipping shots off the fault, much to their opponents surprise, to make certain shots. I'm sure, also, that the crack influenced many a missed shot by unwary players.

On July 4th, a bunch of us sat out on Jims 'Rooftop Gardens' to watch the 'Mad-Minute' go off around the perimeter. The display was awe-inspiring, as usual. Our philosophical question of the evening was:

"During a 'Mad-Minute', there must be several tons of lead fired into the sky almost at once. Where does it go?"

My mouth was almost healed. Doc had taken out the stitches in the second week when the 'self-dissolving' stitches, didn't. I had an angry-looking ½ inch red scar on my lip and a dull ache in my gum where the tooth had been, and my 'gap' whistled, sometimes, when I pronounced S'es, But I was OK.

I'd been fairly successful at avoiding 'Lifers' and had let my mustache grow out, aiming for a 'Handlebar', like the one I'd seen on a Sgt. E-8 in a picture in the Stars & Stripes newspaper. This E-8, it seems, was a Mess Sgt. for a bunch of Generals in Saigon, and he sported this beau-

441

tiful, long, waxed 'Soup-strainer'. I figured if it was OK for the Generals cook, it'd be OK for me. All the guys thought it was 'cool', too.

On July 5th, I was helping re-gravel the motor pool. I was driving the 5-ton truck hauling the rock from the piles stored at the DP. I'd delivered two loads, already, and was turning in at the red gates with the third, and there he was. Sgt. Wilson accompanied by the new XO, Major Payne. They were standing outside the Briefing Room door, chatting. I'd have to drive right past them, and worse, I'd have to salute the officer.

I hoped to be able to just slip by, but they both turned and looked right at me. I tried to mask my new growth with an awkward salute. I thought I'd gotten away with it, for a moment.

"Hudson?"

Wilson's voice.

He was walking briskly alongside my truck.

"HUDSON!" louder.

I pulled up and he stepped up on the running board and peered in at me, like he was making a study of it, or something.

"Hello Top! What's up?" I said, innocently.

He was not put off by my light tone.

"Park this truck in the pool and I wanna see you in the CP! NOW!"

'Oh, shit!'

"OK, Top, be right there."

Five minutes later I walked in and he was seated at his big wooden desk, absently sorting through some papers. He looked up and got a sour expression, as I stood at semi-attention, almost touching the front edge of his desk.

We locked eyes and nothing was said for a full thirty seconds.

"Hudson," he broke first, "You know that mustache ain't authorized in th' Cav."

I explained that it must be, and alluded to the article about the Generals cook, and told him I could show him the picture, even.

If a black man can turn red, he did.

"That man's a E-8, Hudson. He can do anything he wants!" He began, roughly, "Jus' like ME! An' I want YOU to trim that mustache t' look like MINE!"

Like I said, Wilson was a black man, and his mustache consisted of about five little kinky hairs on either side that formed a thin black line above his sneering lips.

I looked at his, and really meaning no disrespect, the words just popped out.

"Top, I wouldn't HAVE one that looked like that."

He clicked his teeth shut and I heard the start of a low growl. I immediately knew that I'd really stepped on it by insulting his vision of manliness, or something.

"I mean…" I started, but never got to finish.

Pushed to his, already intolerant, limit, my last smart-ass remark sent him over the top. He raised up and swung at me; a wide, right swing, with his weight behind it. Had the desk been not as wide, and had I not instinctively dodged my head back as I felt the air from his fist coming, I would have lost some more teeth.

His fist went past, missing by less than an inch, grazing the tip of my offending 'Handlebar'.

Self-preservation instinct kicked in. Before I knew it, while he was stretched across the desk, off balance, his mean face thrust out toward me, I leaned forward and my right fist came up, almost from my knee, and caught him under the point of his big, black chin. The force of the impact surprised even me.

I heard his teeth clack together and saw his eyes roll back in his head and he collapsed backward into his chair, where he lay sprawled for a few seconds before he shook his head and re-focused his eyes. He started to get back up.

I turned, and, I swear to God, I was going to run. Where? I had no inkling. Just away.

There, standing in the doorway, just coming in, was Captain Johnson. He was shaking his head and thrust out his hand, palm out, to stop the First Sgt.

"SERGEANT!" he said.

Top dropped his arms and stood there breathing hard.

I was physically shaking. The consequences for hitting a 1st Sgt. were flashing through my head.

The Captain walked over to his office door and opened it.

"Hudson…in here. NOW!"

I meekly complied.

Now, Captain Johnson liked me, I knew. But, I also knew that he'd just seen me hit the Sgt. Whether he'd seen Top swing first, I didn't know.

He told Wilson to sit down and shut up. He came in and shut the door behind him. I remained quiet and at attention as he assumed his seat behind his desk.

"At ease, Hudson."

I studied his face. I could tell he was upset, but, was that a slight turning-up at the corners of his mouth? He began.

"I understand that there has been some...shall we say, animosity?...between Sgt. Wilson and yourself."

"Yes sir! But I...." He raised his hand.

"I know there is a perfectly good reason you hit the First Sgt., and I don't want to hear it!"

I clamped my lips tight to stifle all the idiotic things I wanted to say.

"I also know that the First Sgt. is aware that I witnessed your action."

"RE-action, sir!" I wanted to say SOMETHING in my own defense.

"Whatever!" he raised his hand for silence. "The Sgt. is going to press me to have you locked up."

Images of prison cells flashed through my brain. I felt like I couldn't breathe.

He thought a minute while I stood there, sweating. Finally, he continued.

"Considering the fact that you are roughly HALF his size, I wouldn't think that you would, purposefully, pick a fight with Sgt. Wilson. Correct?"

I nodded.

"And, having known you, personally, while you were my driver..."

He thought another long, sweaty minute.

"I'm going to concede to the fact that there was no real...malice aforethought, on your part. Am I correct in assuming this?" There was that little smile, again.

"Yessir!....I mean....no sir, no malice at all, sir! A man would hafta be crazy to..." He halted me again.

"I fully agree," he was really smiling, now, "a man WOULD have to be crazy to hit a First Sgt., intentionally." He paused, "Or throw up on him, for that matter."

He let that little barb sink in. I shrugged.

"Therefore, I'm going to handle this right here." He placed his hands flat on the desk. "There'll be no jail-time."

I breathed for the first time in minutes.

"BUT!"

I waited for the ax to fall.

"I will lower your rank to E-1." He paused, "Now, is there anything you'd like to say?"

"Sir," I said, earnestly, "I've got 33 days left in this Army. It makes no difference to me whether I go out an E-5 or an E-1, as long as I go out."

He looked at me intensely for a moment then nodded.

"I thought that might be your reaction. I'm going to instruct Sgt. Wilson to give you wide-berth, and I'll expect the same from YOU? Understood?"

I nodded, vigorously. "Completely, sir!"

"Now, get outta here!"

I saluted and turned to leave.

"One more thing!" he said, "Trim that ridiculous looking mustache!"

I slid out past a glaring Sgt. Wilson and once out the door, I ran on wobbly legs straight to my hootch and cut that 'Handlebar' off. Not as radically as the 1st Sgt. had wanted, but, to regulation.

Three days later, I received orders for 'Disciplinary reduction of rank'. I was back where I'd begun, in the Army, but I didn't care.

In thirty days I'll be a 'Civilian First-class'!"

Twenty nine days. Twenty eight days. Twenty seven. They went by so slowly. I spent most of my energy trying to be invisible.

'If they can't find me, they can't make me do anything foolish!' was my credo.

I was aided in this by the other guys who'd take me out on their details just to get me out of the compound and out of sight. I don't know what Capt. Johnson told Wilson, but the man avoided me like the plague. I gladly returned the favor.

Foxy Lady had six puppies on July 28th. Three white and three black-and-white, like Buddy. Buddy was getting really large, now, and was a proud papa. He always hung around, in case any of his puppies needed protection. Buddy was killed by a 'Deuce', on the perimeter road a week before I left. We were all broken-up and we buried him in the floor of the old French bunker, where he liked to hang-out with the dopers. We still had six reminders of him.

With one week left, I started looking around for someone to take Poopie. Everyone volunteered, but SHE chose Immanuel (Manny) Garcia. She'd sleep on his porch some nights and was always delighted to see him. Manny was an FDC guy with ten months left in his tour, so he'd probably be here, at HQ for the duration, to provide food and shelter for my 'Baby'.

I hated having to leave her. I even inquired about 'Export and Quarantine' laws, but got a big "No Way!" Manny was happy. He loved that li'l dog, more than anyone.

I shipped my stereo and tapes home, along with my only 'war souvenir', the big machete I'd gotten on LZ Becky. I gave away all my poncho liners except the one I wrapped around my stereo for padding. My flare-parachute mosquito net went to Rudy. Fuk, who was getting 'short', too, with twenty-eight days left, took my hand-painted psychedelic posters and my bookrack I'd made from ammo-crates, full of J.D. Macdonald mysteries. Rojeski got my guitar. He'd picked up a few chords from watching Fuk and me at the sing-alongs, and wanted to play. Other small things got distributed to other friends until I was down to the 'Basic Load' I'd come in with.

0700, August 7th, 1970, I went out the front gates of the 'Dirty Thirty' for the last time. Can't say I was sad to go, though I'd miss some of the guys and my dog.

At last! The day eagerly awaited for fourteen long months. All I had to do was get through 'Processing'.

Can't be too hard I assumed.

I'd had my hair cut to regs. I'd trimmed my mustache, actually almost as short as Sgt. Wilson's. I was wearing a new set of fatigues that were actually starched stiff by the gook laundry in PV.

446

I was STRACK!

I wanted nothing to interfere with my exit from Vietnam.

Clark, a fellow Kentuckian, drove me to the airstrip where I'd catch a scheduled flight to Bien Hoa.

"Maybe I'll see you back in Kentucky!" I said as I snagged my duffel from the back of the jeep.

"Wait another 225 days, an' I'll go with you."

My response to this was a hearty laugh and a "No Way!"

"OK, see ya in Kentucky!" he drove off giving me a thumbs-up signal. I returned it.

At 0900, I was in Bien Hoa, leaving me the whole day to 'Process Out' before my plane, tomorrow.

I leisurely strolled out to the main road, asked directions, and soon I was at 1st Cav Division HQ, which took up a large part of the huge base. My first stop was at 'Matériel Return', where I left my steel pot, (sure hated to see THAT go), flack jacket, rifle, all my fatigues except one clean pair and what I was wearing, and I was questioned about 'Contraband'. They searched my belongings for drugs, like I'd be stupid enough to try smuggling out some 'grass' and risk the jail-time.

I retained my ruck, with all my personal stuff, my ball cap and my canteen belt. I was supposed to pick up my duffel bag with my stateside fatigues and khakis, but I was informed that a rocket had ignited a fire in the storage facility, and all those things had burned. Big Deal! The LAST thing I'd need was stateside fatigues.

I asked a Sgt. at the warehouse how to get to '1st Cav Finance', which was the next stop designated on my printed 'DEROS Instruction Sheet'. He went through some elaborate directions, but I was so excited, by now, that I didn't follow him very well, and by the time I was back on the street, I'd completely forgotten.

'Oh, well,' I figured I'd just thumb a ride and, surely, the driver'd know the way.

I walked down a couple of busy streets, crammed with vehicles of every description. I bided my time, taking in sights. One 'sight' I didn't expect was a white, concrete block building with the familiar red and white 'DAIRY QUEEN' sign above it. I was flabbergasted. Hot and flabbergasted. I floated on air, thinking milkshakes, ice cream, sweet, cold! When I got there, I was somewhat disappointed to find that all they had were the little cups of custard, like the ones we'd gotten at recess in elementary school. Complete with the little wooden spoons. Chocolate or vanilla. I bought one, sat on a bench alongside the building and spooned it down, luxuriating in the coldness. It hurt my nose and teeth, but it was good.

After that, I stood on the next street corner and stuck out my thumb. Three vehicles stopped, but none of the drivers knew where 'Finance' was located. The fourth, a ¾ ton, with three guys in front and a canvas rear cover, bearing 1st Cav numbers on the bumper, proved to be of help.

"Can you drop me at 1st Cav Finance?" I asked the driver.

"Sure, man, but you'll hafta ride in th' back, OK?" he returned.

They were laughing and joking. Real jolly guys. I figured 'No sweat'.

I climbed up into the bed and found the back of the truck stuffed full of spools of commo wire. There wasn't room for me to sit on either side bench, so I perched my butt on the top edge of the raised tailgate and held on to the wooden roof brace with my right hand.

I hollered "OK", and he took off. And I DO mean TOOK OFF! The guy must've been a frustrated drag racer. I had my ruck on my back, so both my hands were free, and it took both hands to hold on as he raced from corner to corner, jerking the vehicle through the gears.

'Man, this guy drives like Steve McQueen!' I thought.

We rounded several turns, practically on two wheels, and then a sharp right-hand corner, where he actually had to slow down and down-gear the truck. I let go with one hand to brace myself against a big coil of wire, to keep from being thrown forward. Once around the bend, he jammed the transmission into first and popped the clutch. The truck roared and lurched and I lost my grip with my other hand and realized that the upright tailgate had, somehow, come unlatched and was going down, with me on it. In slow motion, I was ejected out the back.

In mid-air, I saw my feet come up and tangle in a spool of wire. Quick visions of being dragged down the paved road came to me. I sailed out backwards uncoiling the wire as I went. I hit the road on my back, skipped twice, then pulled the coil of wire out with me and slid to a painful halt in the middle of the road. The truck sped on, oblivious to my fate. It rounded the next corner without even slowing, and I swear I heard those guys laughing it up, in the cab. A 'Deuce' had been behind us, skidded to a halt a scant ten feet from me and blasted on his air-horn.

I scrambled, sorely, to my feet and shuffled out of the road, dragging the wire-spool with me, since it was still tangled around my feet. The driver in the 'Deuce' yelled "You OK?" I nodded, though I really wasn't. My rucksack had cushioned my head from impact, but my web canteen belt had rolled up my back when I hit, bunching up my shirt and taking a layer of skin off from my waist to my shoulder blades. I looked down and saw drops of blood in the brown dust alongside the road. 'Shit!'

I was hurt, so I looked around for someplace to get help. When I turned fully around and looked at the building I was directly in front of, I gasped. There, emblazoned above the door, was the sign: 'FIRST CAVALRY FINANCE'

"Jeez, I told him t' 'drop' me at 1st Cav Finance," I muttered, "but I DIDN'T mean DROP!"

I don't know how they could have done it on purpose, or if it was some kinda freakish accident, but it was all just too much of a coincidence.

Now, hurt and pissed off, I kicked the wire roll out of the way and marched through the screen door into a typical Army processing office, with a tile floor, plywood walls and a counter dividing the reception area from the work area. I walked up to the counter and dripped blood across the floor. The Spec-4 clerk had seen me get up out of the road and walk in, and, horrified at me bleeding all over his tile told me to go to the aid station around the corner and get some help.

"I'll go when you're through processing these." I flopped my records down on the Formica. "So do it quick, an' I'll go."

I walked outside, smoked, and bled for ten minutes while he arranged my files. Then he brought them out, for me to sign. I looked over the papers and noticed, right off, PV-2 Hudson, R.W., at the heading. Everything else looked correct.

"I'm a PV-1." I pointed at an obvious mistake that could take DAYS to correct.

"Oh, no, you're an E-2." He said brightly, "I put you in for a Auto-Promo."

'It took a Captain to bust me, but a Spec-4 can promote me?' I was a little confused.

"Say what?" I asked.

"Auto-Promo." He said it like I was so stupid, "According to Reg #, (he rattled off a long number with several decimal points and dashes), a soldier cannot exit a Combat Zone as an E-1. It's an 'Embarrassment to the Army'. Normally, you'd have to stay here, until you were re-promoted through time-in-service."

"The HELL I will!" I burst.

He looked alarmed.

"Oh, no!" he explained, rapidly, "You're ETS-ing. So you get an Auto-Promo that bumps you back to an E-2 pay-grade."

"You're sure?" I was dumbfounded.

"Sure!" he said, brightly.

I couldn't quite believe it. I get dumped off a truck and promoted in one swell foop.

I signed the papers, handed him his copies, stuck mine in my records folder, thanked him, and, to his relief, walked off to find that aid station.

Around the corner and two buildings down was a Medical building with the red cross on the door. I entered and told the PFC at the desk my problem. He summoned a Medic, who took me back and examined and dressed my contusions. Whatever he used for disinfectant, burned like the fires of Hell, but he said it wasn't serious. I had just lost some skin. It'd scab over by morning and hurt a while, if I treated it right. He wanted to know how it happened. I told him to never mind.

When he was finished, I asked him where the DEROS Center was and he directed me. I left and went there. I walked, needless to say.

At the Center, I was assigned a louse-ridden bed for the night and told to be at the mandatory 0800 formation tomorrow.

I left thinking, 'Another bullshit formation!'. Then I realized this would probably be my LAST formation. 'What th' Hell. I can stand it!' I smiled.

I spent that evening at a PX, where they had a row of pinball machines along a wall. I played every game there at least twice. At 10:00, I went back to the DEROS barracks, but it was nearly empty. All the guys were too keyed-up to sleep. After looking at my filthy bed, I decided I was, too.

I wandered around the base for a while. I found an EM club and had a couple beers and some conversation with a couple of PFC clerks. They were envious that I was leaving. They were both 'Newbies', fresh from the states. They had a LONG way to go. I bought them a couple of beers, to help ease their longing to be away from this God-forsaken country. I stayed until they threw me out at closing time, 1:00 A.M.

With nothing else to do, I found my way back to the barracks. I shook out the wool Army blanket on the bunk and lay down fully clothed. I was so wired, I knew I wouldn't sleep, but then I found myself waking up, the gray morning light coming through the screened windows. My Timex, through its almost opaque crystal, said 0700.

'MY LAST DAY!' my first thought.

I cleaned up in the latrine, where, miracle of miracles, there were actual flush toilets. First I'd seen in country. I flushed it twice, just to marvel. I was getting a feeling, a yearning, for normalcy. To be where things didn't blow up all the time. Where the guy down the street won't try to kill you for a political conviction. Where you might have a 'boss', but you can QUIT, if you want. Ah, to be a civilian! I can see it now!

I ate my last powdered egg breakfast at the mess, and formed-up with thirty other DEROSees at 0800 at the CP. We were herded into Army busses. The same ones, obviously, that had met me at the airport on my arrival. We made the trip back to Ton Son Nhut. I saw the same sign above the gate, but from the other side, now. I realized, in the last fourteen months, I'd seen a lot of things from the other side; Life, Death, existence itself.

I decided it was time to get back on the right side of things. I'd survived!

I joined in the wild cheer that arose in the bus when we parked in view of a 727, and the bus doors swung open.

GLOSSARY

AC-----Armored Cavalry

AG-----assistant gunner

APC-----M-113 armored personnel carrier

AV-----Aviation company

Battery-----Artillery company

BEE- HIVE-----XM494 or XM596 artillery round containing thousands of tiny, nail-like 'Fleshettes'. Canister shot.

Blooper-----M-79 grenade launcher

Boonies-----the jungle or the Field

BX-----Base exchange

CAV-----Cavalry

Chinook-----CH-47 transport helicopter

Concertina------coiled barbed-wire

CP------command post

C-Rat-----C Rations

C-4------plastic explosive

DEROS-----fulfill tour of duty

'DEUCE'-----2 ½ ton truck

Dink------same as gook

Doper-----pot smoker

EM-----enlisted man

ETS-----end term service

Fast-movers-----jet aircraft

FNG-----fucking new guy

Frag----fragmentation-type grenade

Gook-----Vietnamese person, (derogatory)

GP-----general purpose

Gung Ho-----itching to fight, (also, John Wayne)

Gunner-----artillery crew leader

H&I------harassment and interdiction

Hard-core------determined

HE------high explosive

'HOT'-----as in 'Hot LZ', active enemy engagement

Huey-----Bell UH-I helicopter
Juicer-----a drunk
KIA-----killed in action
KZ-----killing-zone
Lifer------career soldier
Loach-----light observation helicopter (LOH)
Loader------artillery crew member who loads the round into the gun
LP-------listening post
LRRP-------Long Range Recon Patrol
LZ-----landing zone
MACV------Military Assistance Command, Vietnam
MOS------job or occupation designation
NCO-----non-commissioned officer
NG------National Guard
NVA------North Vietnamese Army
OD-----olive drab
OP------'other peoples', as in cigarettes
Peneprime-----oil surface for dirt roads
Pig------155 Howitzer
Powder-Monkey------artillery crew member in charge of gun-powder
PX-----Post exchange
Rear------safe area away from the fighting
REMF------Rear Echelon Mother Fucker
RPG-----rocket propelled grenade
STRACK-----sharp-looking, in a military manner
Tangle-foot------barbed wire tightly strung between short stakes 10-12" off the ground
WIA------wounded in action
WP------white phosphorus
VC, Victor Chuck, Charlie-----Viet Cong

About the Author

Upon returning to his hometown in 1970, Richard (no longer a Mouse) Hudson resumed his musical career while attending the University of Kentucky. He soon renewed an acquaintance with Shirley, a friend and fellow musician he knew before he went to Vietnam. They married in 1972.

After living out of state for several years, the Hudsons moved back to Kentucky to be near their families. They still reside in Lexington where they run their own businesses and play bluegrass music with friends.

Richard's sense of right and wrong, his ability to relate and identify with people in all walks of life and his general zest for life, he attributes to his brief military service in Vietnam.

Printed in the United States
96081LV00005B/79-81/A

9 781434 306180